TELEVISION

Critical Methods and

Applications

TELEVISION

Critical Methods and Applications

Second Edition

JEREMY G. BUTLER

The University of Alabama

LEA

LAWRENCE ERLBAUM ASSOCIATES, PUBLISHERS

2002   Mahwah, New Jersey   London

Director, Sales and Marketing:	Robert Sidor
Director, Customer Relations:	Nancy Seitz
Acquisitions Editor:	Linda Bathgate
Textbook Marketing Manager:	Marisol Kozlovski
Editorial Assistant:	Karin Wittig
Cover Design:	Kathryn Houghtaling Lacey
Textbook Production Manager:	Paul Smolenski
Full-Service & Composition:	TechBooks, Inc.
Text and Cover Printer:	Hamilton Printing Company

This book was typeset in 10/12 pt. Times Roman, Bold, and Italic.
The heads were typeset in Americana and Americana Bold.

Lawrence Erlbaum Associates, Inc., Publishers
10 Industrial Avenue
Mahwah, New Jersey 07430

Library of Congress Cataloging-in-Publication Data

Butler, Jeremy G., 1954–
    Television : critical methods and applications / Jeremy G. Butler.—2nd ed.
      p. cm. — (LEA's communication series)
    Includes index.
    ISBN 0-8058-4209-8 (pbk. : alk. paper)
    1. Television—Psychological aspects. 2. Television—Semiotics. 3. Television
broadcasting—United States. 4. Television criticism. I. Title. II. Series.

    PN1992.6 .B86   2001
    791.45—dc21

                                             2001023192

Printed in the United States of America
10 9 8 7 6 5 4 3

CONTENTS

Should we take television seriously?

Should we take television seriously as a cultural or aesthetic medium, as a *text* capable of producing meaning? Should we take *When Animals Attack* seriously? Should we commission studies on *As the World Turns'* visual style? Should an interpretation of the discourse of *The Beverly Hillbillies* be permitted in an academic journal? And, most pertinent to this book, should there be college courses on these programs? Should *The Simpsons* be allowed in today's syllabi?

Yes, we should study television in school. And, yes, we should take television seriously. Why? Because television provides meanings, many meanings, as it entertains. There is little doubt that it is the predominant meaning-producing and entertainment medium of the past 50 years. As such it demands our scrutiny. In order to dissect the pleasures and meanings that television affords us, we need an understanding of *how* narrative is structured, and *how* sets are designed, and *how* the camera positions the viewer's perspective, and *how* sound interacts with image.

Television: Critical Methods and Applications supplies the student with a whole toolbox of implements to disassemble television. It explains how television works, how television programs and commercials are made, and how they function as fertile producers of meanings. *Television* does not attempt to teach taste or aesthetics. It is less concerned with evaluation than with *interpretation*. It resists asking, "Is *Buffy the Vampire Slayer* great art?" Instead, it poses the question, "What meanings does *Buffy* signify and how does it do so?" To answer this question brings viewers closer to understanding television as a meaning-producing phenomenon, and thus helps them stay afloat in a sea of frequently contradictory meanings.

The form of analysis stressed here asks the viewer, first, to explore the structures of narrative, non-narrative, and commercial television material. Second, *Television* questions how those structures emphasize certain meanings (and repress others) to viewers. And third, it considers how television's images and sounds work together to create its programs, commercials, and assorted televisual flotsam and jetsam. Thus, this textbook works from the very concrete (light and shadow on an illuminated video screen, accompanied by sound) to the very abstract (discourses on many aspects of the human experience)—and back again.

Accordingly, Part One introduces the student to the principles organizing television's narrative and non-narrative content. Part Two explains how that content is communicated to the viewer through the medium's style, its manipulation of image and sound. Part Three addresses some specific television forms: music video, animation, and the commercial. Part Four departs from *Television's* consideration of television texts to survey the "critical" approaches that have been applied to the medium—as opposed to empirical methods. This part of the book offers the student grounding in fields such as genre study, ideological analysis, feminist criticism, and so on. Finally, the Appendix provides guidance for writing papers about TV. It outlines how the principles of textual analysis developed over the previous chapters may be applied to specific programs.

Television's first edition was written during the year that the World Wide Web fully incorporated images and sounds (1993, when the Mosaic browser was released). We're excited about the new possibilities for TV analysis that the World Wide Web provides, and we've developed a companion Web site for *Television*: www.TVCrit.com. Here you'll find sample student analyses, color versions of all the frame grabs (larger than reproduced here, too), and many additional television materials that we couldn't fit into the book—including video clips. Parts of the site are reserved for *Television* readers and require the following account name and password:

Account name: tvcrit

Password: tvcrit4u

Television was born of the author's frustration as a teacher of television criticism. Many television textbooks deal with the history and structure of television as an industry, but few offer students a way to analyze that industry's products from a critical perspective. Other TV textbooks emphasize the nuts-and-bolts of video production to the extent that they seldom have space to consider television meanings and how they are generated by those "nuts-and-bolts." Textbooks that do address television research and theory are often empirical in their orientation—relying on models first presented in psychology and sociology—and largely neglect the issue of critical interpretation.

The author has relied on nonempirical models for inspiration. Much of *Television* will look familiar to readers who have encountered film criticism textbooks. Moreover, *Television* also bears the marks of literary criticism, semiotics (the study of signs and meaning), and ideological criticism. It draws on each of these approaches where appropriate, but the authors are concerned above all else to analyze television *as television*.

At the time this book is being revised for its second edition (Autumn 2000), the boundaries between television and other media are fast dissolving. When one looks at a "television" screen these days, one could be playing a video game or responding to e-mail instead of watching a TV program. As digital broadcasting and "enhanced TV" become the standard, our TV sets begin to look more and more like our computers. And as CDs and DVDs play through our computers and we digitally edit home movies, our computers begin to look more and more like our stereos, VCRs, and televisions.

This is not just a time of great technological shifts. There have also been huge changes in the economics of television—particularly in the United States. The broadcast networks are under siege from newer media. They no longer command our attention as they did from the 1950s to the 1970s. Some critics have even proclaimed an end to the "Broadcast Era" of television, but the mode of production associated with broadcast television is far from dead. Recognizing the accelerated convergence of comtemporary media, this second edition of *Television* incorporates new sections on digital television, computer-based imaging, and the impact of new digital media like the World Wide Web.

To keep *Television* comprehensible (and a reasonable length), we have had to set some perimeters—even though we occasionally stroll across them. *Television* is still principally a book about *commercial, network* television. And its examples are drawn largely from U.S. television (with occasional reference to Canadian and British TV). It would be dangerous to assume that this particular model of television defines *everything* one sees on the television set or that it is an unchanging monolith or that it is the same throughout the world. Clearly it is not. But still, television originated as a commercial, network medium and will continue to have an impact as such for the foreseeable future.

Television, then, cannot hope to be a comprehensive guide to deconstructing everything that appears on a video screen. No single volume could. It does, however, offer the student a better understanding of television's principal manifestation: the ever-present, ever-flowing, commercial television system.

ACKNOWLEDGMENTS

Blaine Allan and Gary Copeland each wrote one of *Television's* chapters, but their contributions to this project go far beyond that. They were there for the original conceptualization of the project, helped shepherd it through various drafts and rewrites, furnished key examples when my mind went blank, and generally illustrated just how collegial colleagues can be.

We thank our editor, Linda Bathgate, and Lawrence Erlbaum Associates for their diligence in bringing this project to fruition.

Several persons read and provided useful comments on the first edition: David Bordwell, Jim Castonguay, Brent Davis, Maureen Furniss, Carolyn Hales, Michele Hilmes, Lynne Joyrich, Chuck Kleinhans, Ken Kwapis, Tara McPherson, Ellen Seiter, Greg Stroud, Lang Thompson, and Mark J. P. Wolf. We are grateful for their insights.

The Center for Public Television and Radio at The University of Alabama and its director, Tom Rieland, graciously assisted with the preparation of illustrations. Videographer Preston Sullivan set up several illustrative shots, with the help of Brent Davis, Dawn Haskew, Jim Holliman, Glen Richard, and Jason Ruha.

The frame enlargements in this book were created by using a computer to capture individual frames from videotape. Barry Smith ably assisted in this task. Other illustrations were created by Laura Lineberry (drawings), Rickey Yanaura (photographs), Niklas Vollmer (nonlinear editing) and Mark J. P. Wolf

(3D animation). Figure 4.7 is courtesy of MTV. Figure 6.33 is courtesy of The Weather Channel and photographer Richard Grant. Tables 7.1, 7.2, and 12.1 are courtesy of Nielsen Media Research.

Rosemary McMahill industriously compiled the glossary and also provided valuable assistance with the word processing of the manuscript.

My students at the University of Alabama were the first to be exposed to this text, while still a cobbled together manuscript. I thank them for their patience in dealing with *Television* in photocopied form—missing an illustration here and there and lacking a binding that would properly hold it together for a 15-week semester. Their responses and comments helped make this a much more readable book.

Not all support for this book was academic. Both Jeremy and Penelope Butler and Reid and Teresa Butler took me under their wings during a sabbatical and a summer, respectively, in Phoenix—allowing me the privilege of writing time unfettered by concerns of room and board. And Marysia Galbraith buoyed my spirits and steeled my resolve in many ways during the revision process—including her organization of a research retreat at Zamek Dunajec w Niedzicy to study Mexican soap operas on Polish television.

Jeremy G. Butler
Tuscaloosa, Alabama
jbutler@TVCrit.com
November 2000

www.TVCrit.com

Sample analyses
Color Illustrations
Video clips
Online Resources

PART ONE

UNDERSTANDING TELEVISION'S STRUCTURES AND SYSTEMS

CHAPTER 1

Television's Ebb and Flow

Newspapers and magazines that list television programs often use a grid to represent an evening's schedule. In many of them, the channels run vertically down the left side of the grid, while half-hour time "slots" run horizontally along the top. (Fig. 1.1 shows one such grid for a summer day in the 1990s.) The reasoning behind this array is obvious. At a glance, we can fix our location in the grid, noting the axis of channel (say, channel 9) and the axis of time (say, 7:00). After figuring that location, we can quickly see what will follow the current program in time (horizontal) and what is happening on other channels at that same time (vertical).

Grids such as these may help us understand the basic structure of TV and the experience of watching television. Most listings emphasize programming time slots rather than the individual programs themselves. *TV Guide*, with a few exceptions, does not describe TV programs separately from their time slots. Only movies on "premium" cable channels (HBO, Showtime, Disney, and so on) receive special status in this regard.[1] In addition to noting movies in the listings grid, *TV Guide* isolates them from other television programs and indexes them, film by film, in the back of each issue. There is no corresponding index for any other type of television program. The editors of *TV Guide* evidently believe that viewers experience movies differently from other television programs.

The grid in Figure 1.1 and *TV Guide*'s format illustrate that television programs are positioned by network programmers and experienced by viewers as one program within a sequence of other programs in an ongoing series of timed segments. Further, programs are also associated—potentially linked—with other programs by their shared time slot. During the time that a television set is on in U.S. households—$7\frac{1}{2}$ hours per day, on average—we are carried along in the horizontal current of television time, flowing from one bit of TV to the next. Equally important, we may move vertically from one channel to another, creating associations between concurrent programs. A listing grid depicts visually these two axes of television's structure: sequence (one thing after another) and association (connections among simultaneous programs).

FIGURE 1.1

THURSDAY--JULY 2, 1992					PRIME TIME
	7:00	7:30	8:00	8:30	9:00	9:30
Broadcast						
ABC	*The Sting II (movie)*				Prime Time Live	
CBS	Top Cops	Moment of Truth	Street Stories		Bodies of Evidence	
Fox	Simpsons	Michael Jackson	Beverly Hills, 90210		Hunter	
NBC	Different World	Cosby Show	Cheers	Wings	L.A. Law	
PBS	MacNeil, Lehrer		Johnny Shines: On and On		Mystery!	
Cable						
AE	Nature's Kingdom		World at War		Brute Force	
AMC	*Conn. Yankee... (movie)*		*The Big Lift (movie)*			
BET	Desmonds	Video Soul				Generations
CNN	News		Larry King Live		News	
DISC	Carriers	G.I. Diary	Beyond 2000		Coast to Coast	
ESPN	Bowling		Boxing			
FAM	That's My Dog	You Asked For It	Scarecrow and Mrs. King		700 Club	
LIFE	L.A. Law		*To Save a Child (movie)*			
MTV	Day in Rock--Duff				Real World	Duff
NICK	F Troop	Superman	Get Smart	Dick Van Dyke	Dragnet	Alfred Hitchcock
TBS	*Alcatraz: The Whole Shocking Story (movie)*					
TNT	Centennial				*Greatest Show on Earth (movie)*	
USA	Murder, She Wrote		*Young Frankenstein (movie)*			
Premium						
DISNEY	Return to Treasure Island		*Summer Magic (movie)*			
HBO	Steven Wright		*Summer Heat (movie)*			Roseanne Arnold
CINEMAX	*End of Innocence (movie)*				*Lipstick (movie)*	
SHOWTIME	*Victor/Victoria (movie), cont.*		*Commando (movie)*			*Red Shoe (movie)*

We begin with this brief consideration of program listings because it illustrates the fundamental principle of commercial television's structure. As Raymond Williams first argued in 1974, television differs crucially from other art forms in its blending of disparate units of narrative, information, and advertising into a never-ending flow of television.[2] Although we commonly talk of watching a single television program as if it were a discrete entity, more commonly we simply *watch television*. The set is on. Programs, advertisements, and announcements come and go (horizontal axis). Mere fragments of programs, advertisements, and announcements flash by as we switch channels (vertical axis). We stay on the couch, drawn into the virtually ceaseless flow. We watch television more than we seek a specific television program.

The maintenance of televisual flow dominates nearly every aspect of television's structures and systems. It determines how stories will be told, how advertisements will be constructed, and even how television's visuals will be designed. Every chapter of this book will account in one way or another for the consequences of televisual flow. Before we start, however, we need to note three of this principle's general ramifications:

1. Polysemy
2. Interruption
3. Segmentation

POLYSEMY, HETEROGENEITY, CONTRADICTION

Many critics of television presume that it speaks with a single voice, that it broadcasts meanings from a single perspective. During the 1992 presidential election campaign, Vice President Dan Quayle singled out the TV pregnancy of an unwed mother—Murphy Brown (Candice Bergen)—as indicative of television's assault on "family values" (a euphemism for a conservative ideology of the family). For Quayle, the meanings presented on TV had systematically and univocally undermined the idea of the conventional nuclear family: father, mother, and correct number of children; the father working and the mother caring for children in the home; and no divorce or single parenthood. Television's discourse on the family had become too liberal—even decadent—according to Quayle and his supporters.

What Quayle failed to take into consideration, however, is the almost overwhelming flow of programs on television. *Murphy Brown* (1988–1998) is but one show among the hundreds that compose TV flow. And its endorsement of single parenthood, if such indeed is the case, is just one meaning that bobs along in the deluge of meanings flooding from the TV set. The many meanings, or **polysemy**, that television offers may be illustrated by excerpting a chunk of the television flow. Look at the Thursday-night schedule reproduced in Fig. 1.1. Let's presume that a typical viewer might have watched *The Simpsons*, followed by *The Cosby Show*; then taken some time off to put the kids to bed, and concluded the evening with *Roseanne Arnold*, departing from broadcast network television for this HBO special.[3] (Of course, this doesn't even take into consideration the channel switching that might have gone on during a particular program; but for the sake of illustration, we'll keep it simple.) What meanings surrounding the U.S. family, we might ask, do these three programs present?

TV Guide describes *Roseanne Arnold*, the special: "The comedienne comments on women's rights and dysfunctional families in stand-up." Roseanne, in some respects, exemplifies Quayle's comments. Her publicly available private life, frequently represented in television "magazine" programs such as *Entertainment Tonight*, illustrates the decay of the conventional family: her acrimonious divorces, her pregnancy while unmarried (and the child she gave up for adoption), her allegation of abuse as a child, and so on. In this special, she describes her family:

> There's Dad in his greasy T-shirt slopping down a beer and eating a big bowl of Capt'n Crunch. Mom's passed out on the couch while her horrible little dog licks her sweaty feet. My brother's dressing up like a girl, my sister's dressing up like a guy. I'm stealing food out of the fridge hand over fist, while my younger sister, who weighs all of 80 pounds, is upstairs doing jumping jacks for two hours 'cause she just ate a whole can of green beans and thinks she's too fat.

Thus, one meaning connoted by *Roseanne Arnold*, the program—and even Roseanne, the person—is that the traditional family is disintegrating, dysfunctional, and oppressive.

As a premium cable service, HBO promotes itself as providing material that is not seen on broadcast television. HBO's programs contain violent and sexual material forbidden by broadcast networks (ABC, CBS, Fox, NBC, UPN, and WB). It would be misleading, therefore, to assume that *Roseanne Arnold* typifies television's representation of the family. For that we must look to *The Cosby Show* and *The Simpsons*.

On *The Cosby Show* the traditional family is far from disintegrating, dysfunctional, or oppressive. Quite the contrary, *The Cosby Show* illustrates the strengths of the nuclear family—not surprising, considering that producer Bill Cosby has a doctorate in education and uses the program to propound his approach to child rearing. There may be occasional friction within *The Cosby Show*'s family (the Huxtables), but in the final analysis it provides an enclave, a safety zone, of affection and nurturing. In the episode rerun on our sample Thursday, the Huxtables' married daughter, her husband, and their twins are moving out of the Huxtable house. This allows for some joking by the father, Cliff (Bill Cosby), about his pleasure in getting rid of his daughter, but the centerpiece of the episode is a scene in which Cliff babysits the twins alone. This scene reinforces Cliff's skill with children (echoed in Cosby's commercial work for Jell-O) and emphasizes the importance of the (grand)parent–child relationship. In short, Cliff and Clair Huxtable signify all that is positive about the conventional family structure.

Are Quayle's "family values" associated with our final example, *The Simpsons*? Yes and no. *The Simpsons* exists somewhere in the middle of the spectrum that places *The Cosby Show* on one end and *Roseanne Arnold* on the other. *The Simpsons* does chip away at some of the foundations of the conventional family, but in the end it comes to reaffirm those foundations. Homer Simpson, for instance, is a much less satisfactory father figure than is Cliff Huxtable. On this particular Thursday, the Simpson family faces a crisis: The dog is sick and requires a costly operation to survive. Homer's response—typically ungenerous and self-serving—is to tell the children about "doggie heaven" and prepare to put the dog to sleep. Obviously, this is not the behavior of a caring patriarch such as Cliff. After Marge Simpson (a rather conventional mother figure, except for her towering blue hairdo) calculates a plan to finance the operation, Homer finally agrees to it, muttering, "lousy manipulative dog." By the end of the episode, the Simpson family—Homer included—has rallied around the dog, drawing close, as sitcom families always have. The "family value" of the supportive clan with the nurturing mother is reasserted.

As this small portion of the televisual flow illustrates, television contradicts itself frequently and haphazardly. It presents many heterogeneous meanings in any one night's viewing. This polysemy contributes to television's broad appeal. With so many different meanings being signified, we are bound to find some that agree with our world view. Does this mean that television can mean anything to anyone? And how are these meanings constructed? Three axioms will guide our approach to television.

Axiom 1. A segment of the televisual flow, whether it be an individual program, a commercial, a newscast, or an entire evening's viewing, may be thought of as a televisual **text**—offering a multiplicity of meanings or polysemy. When Roseanne describes her family, her words signify, among other things, "my family was dysfunctional." In its broadest sense, a "text" is any phenomenon that pulls together elements that have meaning for readers, viewers, or spectators that encounter it. Just as we read and interpret a book's organization of words in sentences, so we view and interpret a television program's sequence of sounds and images. Thus, narrative and non-narrative structures, lighting and set design, camera style, editing, and sound may be thought of as television's textual elements—those basic building blocks that the makers of television use to communicate with their audience. This book will present ways for students to better understand how these textual devices mount potential meanings for the viewer's consideration.

Axiom 2. The television text does not present all meanings equally positive or strong. Through dialogue, acting styles, music, and other attributes of the text, television emphasizes some meanings and de-emphasizes others. When the Simpson family gathers around their dog, with smiles on their faces and upbeat music in the background, the text is obviously suggesting that family togetherness and sacrificing for pets are positive meanings. But although television is polysemic, not all meanings are equal. TV is not unstructured or infinitely meaningful. Or, as John Fiske writes, "[Television's] polysemic potential is neither boundless nor structureless: the text delineates the terrain within which meanings may be made or proffers some meanings more than others."[4] The crucial work of television criticism is to analyze the medium's hierarchy of meanings. Which meanings does the text stress? *How* are they stressed? These are key questions for the television critic. To answer them requires an awareness of the cultural codes of class, gender, race, and such, that predominate a society. As Stuart Hall has noted, "Any society/culture tends, with varying degrees of closure, to impose its classifications of the social and cultural and political world. This constitutes a *dominant cultural order*, though it is neither univocal nor uncontested."[5] Television always has been a medium encoded with the meanings prevalent in the society to which it appeals. In contemporary U.S. society, many meanings circulate, but some are given greater weight than are others by the dominant cultural order. Correspondingly, although television is polysemic, it must be stressed that it is a **structured polysemy.** There is a pattern or structure implicit in the meanings that are offered on television. That structure tends to support those who hold positions of economic and political power in a particular society, but there is always room for contrary meanings.

Axiom 3. The act of viewing television is one in which the **discourses** of the viewer encounter those of the text. A discourse, in this sense of the term, has been defined by Fiske as "a language or system of representation that has developed socially in order to make and circulate a coherent set of meanings about an important topic area. These meanings serve the interests of that section of society within which the discourse originates and which works ideologically to naturalize those meanings into common sense."[6] We come to a TV text with belief structures—discourses—shaped by our psyche and social position: schooling, religion, upbringing, class, gender. And the TV text, too, has meaning structures that are governed by ideology and television-specific conventions. When we read the text, our discourses overlay those of the text. Sometimes they fit well, and sometimes they don't.

Discourses do not advertize themselves as such. The dominant discourse is so pervasive that, as Fiske suggests, it disappears into common sense, into the taken-for-granted. Consider the common presumption that in the U.S. everyone can become financially successful if they work hard. Most Americans believe this to be a truth, just common sense—despite the fact that statistics show that the economic class and education level of your parents virtually guarantees whether or not you'll succeed financially. The notion of success for all, thus, has a rather tenuous connection to the real world of work. However, it has a very strong connection to the discourse of corporate capitalism. If workers, even very poor workers, believe they may succeed if they work hard, then they will struggle to do good work and not dispute the basic economic system. So we may see that the commonsensical "truth" of the Horatio Alger success story is a fundamental part of a dominant discourse. As critics of television, it is our responsibility to examine these normally unexamined ideals.

INTERRUPTION AND SEQUENCE

Up to now we have depicted television as a continuous flow of sounds and images and meanings, but it is equally important to recognize the discontinuous component of TV watching and of TV itself—the ebb to its flow.

On the Thursday-night grid in Fig. 1.1, we can move horizontally across the page and see, obviously, that an evening's schedule is interrupted every half-hour or hour with different programs. One program's progression is halted by the next program, which is halted by the next, and the next. Within programs the flow is frequently interrupted by advertisements and announcements and the like. And on an even smaller level, within narrative programs' story lines there tend to be many interruptions. Soap operas, for example, often present scenes in which characters are interrupted just as they are about to commit murder, discover their true paternity, or consummate a romance that has been developing for years.

The point is that TV is constantly interrupting itself. Although the flow that gushes from our TVs is continuously television texts, it is not continuously the same type of texts. There are narrative texts and non-narrative texts and texts of advertising and information and advice, and on and on it goes.

Furthermore, we as viewers often interrupt ourselves while watching television. We leave the viewing area to visit the kitchen or the bathroom. Our attention drifts as we talk on the phone or argue with friends and family. We doze. And remote-controlled TV sets permit the most radical interruption of all: random channel switching. With a remote control, we choose the speed of interruption and move along the vertical axis of the grid, creating a mosaic of the texts that are broadcast concurrently. We blend together narrative and non-narrative programs, movies, advertisements, announcements, and credit sequences into a cacophonous supertext—making for some occasionally bizarre juxtapositions (as we switch, say, from a religious sermon to a rap video). The pace can be dizzying, especially for other viewers in the room who are not themselves punching the remote's buttons.

All of these forms of interruption—from television's self-interruptions to the interruptions we perform while watching—are not a perversion of the TV-viewing experience. Rather, they *define* that experience. This is not to suggest, however, that television does not try to combat the breaks in its flow. Clearly, advertisers and networks want viewers to overcome television's fragmentary nature and continue watching their particular commercials/programs. To this end, story lines, music, visual design, and dialogue must maintain our attention, to hold us through the commercial breaks, to quell the desire to check out another channel.

SEGMENTATION

Television's discontinuous nature has led to a particular way of packaging narrative, informational, and commercial material. The overall flow of television is segmented into small parcels, which often bear little logical connection to one another. A shampoo commercial might follow a *Seinfeld* scene and lead into a station identification. One segment of television does not necessarily link with the next, in a chain of cause and effect. In Fiske's view, "[Television] is composed of a rapid succession of compressed, vivid segments where the principle of logic and cause and effect is subordinated to that of association and consequence to sequence."[7] That is, fairly random association and sequence—rather than cause and effect and consequence—govern TV's flow.

TV's segmental nature peaks in the 30-second (and shorter) advertisement, but it is evident in all types of programs. News programs are compartmentalized into news, weather, and sports segments, then further subdivided into individual 90-second (and shorter) **packages** or stories. Game shows play rounds of a fixed, brief duration. MTV comprises mostly individual music videos that last no longer than 5 minutes. Narrative programs must structure their stories so that a segment can fit neatly within the commercial breaks. And even made-for-TV movies—the TV form that comes closest to films shown in theaters—are presented in narrative segments, mindful of exactly when the commercials are programmed. After all, to the television industry, programs are just filler, a necessary inconvenience interrupting the true function of television: broadcasting commercials.

The construction of these televisual segments and their relationship to each other are two major concerns of television's advertisers, producers, and programmers. For it is on this level that the battle for our *continuing* attention is won or lost. We should also be mindful of TV's segmental structure because it determines much of how stories are told, information presented, and commodities advertised on broadcast television.

S U M M A R Y

Televisual flow—Raymond Williams's term for television's sequence of diverse fragments of narrative, information, and advertising—defines the medium's fundamental structure. This flow facilitates the multiplicity of meanings, or polysemy, that television broadcasts.

Our consideration of televisual flow grows from three rudimentary axioms:

1. Television texts (programs, commercials, entire blocks of television time) contain meanings.

2. Not all meanings are presented equally. Textual devices emphasize some meanings over others and thus offer a hierarchy of meanings to the viewer. TV's polysemy is structured, by the dominant cultural order, into discourses (systems of belief).

3. The experience of television watching brings the discourses of the viewer into contact with the discourses of the text.

Televisual flow is riddled with interruptions. TV continually interrupts itself, shifting from one text to the next. And as often as the text interrupts itself, so too do we disrupt our consumption of television with trips out of the room or simple inattention. These constant interruptions lead television to adopt a segmented structure, constructing portions of TV in such a way as to encourage viewer concentration.

The aspiration of this book is to analyze television's production of meaning. We set aside the evaluation of television programs for the time being in order to focus on TV's structured polysemy and the systems that contribute to its creation: narrative and non-narrative structures, mise-en-scene, camera style, editing, and sound.

FURTHER READINGS

The basic principle of television flow stems from Raymond Williams, *Television: Technology and Cultural Form* (New York: Schocken, 1974). This short book is one of the fundamental building blocks of contemporary television criticism.

John Corner, *Critical Ideas in Television Studies* (Oxford: Clarendon Press, 1999) devotes an entire chapter to the notion of flow. John Fiske, *Television Culture* (New York: Methuen, 1987) and John Ellis, *Visible Fictions: Cinema: Television: Video* (Boston: Routledge, 1992) both elaborate on the concept, too. Fiske is also concerned with articulating television's meanings and how they may be organized into discourses. Todd Gitlin confronts television's role in advocating a society's dominant or "hegemonic" discourse in "Prime Time Ideology: The Hegemonic Process in Television Entertainment" in *Television: The Critical View*, ed. Horace Newcomb (New York: Oxford University Press, 2000): 574–594.

Further discussion of how meaning is produced in television texts may be found in the writings of British television scholars associated with the Centre for Contemporary Cultural Studies (University of Birmingham, England). This school of analysis is summarized in Fiske's *Television Culture* and in his "British Cultural Studies and Television," in *Channels of Discourse, Reassembled*, ed. Robert C. Allen (Chapel Hill, NC: University of North Carolina Press, 1992). Students interested in the seminal work in this area should read Stuart Hall, "Encoding/Decoding," in *Culture, Media, Language*, eds. Stuart Hall, Dorothy Hobson, Andre Lowe, Paul Willis (London: Hutchinson, 1980).

The implications of Dan Quayle's comments about Murphy Brown are examined in Rebecca L. Walkowitz, "Reproducing Reality: Murphy Brown and Illegitimate Politics," in *Feminist Television Criticism*, eds. Charlotte Brunsdon, Julie D'Acci, Lynn Spigel (New York: Clarendon, 1997). Walkowitz is concerned with the ideology of "family values" and the representation of women working in television news.

For thoughts on the erosion of broadcast television, see David Marc, "What Was Broadcasting?" in *Television: The Critical View* (2000): 629–648. He is one critic who believes the broadcast-TV era has already come to an end.

ENDNOTES

[1] The bulk of *TV Guide* is comprised of more detailed descriptions of programs than is provided in the grid, but these are also arranged in terms of time slots rather

than stressing first the individual programs. In contrast to this generalization, however, the magazine does emphasize eight or nine programs in its daily "Guidelines" feature, but these programs form a small segment of the television day.

[2] Raymond Williams, *Television: Technology and Cultural Form* (New York: Schocken, 1974), 86.

[3] Although *The Simpsons* and *The Cosby* Show spent two seasons opposed to one another in the same time slot, the latter was shifted to the later time period during the end of its run (Summer 1992).

[4] John Fiske, *Television Culture* (New York: Methuen, 1987), 16.

[5] Stuart Hall, "Encoding/Decoding," in *Culture, Media, Language*, eds. Stuart Hall, Dorothy Hobson, Andre Lowe, Paul Willis (London: Hutchinson, 1980), 134.

[6] Fiske, 14.

[7] Fiske, 105.

CHAPTER 2

Narrative Structure: Television Stories

When asked if he thought films should be a slice of life, director Alfred Hitchcock is reported to have said, no, they should be a slice of cake. We might well pose the same question about television: Is it a slice of life or a slice of cake? The images we see on the screen show us real people and objects, and the sounds we hear are taken from our real experience, with dialogue spoken in a language and idiom with which we are familiar. Often we suspend disbelief and imagine that television characters are real persons, with tangible pasts and a future toward which time is carrying them. We might muse, "I wonder what happened to Steve Urkel after *Family Matters* was cancelled." It seems as if we just happened to drop in on these TV people and witnessed a slice out of their lives.

But we should be aware that for all their seeming reality, the stories we watch are actually slices of televisual confections. As if making a cake, the screenwriters and directors follow storytelling "recipes" that suggest the proper ingredients and their proper amounts for creating a television program. They mix those ingredients in conventionally prescribed ways—adding a chase scene here and a romantic clinch there—to maximize viewer pleasure. Just like the frosting on the top of a birthday cake, a television narrative has been blended to satisfy our appetites.

To understand television narrative, then, we must look beyond the appearance of reality the medium promotes and understand the recipe that created that reality. We may ask of any program, "How is this story put together? What are its narrative components, and how do they relate to one another?" As we begin to look at television's narratives, we will notice a limited number of basic structures, a finite set of recipes for mixing story ingredients. Historically, there have been four principal narrative modes on television:

1. The theatrical film (originally shown in theaters)
2. The made-for-TV film and miniseries (also known as the MOW)
3. The series program
4. The serial program

This chapter charts these four structures and explores the differences and similarities among them.

THE THEATRICAL FILM

From Antagonism to Alliance

When television experienced its first growth spurt in the years after World War II, the U.S. motion picture studios and the television industry were mutually antagonistic. TV, an upstart medium, stole the cinema's customers and undermined the studio system that had dominated North America's narrative market. Indeed, the entire world depended on Hollywood for its stories. But the 1950s would be the last decade that U.S. viewers would rely so heavily on the cinema for their entertainment. By 1960, television had replaced the cinema as America's primary form of entertainment, and many within the film industry were bitter about this loss of control. Just as film executives resented television's intrusion into their domain, so were their counterparts in the television industry hesitant to deal with the film studios. Television producers wanted to create their own material and not have to depend on the whims of the film industry for their product.

What began as antagonism between the film studios and the television industry soon evolved into a wary alliance. Television was hungry for narrative product; the studios controlled thousands of movies. After their initial runs, these films were warehoused, seldom heard from again, and thus not a financial asset. RKO, Monogram, and Republic—three of the smaller studios—were the first to begin leasing their older movies to television. Soon the major studios were compelled to join in. It wasn't long before newer and newer films began making their way to television more and more quickly. The ratings success of NBC's *Saturday Night at the Movies* (1961–) led to all of the broadcast networks featuring "nights at the movies." By the end of the decade there were recent theatrical films running on television just about every night of the week.

Since that time, the relationship between theatrical filmmaking and television has become more complex. Rather than disdaining television, most of today's film studios also own and operate television production facilities, blurring the economic distinction between the two media. Bringing film and television even closer together are the VCR and DVD player, which were introduced to the home market in the late 1970s and late 1990s, respectively. Indeed, in the late 1980s videocassette rental revenue bypassed theatrical box office receipts. Nowadays more viewers see a videocassette or DVD of a movie on their television sets than go to see a film projected in a theater.

Although the VCR/DVD and premium cable channels (HBO, Showtime, etc.) have radically changed the way we view/consume movies and have virtually eliminated programs such as *Saturday Night at the Movies*, theatrical films continue to play a major role in television programming. Most local stations and many cable satellite stations such as WGN, WWOR, and WTBS continue to use theatrical films to fill much of their schedule. (Television mogul Ted Turner, for example, now owns—not leases—the MGM film library, and has based his

TNT and Turner Classic Movies channels on that collection.) Moreover, the narrative structure of the theatrical film is still used as a standard by which other TV programs are judged. It is important, therefore, to consider how the theatrical film structures its stories and how those structures are modified when they appear on broadcast television.

The Classical Paradigm

The theatrical cinema was not always a powerful narrative machine. Around the turn of the century film stories were in a rather primitive state. Some early movies told no stories at all: a baby is fed, a train arrives at a station, a wall falls over. Viewers were so enthralled with the mere sight of movement on the screen that characters and plot were superfluous. However, cinema viewers soon developed an obsession with narrative, and the young film industry was more than willing to provide it. When D. W. Griffith's milestone, *Birth of a Nation*, was released in 1915, the cinema had already established itself as an accomplished, mature art form, a specifically narrative art form. The popularization of sound a little over a decade later threw the industry into upheaval and forced the cinema to readjust its storytelling methods. But by 1934 American movies had settled on a certain way of constructing stories as well as a conventional style of editing, visual composition, dialogue and music, and so on. This filmmaking method has come to be known as the **classical Hollywood cinema**, or, more simply, **Hollywood classicism**.[1] Classical narrative structure is the concern of the present chapter. Classical editing and sound are discussed later.

In order to avoid one possible point of confusion, it is important to note that "classical" film, in this sense, does not refer simply to well-established and admired films that have maintained their appeal over the decades. Calling *Casablanca* (1942) or *Gone with the Wind* (1939) a "classic" is not using the term as we will be using it here. Rather, classical in our sense refers to a specific mode of filmmaking and can be applied to almost all films made in Hollywood since the 1930s. *Casablanca* and *Gone with the Wind* are classical films, but so are *What! No Beer?* (1933), *Showgirls* (1995), *Ishtar* (1987), and *Basket Case* (1982), not to mention *Basket Case II* (1989). Moreover, of the theatrical films shown on broadcast television, only the very rare exception is not a classical film. Nonclassical films find a home on cable channels such as Sundance, the Independent Film Channel, Bravo, and Arts and Entertainment (A&E). The foreign-language "art" and U.S. "independent" (i.e., independent of the major studios) films are often aggressively anticlassical. Although they have little impact on network narrative television, one can see their influence in music videos and television commercials.

What binds together the thousands of classical films that have been made over the decades? The seven basic components of classical narrative structure are listed here. As we outline these components, we will illustrate them mostly with examples from *Raiders of the Lost Ark* (1981). *Raiders* was chosen because it is one of the most widely viewed films in the history of the cinema (as of 2000 it was still one of the 20 highest-grossing films of all time) and because it exemplifies classical principles so clearly.

1. Single Protagonist. The protagonist is the central character in a film, book, TV program, or other fictional mode. The story revolves around him or her. Classicism has usually limited a movie's protagonist to just one or, at most, two characters. Filmmakers reason that this facilitates viewer identification and streamlines the narrative action. Viewers can identify with one person more readily than with a dozen and can comprehend a single character more quickly than several mixed together at the beginning of the film.

This seems commonsensical enough, but narratives do occasionally use more than a single protagonist. Soap operas usually feature a dozen protagonists at any particular point in the story. Russian silent filmmakers such as Sergei Eisenstein argued that an entire class of people could be the protagonist. In Eisenstein's *Strike* (1924) and *Potemkin* (1925) masses of people serve as the narrative focus. Of course, there are even classical films that break this "rule" of the single protagonist, but instead of splintering the story, these films often unite several characters with a single purpose so that they function as a united force within the narrative. The four "ghostbusters" in the film of the same name (1984), for example, work together to destroy the ghosts.

2. Exposition. The exposition introduces the viewer to two components of the story: (a) The principal characters' personas, their "personalities," and (b) the space or environment the characters inhabit. Every story must have an exposition, but not necessarily at the beginning of the film. Many movies, especially murder mysteries, start in the middle of the action and then later explain who the characters are and what their space entails. Stories that open in such a fashion are said to begin *in medias res*. *Raiders of the Lost Ark* begins *in medias res*; the hero, Indiana Jones ("Indy") is nearly crushed by a huge rolling boulder and is then pursued by angry natives. All of this occurs before we know who he is, where he is, and why he is doing what he's doing. Once Indy escapes from the jungle, the film's exposition begins. His profession and motivation are established when we see him lecturing about archeology; and the entire story (its characters and their locations) is mapped out by the government bureaucrats who visit Indy and pique his interest in the Ark of the Covenant.

3. Motivation. In any classical story, something must catalyze events. The action must have motivation. Here the importance of the single protagonist is reemphasized, for classical narrative is motivated by the desire of a single character to attain a goal or acquire something (or someone). *Raiders of the Lost Ark* illustrates this unequivocally: Indy desires to acquire the Ark of the Covenant. The protagonist's desire—his or her lack of something or someone or some emotion—catalyzes the story, provides a reason for events to happen, and establishes the narrative's central enigma.

4. Narrative Enigma. Early in any classical film a question is explicitly or implicitly asked. This question forms the central enigma of the classical story. In *Raiders* the questions is: Will Indy find the Ark and prevent the Nazis from using it? There may be secondary enigmas (What is in the Ark? Will Indy get together with Marion?), but every other aspect of the story stems from the one central enigma. It is essential to classical narrative that the enigma must not be solved immediately. If it were, there would be no story. Imagine how short *Raiders of the Lost Ark* would be if Indy found the Ark in the first 10 minutes.

Consequently, *Raiders of the Lost Ark* and all classical narratives rely on a series of delays that forestall the solution of the enigma.

Chief among the delaying tactics of the classical cinema is the introduction of a character who blocks fulfillment of the protagonist's desire—and, thus, blocks the resolution of the narrative enigma. This blocking character is known as the **antagonist**. The antagonist can be as simple as a solitary character with whom the protagonist battles or competes—for example, Belloq, Indy's nemesis, to whom he loses an idol in the opening scene. Or, the antagonist may take the shape of the character's environment: for example, the Civil War in *Gone with the Wind* or North Atlantic icebergs in *Titanic* (1997). Some classical films even pose the antagonizing force as being within the protagonist—as in *Jerry Maguire* (1996), where the title character faces a moral crisis about his life and his career as a sports agent. These narrative conflicts are not mutually exclusive. A film may contain a combination of them, as when, in *Ordinary People* (1980), Conrad deals with his internal conflicts about his brother's death at the same time he works through his antagonism with his mother.

In any case, the conflict created by the antagonist delays the resolution of the enigma until the end of the film. These delays form the basis of the chain of cause–effect actions that compose the main body of the film.

5. Cause–effect Chain. Once the exposition has established the characters and their space, and the protagonist's desire has sparked the forward movement of the story, the narrative begins a series or chain of events that are linked to one another and occur over time. Events do not occur randomly or in arbitrary order in classical films. One event causes the next, which causes the next, which causes the next, and so on (Fig. 2.1). *Raiders of the Lost Ark* illustrates this: The visit by the bureaucrats causes Indy to go looking for the Ark, which causes him to track down Marion Ravenwood to find a clue to the Ark's location, which causes him to become realigned with her and take her to Cairo, which causes them to battle the Nazis in the Cairo market, and so on. Link by link the narrative chain is built.

Each single narrative event is commonly called a **scene** or **sequence**. A scene is a specific chunk of narrative that coheres because the event takes place in a particular time at a particular place. The space of a scene is consistent, and time passes in a scene as it does in real life. Contemporary narrative theory has renamed the scene the **syntagm**. The order in which the scenes or syntagms transpire is the film's **syntagmatic structure**.

FIGURE 2.1

The Cause–Effect Narrative Chain

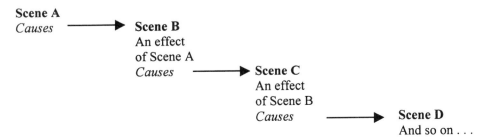

In a single scene time is continuous, as it is in life; but as we make the transition from one scene to another, the potential for manipulating time arises. Time in film does not match time in reality. If it did, it would take months to watch *Raiders of the Lost Ark*. **Story time**, several months, in this case, is rarely equivalent to **screen time**—*Raiders of the Lost Ark*'s 115 minutes. To maximize narrative impact, the duration and order of story time are manipulated as it is converted into screen time.

Most commonly, screen time's duration is shorter than that of story time. Very few films last as long as the actions they represent on the screen. Obviously, films must compress time in order to tell their stories without taxing the viewer. Only occasional oddities equate screen time with real time. For example, in *High Noon* (1952) 82 minutes in the life of a sheriff are presented in 82 minutes; *Rope* (1948) is presented as if it were one long, continuous shot; and *Time Code* (2000) shows us four screens of continuous action simultaneously. Further, screen time is not always shorter than story time. This is less common than is the reverse, but certainly not unheard of. In *Fantastic Voyage* (1966), a tiny submarine passes through a human heart in 57 seconds of story time, as we are told by the characters. But this 57 seconds of story time elapses over 3 minutes of screen time. Thus, the duration of time may be manipulated to maximize narrative effect.

The order of screen time may be similarly manipulated. In most classical films, the events shown in the second scene occur after those that appear in the first scene, those in the third scene occur after the second, and so on—that is, the temporal structure is normally chronological. However, it is not uncommon for films to use **flashbacks** or, less often, **flashforwards**, to rearrange a story's temporal structure. In classical film these departures from chronological order are clearly marked with special effects so that we are certain when we are shifting into the past: The image goes wavy, the focus shifts, smoke appears before the lens, or the character's voice fades out. In nonclassical films, such as those by Alain Resnais and Luis Buñuel, the past is jumbled up with the present and the future in challenging and sometimes contradictory ways.

Also important to consider is the increasing intensity of events, the basic dynamic force of the narrative. As the enigma's resolution is delayed again and again, the narrative level escalates. As Indy comes closer to the Ark, his battles become more and more death defying. Eventually, this results in the film's climax.

6. Climax. At a classical film's climax the narrative conflict culminates—necessitating a resolution. The film's central enigma, which has been delayed for 90 minutes or more, demands to be solved. At the climax of *Raiders of the Lost Ark*, the conflict between Indy and Belloq peaks as Indy and Marion are tied to a stake while Belloq and the Nazis open the Ark. The central enigma (Will Indy find the Ark and prevent the Nazis from using it?) and its subsidiary (What is in the Ark?) are solved in this scene: Apparently the wrath of God is contained in the Ark and consequently the Nazis are destroyed when they open it.

Climaxes are the most concentrated moment of the narrative conflict, but typically they are not the very end of the film. Classical films normally incorporate a short resolution to answer any outstanding questions.

7. Resolution or Denouement. Up to the point of the resolution, the enigmas have been consistently delayed and the narrative action has constantly risen. In the resolution, in contrast, the enigmas are solved and the narrative action (or conflict) declines. After the apocalyptic destruction of the Nazis, *Raiders of the Lost Ark* resolves by showing us the Ark being stored in an anonymous crate in a huge warehouse, and Indy and Marion getting together for a drink. The questions about the Ark's contents and the Nazis' use of it are answered. Also answered is a subsidiary question about whether Indy and Marion will reunite. There is a strong sense of **closure** at the end of this and most classical films. The enigmas that had been opened at the start of the film are now closed off, secured. The narrative's questions are answered.

If a narrative concludes without answering its questions and the ending is ambiguous or open, this is an instance of narrative **aperture**. For the most part, narrative aperture exists only in nonclassical films. Jean-Luc Godard's *Vivre sa Vie* (1962), for example, concludes with the protagonist being suddenly shot and killed, with no subsequent explanation. There are very few films that follow classical conventions up until the very end, and then tantalize us with an ambiguous finish. The horror genre contains most of these films. *Halloween* (1978), with the mysterious disappearance of the killer's body, is one example. There are, of course, economic reasons for the openness or aperture of horror films. An open ending facilitates the return of the killer in sequels. But aperture also suits the horror film's raison d'être, which is to call into question the stability of rational life. An ambiguous ending undermines the narrative equilibrium that is the goal of most classical films. The horror film does not share that goal.

Theatrical Films on Television

The transition from theater to television can have significant effects on feature film narrative. The most drastic of these effects is the shortening of a film to fit it into a television time slot. Large parts of the narrative are excised in this process. A Chicago station once ran the 118-minute *From Here to Eternity* in a 90-minute time slot. Subtracting more time for commercials, station promotional materials, and other interruptions left about 75 minutes for the film itself. The Artists Rights Foundation tracks the time cut from theatrical films. It notes, for example, how *The Silence of the Lambs* lost 29 minutes when broadcast on the WB network. Obviously, cutting this much time from any film is going to severely affect the coherence of its narrative chain. Characters appear and disappear unpredictably and entire subplots cease to exist. The cause–effect linkage of classical films is disrupted, sometimes to the point of incomprehensibility, when films are edited in this fashion. Specific scenes that the Artists Rights Foundation noted were missing in the 1999 CBS screening of *Dead Man Walking* (1995) included:

1. Sister Helen Prejean (Susan Sarandon) entering the prison—flashback scenes of the murders that Matthew Poncelet (Sean Penn) was found guilty of committing and that he will be put to death for.

2. Four separate scenes that show Sister Helen working to get Pancelet a new trial.

3. A court room scene that denies Matthew Poncelet the right for a new trial.

4. A scene with Sister Helen asking the prison priest to be Matthew Poncelet's spiritual advisor. At this time, we learn she will be the first woman to advise a prisoner on death row.

5. Three separate scenes with Sister Helen speaking with the murdered victim's families.[2]

Movies shown on broadcast television are also shortened for reasons other than time concerns. Typically, broadcast standards for television are stricter than U.S. obscenity laws for motion pictures. Images, language, and even entire scenes that television networks deem unfit for family viewing will be excised. *Slap Shot* (1977), *Raging Bull* (1980), and the originally X-rated *Midnight Cowboy* (1969) have all been ravaged when broadcast on commercial television.[3] Even when movies are shown on cable premium channels there is no guarantee they will not be edited. When Showtime—a pay service that boasted running films "uncut and uninterrupted"—presented *Montenegro* (1981), it removed a sexually suggestive scene involving a motorized toy tank.

Thus, various bits and pieces of theatrical films are missing when they are presented on commercial television. Of course, the portions of the film that remain are not presented without interruption—except on rare occasions (e.g., the initial screening of *Schindler's List* [1993]). U.S. television inherited from radio the convention of interposing commercials within the body of movies and programs. Commercials and their impact will be considered later; but we may note here that the appearance of TV commercials within classical films adds a distracting, narratively detrimental element that is absent from the film's presentation in the theater.[4]

The abbreviation and interruption of classical film narrative are not the only ways that film stories are modified on television. In somewhat uncommon circumstances, theatrical films are sometimes actually lengthened when presented on television. Network TV added 49 minutes to *Superman* (1978) and 19 minutes to *Superman III* (1983) when they were originally telecast.[5] In one of the strangest of such incidents, a 1980s telecast of *Rear Window* (1958) extended its running time by presenting the credits in slow motion and inserting a dream sequence that had not existed in the original film! The narrative effect of such alterations varies from film to film, but it is seldom beneficial.

Hence, for a variety of reasons the movies seen on broadcast television and cable premium channels may substantively differ from the versions shown in theaters. Narrative can be a fragile component of the movies and often is distorted beyond recognition in the transition from theater screen to television screen. However, theatrical films are not the only "movies" appearing on television. There are, of course, many films that were specifically designed for the electronic medium.

THE MADE-FOR-TELEVISION FILM OR MOW

Until the mid-1960s, the only movies shown on television were ones that had originally been designed for theater audiences. The early 1960s success of "nights at the movies" made networks hungry for more, cheaper films—ones that might also serve as springboards for television series. Consequently, the made-for-TV movie was born, and, within the industry, christened the **MOW** (for "movie of the week"). *See How They Run* inaugurated this new form in 1964. Since then, MOW films have been mixed with theatrical ones on networks' film programs in increasing numbers. In the 1978–79 season, more MOWs were broadcast than were theatrical films, which continues to be the case.[6] Viewers seem to distinguish less and less between the two. Of the two highest-rated movies in the history of television, one is a theatrical film (*Gone with the Wind*) but the other is a made-for-television film (*The Day After* [1983]). Moreover, the made-for-TV/theatrical dissimilarity is becoming increasingly difficult to maintain because U.S. made-for-TV movies are often shown theatrically in Europe (e.g., the pilot for *Twin Peaks* [1990]) and films shot for European television are sometimes shown in U.S. theaters (e.g., *The Full Monty* [1997] was co-produced by Channel 4 TV [U.K.]).

Are there substantive differences in the narrative structure, then, between theatrical and MOW films? What is it about the latter that marks them as being produced specifically for television?

Narrative Structure

As we might anticipate, there are more similarities than differences between the narrative structure of the made-for-TV film and that of the theatrical movie:

1. Single protagonist.
2. Exposition establishes characters and space.
3. Protagonist's desire catalyzes story.
4. Central enigma underpins story.
5. Narrative progresses by antagonist delaying enigma resolution.
6. Conflict peaks in a climax.
7. Closure assured in the resolution.

With so many similarities, what is it that distinguishes the two forms? The distinctions arise from the MOW's recognition of interruption as a sustaining force on television. In short, MOWs are designed to be interrupted. Their narrative chain is segmented to take advantage of commercial breaks. Rather than a continuous chain of events in cause–effect relationship with one other, the MOW often (though not always) halts the action and provides a small climax just before the commercials begin. This climax does not resolve the enigma, as does the final climax of a theatrical film. Instead, it heightens the enigma, posing questions that entice the viewer to stay with this channel through the commercials to find out what happens next.

Theatrical films have these small climaxes on occasion, too, but they are not coordinated with television's commercial breaks; they don't occur with regularity every 15 minutes or so. MOW narrative structure aligns itself with the rhythm of television, taking advantage of the pauses to heighten narrative suspense. Television's rhythm also determines the length of most MOWs. To fit into a 2-hour time slot with an average of 15 nonprogramming minutes per hour, they must run 90 minutes—with little room for variation. Theatrical films typically run 90 to 120 minutes, with the nature of the story determining the film's exact length. In contrast, the 90-minute precondition for MOWs strictly determines the length of the story, as it must be made to fit this time slot. Screenwriters and directors working within the MOW form must plot their films with this rigid time limit in mind, just as poets must confine themselves to the rhythmic pattern of the sonnet and painters must cope with the usually rectangular shape of a frame.

Many MOWs are used as **pilots**—programs that introduce new series. This function of some MOWs affects their narrative structure, distinguishing them from the classical model. Classical films end with a strong sense of closure. Questions are answered; enigmas are solved; couples are united. Those MOWs that do double duty as pilots for projected television series cannot tolerate this narrative closure. Instead, they serve to open the narrative of the series to follow. Typically, a pilot will resolve some narrative issues, but, more important to its producers, it must establish ongoing enigmas that will underpin the program during its regular run. Thus, the 2-hour pilot for *Miami Vice* (1984) establishes the characters of Rico Tubbs and Sonny Crockett, and, through the death of Tubbs' brother, provides the motivation for Tubbs moving to Miami. But the pilot concludes without Tubbs apprehending his brother's murderer—as would have been typical for a classical film. There is no closure to the pilot's central enigma: Will Tubbs capture the killer? We had to wait until several weeks into the season before the murderer was punished during the run of the series. The pilot, which is frequently presented as if it were a stand-alone movie, uses a certain degree of narrative aperture to engage us, drawing us into the narrative structure of the regular run of a series.

In sum, the MOW shares many attributes with its theatrical counterpart. The two are getting harder and harder to tell apart. And yet, the MOW's narrative structure does reveal the traits of having been "made for television." It recognizes television's interruptive form, and it has developed narrative strategies to cope with it. These strategies are even more evident in the television series, a format that is quite distinct from the movies, whether theatrical or MOW.

THE TELEVISION SERIES

Early television drew on a variety of sources for its programming material: theatrical movies, sports events, vaudeville-style music and comedy skits, and such. In many regards the infant medium relied most heavily on its broadcasting predecessor, radio, for programming strategies and narrative forms. Indeed, the influence of radio was so strong, and the television image in the 1940s so poor, that early television was little more than radio accompanied by fuzzy, indistinct, black-and-white pictures—with the emphasis on sound rather than image. Television has changed a good deal since then, but the basic narrative form that TV inherited from radio endures to the present day: the **series**.

There are precedents for the television series in both literature and the cinema. Literary series have been published that center on figures such as Tarzan, the Hardy Boys, and Nancy Drew; and theatrical film series have featured a variety of characters: Tarzans (dozens since Elmo Lincoln first did the role in 1918), sophisticated detectives (the "Thin Man" films, 1934–47), homicidal maniacs (Freddy Krueger of *Nightmare on Elm Street*, beginning in 1984), sports heroes (Rocky, beginning in 1976), and so on. Even so, the series has never been as important to literature or film as it is to television. Each season, the list of the top 10 rated shows is dominated by series (see, for example, the 1998–99 season, Table 7.1). What characterizes the narrative television series, and how is it particularly well-suited to the form of television? We can begin to answer these questions by examining the series' narrative structure.

Narrative Structure

The television series is a narrative form that presents weekly episodes with a defined set of recurring characters. For example, the five most popular series during the 1998–99 season were *Friends, Frasier, Jesse, Veronica's Closet,* and *Touched By an Angel* (Table 7.1). In series such as these, each week's episode is basically self-contained. Although they will occasionally have two-part episodes or a narrative arc that recurs, the narrative does not consistently continue from one week to the next. Each episode does not begin where the previous one ended, as episodes do in the television **serial**. The series and the serial forms have gotten progressively closer to one another over the years. *Friends* exemplifies this. It's a program where narrative arcs (such as Ross's numerous marriages) do persist over the course of several episodes, but the bulk of the issues raised on it each week are resolved by the end of the episode. It is thus considered a series even though it contains some serial aspects. We'll use it as our principal source of examples as we discuss the characteristics of the series.

In some respects, the television series resembles the classical film. After all, series do present chains of events driven by enigmas. But the pressures of constant interruption and of repetition, of a weekly appearance before the viewer, force the television series to rely on some distinctly different narrative strategies.

1. Multiple Protagonists. Many series center on a single protagonist: Mary Richards (*The Mary Tyler Moore Show* [1970–77]), Jessica Fletcher (*Murder, She Wrote* [1984–96]). But it is more common for a TV series to use a pair of protagonists or even an ensemble cast of five or six main characters. Christine Cagney and Mary Beth Lacey (*Cagney and Lacey* [1982–88]) held equal narrative importance, as did the central characters on *Cheers* (1982–1993) and *Friends* (1994–). The main function of these multiple protagonists is to permit a variety of plots within the same environment. One week *Friends* was concerned with Phoebe giving birth to triplets (October 8, 1998). The next week Joey appeared on a PBS telethon, disappointed that he wasn't hosting it; Ross decide to move to London to marry Emily; and Phoebe's triplets were nearly forgotten. Narrative emphasis shifts from one episode to the next, but the core characters remain the same.

2. Exposition. The constancy of the series' central figures means that each episode needs only a brief exposition. Most of the characters and their space are known to the viewer from previous episodes, and often they are reestablished in the program's theme song: for example, "Come and listen to my story about a man named Jed, a poor mountaineer, barely kept his family fed . . ." (*The Beverly Hillbillies* [1962–71]). Only the particulars of the current episode's characters and any new locations must be established. We rely on the consistency of characters and space; it is part of what makes the show comfortable to watch. We know that every week—or every day in syndication—the characters of *Friends* will congregate at the Central Perk coffee house, and that Andy Taylor and Barney Fife will preside over their jail (*The Andy Griffith Show* [1960–68]). Only new characters and new locations need be established in the exposition. Obviously, this is different from a one-time presentation such as an MOW, which must acquaint the viewer with an unknown cast of characters and an unfamiliar setting.

Series characters have a personal history of which we are usually conscious and to which references are occasionally made. In *Friends*, for example, the humor of each of Ross's marriages depends on our knowledge of his previous marital failures. On most series programs, however, these personal histories are rather vague and ill defined. The past is a murky region in series television. The present tense of a specific episode is usually all that matters. In the 1986–87 season of *Miami Vice*, Detective Larry Zito was murdered—a narrative event important enough to warrant a two-episode story. Subsequent episodes of the program, however, seldom mentioned Zito. That segment of the program's past virtually ceased to exist, except in reruns. Thus, series characters do have an established past, and their characters do not need reestablishing each week; but they often misplace this past and, in any event, it is usually not necessary for our enjoyment of a specific episode for us to know the details of the characters' pasts.

3. Motivation. The constancy of a series' characters and setting establishes a narrative equilibrium. A state of balance or rest exists at the beginning of each episode. However, if this balance were to continue, there would be no story. Something needs to disturb the balance to set the story in motion, to catalyze it.

The most common narrative catalyst, as in the classical cinema, is the lack or desire of the protagonist. Since the series incorporates multiple protagonists, this permits it to shift the narrative catalyst function from one character to another. The desire of one protagonist may dominate one week; the desire of another may arise in the next episode. In the episode of *Friends* titled "The One With Chandler's Work Laugh" (January 21, 1999), several characters have desires that motivate the narrative: Will Rachel discover Monica and Chandler's secret romance, and will that affect their friendship? Will Monica continue to love Chandler—despite his obsequious demeanor around his boss? Will Ross find true romance? Each lack (of the truth, of commitment in a relationship, of romance) raises the question of whether the protagonist's desire will be satisfied. In short, each raises a narrative enigma.

4. Narrative Problematic. Questions such as these underpin the narrative of a series and capture our attention (if they are successful). But, of course, as in all narrative forms these enigmas must not be immediately resolved. There must be a counterforce that prevents their instantaneous resolution, or there would be no story to tell. In the *Friends* examples, there are several counterforces. Monica functions as the **antagonist** for Rachel's desire for the truth—lying to her and concealing the relationship. Chandler's boss and his behavior around the boss are counterforces to Monica's commitment to him. And Janice—an ill-suited date for Ross—delays his attainment of love. As with the classical film, the counterforce need not be a single individual. It may also be the protagonist's environment or an internal, psychological element within the protagonist. The main point is that the protagonist's acquisition of his or her goal must be postponed, deferred, so that the narrative may develop further complications.

Thus, the narrative focus shifts from one week to the next, but it is important to recognize that these individual desires and enigmas exist within a larger narrative problematic. Because fundamentally the series is a repeatable form, there must be some narrative kernel that recurs every week. In effect, the program must ask the same question again and again to maintain consistency and viewer interest. Of course, we wouldn't watch exactly the same material each week (although the number of times we watch a particular episode in syndication contradicts this), so there must be some variation within that consistency. But, still, every series must have some recurring problematic, some dilemma with which it deals in every episode.

For *Friends* the dilemma revolves around issues confronting friends in their 20s—just out of college, but not yet fully settled into a career. We might think of that dilemma as: Will the friends' camaraderie be disrupted? That is, will the friends stop being friends? Related questions include: Will Chandler/Joey/Monica/Phoebe/Ross find romance? Will Chandler/Joey/Monica/Phoebe/Ross find fulfilling work? Almost every week the program tests the bond among these six friends. To take another example—this time from a police drama—the problematic of *Miami Vice* is: Will Crockett and/or Tubbs surrender to the temptations (the "Vice") they are immersed in and become villains? Individual episodes counterpose various antagonists against Crockett and Tubbs, but overriding these specific concerns is the more general issue of their moral character.

Each episode, drawing on the multiplicity of protagonists in series TV, poses a slightly different narrative enigma. As John Ellis has noted, "The basic problematic of the series, with all its conflicts, is itself a stable state."[7] Specific enigmas come and go—briefly igniting the viewer's interest—but the fundamental problematic remains firm, sustaining the viewer's ongoing attachment to the program.

5. Cause–effect Chain. As in the classical film, events do not happen randomly in series television. One scene leads into the next, and the next, and the next. A cause–effect chain is erected scene by scene. However, this chain must be broken at least once during a half-hour program, and at least three times during an hour–long program, for the insertion of commercials. The TV chain is not continuous as it is in the cinema.

The series deals with this discontinuity by segmenting the narrative. That is, the story is broken into segments that fit between the commercial breaks. These between-commercial segments, sometimes called **acts**, consist of one or more scenes that hold together as strongly as classical scenes do. They end with their own small climax, which leads into the commercial break. The function of this precommercial climax is not to resolve narrative dilemmas, but instead to heighten them, to raise our interest in the narrative as we flow into the commercials. New, minor enigmas may even be posed just before the segment ends.

In "The One With Chandler's Work Laugh," for example, Ross is despondent about his failed marriage to Emily. As act one ends, Monica, Joey, Rachel, and Phoebe quiz him about being out all night. He is evading their questions when Janice enters the room—revealing that Ross was with her. As the segment fades to black with a shot of an embarrassed Ross, the viewer is left with the enigmas: Were Ross and Janice romantically involved the night before? Following the commercials, this question is answered in the very first scene (yes, they were) and the narrative chain resumes.

In sum, the segmentation of the series narrative interrupts the rising curve of increasingly intensified action that we see in classical cinema and replaces it with portions of narrative equipped with their own miniature climax—in a sense, a series of several upward curves. In this way, television narrative more closely resembles the play, with its division into separate acts; or the mystery novel that ends each chapter on a note of suspense. The chain is slightly ruptured, but not sundered by the so-called commercial breaks.

6. Climax. Series episodes do have a final climax, where the action finally peaks and asks for some form of resolution. In the final scene of "The One With Chandler's Work Laugh," Ross' whining annoys Janice, and she breaks off their relationship. However, series programs' climaxes are undercut by one main factor: the repeatability of the program, its need to return the following week with the same problematic. The conflict reaches its peak, but there is no final resolution. In this example, we learn that Ross and Janice's relationship is over, but we don't know about Ross' future romances or the possibility of Janice reappearing on the show. The small question: "Will Ross find romance with Janice?" is answered. Larger questions such as "Will Ross *ever* find romance?" or "Will romance and marriage take him away from his friends?" are not fully resolved. The last shot of the episode shows Janice teasing Joey, the one male "friend" with whom she has not slept, that he might be next. And so future complications are already being seeded.

7. Resolution/Denouement. Series episodes can have no final resolution, no narrative closure, because to do so would mean the end of the series itself. If there were no more threats to the friends' camaraderie, if they were all happily coupled up and satisfied with their jobs, or if the moral character of Crockett and Tubbs were assured, there would be no more conflict on which to base *Friends'* and *Miami Vice's* narratives. Consequently, the ending of each episode must leave us in doubt as to the ultimate resolution of the series' overarching conflict. There must be a sense of narrative openness, a limited aperture. We know about Ross and Janice, but we do not know about Ross and Joey and their future relationships. And, most important, we don't know if further rifts will develop among the friends.

On rare occasions, television series will conclude the program's run by providing true narrative closure. *M*A*S*H* ended the fictional doctors' and nurses' conflict with the Korean War by presenting a $2\frac{1}{2}$-hour episode (February 28, 1983) of the war's end. With no more war to play antagonist to the medical protagonists, the narrative motor of the program ran out of fuel. Its repeatable problematic had finally been resolved—after 11 years and hundreds of episodes.

Most series, however, do not close in this fashion. One moment they are part of the weekly schedule and the next they are gone. Their abrupt departure sustains their narrative aperture, which is helpful if they are sold into **stripped syndication**, where their problematic is *re*-presented daily.

THE TELEVISION SERIAL

The serial is another form of storytelling that successfully made the transition from radio to television. Even before radio made use of the serial, there were examples of it in literature and the cinema. Nineteenth-century novels, such as those by Charles Dickens, were often originally published chapter by chapter in magazines. Silent movie serials such as the hugely popular *Fantômas* (1913) in France and *The Perils of Pauline* (1914) in the U.S. entertained audiences during radio's infancy. Neither of these forms, however, would reach an audience as enormous as the TV serial's.

Unlike the *series*, the *serial* expects us to make specific and substantial narrative connections between one episode and the next. In the series, the link between each week's programs is rather vague. In the serial, the connection is fundamental to its narrative pleasures. The main difference between the series and the serial is the way that each handles the development of the narrative from episode to episode.

With the exceptions of *Dallas* (1978–91), *Dynasty* (1981–89) and *ER* (1994–), the serial has seldom been as important as the series to the broadcast networks' prime-time schedules. In contrast, the narrative series has never been a significant factor in the networks' daytime schedules; there, the serial—in the form of the soap opera—reigns supreme. The television serial has long been the least respected narrative form. There is a creeping sexism in this attitude, for it assumes that soap opera is something that only "housewives" could find interesting. More recently, however, critics have begun to reevaluate the serial, with intriguing results; and producers/directors have reworked the form in sophisticated, sometimes quirky serials such as *ER*, *St. Elsewhere* (1982–88) and *Twin Peaks* (1990–91). Moreover, *ER* was a ratings champion throughout the late '90s—often triumphing as the highest rated show of the season.

How is it that serials tell their stories? What is their narrative structure, and how does it differ from both the classical cinema and the television series?

Narrative Structure

1. Multiple Protagonists. In our discussion of series programs, we noted an increased tendency toward multiple protagonists. The serial—especially the daytime serial—uses an even larger number of protagonists, each of whom is equally important to the narrative structure. Hour-long soap operas typically have 15 to 20 central characters—many more than the classical film, and even more than multiple-protagonist series such as *Friends* (whose main characters number just six). Soap opera casts are the largest of any program on television.

The multiplicity of protagonists permits a variety of simultaneous story lines within the narrative world of a serial. And, more important, the quantity of characters decreases the importance of any one character. Indeed, soap opera characters lead a precarious existence. They come and go with a swiftness that is uncommon in other fictional forms. This is due partly to economics. Most soap opera actors work under contracts that may be cancelled every 13 weeks. If the producers feel that actors are not generating enough viewer interest, they may suddenly disappear, along with their characters (although characters are also frequently recast). However, economics is not the only reason for the large number of protagonists. Soap opera relies on a multiplicity of characters to create a narrative web in which most characters are connected with one another.

2. Exposition. As does *Raiders of the Lost Ark*, the television serial begins each episode *in medias res*. The story has already begun, the action joined in progress. This is especially remarkable for daytime serials whose story may have begun decades before. *Guiding Light* has been developing its story on radio and television for more than 60 years—making its radio debut on January 25, 1937. *As the World Turns* has been constructing its narrative since April 2, 1956. If these were classical films they would have lasted thousands of hours and their exposition would have occurred years ago!

Few, if any, viewers have watched these serials since their inception. And the programs are always adding new viewers. So how do serials cope with viewers who have missed episodes or are new to the program? The answer is that serials, particularly the long-running soap operas, contain a large quotient of redundant narrative information. Character A has coffee with character B and they discuss how C has fathered a child with D. This narrative fact is now established. But in a later scene (the next day, perhaps) we will see character B at the nurses' station discussing the situation with two more characters. The information is redundant to the regular viewer, but serves as exposition for the viewer that has missed the previous scene. Through this redundancy the soap opera constantly *re*-establishes its characters and their situations.

Part of the redundant information that is regurgitated in the serial is the pasts of the characters. Serial characters carry a specific, significant past—much more so than do the series characters. In the series, as we previously discussed, the past is obscure and indefinite; but in the serial, characters constantly refer to it. Previous love affairs and marriages, murders and double-crossings, pregnancies and miscarriages, are layered on top of the current goings-on. For the regular viewer in particular this creates a remarkably dense, multilayered narrative. A casual remark between two characters can be loaded with repressed, unspoken associations. A kiss hello can signify years of ill will or unrequited lust. A complex weave of character relationships exists from the very first second of a day's episode of a daytime serial.

This is not to say that new characters are never introduced on serials. Obviously, they must be, to keep the narrative fresh and interesting. These characters all undergo a conventional exposition, as does a character entering a classical film. However, daytime soap operas frequently abbreviate this exposition by providing familial associations for new characters. Often, new characters will be someone's never-before-seen cousin or uncle, or even sister or mother. The use of familial relations quickly incorporates new characters into the story lines associated with those families. Their characters are established as being similar to, or different from, the rest of the family's overall character.

3. Motivation. Like the exposition, the original catalyst for long-running television serials took place years ago. In the episodes we watch day after day, or week after week, the many protagonists' desires and lacks are mostly already established. Only the occasional new desire/lack is introduced to maintain the narrative diversity. In both daytime and nighttime serials, these lacks/desires normally concentrate on heterosexual romance and familial relations (especially paternity). In the 1980s and 1990s, however, the serial diversified, with *Dallas* leading the serial into themes of corporate greed, and *General Hospital* (1963–) introducing international intrigue and science fiction (the "ice princess") into the soap opera world.

4. Narrative Enigma. The serial is saturated with enigmas. It thrives on them. Will Luke reunite with Laura (*General Hospital*)? Will Tad conquer amnesia and marry Dixie (*All My Children*)? These are just two of the thousands of enigmas that have been posed on daytime serials. Indeed, the multiplicity of protagonists ensures that several—up to a dozen or so—enigmas will be running on any one program at any one time. Unlike the classical film or the TV series episode with their one central enigma, the serial nurtures multiple enigmas. They are its foundation. The multiplicity of enigmas ensures that serials will never lose their narrative momentum. If one enigma is solved, many others still remain to slowly pull the story forward.

5. Cause–effect Chain. The narrative chain of daytime serial television is interrupted more frequently than that of series television. There are more commercial breaks per program minute in daytime soap operas than there are in nighttime series. (It is no coincidence that soap operas are the most consistently profitable programs on television.) In an hour-long episode, almost 20 minutes are taken up with commercials and other non-narrative material. Indeed, barely 9 or 10 minutes of story material elapse between commercial interruptions.

Serials adapt to this constant interruption much the same way that series do. They segment the narrative. Each serial narrative segment ends with a small climax, which raises new enigmas rather than leading to resolutions. We enter, or "flow" into, a commercial break on the heels of a question mark. Will Betsy arrive home in time to see Craig walking around the house—him having forgotten that he's faking paralysis to trap her in a loveless marriage (*As the World Turns*)? After we return from the world of commerce, we'll get our answer to this small enigma (no, she doesn't), but the overarching enigma is sustained.

6. Climax. Eventually, individual story lines do climax on serials. If they didn't, we would probably stop watching out of total frustration. So we do have fairy-tale weddings in which long-separated lovers are united, and climactic gun battles in which evil characters are dispatched. But these climaxes never result in narrative resolution.

7. (The lack of) Resolution. Almost by definition, serials cannot have total resolution. They cannot resolve *all* of the enigmas. If they did, there would be no reason to tune in the next day. Climaxes are used to generate new enigmas, rather than resolution. The fairy-tale wedding raises questions about whether the groom will realize that the bride is pregnant by the altar boy. The gun battle raises the question about whether the protagonist will be imprisoned for life. Even death is not a certainty—as was illustrated by Bobby Ewing's return to *Dallas* after "dying" in front of Pam's eyes. (Apparently it was just a dream of Pam's—a dream that lasted an entire TV season!) Many serial characters have returned from (presumed) death two and three times. So even death is not a permanent resolution on the soap opera.

On the extremely rare occasions when a serial story line does achieve relative narrative closure—say, a couple marries and leaves the program—it is still of little consequence to the enigma structure of the program because of the abundance of other enigmas. For example, the sixth season of *ER* ended with Carol joining Doug in Seattle—the conclusion of a very rocky relationship spanning several years. Since both actors have left the show, it seems unlikely there will be further developments in their relationship, but the show has no lack of ongoing enigmas (e.g., Carter's drug addiction and Benton's romantic life). With numerous protagonists, someone is certain to be lacking or desiring someone or something at any point in time on *ER* and other serials. The one imperative of the serial is that the story must continue.

SUMMARY

Narrative forms must share television time with all sorts of other material: news, commercials, game shows, public service announcements. And yet, stories are what principally draw us to television. Theatrical films, made-for-TV films (MOWs), series programs, and serial programs lure us with the promise of entertaining stories. These television narratives share certain characteristics. They all present protagonists—established by an exposition—in a chain of events motivated by desire. There are always antagonists—individuals, environments, or internal—that prevent the attainment of that desire. The chain in each narrative mode is comprised of actions connected to one another by narrative enigmas that pull the story toward a climax. All of these aspects are necessary for conventional storytelling, though their order and emphasis may differ from mode to mode.

However, important distinctions separate the narrative modes. Series and serials rely on a viewer foreknowledge of characters that is not possible in individual films, whether made for TV or not. The MOW, the series, and the serial adapt themselves to television's constant interruptions through narrative segmentation, to which theatrical films are not accustomed. Each mode handles enigmas and resolutions somewhat differently—depending on whether the mode must be continued the next week/day or not. On one end of the spectrum is the classical film, with its firm narrative closure; on the other is the soap opera, with its never-fully-closing narrative aperture.

We should resist the impulse to use the classical film as our yardstick to measure these individual narrative modes. Instead, we should understand them on their own terms as television narratives. Every narrative form on TV must somehow conform to television's flow, interruption, and segmentation. The daytime serial—with its extreme segmentation, multiple protagonists, multiple enigmas, and lack of full resolution—owes the least to the classical film or the 19th century novel and is perhaps the most televisual of the narrative modes. The theatrical film is, obviously, the least suited and consequently suffers the most. The series and the MOW each has its own way of accommodating the medium. And still, all are television stories.

FURTHER READINGS

The most cogent overview of television narrative, especially as it compares with the narrative of other related media, is John Ellis, *Visible Fictions: Cinema: Television: Video* (Boston: Routlege, 1992), although his references are becoming a bit dated. Another and more theoretical overview is provided by Sarah Kosloff's chapter, "Narrative Theory and Television," in *Channels of Discourse, Reassembled*, ed. Robert C. Allen (Chapel Hill, NC: University of North Carolina Press, 1992). Kosloff includes an annotated bibliography of narrative theory of literature, film, and television. Using *Star Trek's* holodeck as a portent of the future, Janet H. Murray details the development of narrative in the digital age in *Hamlet on the Holodeck: The Future of Narrative in Cyberspace* (Cambridge, MA: MIT Press, 1997).

Analyses of the narrative structures of film and literature can often provide insights into those of television. David Bordwell and Kristin Thompson have written frequently on narrative systems in film. Their *Film Art: An Introduction*, 6th ed. (New York: McGraw-Hill, 2000) offers chapters that summarize their work elsewhere. David Bordwell, Janet Staiger, and Kristin Thompson, *The Classical Hollywood Cinema: Film Style and Mode of Production to 1960* (New York: Columbia University Press, 1985) is a meticulous analysis of the evolution of classical film narrative form as a mode of production. Edward Brannigan, *Narrative Comprehension and Film* (London: Routledge, 1992) examines both narrative structure and our interpretation of it in film. Seymour Chatman's *Story and Discourse: Narrative Structure in Fiction and Film* (Ithaca, NY: Cornell University Press, 1978) provides a summary of narrative analysis in those two media.

For discussions of the narrative structure of specific television genres and formats, see Robert C. Allen, *Speaking of Soap Operas* (Chapel Hill, NC: University of North Carolina Press, 1985); Paul Attallah, "The Unworthy Discourse: Situation Comedy in Television," in *Interpreting Television: Current Research Perspectives*, eds. Willard D. Rowland, Jr., and Bruce Watkins (Beverly Hills: Sage Publications, 1984); and Elayne Rapping, *The Movie of the Week: Private Stories, Public Events* (Minneapolis: University of Minnesota Press, 1992). Of course, television narratives do not exist in isolation from one another. Mimi White, in "Crossing Wavelengths: The Diegetic and Referential Imaginary of American Commercial Television," *Cinema Journal* 25, no. 2 (Winter 1986): 51–64, explains just how narratives may bounce off one another in television.

ENDNOTES

[1] For an exhaustive consideration of classicism, see David Bordwell, Janet Staiger, and Kristin Thompson, *The Classical Hollywood Cinema: Film Style and Mode of Production to 1960* (New York: Columbia University Press, 1985).

[2] "Film Victim of the Month," *Artists Rights Foundation* January 1999, Available: http://www.artistsrights.org.

[3] Midnight Cowboy is so butchered when it is shown on television that Leonard Maltin advises, ". . . please don't watch it on commercial TV: the most lenient prints run 104 m. [out of an original running time of 113 minutes] and are ludicrously dubbed to remove foul language." *TV Movies and Video Guide* (New York: Signet, 1990), 719.

[4] Recently U.S. theaters have begun running commercials with the films, a practice that had long been done in Europe. Still, theatrical movies are not interrupted by the commercials, as they are on television. Instead, the commercials are always shown before the feature begins.

[5] Maltin, 1081–2.

[6] Tim Brooks and Earle Marsh, *The Complete Directory to Prime Time Network TV Shows*, 7th ed. (New York: Ballantine, 1999), 687.

[7] John Ellis, *Visible Fictions: Cinema: Television: Video* (Boston: Routlege, 1992), 156.

CHAPTER 3

Building Narrative:
Character, Actor, Star

The previous chapter discusses television narrative as if the characters involved were pieces in a jigsaw puzzle, depersonalized components fitted into abstract patterns. This is misleading. While it is, of course, important to understand narrative structures, it is equally important to understand the characters that inhabit those structures. In a sense, these characters can exist even before the narrative action begins. The first time we see Dr. Mark Greene in the first shots of *ER*'s pilot episode (1994), we immediately begin to construct an idea of his character: a dedicated, overworked doctor (Figs. 3.1–3.3). Even before this character *does* anything in the plot structure, we begin to make assumptions based on setting (the hospital room), props (the bed, his glasses), and his appearance (disheveled). Furthermore, characters such as Dr. Greene exist *after* the narrative action concludes each week. For instance, when we pick up a copy of *TV Guide* because we respond to a picture of Dr. Greene, we are carrying his significance beyond the story lines of *ER*. Dr. Greene has begun to take on a "life" of his own. Additionally, such magazine coverage of television introduces us to the actors who embody the roles, and it nurtures the process of turning common actors into genuine stars. The *TV Guide* issue is as much, or more, about actor Anthony Edwards as it is about character Dr. Mark Greene.

To put it bluntly: Without characters there could be no television narrative and no television stars. Correspondingly, without actors there could be no characters. Characters, actors, stars: these three intertwining phenomena will be the focus of this chapter. We will begin by charting the mechanisms used to construct characters on television. Among these is the performance of the actor, which will be discussed in terms of contrasting acting strategies. The significance of the actor does not end with his or her performance within a televisual text, however. An actor, such as Edwards, may also appear in other **media texts:** magazines, movies, newspapers, public appearances at shopping malls. As the image multiplies, the actor evolves into a television star.

FIGURE 3.1

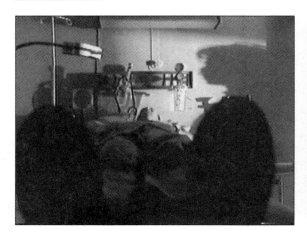

FIGURE 3.2

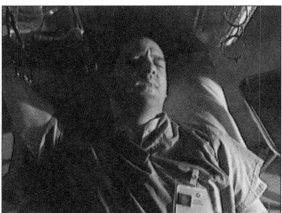

FIGURE 3.3

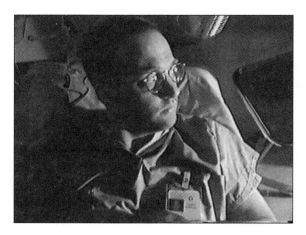

BUILDING CHARACTERS

Because characters typically assume human form, because they look like us, talk like us and, in some sense, behave like us, it is easy to mistake characters for real people, with real lives beyond the boundaries of their television programs. Most of us realize that Buffy Summers is not a real person, that writers have designed her words and directors have chosen camera angles to present her. But still we willingly set that knowledge aside, suspending disbelief while watching *Buffy the Vampire Slayer*. Or, more accurately, the program endeavors to hide the work that went into creating Buffy, to render invisible the making of a character. If it succeeds, we accept Buffy as a plausible human being (even if her slaying actions may seem fantastic). If it fails, we respond with annoyance or amusement: "People don't talk like that!" or "They want us to believe that teenagers could save us from demons? Get real!"

Annoyance at television's implausibility, its "fakery," is a first step toward viewing the medium critically. However, to systematically analyze TV, we must channel the occasional awareness of television's "fake," constructed nature into a systematic critique of how those narrative constructions operate. In this case, we need to ask how characters are manufactured and how we come to understand the meanings associated with them.

Fabricating characters is the day-to-day work of writers, directors, producers, and other craftspersons. Indeed, it's the principal work of the entire televisual medium—creating **signs of character** that signify the character to us. We, in turn, interpret or **read** these signs according to a variety of factors:

- Our understanding of the world, of television, of genre.
- The context (i.e., program) in which the character appears.
- The viewing situation itself (Did we have a large meal just before turning on the television? Is the room too brightly lit? How large is the television? And so on.).

All these variables can influence how we perceive a character. They make character construction an imprecise science. Still, we can better understand how characters are constructed if we identify the types of signs that signify character and investigate the **code** of character construction. This code comprises certain "rules" that govern what meanings a character signifies to us and how those meanings are created.

Both producers and consumers of television have learned this code. In fact, we learn it so well that we take it for granted. Television producers (and writers and directors) unthinkingly use this code to construct characters; and television consumers (we, the viewers) incorporate it into our commonsense understanding of the medium. Producers and consumers alike understand, for example, that a character such as Dr. Greene who wears eyeglasses is supposed to be more intellectual or sensitive than other characters. If characters smoke, they will likely be evil or immoral. When Dr. Greene smokes, for example, it suggests that he's losing his grip. These conventions of costuming and props are part of a code that is so taken for granted as to become nearly invisible. It is the analyst's task, then, to make it visible again. In so doing, it is important to remember that this so-called code is both *historical* and *cultural.* That is, it changes over time and is not fixed; and it differs from one culture to another and is not universal.

Although the historical and cultural nature of the code is true of all aspects of character construction, it is most obvious in the case of costuming. The skinny ties worn by Sergeant Friday in the 1950s and 1960s program *Dragnet* (1952–59, 1967–70) were part of a total costuming style that signified moral and political conservatism. When that same style of tie was worn by musicians such as Elvis Costello in music videos in the early 1980s, it had liberal and hip connotations—perhaps even reflecting the styles of 30 years prior. Time had changed the meaning of that visual signifier (the tie). As well as being bound to a certain time, such specifics of costuming are also culturally determined. The width of Sergeant Friday's or Elvis Costello's ties would not mean much to a traditionally attired African, for instance, whose code of dress does not normally include neckwear.

To provide a less frivolous example of the cultural significance of dress, consider that in the Western world black is recognized as the color of mourning. It has come to signify death. In contrast, in Asian countries mourners wear white. Hence we may see that no costuming convention is universal. The code changes from one culture to another.

As we begin to examine the conventionalized code of character construction, we will rely heavily on a typology of character signs articulated originally by Richard Dyer in his studies of cinema stars.[1] Most of Dyer's comments on film characters may be imported into our consideration of television characters, but television is not the cinema, and the following typology alters Dyer's scheme where appropriate.

A Typology of Character Signs

Viewer Foreknowledge. Before watching a single episode of a television program, we are provided with signs that signify the characters to us. Advertising on television and in print describes and promotes the program in terms that capitalize on our familiarity with the program's genre, its stars (if famous enough), and, in the case of programs spun off other programs, its parent show. If a program is advertised as a new police drama, then we can expect certain genre character types: the foolish rookie, bitter veteran, helpless victims, and so on. If it features Andy Griffith, as when he appears in *Matlock* (1986–), then we are prepared for a character articulated by Griffith's homespun star image. And if the program is a spinoff, such as *A Different World* (1987–93), then we have already seen some of the characters (e.g., Denise Huxtable) in previous stories, although in a different context (*The Cosby Show*). Such aspects of genre, star, and parent program generate a **narrative image** of the program—an enticing representation of what the program's characters will be like—that functions to lure us to a new program.[2]

Of course, once the program has been on for a few weeks (or months, or years), viewer foreknowledge before each individual episode rises to the point where the characters become as familiar as figures from literary and cinematic series, such as Frankenstein's monster or Nancy Drew or Tarzan. An established program often plays on our familiarity by using its credit sequence to rehearse character relationships. The credit sequence of *M*A*S*H*, for instance, presents us with each of the major characters and their milieu. Even though we are, most likely, already familiar with these characters, this short prenarrative segment re-presents the program's cast and diminishes the need for a full exposition to establish the characters.

Character Name. Characters' names distinguish them from the rest of the cast and, more important, signify certain character traits to us. These traits may be as program-specific as the character's familial bonds: Alex Keaton is obviously related to Elyse and Steve Keaton on *Family Ties* (1982–90). (Familial relationships are particularly important to soap operas.) Names also carry significance within the general culture. The name Ricky Ricardo (*I Love Lucy* [1951–61]) carries Hispanic connotations. Miles Silverberg (*Murphy Brown* [1988–98]) conveys Jewish associations. Each of these names raises expectations that the character will either fit into ethnic/religious stereotypes, defeat those stereotypes, or perhaps select particular stereotypical connotations while rejecting others.

Character names connote meanings other than religion and ethnicity, too. On *Murphy Brown*, the title character's name is distinctive enough within U.S. culture (a family name, Murphy, used as a first name) to imply an extraordinary woman: unusual name = unusual character. And, on the same program, the name Corky Sherwood is used to diminish that character's seriousness by using the diminutive and, for a broadcast journalist, overly familiar, -y ending (cf. Buffy, Tippy, Candy). Further, when Corky married a man named Forrest, she became Corky Sherwood Forrest—the pun on her married name creating humor at the character's expense.

Appearance. Appearance can be broken down further into three components: the **face** (and hairstyle), the **body** (build and posture), and **costuming**.

Television's reliance on the close-up favors the face as a signifier of character. Unfortunately for the purposes of analysis, the meanings of facial characteristics are ephemeral and difficult to pin down. Aside from clear-cut racial characteristics, it is hard to particularize the meanings of a face—although we unthinkingly make these interpretations a thousand times a day. What does Tom Selleck's or Burt Reynold's moustache "mean"? What does David Leterman's tooth gap signify? These are questions that cannot be answered with any rigor. And yet, there are some facial characteristics that become significant because of their difference from facial norms: Farrah Fawcett's copious amount of blond hair in her *Charlie's Angels* days (1976–77) signified "blondness" and a specific type of "sex symbol" to many viewers (Fig. 3.4). Her blond hair linked her to other female sex symbols and thus signified a certain sexual availability and vulnerability in the Marilyn Monroe tradition. It is the variation from the norm that not only makes a characteristic noticeable, but also creates meaning.

Corporeal (bodily) attributes carry clearer meanings than facial ones. Selleck's robust physique conveys strength and masculinity. In contrast,

FIGURE 3.4

FIGURE 3.5

Roseanne's physique during the early years of her sitcom (1988–97) associates her with the "mammy" stereotype—the overweight woman who is sexually neutral but an expert at caring for others (Fig. 3.5). These actors' physiques and the way they carry them quickly signify aspects of their characters to the viewer.

As we have mentioned, costuming is a significant component of character construction. Within television there are two very active overlapping codes determining our understanding of costume: the code of dress predominant in a specific culture at a specific time, and the code of dress specific to television and television genres. Our earlier example of skinny ties in *Dragnet* and music video is one instance of a fashion element that was part of the culture at large and was incorporated into television programs. Narrow ties would have existed with or without TV. Certain genres, however, develop a code of costume that is not shared by the contemporary culture. Westerns, private eye shows, and science fiction programs each have developed clothing items that hold specific meaning. The gambler's fancy vest in the Western, for example, has come to signify his greed and untrustworthiness. Costuming is closely related to, and often overlaps with, our next sign of character.

Objective Correlative. Objective correlatives are objects (or sometimes animals) that are associated with characters and convey something about them. Objective correlatives include the environment that is the home or work place of a character. The living room and neighboring junkyard of *Sanford and Son* (1972–1977) help establish Fred Sanford's social class and lifestyle. Sitcoms, in particular, rely heavily on a limited number of sets; and those settings come to be as familiar to regular viewers as their own living rooms.

Even more distinctive than these sets are objective correlatives that are individual objects linked to characters: Lucas McCain's rifle in *The Rifleman* (1958–63), Ricky Ricardo's conga drum in *I Love Lucy*, Bart Simpson's skateboard on *The Simpsons* (1989), and so on. In each instance the object comes to signify something about the character. Bart's skateboard, for example, connotes that he's a bit reckless and brash (Fig. 3.6).

FIGURE 3.6

Dialogue. What characters say and what other characters say about them determine a good deal about our understanding of that character. These meanings range from the direct (character A saying that character B is a murderer) to the oblique (the inflections of Jerry Seinfeld's voice as he cracks a joke). In each case, meaning about the character is communicated to the viewer.

Lighting and Videography or Cinematography. Some of the more technical aspects of filming or videotaping an actor also contribute to our sense of character. These are discussed more fully in the chapters on visual style, but we may note here a few ways that television technique affects character.

Deviations from the standard of broad, even lighting have come to signify aspects of character. When actors are lit from below, their characters are thought to be sinister. When lit entirely from behind, the resulting silhouette conveys a sense of mystery. Other, more subtle lighting effects also serve to represent character. In the *ER* example above (Figs. 3.1–3.3), the repeated intrusion of light into the dark hospital room (also note the nurse's silhouette in Fig. 3.1) and the strong side-lighting of Dr. Greene contributes to the sense of his discomfort and disturbance.

Similarly, camera lenses and other technical devices (see chapter 6) may influence character development. Close-ups taken with a wide-angle lens may distort actors' features, making them appear strange or goofy. The odd, low camera angle of Dr. Greene (Fig. 3.1), for example, emphasizes his feet and his reclining position, but conceals his face until we cut to the high-angle shot (Figs. 3.2–3.3). The first shot effectively intrigues us as to his character and pulls us into the narrative (remember, this is the very first shot of the program's first episode).

Most viewers are not actively aware of such technical manipulations. Nonetheless, they do affect our understanding of character, and it is the analyst's responsibility to remain sensitive to these uses of television style.

Action. What characters do in a story—that is, their actions—determine in the final analysis what characters mean. Characters who do evil things come to signify evil.

BUILDING PERFORMANCES

We have discussed the character as a fairly static object: a human being of a certain appearance, associated with certain objects, who is presented in a certain way, and fits into a narrative structure. What we have ignored thus far—and what is frequently overlooked in television studies in general—is the work of the actor in the creation of character. Acting and performance, as we will use the terms, refer to how a line of dialogue is spoken and how a gesture is made and how a smile is smiled. It is what the actor does that is distinguishable from the scriptwriter's lines or the director's positioning of the camera. Consequently, performance is often difficult to isolate from other aspects of character and is even tougher to describe.

Our approach here, first of all, scraps any attempt to evaluate or judge acting. The evaluation of acting is clouded by ever-changing codes of good and bad acting and the mercurial psychology of the individual viewer or critic. What is considered good acting at one time and place seems strange or exaggerated at another. Moreover, acting is not like the physical sciences; there is no such thing as progress in the art of acting. Acting does not get better and better. There are only different types of acting and different eras and different cultures that view certain types as better than others. For instance, there is a long-standing prejudice within U.S. culture that rates television acting below that of the theatrical film, and both television and film acting below that of the live theater. (And acting in daytime television is rated below that of prime time.) While there may be minor distinctions among the performances in these media, the main determinant in these judgments is a cultural elitism underscored by economic class prejudice; only relatively wealthy persons can afford to see live theater today. Consequently, television and film have become the cultural upstarts that have undermined the theater's dominance of the acting arts.

Elitism aside, the judgment of acting is a subjective business—inevitably anchored in deep–rooted drives and desires of which the viewer–critic is barely aware. In this book we will set aside the elitism and the subjectivity of judging acting in favor of trying to understand how we interpret acting and how performance conveys meaning. To this end, we will start with the raw material of acting—what Dyer calls the **signs of performance**—and then we will consider some of the strategies of performance that greatly determine how we interpret acting.[3]

A Typology of Performance Signs

When actors construct performances, they have two raw materials to work with: voice and body. How these materials are used is what defines performances. Further, in studying performance it is useful to divide these materials into four types of performance signs:

    1. Vocal

    2. Facial

    3. Gestural

    4. Corporeal[4]

It may appear that there is some overlap here between performance signs that depend on the actor's body and the previously discussed character signs. The difference between the two is that performance signs deal with how the raw material is used; the discussion of character signs focuses on what material is selected and how it appears, even before being animated through performance.

Before considering briefly some of the specific ways that performance signs function, we should note that actor performance, more than any one character sign, contains the principal signifiers of a character's presumed emotional state. The way an actor talks or moves or smiles signifies how the character feels. In television, unlike the novel, we seldom have direct access to a character's emotions. The novel may represent emotions simply by describing them verbally: "Christine felt sad the day she murdered Bob." But a television program—unless it uses voiceover narration or characters talking about their mental health—must signify these emotions principally through performance signs. It is worth reiterating, however, that characters are not real people, that they do not feel emotions. Instead, emotions are represented through character and performance signs, which the viewer interprets as signifiers of emotion: a particular look in Christine's eye while she murders Bob equals sadness. This difference between the emotions of characters and the emotions of real people is more than just semantics. It is a distinction we must keep in mind to distance ourselves far enough from character emotions so that we can analyze how they function in the narrative structure, how they motivate the story.

Vocal Performance. There are a number of vocal qualities that may be manipulated in the construction of a performance: principally, **volume**, **pitch**, and **timbre**. Just as in a musical performance, these qualities may be organized for specific effect.

The meanings of **volume** are varied. Loudness may signify strength, or it may signify shrillness or terror. Softness may signify meekness, or it may signify a control so total that speaking loudly is not necessary. As usual, context determines meaning.

Pitch in music is how high or low a note is. Vocal pitch within our culture tends to convey gender-oriented meanings. A higher pitch is associated with the feminine and a lower pitch with the masculine. Higher voices are also linked with childlike characters. The deep bass voice of William Conrad helped create the tough, masculine character of Detective Frank Cannon (*Cannon* [1971–76]). Georgia Engel's high voice contributed to Georgette Baxter's femininity in *The Mary Tyler Moore Show* (1970–77). The gender significance of pitch is rooted in obvious biological differences between men's and women's vocal chords, but gender is also culturally determined. Individual men's voices are not necessarily lower than individual women's, and vice versa. And since pitch significance is part of culture, not just nature, female actors may use lower pitch to signify masculine characteristics, while male actors may use higher pitch to signify feminine ones.

The final aspect of vocal quality that actors use in creating a performance is **timbre**, which is the most difficult to describe. Timbre is the tonal quality of a sound. Aside from being high or low, soft or loud, is a sound harsh or mellow or nasal or smooth? In short, what type of tone does it have? The harsh, nasal tone of Fran Drescher's voice augments the tough, street-wise attitude of her character in *The Nanny* (1993–99). Sharon Gless's throaty delivery underlines the sexual potential beneath the police detective exterior of Chris Cagney (*Cagney and Lacey* [1982–88]). Different tonal qualities convey a myriad of connotations within our culture. To describe them all would be nearly impossible, but still, the analyst needs to remain alert to them.

In addition to vocal quality, the performance of dialogue is also affected by the rhythm of the speech. Bob Newhart's trademark of halting, interrupted speech signifies his characters' lack of confidence (in *The Bob Newhart Show* [1972–78], *Newhart* [1982–90], and *Bob* [1992–94]). Peter Falk's slow delivery of crime scene analysis in *Columbo* (1971–77) masks his quick and clever deductive skills. Lucille Ball's rapid-fire delivery of dialogue in *I Love Lucy* marked her wacky nerviness. In each case the rhythm of the vocal performance conveys meaning to the viewer.

Facial Performance. Facial performance is the way that facial appearance is used. Facial appearance—for example, Fawcett's hair in Figure 3.4—is a character sign. We may also think of it as a performance sign in terms of how Fawcett moves her hair. Fawcett's hair is not just larger than normal, it is also emphasized by the performer, which accentuates its significance. With each toss of Fawcett's head, the meaning of these signs (Fawcett's "blondness") is re-emphasized.

Most facial performance is not as large as Fawcett's, obviously. Minuscule movements of facial muscles can have significance. The viewer easily distinguishes the different meanings suggested by tiny variations in facial movement. A certain type of smile can mean amusement, while another can mean condescension or disbelief. In the context of the scene from which Figure 3.4 was taken, Farrah's smile signifies flirtation as she plays dumb with a group of men Charlie's Angels are investigating. Her exaggerated performance in this scene also signifies to the viewer that her flirtation is a put-on, that it is just part of her disguise. In contrast, Marlon Brando's smile in *A Streetcar Named Desire* is quite predatory as he sizes up his sister-in-law (discussed below, Fig. 3.10). Of all the performance signs, the facial presumably signifies the most about character emotions—which is why soap opera, the genre most concerned with emotion, contains the most intense examination, in close-up, of facial performance.

Gestural Performance. The significance of human gestures to a performance has been discussed since at least the late 19th century, when a French teacher of elocution, François Delsarte (1811–71), codified gestures into the Delsarte System of performance. In the Delsarte System there is a strict vocabulary of gesture: a raised fist means "determination or anger" and an open hand tilted downward means "apathy or prostration."[5] However, the meanings of gestural performance are not as clear-cut or universal as Delsarte maintained. Instead, gestures convey meanings in more ambiguous fashion and in a way that changes over time and from culture to culture. (Hand gestures, for instance, differ markedly from one country to another). While Meg Ryan was on *As the World Turns* (1982–84), her performances featured gestures that sometimes caught the camera operators by surprise. For example, in one shot she waves good-bye to a friend and does it so broadly that her arm extends beyond the frame of the image (Fig. 3.7). What meaning are we to assign to this arm movement? Perhaps

FIGURE 3.7

we can say that this odd gesture contributes to the quirkiness of her character, but that is nowhere near as precise as Delsarte's strict code of gesture.

Corporeal Performance. The stance and bearing of an actor's body communicate meaning to the viewer that, obviously, ties in with the actor's gestures. The rigidly erect posture of Bebe Neuwirth (Fig. 3.8) signifies the emotional stiffness of her character, the psychiatrist Lilith on *Cheers* (1982–93) while Ted Danson's casual stance and fluid movement (Fig. 3.9) on the same program represent the moral laxity of Sam Malone. Neuwirth holds her body stiffly and gestures minimally; Danson leans and slouches and often gestures comfortably.

Strategies of Performance

Most of the time, we do not concern ourselves with the work that the actor used to create the performance. Indeed, the television program erases the marks of

FIGURE 3.8

FIGURE 3.9

that work by emphasizing the character as a "real" human being rather than a constructed collection of character and performance signs. However, our understanding of performance signs is often affected by presumptions of how the actor came to create those attributes. And discussions of acting inevitably return to questions of performance strategies: principally, how did the actor create the performance? As this is also the main concern of acting schools, it seems appropriate to deal with this issue here. To best understand the different approaches to acting, it is necessary, however, to place acting strategies into a historical context—since one style often reacts against another. It also becomes necessary to stray into the related media of film and live theater to place performance history in context.

The danger in studying strategies of performance, however, is that it presumes that what is going on in the actors' minds is going to be evident in the way they perform. This, obviously, is a hazardous interpretive leap. Actors may be performing emotionally charged scenes and be thinking about what they will have for lunch that day. There is no way we can truly know an actor's mental processes. And yet, what we assume about those processes can be a key element in understanding how we interpret acting.

Fundamentally, there are two approaches to performance in fiction television: the **naturalist** and the **anti-naturalist**. In naturalistic performance styles, actors struggle to create a performance that we will accept as a "plausible," "believable" character—as human beings, and not actors trying to look like someone they are not. Anti-naturalist performance styles reject the notion of a believable character, but they do so for a broad variety of reasons that will be discussed in due course.

The Naturalists

There are, of course, many schools of thought regarding the production of a naturalistic performance. Limiting our scope to the 19th and 20th centuries we will consider two types of naturalistic performance: **Repertory** and **Method**.

It must be noted at the outset, however, that these two strategies do not exist in pure form. Any performance is an impure mixture of approaches.

Repertory Performance. In repertory theater, a set group of actors performs a series of different plays during a season. One week the group might perform Ibsen's *A Doll's House* and the next week perform Shakespeare's *Macbeth*. As a result, the actors are constantly assuming new roles. To facilitate this ongoing change of roles, a repertory-style performance sees acting as a process of selecting particular gestures and spoken dialects and constructing a performance from them, although it does not rely on a code of gestures set out in an acting manual. The work of the actor is to study human gesture and speech and borrow gestures and dialects from life in the construction of characters. Repertory actors are dispassionate in this assemblage of movements and accents. They don't become emotional while acting, but instead use the gestures/accents that signify emotion.

For example, when Larry Drake began the role of the mentally challenged Benny Stulwicz on *L.A. Law* (1986–94), he observed psychiatric patients to see how they moved and spoke. Armed with this information, he could signify mental retardation by reenacting the gestures and speech patterns of the mentally challenged. Some film actors are also particularly well known for this performance strategy—Laurence Olivier and Meryl Streep, for example.

Even though repertory acting today does not rely on the Delsarte System of performance, it would be inaccurate to say that repertory performances are not in a sense "coded." True, there is no clearly delineated code such as Delsarte believed in, but repertory acting does draw on the rather flexible code of human gesture and dialect that operates in a society at a particular time. An actor's selection from life of gesture and dialect depends on certain common sense presumptions about how people move and speak. Even when an actor such as Drake takes special pains to study a certain type of person, his perception is still filtered through assumptions of which gestures and dialects are significant and which are not. So-called body language follows certain conventions that shift over time and cultures.

Method Performance. The style of performance most generally known in the U.S. is called simply "The Method." Method acting differs sharply from the repertory style. Rather than stressing the selection and assembling of gestures and dialects, Method acting encourages actors to *become* the characters, to fuse their personalities with the roles, to relive the characters. Method teachers argue that once the actor becomes the role, then the gestures and dialects necessary for the performance will organically grow out of that union of actor and character. Repertory performers are accused of mechanical acting by Method believers, because non-Method performance relies on a machine-like fitting together of techniques.

Three tactics that Method actors use to encourage the actor–character fusion are **emotional memory**, **sense memory**, and **improvisation**. Using emotional memory, actors draw on their memories of previous emotions that match the emotions of the characters. To encourage those memories, the actor can use sense memory to remember the physical sensations of a particularly emotional event. Was it hot or cold? How did the chair they were sitting on feel? Thus, sense memory is used to generate emotional memory. Improvisation is mostly used during rehearsal in Method acting. Actors imagine their way into the "minds" of characters and then place those characters into new situations, improvising new lines of dialogue based on this actor–character union.

According to Method advocates, if actors successfully tap into deep-rooted emotions and "become" the characters, then their performances will express a higher degree of "truth" because the actor is feeling what the character is feeling and behaving appropriately. For better or worse, this has become one of the principal criteria for judging acting: Do the actors appear to be fully submerged into the characters? Do they feel what the characters feel?

Judging performance in this fashion can be dangerous. It rests on the ability to read the actor's mind during a performance—an impossible task. For this reason, the evaluation of acting based on Method acting criteria remains dubious.

Method acting initially came to the attention of the U.S. public at about the same time that television enjoyed its first growth spurt: the late 1940s and early 1950s. At that time, director Elia Kazan brought Marlon Brando to the stage

FIGURE 3.10

and then to the screen in *A Streetcar Named Desire* (1951, Fig. 3.10), which was followed by *On the Waterfront* (1954). Brando was the most visible of several distinctive new actors who were advocating the Method. Brando, James Dean, Montgomery Clift, Julie Harris, and others had been trained by Method teachers such as Lee Strasberg (at the Actor's Studio) and Stella Adler (Brando's principal teacher). However, the Method was being taught in the live theater long before this crop of actors made their impact on U.S. cinema. The technique originated in Russia at the end of the 19th century, when Konstantin Stanislavsky founded the Moscow Art Theater in 1897. Stanislavsky disdained any acting other than that of the live theater. He barely tolerated film actors and died in 1938 before television became a mass medium. Still, the impact of the Stanislavsky system on television has been immeasurable.

The Method made a remarkably early incursion into television performance. The musical variety programs, Westerns, sitcoms, and soap operas—and, moreover, the bulk of 1950s television—had little to do with the Method, but 1950s television also hosted the so-called golden age of live television drama. Stage-trained actors and theatrical productions were imported into television to be broadcast live on programs such as *Playhouse 90* (1956–61) and *Philco Television Playhouse* (1948–55). The latter was initially sponsored by the Actor's Equity Association (the principal theatrical actors union in the U.S.) and dealt directly with Method-influenced performers. One such actor was Rod Steiger, who trained alongside Brando at the Actors' Studio and brought the Method to the title role of *Marty*—broadcast live on *Philco Television Playhouse* May 24, 1953 (Fig. 3.11).

In some respects, the 1950s live television dramas more closely resembled theatrical presentations than did the cinema of that time. In both theater and live television, each scene was played straight through, not broken apart and then edited together as it would be in a film production. And 1950s television drama was also shot on an indoor sound stage—equivalent to the theatrical stage—rather than the location work that was becoming popular in film at that time. In many respects, 1950s actors must have felt more

FIGURE 3.11

comfortable in a television studio production than on a movie set. As previously suggested, however, *Playhouse 90* and the like were not typical of programs on the infant medium, and Method acting was definitely the exception rather than the rule. Since that time, though, Method acting has found a home on television in dramatic programs such as *Hill Street Blues* (1981–87) and *Law and Order* (1990–), made-for-TV movies and, in diluted form, many other programs.

In theory, emotional and sense memories may be used to access a broad range of emotions, both negative and positive. The history of Method performances in television and film, however, has been heavily weighted toward darker emotions, anxieties, and quirky neuroses. It is no small coincidence that the Method was popularized at roughly the same time as Freudian psychology—psychoanalysis—became part of everyday language. Just as in Freudian theory, the Method presumes that negative emotions are somehow more authentic than positive ones; that sorrow, depression, and doubt are more realistic than joy, elation, and self-confidence. This, however, is a dubious assumption, because positive emotions appear in reality also; they are thus no less real. Nonetheless, the Method's emphasis on emotional discord is a large part of the reason it has not been used much outside of television drama. These sorts of emotions find little expression in sitcoms and the like.

Aside from the emphasis on gloom and melancholy, Method performances historically also have been marked by a specific use of performance signs. In the 1950s, the vocal performance of Brando, Dean, Clift, et al., was often remarked on. In comparison to contemporary acting norms, they used odd speech rhythms (offbeat, faltering); overlapped dialogue; and slurred or mumbled their lines. Their movements were similarly offbeat and quirky, when compared to the norm of the time.

Thus, Method acting was initially described as a technique that actors used to create a performance, but it has also developed its own conventions, its own code of performance. It has come to rely on the creation of negative emotions and has been marked by odd performance signs.

The Antinaturalists

Naturalism can thus be seen to dominate how most people—critics and everyday viewers alilke—think about acting. But it would be wrong to assume that we always demand naturalism from television performers. Sometimes it's quite clear that the actors are "faking" it, that they are separating themselves from the roles they play and pointing to the mechanics of their performances. It's as if they were winking at the viewer and implying, "You and I both know that I'm not *really* this character. I'm only performing a role." When actors distance themselves from their roles, they reject the basic tenet of the Method. They don't become the characters, they just present them to us. This style of performance can be traced back hundreds of years to broad comedy traditions in the theater, but we'll limit this overview to two 20th century antinaturalist approaches: vaudeville and Bertolt Brecht's theory of epic theater.

Vaudeville Performance. Vaudeville was a style of theatrical presentation that was built around song-and-dance numbers, comedy routines, and short dramatic skits and tableaux (the cast freezing in dramatic poses). Vaudeville was at its most popular in the late 19th and early 20th centuries, but by the 1920s was eclipsed by the competing mass entertainment forms of radio and the movies. Even though vaudeville as a medium no longer exists, the style of performance it used survives in many television forms.

Significantly, vaudeville performance does not demand that we forget the presence of the actor within the guise of the character. That is, vaudeville performance frequently reminds us that we are watching a performance and that the characters before us are not real people. This is largely achieved through the *direct address* of the viewer. Vaudeville actors often look straight at the audience and make comments to them. This violates the theatrical concept of an invisible "fourth wall" that separates audience from characters. In conventional theatrical performances, we observe the action without being observed ourselves. In vaudeville, our presence is repeatedly acknowledged. And if we are acknowledged as viewers, then the entire illusion of the fiction is undermined. The naturalist concept of the believable character becomes immaterial to the vaudevillian.

At its beginnings television bore the legacy of vaudeville. Musical variety programs—mixing vaudevillesque music, acrobatics, ventriloquism, and comic skits—dominated early television. *The Milton Berle Show* (1948–67), *The Ed Sullivan Show* (1948–71) and *The Jackie Gleason Show* (1952–70) are just three of the long-running variety programs that were popular during that time. In each, a host spoke directly to the viewer, introducing the short performances that constituted the weekly show. And the performances themselves were also directly presented to the viewer. Even the comic narrative pieces featured the performer looking directly at the camera (a taboo in dramatic television) and implicitly or explicitly addressing the viewer.

In the 1970s the musical variety program fell from favor with the U.S. audience, but vaudeville-style performance continues in programs such as *Saturday Night Live* (1975–) and in comic monologues such as those that begin late-night talk shows and litter the many stand-up comic programs on cable television.

Brechtian Performance. German playwright and theorist Bertolt Brecht once posed rhetorically, "What ought acting to be like?" He then answered:

> Witty. Ceremonious. Ritual. Spectator and actor ought not to approach one another but to move apart. Each ought to move away from himself. Otherwise the element of terror necessary to all recognition is lacking.[6]

Brecht's theories, as exemplified by his plays, abandon the naturalistic ideal of a believable character with whom we can identify. In his so-called **epic theater** (which has little to do with the traditional epic), we are alienated from the characters rather than identifying with or "approaching" them. Actors do not relive characters as in the Method, but rather quote the characters to the viewer, always retaining a sense of themselves as actors, as separate from the characters. In other words, the actor presents the character to the viewer without pretending to actually be the character. Viewer and actor alike are distanced from the character; hence the term Brechtian **distanciation.**

What is the purpose of this distanciation? Brecht argues that conventional dramatic theater narcotizes the spectator. We immerse ourselves in a story for 2 hours and then emerge from the theater as if waking from a drug-induced nap. Brecht contends instead that we should be confronted, alienated. His is a Marxist perspective that believes that the theater should be used to point out social ills and prompt spectators to take action about them. He advocates nothing less than a revolutionary theater.

Brechtian performance theory has found fertile soil in the cinema of filmmakers such as Jean-Luc Godard, whose 1960s work aspired to transpose the epic theater to the cinema. But its significance to broadcast television is, admittedly, marginal. However, Brecht has influenced avant-garde video production of the past 20 years, including works done in that medium by Godard and video artists such as Nam June Paik.

We can find small instances of Brecht skulking about the edges of commercial television, if we look hard enough. In the music video for the Replacements' *Left of the Dial*, for instance, all that is seen is a black-and-white shot of an audio speaker in a room. The video begins with a tight close-up of it; then it starts to vibrate as the music begins. The camera pulls back to reveal a record player, a few albums, nothing spectacular. A person walks in front of the speaker, and we see his arm while he smokes a cigarette, but his face is never in frame (Fig. 3.12). The video ends without the band ever appearing, as is the convention in, say, 90% of music videos. So, to start with, there's really no one to identify with. Beyond that, however, *Left of the Dial* breaks some of music video's other conventions by refusing to create a spectacle. Nothing really happens. We are left to amuse ourselves, to think about the video and the conventions it's breaking. There's nothing for us to identify with: no spectacle, no characters (i.e., band members). This, we would argue, could be considered Brechtian television.

It is also possible to contend that the comic remarks made directly to the viewer by characters on *It's Garry Shandling's Show* (1988–90) and *Malcolm in the Middle* (2000–) are a watered-down form of Brechtian distanciation, although,

FIGURE 3.12

in the final analysis, they're probably closer to the direct address of vaudeville and musical variety.

Thus, even though there is actually little Brechtian television to be found, we should still be aware that alternatives to naturalism do exist and, in film and theater, are actively investigated.

THE STAR SYSTEM?

Not everyone who appears on television is a television star. Stars, as we will be using the term, are actors or personalities whose significance extends beyond the television program on which they appear. If actors' images do not range beyond their programs, then they are just actors trapped within the characters they've created—as are many soap opera actors, whose names are never known to viewers. A true **star image**, in contrast, circulates through the culture in a variety of media—magazines, newspapers, Web sites, other television programs—and has culturally delimited meanings associated with it.

Of Texts and Intertextuality

Often it seems as if we know stars personally and intimately. We see them weekly (or daily) on our television screens, read about them in magazines, and hear them discuss themselves on talk shows. A large part of our conversation about television focuses on the personal lives of the stars. Wherever TV viewers congregate—the office water cooler or the high school lunch table—stars are a topic of conversation: "Do you think Jerry Seinfeld should marry someone so much younger than him?" or "Isn't it sad that Michael J. Fox has Parkinson's disease?" This illusion of intimacy is encouraged by television and other media, but it should not be confused with actual knowledge of someone's personality. We can never know stars' authentic natures because our knowledge of them is always filtered through the media. Magazine articles and the like often claim to present genuine knowledge about the star's inner self, but media-produced information about stars is like the layers of an onion. One article will discuss the "truth" about Pamela Anderson's feelings regarding her break-up with Tommy Lee and the circulation on the Web of their sexually explicit videotape; and then, inevitably, another comes along and undercuts that particular "truth" and proposes its own "truth," which is then countered by another article with its version of Anderson's emotions. We viewers can never cut through all of the layers of the onion and have direct knowledge of the star's psyche. But, for our purposes, the "true personality" of a star is a moot point. What we are concerned with here is how a star's image is built and how it fits into television's narratives.

In this regard, it is helpful to think of a star as a "text," as a collection of signifiers that hold meaning for the viewer. Various meanings cluster around stars. Their polysemy (literally: "many meanings") is generated by their appearance in several media texts: television programs, commercials, magazine articles, and the like. Roseanne, for example, appears in the sitcom *Roseanne*, but her presence is not limited to that program, which is currently in syndication. She is also the subject of numerous articles in popular magazines (from *The National Enquirer* to *People* to *Time* and *Newsweek*), has starred in a feature film (*She-Devil* [1989]), has authored an autobiography, and has performed on HBO comedy specials and television programs other than *Roseanne* (including *The Roseanne Show* [1998–2000], her own syndicated talk show). Her star text, an image of how she lives and what she thinks, is constructed from the representation of her in all of these media texts. Thus, she has an **intertextual** presence in U.S. culture that creates a sense of her publicly available private life. Her **intertextuality** separates her from other actors and establishes her as a star. For our purposes, intertextuality is the main component distinguishing a star from an actor. Without intertextuality, an actor is "just" an actor.

The different types of media texts in which stars appear may be clustered into four sometimes overlapping groups:

1. Promotion
2. Publicity
3. Television programs (and films)
4. Criticism of those programs/films[7]

By examining the stars' appearance in these media texts, we may better understand their intertextuality and how their polysemy evolves.

Promotion. Promotional texts are generated by stars and their representatives: agents, public relations firms, studios, networks, and so on. Principal among promotional texts are press releases containing information in the star's best interests, print advertisements in television listings such as *TV Guide* (one of the highest circulation magazines in the world), promotional announcements on television (whether created by a network or a local station), and appearances on talk shows and news/informational programs (e.g., *Entertainment Tonight* and the *E!* cable channel). Promotional materials represent the deliberate attempt to shape our perception of a star.

The majority of promotional texts place stars in the contexts of their television characters. Promotional announcements on television especially focus on the character and the program in which a star appears—sometimes excluding the star's name altogether. The strength of the star's influence determines whether star or character will be emphasized. Genie Francis, probably the biggest soap opera star of the late 1970s and 1980s, left her role of Laura on *General Hospital* and began appearing on other, competing soap operas. The new networks then promoted her character as "Genie Francis in . . ." This was extremely unusual for soap operas, and indicated just how major a star image Francis was. Prime-time programs' promotional material stresses stars more than does daytime drama's, but the star's character always governs how the star will be presented.

Publicity. We will here separate publicity from promotion, although the two are often indistinguishably intertwined. For our purposes, publicity will be used to designate information beyond the control of stars and their entourage: news reports about scandalous events in the stars' lives, unauthorized biographies, interviews in which stars are embarrassed or confronted with some unsavory aspect of their lives, and so on.

There have been many instances in the history of celebrity where promotion posed as publicity. Indeed, the career of the very first film star, Florence Lawrence, was launched by her producer spreading a false rumor that she had been killed in a streetcar accident. He then took out an advertisement declaring, "We Nail a Lie," in which he vigorously denied the rumor (Fig. 3.13). On a more mundane, day-to-day level, newspapers and magazines often publish verbatim the promotional press releases sent to them by the networks. Thus, often what

FIGURE 3.13

appears to be a news story (that is, "publicity") is actually the work of a star's publicist ("promotion").

The distinction between publicity and promotion is not always clear, but there are some instances when it is quite obvious. When a tabloid magazine learned that Roseanne had had a child before she was married, had put her up for adoption, and hadn't seen her in years, it published the story even before Roseanne could speak directly with her daughter. The articles about this event in Roseanne's publicly available private life constituted information beyond her influence. Publicity such as this raises interesting questions about the tensions and conflicts within stars' images—aspects that contrast with the official narrative of their lives. In the instance of Roseanne's child, the publicity relates to her on-screen image as a mother. In her television program she's represented as a tough, but ultimately loving mother. In contrast, the publicity represented her as a woman who abandoned her child. The tension between these two representations of Roseanne, and her bringing them together in a single person, illustrates how a star may reconcile a variety of sometimes conflicting meanings.

Television Programs. As we have previously noted, the characters a star plays in television programs determine much of how a star is perceived. However, to qualify as stars within our definition, stars must first of all have images beyond that of their characters. Francis and Roseanne are obviously stars. Their cultural currency extends beyond the texts of *General Hospital and Roseanne*. But an actor such as Jon Hensley—who plays Holden Snyder on *As the World Turns*—is not, because he is not recognized outside of his role.

When stars play roles, their polysemies may fit those characters in a variety of ways.[8] Often, as in the case of **typecasting**, the star image perfectly fits the character. For example, Don Johnson's former abuse of alcohol and generally dissipated life, and the meanings associated with that, made for a perfect fit with his character Sonny Crockett's background of alcoholism and degradation (*Miami Vice*). Johnson's publicly available private life and Crockett's "past" greatly resembled one another. Critics of television often presume that this **perfect fit** is the only way that stars are used in television. However, such is not the case.

Often there is a **problematic fit** between a star's polysemy and the attributes of the character he or she is playing. When a character is cast against type, the star image contrasts with the character. When Farrah Fawcett, whose image centered around her physical attractiveness and implied a certain empty-headedness, was cast as the abused wife in the ambitious MOW *The Burning Bed* (1984), there was a problematic fit between her image and the character portrayed. Similarly, during the 1970s, soap opera star Susan Lucci was represented in the press as a loving, devoted mother at the same time that her character, Erica on *All My Children*, was a manipulative woman who secretly took birth control pills to prevent conception.

Perfect and problematic fits of star image to role are less common than the **selective use** of the star's polysemy in the character's attributes. Larry Hagman, for example, has been represented in the press as an unpredictable man with a strong interest in spirituality and Eastern religions. His character of J.R. in *Dallas* selects Hagman's unpredictability, but ignores or represses his spirituality. In this fashion, Hagman's star image is partially used in the construction of his character. This is probably the most frequent use of star image in characterization.

Criticism. The final media text contributing to a star's image is the commentary on stars and their programs that appears in print, on Web sites, and on television itself. Critics and fans who create Web sites are presumed to operate independently of studios, networks, and other promotion-generating organizations. And, although many a review has been written out of a network's press kit, critics write about stars from a viewer's point of view, evaluating their images and their use in television programs. Thus, critics and fan-generated Web sites often share in the dissemination of a star image or help to change it.

Although the start of each television season does see a host of reviews and previews of the new programs, TV **criticism** is not as important to television as film criticism is to the movies. Film criticism is an institutionalized part of the promotional hoopla that leads to a film's release; it helps to create a narrative image of what the film will be like; and critics' comments are an essential part of the marketing of a film on videocassette and DVD as well. Television criticism, in contrast, is likely read or seen after the program has been broadcast. We may already have developed an opinion of the program before we read a review of it. Still, some programs—such as *Hill Street Blues, Twin Peaks* (1990–91), and *Everybody Loves Raymond* (1996–)—have benefitted greatly from critics championing their virtues.

Intertextuality and Polysemy: Roseanne

To illustrate how a polysemic star image (or text) develops through intertextuality, we will focus on Roseanne—one of the most striking and sometimes controversial television stars of the late 1980s and 1990s. Her image is particularly instructive because the connection between her publicly available private life and her on-screen character is so strong. After all, the program's main character (Roseanne Conner) shares Roseanne's name. And yet, there are still important divergences between Roseanne and Roseanne Conner.

Roseanne's image has developed through three main sources: her stand-up comedy routine, *Roseanne* (the television program), and the scores of articles about her in the mainstream and tabloid press. Born in Salt Lake City, Roseanne began performing in clubs in Colorado in the early 1980s as Roseanne Barr. Eventual success at Los Angeles's Comedy Store around 1985 led to appearances on *The Tonight Show*, at Caesar's Palace (Las Vegas), and on a Rodney Dangerfield HBO special. Her first solo television exposure was HBO's *The Roseanne Barr Show* (1987), which included narrative segments of her as a disaffected housewife among the stand-up comedy routines. The following year *Roseanne* premiered (October 1988) and quickly became a top-rated sitcom, despite the controversies surrounding Roseanne.

A history of the publicity surrounding Roseanne would be much harder to trace, simply because there is so much of it. Early on, aspects of Roseanne's publicly available private life were both reported and, occasionally, invented. Roseanne's life violated many taboos, and the press was quick to pick up on all of the ways that Roseanne deviated from the mainstream: her Jewish/Mormon religious training, her institutionalization in a psychiatric hospital, the birth (while she was still single) of a daughter that she gave up for adoption, her sexually charged relationship with ex-husband Tom Arnold and her championing of his career, her working-class roots, her problems with her own children (one of whom was treated for alcohol abuse), her charge that her parents sexually abused her, her off-key rendition of the National Anthem at a baseball game, and the list goes on. Almost all of the publicity storm swirling around Roseanne has centered on how she violates convention, does not fit in, and does not behave in a seemly manner. She is, as one critic put it, an "unruly woman."[9] It might seem somewhat strange, therefore, that she has become such a major star.

What is the ideological function of a star? How do stars embody taken-for-granted assumptions about how the world works? We can begin to answer these questions as we examine Roseanne's polysemy, the meanings that constellate around her image. It is arguable that three central themes run through Roseanne's image: ordinariness, feminism, and body image (her weight).

Central to the appeal of *Roseanne* is its working-class milieu. The difference in economic status between the Conner family and that of the 1980s' premiere television family, the Huxtables (*The Cosby Show*), has frequently been commented on. Indeed, *Roseanne* breaks with a long tradition within the television domestic comedy of upper-middle-class families—as was evident in earlier sitcoms such as *Father Knows Best* (1954–63) and *The Donna Reed Show* (1958–66). Roseanne Conner's jobs as factory worker and waitress carry marks of "ordinariness." They signify "middle America" and "normalcy." The working-class origins of Roseanne, the actor, are likewise stressed in the publicity attending her—as in magazine articles chronicling her time living in a trailer while her first husband worked as a garbage truck driver and mail carrier. Even though she is now a wealthy star, she is still presented as being "one of us."

In Roseanne's "feminism" we can see many of the tensions that her star image contains. On the one hand, she has been championed by feminists for humor that is critical of patriarchal assumptions about the woman's position within the home. Some of her wisecracks regarding housework include: "If the kids are still alive when my husband comes home, I've done my job" and "I will clean house when Sears comes out with a riding vacuum cleaner." Her feminism is apparent in her anger about the treatment of women. In a *Ms.* magazine interview she said, "I think of my mother, I think of all the women in the nuthouse, I think of all the women all the time. And I go, 'Hey, I will not be insulted anymore. There is no way to beat me, because I am so pissed.' "[10] On the other hand, there are aspects of Roseanne's image that contradict feminist principles. Even though Roseanne the woman ridicules aspects of the conventional nuclear family, *Roseanne* the program relies on an underlying belief in the validity of that family structure. The family is still the ultimate source of love and support, even amid all the sarcastic remarks.

Roseanne's weight is the center of another ideological conflict. Her large size (Fig. 3.5) links her with the stereotype of the "mammy," one of the greatest nurturing figures in U.S. culture. The Aunt Jemima figure is a middle-aged black woman, whose origins stem from the enslavement of African Americans. She nurtures her own children, her owner's children, and even the adult slave owners. Her large, shapeless form connotes her skill at cooking and also neutralizes her sexual attraction. The mammy is presumed to be fertile, a baby machine, but not sexually active or possessing her own desires. Rather, her desire is displaced into caring for others. Roseanne is signified as a nurturer, as exceptionally fertile, but one of the most controversial aspects of her image has been her unwillingness to be sexually neutered. This is evident in Roseanne Conner's relationships with her husband, which often has sexual overtones. It is also evident in Roseanne's extremely sexual relationship with Tom Arnold (before and after they were wed), which was widely reported both in the tabloid press and more mainstream magazines such as *People Weekly*. As an overweight woman with sexual appetites she disrupts many assumptions about overweight women. She also disrupts the mass-media convention that only slim people are sexually desirable or sexually active.

In sum, Roseanne's polysemy is fissured with ambivalence: mother and antimother, sexually neutral and sexually active. She thus brings together conflicting meanings. This is often the function of stars within U.S. culture. They unite opposite elements within our ideology and, through their single images, manage an almost magic reconciliation of them. Roseanne is a raucous, unruly woman, a woman who has been roundly condemned as vulgar, blasphemous, antifamily and even unpatriotic. And yet, she was also the matriarch of the best-loved television family of the 1990s. Her power to unite all of these contradictions is part of what marks her as an important television star.

SUMMARY

Our relationship to the human figure on the television screen is a complicated and conflicted one, and we may never completely decipher its intricacies. However, it is possible to break down character, performance, and star images into their building blocks. Characters in narrative, actors acting, and star images lure us to the television set. The analyst must step back from that lure and ask how character, performance, and star image are constructed, how they function in narratives.

We have adopted a semiotic approach in this endeavor. Characters are made up of character signs—a variety of signifiers that communicates the character to the viewer. Acting is a matter of performance signs—facial, gestural, corporeal, and vocal signifiers that contribute to the development of character. And star images have been presented as texts fabricated through the media texts of promotion, publicity, television programs, and criticism. The existence of stars as real people has been de-emphasized in favor of their signifying presences within U.S. culture, as is exemplified in the case of Roseanne.

We have also briefly explored two different schools of performance construction: naturalist and antinaturalist. The former dominates television, film and theater—relying on the principals of repertory performance and the Method. The latter is less well known, but we can still see the influence of vaudeville and Brecht on television programs.

FURTHER READINGS

The significance of characters to the television text is explained in John Fiske, "Cagney and Lacey: Reading Character Structurally and Politically,"

Communication 9 (1987): 399–426. Fiske continues and enlarges on this discussion in *Television Culture* (New York: Methuen, 1987).

The few substantive writings on television actors as stars have focused on female performers. Patricia Mellencamp, "Situation Comedy, Feminism and Freud: Discourses of Gracie and Lucy," in *Studies in Entertainment: Critical Approaches to Mass Culture*, ed. Tania Modleski (Bloomington, IN: Indiana University Press, 1986) applies Freudian psychology to Gracie Allen's and Lucille Ball's television performances. Denise Mann, "The Spectacularization of Everyday Life: Recycling Hollywood Stars and Fans in Early Television Variety Shows," *Camera Obscura*, no. 16 (January 1988): 49–77, explores the significance of performers like Martha Raye to television in the decade after World War II. Roseanne has been discussed in several essays, most notably Kathleen K. Rowe, *The Unruly Woman: Gender and the Genres of Laughter* (Austin, TX: University of Texas Press, 1995).

Discussion of women performers in music videos can be found in E. Ann Kaplan, *Rocking Around the Clock: Music Television, Postmodernism and Consumer Culture* (New York: Methuen, 1987); and Lisa A. Lewis, *Gender Politics and MTV: Voicing the Difference* (Philadelphia: Temple University Press, 1990). Kaplan is most interested in Madonna as a figure who blends aspects of popular culture into a postmodern puree. Lewis examines Madonna, Pat Benatar, Cyndi Lauper, and Tina Turner principally in terms of their fans and the relationships between the fans and the stars. Madonna has been discussed in numerous critical essays and empirical studies—including Jane D. Brown & Laurie Schultze (1990) "The Effects of Race, Gender and Fandom on Audience Interpretations of Madonna's Music Video," *Journal of Communication* 2 (1990): 88–102. For an overview of academic writing on Madonna and the controversy it has raised, see Laurie Schulze, "Not an Immaculate Reception: Ideology, The Madonna Connection, and Academic Wannabes," *The Velvet Light Trap* 43 (spring 1999): 37–50.

The student of television who is interested in the star phenomenon should also investigate the body of literature on cinema stars that has been developing since the late 1970s—especially since many television stars cross over into other media (e.g., Tom Hanks, Madonna, Tom Selleck, Meg Ryan). Some of the work done on the cinema may be transferred, with caution, to television studies. Richard Dyer, *Stars* (London: British Film Institute, 1998), remains the best introduction to the study of stars and characters. Originally published in 1979, it laid the groundwork for most star discussion of the 1980s and 1990s. He has augmented that book with *Heavenly Bodies: Film Stars and Society* (New York: St. Martin's Press, 1986), which approaches Marilyn Monroe in terms of sexual discourses, Paul Robeson in terms of racial discourse, and Judy Garland in terms of her reception by gay viewers.

Although not an actor per se, Princess Diana has been called the "first icon of the new age of the electronic image and the instantaneous distribution of images" by Nicholas Mirzoeff. His essay, "Diana's Death: Gender, Photography and the Inauguration of Global Visual Culture," addresses many of the issues of stardom and performance (in *An Introduction to Visual Culture* [London: Routledge, 1999]: 231–254).

A variety of key essays on performance and star image may be found in two anthologies: Jeremy G. Butler, ed., *Star Texts: Image and Performance in Film and*

Television (Detroit: Wayne State University Press, 1991) and Christine Gledhill, *Stardom: Industry of Desire* (New York: Routledge, 1991).

E N D N O T E S

[1] Richard Dyer, *Stars* (London: British Film Institute, 1998), 106–17.

[2] John Ellis, *Visible Fictions: Cinema: Television: Video* (Boston: Routledge, 1992).

[3] Dyer, 134–6

[4] Several authors have discussed performance signs. The terms here are Barry King's, as quoted in Andrew Higson, "Film Acting and Independent Cinema," *Screen 27*, nos. 3–4 (May–August 1986), 112.

[5] Reproduced in Dyer, 138.

[6] Bertolt Brecht, *Brecht on Theatre: The Development of an Aesthetic*, edited and translated by John Willett (NY: Hill and Wang, 1964), 26.

[7] See Richard Dyer's classification of film stars' media texts. Dyer, 60–63.

[8] See Dyer, 126–31.

[9] Kathleen K. Rowe, "Roseanne: Unruly Woman as Domestic Goddess," in *The Unruly Woman: Gender and Genres of Laughter* (Austin, TX: University of Texas Press, 1995): 50–91.

[10] Susan Dworkin, "Roseanne Barr," *Ms.*, July–August 1987, 206.

CHAPTER 4

Beyond and Beside
Narrative Structure

Sometimes it seems as if everything on television tells a story. Commercials are filled with miniature narratives. Nightly newscasts and news magazine programs such as *60 Minutes* (1968–) contain segments called "stories" that resemble narrative in the way they structure conflict and pose enigmas. *Survivor* (2000–) and other so-called "reality-TV" series are sold like soap operas—emphasizing dramatic conflict. As Fox executive vice president of programming, David Nevins, said about *American High* (2000), "We need to market the characters and the stories like you would market a good quality drama."[1] It all makes us wonder if there is anything real on TV, or if it is just one big fiction.

The simple response would be, no, there is nothing real on TV. The makers of television programs do not and cannot present a portion of reality (a car wreck, a football game, an earthquake) without first recasting it in the language of television and thereby modifying or "fictionalizing" it to some extent. They will necessarily present it from a certain camera angle and within a certain context of other shots. It will be accompanied by certain sound effects or music, and perhaps even narrated in a certain fashion. In their transition from reality to television, images and sounds are massaged, manipulated, and placed in new contexts. They are transformed into television material, cut to the measure of television.

But television's relationship to reality is not that simple. Many programs would not exist if we did not believe they were presenting some form of reality. The quiz shows of the 1950s, for example, based their enormous success on the believable illusion that real contestants (i.e., ordinary people) were competing in an impartial, improvised contest, in real time, with an outcome that was not predetermined by a scriptwriter. When it was revealed that the contests were rigged—staged to maximize dramatic impact—viewers were appalled and congressional investigations begun. Obviously, the illusion of reality was paramount to quiz shows then. It continues to be a fundamental component of *Who Wants to Be a Millionaire* (1999–) and the current crop of game shows, as well as news and sports programs and some commercials. Although all of these programs are fictionalized and manipulated on some level, each is also a "fiction (un)like any other"—as Bill Nichols has suggested, using a tricky bit of punctuation.[2] They may not be pure reality, as they sometimes advertise themselves, but they are still distinct from standard television fiction.

It begs the issue, therefore, to say that all television is fiction or that every program tells stories. What is crucial is an understanding of how TV constructs its illusions of reality, its representations of the real; in other words, how some of its fictions are unlike other fictions. This chapter treads that slippery slope, suggesting some of the ways that **non-narrative television** (for lack of a more accurate term) represents reality. We discuss the aesthetic principles that undergird that representation, the economic choices that are made in the process, and the technological limitations to television showing reality "as it really is." Moreover, we need to remain mindful of television's basic structure of flow, interruption, and segmentation, and the restrictions it places on representing the real.

To accomplish these goals, we begin this chapter with some global considerations of television, reality, and "reality television." We then address the modes of non-narrative television and some of its particular genres (news, sports, and game shows). Non-narrative commercials are considered in a later chapter, in the context of commercials in general.

TELEVISION'S REALITY

Everyone has his or her own commonsensical understanding of "reality." Most of us think of it as the world that all people exist in, where events—some caused by other events, some seemingly random—occur all the time everywhere. Reality has no inherent meaning; or perhaps its meanings are so varied that they are virtually limitless. Things just keep happening, regardless of human attention or inattention to them: a woman drives to work, moss grows on a tree, a political prisoner is killed in a jail, a cat naps, the Soviet Union dissolves, two men play checkers, a president is elected. The real is "polymorphous," as John Fiske suggests.[3] It assumes many shapes and styles, and is open to many interpretations.

Most important for our study, reality does not itself suggest interpretations or emphasize one event over another. A musical crescendo did not accompany the dissolution of the Soviet Union. A spotlight did not suddenly appear on the voting booth of the person who cast the deciding vote in the last presidential election. The meaning, the importance, the televisual and cultural significance of reality's events are determined by the makers of non-narrative television—as well as historians, newspaper columnists, textbook writers, and other cultural workers. These persons re-present a global reality back to all of us living in one small portion of it. Since we cannot experience all of reality directly, we must rely on television, magazines, newspapers, books, and movies to re-present it to us. Thus, our knowledge of the reality beyond our own personal sphere is always filtered through the mass media. In a very substantial sense, the media determine what is real and what is not, emphasizing certain events and ignoring others.

Equally important, the media manipulate and process those events that they have selected for us. Reality is mediated according to technological abilities (cameras cannot capture what occurs in darkness) and economic imperatives (footage of moss growing will not earn advertising dollars). It is also mediated according to ideological, institutionalized parameters such as the Radio-Television News Directors Association (RTNDA) code of ethics. From where we viewers sit it is often difficult, if not impossible, to isolate the actual events from their processed version. We are often unable to "separate reality from reality-as-described" because we have no direct knowledge of that reality.[4] We are only exposed to its description, to reality-as-described. That is, the only alternatives to the media's description of reality are other descriptions generated by other media. For instance, most of our knowledge of the U.S. war with Iraq over the invasion of Kuwait in 1990–91 was based on television news reports, which were tightly controlled by the U.S. government. These reports initially presented one description of the events: a clean, honorable, practically bloodless rout of Iraqi forces by U.S. troops, aided by their technologically advanced weaponry. Alternative descriptions of a different reality eventually surfaced—reports that detailed the burying alive of Iraqi soldiers by U.S. Army bulldozers and the high percentage of U.S. soldiers who were killed or wounded by so-called friendly fire. The point is not that these later reports were more real than the early ones, but that *both* were incomplete descriptions of reality that emphasized some events and ignored others. We viewers had to counterbalance one reality-as-described with another—as we must constantly do when watching nonfiction television. Short of traveling to Kuwait, personally examining the battlefields, interviewing Iraqi and U.S. soldiers, and perhaps shuffling through the memos of Iraqi leader Saddam Hussein, President George H.W. Bush, and their generals, we viewers will never be able to generate our own description of this war. We have no choice but to rely on its varying and incomplete representations in the media.

This chapter does not offer analytic methods that will allow the reader to glean reality or truth from media representations of the real world. But it does examine the structure of those representations, allowing the reader to better understand them as such rather than as reality itself.

Before we start, however, it may be helpful to adopt two of Bill Nichols's terms for discussing the reality depicted by television.

First, Nichols prefers the phrase **historical world** or **historical reality** over the term reality. This distinction helps him stress that nonfiction television is not able to represent an *unmediated* reality. Instead, nonfiction television is always signifying a processed, selected, ordered, interpreted, and incomplete reality. Just as historians fashion a narrative out of reality's jumble of events, so do nonfiction television texts denote a particular reading of reality. The terms *historical world* and *historical reality* do not refer solely to events of major significance, as when a sports reporter announces that the breaking of a record is a "historical event." Rather, historical in our sense of the term refers globally to all the events that could be represented on television—that is, to those aspects of the real world that may be used to tell stories.

Second, Nichols introduces the term **social actor** into the debate on nonfiction television and film. As he explains, "This term stands for 'individuals' or 'people.' ... I use 'social actor' to stress the degree to which individuals represent themselves to others; this can be construed as a performance. The term is also meant to remind us that social actors, people, retain the capacity to act within the historical arena where they perform."[5] When we see people in nonfiction television programs, we see them as social beings, as individuals functioning within a society of other individuals. Whether the individuals on TV are anonymous persons describing car accidents or Michael J. Fox announcing his contracting Parkinson's disease, their appearances on television are warranted by their social significance, their significance to society. And, as Nichols implies, persons on television act according to social codes of behavior to represent themselves to others. In a sense, we all perform according to certain conventions in public; we all act conventionalized social roles. When we go to a restaurant, we wait to be seated, eat food in a certain prescribed order (salad, entree, dessert), and pay in response to the presentation of the bill. Each of these actions is part of a learned behavior, a role, that we perform in a particular social setting. Persons who deviate too greatly from these socially approved roles are removed from society and placed in prisons or psychiatric hospitals.

In sum, then, nonfiction television presents to the viewer the interaction of social actors in the historical world. In parallel fashion, fiction television presents the interaction of constructed characters, portrayed by professional actors, in a narrative world. It's easy to see how the two might become blurred—as was illustrated by the historical world's presidency of professional actor Ronald Reagan. Moreover, television frequently encourages the confusion of social actors and professional actors, as in commercials where actors wear lab coats and imitate scientists or where professional wrestlers have scripted storylines that take precedence over uncontrolled competition. Despite television's common meshing of historical world and narrative world, much programming still depends on distinguishing between the two. News and sports programs would be disdained and ignored if they lost contact with the historical world. Our goal is to better understand how the contact between the historical world and the narrative world of television is depicted.

REALITY TELEVISION: FORMS AND MODES

The defining characteristic of nonfiction television is its apparent relationship to the historical world. Unfortunately, there is not much agreement among television theorists regarding this fundamental relationship. This causes much confusion, as you can imagine. For our purposes, it is best to rely on a strategy devised by Nichols and elaborated on by Julianne Burton.[6] Using and modifying slightly their approach, we may distinguish nonfiction television's four principal **modes of representation**—the ways that it depicts historical reality and addresses itself to the viewer about that version of reality:

1. Expository (or rhetorical)
2. Interactive
3. Observational
4. Reflexive

FIGURE 4.1

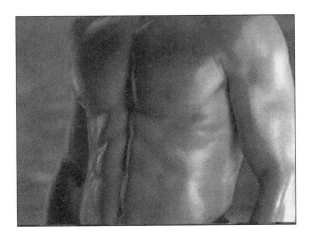

As we consider each mode we will examine how the television text corresponds to the historical world it appears to represent. Individual nonfiction genres (news, sports, game shows, etc.) are not limited to one single mode, but instead draw on each as needed. We will particularize some of these genres and their uses of these modes below.

Expository Mode. The essential component of an **expository** television text is that it presents an argument about the historical world. It assertively or even aggressively selects and organizes the "facts" of that world and presents them to the viewer in a direct address. For example, a commercial for the exercise videotape, *8 Minute Abs*, presents a shot of rippling abdominal muscles (Fig. 4.1), and the narrator announces "Over 1,000,000 stomachs have gotten tighter with *8 Minute Abs*!" The commercial is choosing evidence from the historical world to give credence to its argument—as well as repressing counter evidence (perhaps just as many stomachs failed to get tighter). In this case, the evidence for the tape's effectiveness is both visual (the image of a muscular abdomen) and verbal (the narration)—and is emphasized through the conjunction of the two.

Note that even though this exercise commercial is manipulating material from the historical world, it is not relying on narrative form to guide its manipulation. The logic, the guiding principle, of this commercial is rhetorical rather than narrative. There are many ways that rhetoric, arguments, may be structured. In this case, evidence (a series of images and words) is presented and then a conclusion is propounded ("Call now to buy this tape!"). In other expository texts the conclusion may come first, or a question will be rhetorically posed ("Should you buy this tape?") so that the argument may answer it ("Yes, you should!"); or perhaps emotional appeals will be made rather than evidence cited. Even narrative may be put in the service of rhetoric. A commercial may tell a story to illustrate a point, for instance. But narrative is not absolutely necessary for expository texts; plenty of them argue a position without telling a story. Thus, even though the *8 Minute Abs* commercial is not an unvarnished, unmediated chunk of the historical world, it is still not narrative and not fiction, in the narrow sense of the words.

Note also that this commercial, as in many expository texts, addresses its argument directly to us. In effect, it is saying, "Hey *you*! Here is the proof for my argument. Now, *you* come buy this tape!" This contrasts sharply with the address of narrative television, which speaks to us indirectly, obliquely. Most narrative television programs do not acknowledge the viewer (excepting shows such as *The George Burns and Gracie Allen Show* [1950–58] and *Malcolm in the Middle* [2000–] where characters speak to the camera). Instead, the characters interact as if there were no one watching. This is a charade, of course. There are millions watching. But the point is that the characters do not speak directly to us, as they often do in expository texts. Characters in narrative TV address one another. They are sealed within their narrative or diegetic worlds. Thus, we are not the direct target of the dialogue, as we are in many rhetorical texts.

There is little doubt that commercials are based on rhetoric, argument, and persuasion; but what of other nonfiction television such as network news? Nichols contends that network news also falls within the expository mode. His point is that reporters and anchorpersons make sense of the chaotic and semantically overloaded historical world. They select facts from that world and organize them into a coherent presentation. And while doing that, reporters are arguing implicitly for the validity of their specific selections and their organization; often they are even arguing explicitly for a specific interpretation of these facts. The news anchor, for Nichols, is the ultimate structuring authority in the expository mode. Walter Cronkite, who anchored CBS's evening newscasts for nearly two decades (1962–81), proclaimed "And that's the way it is" at the end of each program. He was certifying the truth value of CBS News's selection and arrangement of the material (its evidence) drawn from historical reality.

One other aspect that establishes the news as an expository text is its use of direct address. In television news, the anchors face the cameras directly and present their argument to us—just as an advertisement presents its claims. Their gaze at the camera is facilitated by the **TelePrompTer**, an inventive bit of technology that is placed directly in front of the lens, seemingly blocking it (Fig. 4.2). The copy is displayed on a video monitor pointed upwards, which is reflected in an angled, two-way mirror. The camera shoots right through it. This renders the copy invisible to the camera and us, but allows the anchor to see it (Fig. 4.3). As Mike Budd, Steve Craig, and Clay Steinman contend, the TelePrompTer "makes it possible for anchors and others to appear to be telling us things that come from them rather than from something they are reading."[7] It thereby lends authority to the claims they make about historical reality. (Politicians commonly use similar devices when making speeches to heighten their contact with the audience.)

Anchors also introduce us to field reporters, who then present their reports directly to us. At the beginning and end of reporters' stories or **packages**, as they are sometimes called, they may speak to the anchor (and not to us); but the majority of the newscast is addressed directly to the viewer. Thus, news does not use the form of address most common to TV narrative, but rather shares its mode of address with the commercial.

Interactive Mode. The **interactive** text represents the mixing of the historical world with the realm of the video/film maker. This mingling occurs

FIGURE 4.2

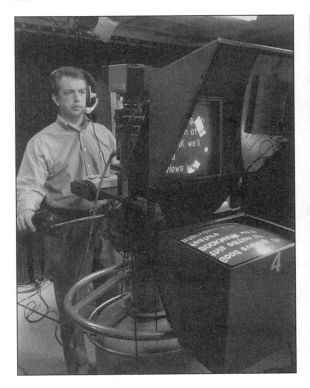

FIGURE 4.3

in one of two ways: The social actor is brought into a television studio (e.g., talk shows, game shows); or a representative of television goes out into the historical world to provoke a response from social actors (e.g., the investigative reports of *60 Minutes* and *Dateline* [1992–]).

Thus, the interaction between social actors and television may occur on television's turf or out in historical reality.

In either case, the interactive mode differs from the expository mode in terms of how it addresses the viewer. Like narrative television, the address of interactive texts is not directed toward the viewer. The social actors within the text speak with the television producers rather than to us. When Mike Wallace confronts a corrupt politician and the politician argues with Wallace, the two are addressing each other, not us. We may identify with Wallace (or with the politician, depending on our sympathies) and thus feel that the politician's responses are indirectly aimed at us. But these politicians are not speaking directly to us. They indirectly address us through our emissaries, the TV reporters.

In other cases, the social actor can become our textual representative—as in game shows such as the long-running *The Price Is Right* (1956–1965, 1972–), where participants are chosen from the audience (Fig. 4.4). We presumably identify with the participants, who are, like us, members of the historical world. Through the contestants we interact vicariously with the host, Bob Barker. Thus, when Barker addresses participants at their podiums (Fig. 4.5) and asks them to guess the price of a toaster, he is indirectly addressing us (Fig. 4.6). Regardless of with whom we identify in an interactive text (social actor or television producer),

FIGURE 4.4

FIGURE 4.5

we are not placed in the same viewer position as in the expository text, where we are often addressed directly.

When social actors enter the realm of television, they are representatives of "our" world, of historical reality, but it would be naive to suppose that social actors are not affected by their contact with television. Any social actor appearing on TV is subjected immediately to the medium's rules and conventions. Contestants on game shows or "guests" appearing on interview programs (whether *The Oprah Winfrey Show* [1984–] or *Nightline* [1979–])[8] are screened before the show; those unsuited for television's needs (based on visual interest, verbal skill, suitability to a particular topic) are filtered out early. Once the cameras are on, these social actors are permitted to speak "in their own words." However, the framing questions are Barker's and Winfrey's and Ted Koppel's; the rhythm of the show is strictly controlled by the hosts; and the final edit belongs to the producer. Even more than talk shows, game shows rigidly limit improvisation by situating the social actor within a tightly structured competition.

FIGURE 4.6

Hypothetically, there are many ways that television people could interact with social actors. They could touch one another or write letters or gesture with their hands. But, of course, the principal form this interaction takes is speech, dialogue, conversation—in short, interviewing. And it is in the interview that we may locate the rudimentary logic of the interactive text. Where the expository text is governed by the logic of the argument and gathering evidence, the interactive text's logic is largely shaped by how the interview is structured. Even game shows, which adhere to a logic of competition and the format of the specific game, also contain instances of interviewing between the host and the social actors—though obviously they are much less central than are interviews in talk shows and the like.

We particularize two basic types of interviews. They are grounded in the degree to which the interviewer is present, visually and verbally, within the text:[9] the dialogue and the pseudomonologue.

In a **dialogue**, the voices of the interviewer and the interviewee are both heard, and both persons may be visible on camera—as in Barbara Walters' interviews of celebrities. The participants exchange comments, speaking "freely" to one another. Of course, interviewers are always in positions of relative power, since they determine which questions to ask and how to frame them. The interviewers, or their bosses, also decide who shall be interviewed to begin with and thus who has the televisual clout to warrant an invitation. A television dialogue doesn't begin unless the interviewer chooses to point the cameras in the direction of a particular social actor. Because of this unequal power relationship the dialogue can never be truly free. It always fits within the constraints of television.

In a **pseudomonologue**, a similar interchange occurs between a social actor and a television representative, but it is presented differently. Interviewers and their questions are not evident in the text. Only the interviewee's answers are included. Thus, it makes it appear as if social actors were speaking directly about their experiences or opinions, even though they have been prompted by the interviewers' questions. This approach is commonly used in news stories about disasters. We don't see or hear the reporters' questions about how the disaster affected the victims and witnesses, but we see and hear their responses to the questions. The reporter remains invisible and unheard, thus making it seem as if social actors were speaking without prompting—in their own voices.

The pseudomonologue blurs the line between expository and interactive nonfiction. What is presented to us as monologues of interviewees' comments, an unmediated expression of their thoughts, is actually the result of interactive dialogues between the interviewers and the interviewees. That is, the pseudomonologue often appears as if the social actor were speaking directly to the viewer, as in exposition; but most viewers know pseudomonologues were originally addressed to reporters constructing their stories. The news reporter will tell us that the hurricane has wrought devastation. The story will then cut to pseudomonologues of hurricane victims describing their plight—seemingly to us directly. Hence, the pseudomonologue is often used as evidence in the ordering of "reality" into a comprehensible logic and the development of a television argument about the historical world. It is not surprising, therefore, that numerous commercials have used pseudomonologues as testimonials for their products' superiority.

Observational Mode. Expository and interactive modes dominate non-narrative television, but there are occasions when the presence of television producers becomes nearly invisible and where their manipulation of the historical world is relatively minimal. In **observational** mode the producer observes rather than argues about (exposition) or mixes with social actors (interaction). Of course, this is always something of a sham. The moment a camera begins to select one view, and consequently neglect another, manipulation and argument begin. And just by being in the same room with social actors, videographers will begin to interact with them, influencing behavior—even if they don't speak with each other. Still, there are nonfiction programs that invite us to suspend our distrust of television's "devious" ways. For their impact, these programs depend on our belief in the television producer's nonintervention.

The most famous television experiment along these lines was *An American Family* (1973), a 12-part PBS series that observed the family of Pat and Bill Loud. Cameras recorded over 300 hours of the day-to-day life of what was supposed to be a stable, average U.S. family. Direct interaction between the filmmakers and the family members was minimized. Over the course of the filming, however, the family fell apart—the parents decided to divorce and one son announced that he was gay. Rather than organize this raw material into a treatise on the decay of the U.S. family, however, the producers presented it mostly without explicit commentary in the form of voice-overs or direct interviews with the family members. It was as close to pure observation as television ever gets.

More recently, other programs have toyed with this concept. *Cops* (1989–) is presented as if we were patrolling U.S. streets with police officers, observing their daily experiences. The show does includes some pseudomonologues of officers explaining (to us) what is occurring. But the bulk of the program is videotape of them in action, interacting with lawbreakers rather than with the camera. Significantly, there is no narrator providing an overall continuity to the program. The social actors speak for themselves. MTV has had great success with the observational mode in *The Real World* (1991–). Its premise is announced at the start of each episode: "This is the true story of seven strangers, picked to live in a house and have their lives taped, to find out what happens when people stop being polite and start getting real." The situation is clearly contrived by Bunim/Murray Productions for MTV, but the videotaping is mostly done in observational mode: no narrator, few interviews (pseudomonologues), little interaction between the videographers and the "subjects" (Fig. 4.7).

Furthermore, *The Real World* illustrated just how artificial the division between videographers and a cast of social actors can be. During a Jamaican segment in the first season, one male producer and one female cast member crossed the line and became romantically involved. MTV handled it by removing the producer from the project—and putting him in front of the camera, videotaping him socializing with the woman. He wasn't permitted to be both part of the television world (as a producer) and part of the historical world (as a cast member). One cannot observe and participate at the same time, according to the logic of the observational mode.

The observational mode was influenced in the 1990s by the ever-shrinking technology of surveillance cameras and microphones. Their inconspicuous size

FIGURE 4.7

has enabled TV producers to observe human behavior without betraying the presence of the camera—unlike *Cops* and *The Real World* where the cameras are never totally invisible (note the intrusive camera in Fig. 4.7). Programs such as *Busted On the Job: Caught On Tape* (1996–) and *Taxicab Confessions* (1995–) rely on such technology. The former uses actual surveillance videotape of employee misbehavior. The latter places lipstick-sized cameras in a taxicab where the drivers encourage their passengers to talk intimately about their lives (Fig. 4.8). In both situations, the persons on tape do not realize they are being recorded, which is the ultimate goal of the observational mode. However, *Taxicab Confession* is not purely observational, since it places an undercover TV "host" in the cab with the unsuspecting passengers. By provoking the passengers, these hosts violate the principal of the observers not affecting the observed.

Reflexive Mode. Certain non-narrative programs invite the viewer to examine the techniques of television production and the conventions of non-narrative programs themselves. These texts could be said to reflect back on their own devices. Hence, they may be called **reflexive** programs.

Reflexive texts differ from other modes of non-narrative television in their relationship to the historical world and its representation. A reflexive text does

FIGURE 4.8

not just depict that world—making an argument about it or interacting with it or observing it—as most non-narrative TV does. Rather, it draws our attention to the process of depiction itself, shifting the focus away from historical reality proper to the text-reality relationship. In Errol Morris's *The Thin Blue Line* (1988), for example, some facts are presented about the murder conviction of Randall Adams, a social actor in the historical world. But the essence of the program is the different narratives surrounding the murder, which Morris presents to us in ambiguous, stylized recreations. Morris does not advocate a single truth as much as he critiques the idea of finding truth and implicitly breaks down the mechanisms that are used to tell stories about historical reality. It is a film both about truth and about the tendency of TV and film to represent reality by transforming it into narrative.

Not surprisingly, *The Thin Blue Line*, which was shown on PBS after an initial theatrical run, belongs to a rare breed of documentary television. Not many programs are willing to call into question their basic assumptions, as *The Thin Blue Line* does. To do so often raises doubt about a program's truthfulness, which is dangerous to any documentary. So the reflexive mode remains on the edges of documentary television, the result of somewhat avant-garde experimentations with the medium.

Reflexivity is less menacing to the foundations of commercials and non-narrative comedy programs, where it reveals itself in parody and pastiche. *The Late Show with David Letterman* (1993–), for example, reflects back on the conventions and devices of talk shows for much of its humor. In typical reflexive fashion, it is both a talk show and a parody of one. The targets of Letterman's parodies extend from talk shows to the whole of television. *The Late Show's* debut featured old shots of Ed Sullivan (whose variety show was broadcast from the same studio decades earlier) cut together so that it appeared he was still alive and was introducing Letterman (Fig. 4.9). Later in the same episode a clip of Sullivan was also used in a comic bit involving his "spirit" and Paul Newman (Fig. 4.10). A large part of the humor in these bits derived from their implicit reference to televisual figures, devices, and conventions. The same sort of reflexivity

FIGURE 4.9

FIGURE 4.10

operates in other non-narrative television comedy—such as many of the skits on *Saturday Night Live* (1975–). To pick one recurring skit from many, "Wayne's World" is obviously a TV parody—choosing low-budget, public-access cable television programs as its target.

Television comedy's self-parody and reflexivity are parts of a long-standing tradition, one which is essential to television's evolution. As a television device or convention ages, it is ridiculed through parody, and then replaced with a modification of it. Thus, while reflexivity is relatively rare in non-narrative documentary works and can endanger basic assumptions about truth and historical reality, it is quite common in non-narrative comedy—refreshing the form and rejuvenating stale conventions.

REALITY TELEVISION: GENRES

These non-narrative modes—expository, interactive, observational, reflexive— find expression in a broad variety of television programs. We may make some sense out of the chaos of non-narrative programs by categorizing them into specific **genres**. Much as we might categorize narrative programs into such genres as the soap opera and the sitcom, we will specify three types of non-narrative material:

- Newscasts
- Sports programs
- Game shows

This is not a comprehensive list. There are other non-narrative genres (e.g., talk shows and science programs such as *Nova* [1973–]), but these three will serve to illustrate the diversity in non-narrative television. We will, however, return to non-narrative genres when we discuss commercials in the following chapter.

The categories above are echoed by economically based divisions within the TV industry and its ancillaries. Completely separate staffs at the networks and the syndication studios are assigned to handle news, sports, and "entertainment" (as if news and sports weren't entertaining). Beyond the industry's view of itself, however, the viewer/critic can make important distinctions among these genres, based on the non-narrative texts themselves and their relationship to the viewer.

Network and Local Newscasts

The newscasts produced on national networks (both broadcast and cable) and on local stations all share a common assumption about historical reality: An event is not significant, is not newsworthy, unless it disrupts the ordinary, day-to-day functioning of life on earth. Presumptions of newsworthiness immediately channel TV news away from the common incidents in reality and direct it toward the odd, the unusual, and the unsettling. Once an incident ceases to disrupt the norm, it stops being "news" and disappears from the television screen. We are not likely to see a newscast begin, "Gravity: It's still holding things down!"

Typically, network news producers select the following types of events from the enormous miscellany of the historical world:

- Catastrophes: natural and otherwise.
- International relations: political and armed conflicts.
- National politics: legal and judicial activities, election campaigns, politicians' other enterprises.
- Law and order: crime and the activities of criminals.
- Economics: financial trends.
- Celebrities: marriages, scandals, deaths.

Local newscasts deal with many of the same subjects but on a smaller scale. The catastrophes are car accidents and house fires rather than earthquakes, and the politicians are governors and mayors rather than presidents, but the approach is modeled on the national newscasts. Local newscasts also incorporate sports and weather information that the national networks do not address.

Newscasts largely use an expository mode to present information collected from the historical world. That is, evidence is displayed to support a reporter's or editor's particular interpretation of events. Inevitably this evidence is arranged, ordered, into some form of conflict: Democrat versus Republican, individual versus institution, police versus killer. The basic logic of most news stories is an argument where the historical world is explained as a series of conflicts.

Conflict is normally most obvious and deadly in the case of international warfare—pitting one nation against another. NBC's and CBS's coverage of a particular international incident may illustrate the expository nature of TV news. The Balkan war of 1991 to 1995 was a particularly difficult one for TV news to fit into a simple structure of "A versus B." Battles raged among Serb, Croat, and Muslim factions in the Federation of Bosnia and Herzegovina (parts of the former Yugoslavia). Moreover, peace-keeping forces from NATO and the UN were thrown into the middle of this complicated situation. In September 1992 a UN plane flying relief supplies was shot down in Bosnia. CBS and NBC both featured Bosnian relief efforts in their nightly newscast—highlighting attempts to bring food and medicine to the town of Gorazde.

As in most incidents outside North America, CBS and NBC relied on exactly the same video footage from Bosnia. The only differences in the two stories were the editing and the voice-over added by CBS's and NBC's reporters based in London: Tom Fenton and Keith Miller, respectively. The CBS story includes footage of decaying Serb bodies that are excluded from the NBC story (Fig. 4.11). And the CBS story ends with shots of Muslim fighters on a hilltop (which are also excluded from the NBC story), with Fenton commenting, "Now the main concern will be to keep a lifeline open for the newly liberated town. That will depend on if the Muslims can continue to hold on to the high ground around them" (Fig. 4.12). In contrast, NBC chose to end with a shot of the deserted airport runway and the remark, "If the plane was shot down, then the UN will somehow have to eliminate the threat" (Fig. 4.13).

Remembering that reporters Fenton (CBS) and Miller (NBC) worked from the same video (the same images of historical reality), what differences can we observe in the "arguments" they present about that reality? NBC's story argues that the main conflict in this incident is between UN relief workers and the forces that shot down the plane—forces that were not yet determined.

FIGURE 4.11

FIGURE 4.12

FIGURE 4.13

CBS includes that conflict as a major part of the story, but Miller's editing and voice-over add a different perspective. Miller argues that the Muslims are valiant freedom fighters by placing them literally and figuratively on the "high ground" (Fig. 4.12). They are "liberating" the town, forcefully pushing back the Serb paramilitary forces (resulting in decomposing bodies in the road [Fig. 4.11]).

Since none of CBS's or NBC's viewers were actually in Gorazde that day, they have no way to authenticate either of these reports through personal experience. They have only these "stories," told in an expository mode, on which to make their judgments. However, by remaining alert to the connotations of terms like "liberated" and "high ground" viewers may better understand how news organizations are constructing their arguments about the historical world.

Reporters are encouraged to view the historical world in terms of conflicts and not cooperation or collaboration. They are trained to present an issue "in a way that is balanced, accurate and fair"—as it is stated in the RTNDA code of ethics. Let's examine for a moment what it means to be "balanced." A balanced presentation presumes two sides that are in conflict. It is the reporter's job to argue each side without prejudice. Consequently, reporters seek the core conflict of an issue and then use the expository mode to articulate each side of that conflict. Just as television narrative is fueled by conflict, so is television news.

Further, most news stories find a way to reduce the conflict to the impact on or the opinions of particular individuals—regardless of how abstract and general the topic may be. Complicated economic developments are illustrated by the inability of a specific person to find work. Airplane crashes are related in the words of the individual survivor—or dramatized in the fate of the specific victim. Reporters "cast" social actors in roles that illustrate abstract topics.

Despite the development of cable news channels during the 1980s, the format of U.S. broadcast newscasts (national and local) has not changed much recently. At the center of this format is the news anchor (or anchors; many newscasts use two). The anchors serve several purposes. Principally, they maintain the television flow, introducing **packages** (news stories), as well as weather and sports components, and guiding the viewer into commercial breaks with **teasers** (brief announcements of upcoming stories). Because anchors frame every element of the newscast (setting them up beforehand and often commenting afterward) they are also represented as authenticating and authorizing the views of the historical world that the reporters and meteorologists deliver. This is regardless of whether the stories were actually chosen by the newscast's producers or someone other than the anchors. As the newscast's authority figures, the anchors offer to make ideological sense out of the day's random events, as Cronkite's "And that's the way it is" suggests. They serve as the central spokespersons for the newscast's exposition. Reporters out in the field create expository packages about the historical world, and the anchors stamp them with their approval.

Television newscasts differ in form depending on when they are telecast during the day, where they fit into television's flow. Morning newscasts emphasize the weather and the time of day; late-night newscasts summarize the day's events. The preeminent network newscast is broadcast in the evening at

5:30 or 6:30, depending on the viewer's time zone. Local news usually follows, and often precedes, this newscast. These network and local newscasts share the basic organizing principle of an anchor providing continuity to a program, but their form differs in its structure because the local newscast is designed to complement the national newscast, to fill in regional information not pertaining to national interests. It's as if the network and local evening newscasts must be taken together to provide the "total" picture of the historical world. We may make some generalizations about how each evening newscast organizes the material it presents.

In day-to-day news production, it is the producer, not the anchor, who establishes the structure of a newscast by setting the order of the stories. (Some anchors, such as Dan Rather, also hold the title of executive producer.) This order is determined by journalistic principles, aesthetic factors, and economic determinants. The basic journalistic guidelines, which television shares with print journalism, are:

- Timeliness (How recently did the event occur?)

- Prominence (How famous are the participants?)

- Proximity (Did it occur close to the viewers?)

- Pertinence (Will it affect viewers' lives? Sometimes abbreviated as WIIFM impact. I.e., there should be a clear answer when viewers ask, "What's in it for me?")

- Unusualness (Is it a common event or something unique?)

- Conflict (Will it lend itself to the news' structure of "pro versus con"?)

Other practical and logistical factors that also influence TV news priorities include:

- Visual impact (Are there strong, affective video images available?)

- Cost (For example, was a video truck rented to do a live, remote broadcast?)

- Promotional value (Does the story boost the station's/network's prestige? For example, is it an exclusive interview that illustrates the superior news-gathering ability of the station or network?)

If all of these factors are equal, network news programs tend to move from the general to the specific, from the international to the national to the regional—including editorial material toward the end of the newscast.

Also, network news tends to begin with **hard news** and move toward **soft news** at the program's end. Although these terms are not very well defined, hard news is generally thought of as stories addressing the *social*—examining events that affect U.S. society as a whole (e.g., national and international relations). Soft news deals with the *personal*—gossip, scandal, murder, mayhem, and so-called human interest stories (which is something of a misnomer since all news stories interest some humans). Hard news, it is presumed, appeals to viewers' intellect; soft news attracts the emotions. Soft news also includes weather and sports.

Significantly, soft news often does not fit the journalistic criteria of timeliness, prominence, proximity, or pertinence that is applied to "real," hard news. A soft news story about a gourd the shape of Michael Jackson's head, for instance, is neither timely, prominent (it doesn't involve Jackson directly), nearby, or pertinent to most viewers. Because it lacks these qualities, it often is placed at the newcast's conclusion. It serves as filler and may be cut if other packages run long.

Television inherited this hard/soft notion from the print media, where we find hard news on the front page of *The New York Times* and (extremely) soft news in *The National Enquirer*. Hard news is the better respected of the two, which is indicative of journalism's trivialization and neglect of the personal. There may also be some sexism lurking in this distinction, as women's issues often exist within the realm of the personal.

The mixture of material in local newscasts and its categorization are different from the national newscasts. On a local level, the newscast is categorized into segments of news, sports, and weather. This division is somewhat artificial, however, for all three segments are, in a sense, "news." Each represents aspects from the historical world to the viewer. Thus, "sports" is more accurately "news about sports events"; and "weather" is "news about weather events." This arbitrary categorization of the news is not limited to television, of course. It can be traced back through radio to the newspaper (e.g., its separate sports section). Though it is not unique to television, it is particularly well suited to television's need for segmentation.

Typically, a local newscast is segmented—interrupted—by four or five commercial breaks. The division of a newscast into news, sports, and weather helps to justify those breaks. It provides a rationale for suspending the program flow at a particular point to begin the flow of commercials. And, since weather and sports are two popular elements of the newscast, their position late in the program may be used to "tease" us into continued viewing.

In many local newscasts, the structure of flow and interruption results in the following segmentation:

- News block
- Commercial break
- News block
- Commercial break
- Weather
- Commercial break
- Sports
- Commercial break
- News block

This structure is typical of many local newscasts: news first, then weather and sports, followed by a final news update (or soft news feature)—all interspersed with commercials. We may see these elements in Table 4.1, an outline of an NBC affiliate's newscast (WVTM, channel 13 in Birmingham, Alabama) on a typical fall day. Also included in this table are other newscast components: the opening and closing, station promotional announcements ("promos"), and teasers.

Though we have labeled the commercials as interruptions, we could just as easily look at newscasts as a flow of commercials that are interrupted by news blocks. For, in many local newscasts, commercials and promos (which are just

TABLE 4.1

A Local Newscast

6:00 P.M., Friday, September 4, 1992, WVTM
(NBC affiliate, Birmingham, Alabama)

LEN.*	CATEGORY	DETAILS
15	Opening	
120	News	Car accident (cheerleaders on a bus)
30	News	Murder suspect arrested
60	News	Wells Fargo truck attacked
90	News	Vice-presidential candidate Al Gore campaigns locally
10	News	President George Bush's son, Jeb Bush, campaigns locally
15	Teaser	
30	Commercial	Marks Fitzgerald furniture
30	Commercial	Starving Artist painting sale
10	Commercial	Mazer's department store
90	News	Background story on child abuse film
60	News	Complaint against a hospital
120	News	Sewage problem, environmental issue
15	Teaser	
30	Promo	
30	Commercial	Nissan
10	Promo	
30	Commercial	Food World
30	Commercial	Milk
10	Promo	
165	Weather	
15	Teaser	
30	Commercial	Marks Fitzgerald furniture
30	Commercial	Winn Dixie grocery stores
10	Promo	
30	Commercial	Alabama Power
30	Commercial	Edwards Chevrolet
230	Sports	
30	Commercial	Marshall Durbin chicken
10	Commercial	Midas muffler
30	Commercial	Delchamps grocery
10	Promo	
30	Commercial	Shoe City
30	Commercial	ServiStar hardware
50	News	Accident, child abuse updates
80	Closing	Credits over high school football footage

*Length in seconds.

commercials for the station itself) occupy nearly as much time as the news proper. In the newscast in Table 4.1, 9 minutes and 20 seconds were devoted to commercial and promotion time in this half-hour newscast. In comparison, just slightly more time (10 minutes, 30 seconds) was allocated to news—although about 17 minutes were spent on news, sports, and weather combined. (Table 4.2 ranks the time spent on each component of that newscast.) Thus, communicating information about the historical world—the presumable

TABLE 4.2

Local Newscast Timings

| | DURATION | | |
COMPONENT	SEC	MIN:SEC	PERCENTAGE
News Stories	630	10:30	38.3
Comercials	410	6:50	24.9
Sports	230	3:50	14.0
Weather	165	2:45	10.0
Opening/Closing	95	1:35	5.8
Promos	70	1:10	4.3
News Teasers	45	0:45	2.7
Totals	1645	27:25	100.0%

purpose of newscasts—is barely given more time than the advertising of that world's products.

From one perspective, the difference between the news and the commercial is blurry, more so than the difference between the narrative program and the commercial. Recall that both news and commercial, in Nichols's terms, are expository forms. Both present evidence to the viewer that is designed to support an argument about the historical world. In this regard, then, commercials could be considered "news" about products and services. Television journalists would dispute this interpretation, asserting that anchors and reporters are not trying to sell the viewer anything. It could be argued, however, that to survive, a newscast must market its interpretation of the historical world as accurate and true. A newscast's vision of the world is sold directly through its promotional spots ("Thirteen News: Alabama's news, from people who *care*.") and indirectly through the arguments about the world that it expresses in its news reports. In this regard, television news differs from fiction programming, whose structure is narrative rather than expository, and thus does not share this kinship with commercials.

Sports Programs

Sports events differ from the events shown on newscasts that we have discussed so far, even though both originate in the historical world. Sports activities, particularly those at the professional and college levels, are commodities designed for spectators—even before television enters the equation. People who "witness" a professional football game in person, for instance, have purchased that privilege. They are seated in a stadium designed for spectator comfort and the optimum display of the playing field. The game is organized according to rules that maximize its entertainment value for the spectator. Spectator sports such as U.S. professional football do not occur randomly, for free, in uncomfortable, inconvenient locations, with unsuspecting, disorganized participants—as do most other historical world events (earthquakes, traffic accidents, wars, etc.) that are deemed newsworthy.

Sports programs, thus, are presenting to the viewer a commercial event, a spectacle really, that has already been contrived to please spectators and marketed to attract an audience. This has obvious economic implications for television sports, but it also affects the form of the programs in less obvious ways.

First, economically speaking, the right to broadcast sports events must be purchased from sports leagues and team owners, unlike the right to broadcast the sort of historical world events we have been discussing so far. These rights do not come cheaply. The national TV networks will pay the National Football League $17.6 billion for broadcast rights during 1998–2005 (which is always subject to renegotiation). These expensive contracts mean, plainly enough, that networks and individual stations have a vested interest in promoting—in emphasizing the importance and entertainment value of—the sports events they've purchased. Moreover, some networks and stations have more than just a passing financial interest in professional sports because many media corporations wholly own sports teams. The Atlanta Braves, for example, is owned by Ted Turner, who also owns numerous media outlets. And XFL football was jointly created by NBC and the World Wrestling Federation.

As you might expect in such a financial climate, journalistic notions of objectivity become a little twisted. Network coverage of sports tries to maintain a distance between the commentators and the teams, but the former still need to emphasize the significance of the event and try to maintain our interest during the game. Local coverage need not even preserve that level of objectivity. Often the commentators will be employed by the team itself—common practice in professional baseball since radio days. These announcers do not just offer expert commentary; they also boost fan support for the sponsored team. When a commentator such as the Chicago Cubs's Harry Caray exclaims "Holy cow!" at a Cubs' home run, he is supporting the team that pays his salary. It's hard to imagine Dan Rather making a similar remark at a news story.

Television producers and announcers have come to rely on the ratings success of sports events. Professional and college sports associations have come to depend on television money to survive. TV and sports have thus become mutually dependent and have fashioned various financial liaisons. They have formed into what Sut Jhally calls a sports/media complex.[10] His point is that spectator sports and the electronic media, especially television, have become so enmeshed that it's becoming impossible to separate the two. Only a small percentage of the viewers of professional football and baseball, for example, actually see games in arenas or stadiums. For the vast majority of sports fans, pro sports are always experienced through television. This has resulted in certain aesthetic adjustments to spectator sports.

The aesthetic structure of television sports is best seen as the blending of television form with the preexisting form of the particular sport. Most sports on television existed long before TV was invented and had already evolved rules to govern a game's fundamentals:

- Time (e.g., four 15-minute quarters in football);
- Space (e.g., the layout of a baseball diamond and players' movements around it); and
- Scoring/competition (i.e., how one wins).

These rules/structures presumed, of course, that the sport would be viewed in an arena or stadium.

When television began broadcasting sports events it soon adapted itself to shooting games in their natural settings. Multiple-camera shooting styles—using powerful telephoto lenses—quickly developed to capture a sport's essential action. But this adaptation process was not one-sided. If a sport was to successfully attract a large television audience, it too had to adapt. As a result, all of the major television sports in the United States, especially football, baseball, and basketball, have adjusted their rules to accommodate television's form. In particular, these sports have found ways to adjust to the medium's organization of time and space.

Let's take professional football as an example. During the 1970s, pro football turned into a major force on U.S. television. As of 2000, the NFL Super Bowl programs accounted for 10 of the 20 highest-rated programs in the entire history of the medium. The immense popularity of pro football on television is obviously due to many different factors, but what concerns us here is how football and television accommodate each other structurally.

The Organization of Time. The rhythms of football are inherently well suited to televisual flow and interruption. The lull after each play while the teams huddle provides the opportunity for television to insert itself, "interrupt" the game, and present slow-motion "instant replays," accompanied by commentary. Football's many time-outs provide convenient stoppages in action for television to cut to commercials. These time-outs were not frequent or long enough for television's needs, however, and the NFL accommodated TV by adding "television time-outs." Charged to neither team, they may be called by officials during the first and third quarters if there has been 9 minutes of play without interruption.[11] In addition, all time-outs have been lengthened to ensure enough time for commercials. Other sports, such as soccer, suffer because their constant play minimizes the opportunity for replays and commercial breaks.

There are other ways that football time has been manipulated to serve the needs of television. The starting time of games depends nowadays on where they will fit into the television schedule. The most radical shifting of game time was when games were moved from the weekend to Monday evening solely for the benefit of ABC's prime-time schedule (with *Monday Night Football* [1970–]). The introduction of sudden-death overtime to the NFL (1974) was also a concession to television time, providing a quicker ending to drawn-out games (as with the tiebreaker in professional tennis). Time is a commodity on television; it's what is sold to advertisers. A sport must adjust to the restrictions of television time if it is to flourish on the medium.

This manipulation of time is modulated by the announcers. Most television sports use two types of announcers: **color** and **play-by-play**.

Color announcers such as John Madden and Terry Bradshaw are often former athletes and/or coaches, with firsthand expertise. Their analysis serves both expository and narrative functions.

First, in the expository mode, they are arguing for a specific interpretation of the action. A basketball team, it might be suggested, is losing a game because its passing has broken down. Announcers back up their arguments with evidence for their specific interpretation: replays, statistics, electronic "chalkboards" that allow them to draw Xs and Os right on images of the players. Statistics are an interesting aspect of sports in this regard. They legitimize a particular event as part of the history of sport by comparing or contrasting a current game with games past, and they provide seemingly objective evidence of the game's significance, or lack thereof. Every year there seems to be more and more types of statistics to absorb. They can be commonplace—for example, football's rushing yardage—or more and more specialized—for example, the number of games in a row that a batter has gotten a hit in the baseball games after the regular season has ended.

Color announcers add quasi-narrative elements to a game, helping to convert athletes—who are social actors—into characters that television can better utilize. Announcers dispense details about the athletes that serve to "characterize" them, to turn them into recognizable sports character types; stereotypes, really. For example, baseball's Nolan Ryan (a record-setter for longevity) was characterized as the crafty, battle-scarred veteran at the end of his career. His experience was counterposed against more agile but inexperienced rookies—another familiar character type. Sometimes it seems as if each sport on television has only six or seven character types into which each athlete is fit. The game thus becomes, in one sense, a narrative of stock characters constructed by, among other things, the comments of the color announcer.

Play-by-play announcers function similarly to news anchors. They serve as the program's apparent authority figure and guiding force—even though a producer or director back in the satellite truck is really in control. Play-by-play announcers narrate the events of the game, prompt the comments of the color announcers, and reiterate (over and over and over) the score and the play-by-play passage of time. Compared to color announcers, play-by-play announcers are slightly distanced from the athletes. Color announcers were athletes and as such possess special experiential knowledge, born of their locker room camaraderie. They are in essence part of the sport that is being covered (often their past exploits will be referred to). In contrast, play-by-play announcers are seldom former players or coaches. Instead, they are usually professional broadcasters such as Chris Berman, Marv Albert, or Brent Musberger. Since they are not actually part of the athletes' world, they may operate as an intermediary between that world and ours. Like the news anchor, they place historical reality into context for the viewer and regulate reality's flow so that it matches the flow of television.

The Organization of Space. The space of any sport is strictly delineated on its playing field or court. In sports such as football, basketball, and hockey, this space is premised on notions of territory, where one team invades the other's turf and attains a goal of some sort. Television has had to find ways to represent this territorial dispute clearly and dynamically. To facilitate this, stadiums and arenas that have been built since the advent of television have made provisions for television cameras and announcers: announcers' booths, special camera platforms at particular vantage points, and the like.

The playing field or court itself is not often changed for television presentation.[12] But there have been television-accommodating rule changes that affect the players' appearance and their movement around these fields or courts.

Names on football uniforms, a recent addition to the NFL, do not make much impact on viewers in the stands. But they are significant in television coverage—making it easier for announcers to identify individual athletes as part of the process of turning them into character types. The NBA's rules permitting three-point shots and outlawing zone defenses (which forces teams to play man-to-man) alter the way that the space of basketball is utilized. Man-to-man defense speeds the pace of the game (as does the 24-second clock)[13] and highlights the confrontations between individual players, making it easier for TV to transform the game's team conflict into a conflict between individuals. For example, NBA games between the Los Angeles Lakers and the Chicago Bulls during the 1980s were often described largely in terms of a battle between individual stars Magic Johnson and Michael Jordan. Viewing from a distance in arenas and stadiums emphasizes team play, downplaying the importance of the individual. Television coverage in contrast reduces sports to the conflict among individuals.[14]

Those individuals highlighted by television are not necessarily the ones who are athletically superior. As Jimmie Reeves has noted, "... personality, character, and color are as interesting to [television] audiences and as crucial to media stardom as run-of-the-mill competitive superiority."[15] Television needs distinctive individuals, not just athletically capable ones. In the 1992 Olympics, for example, U.S. volleyball player Bob Samuelson became a major television figure not so much because of his athletic ability, but because he had overcome a childhood illness (which left him bald) and because of his feisty arguments with officials. When one such argument cost the team a game, every member of the U.S. volleyball squad shaved their heads in a show of support for Samuelson's actions. This group shearing brought the team even more television attention, and their distinctive appearance became as significant as their playing ability. Similarly, Anna Kournikova was a Russian tennis player of modest skills, but television (and other media, too) assigned her the role of glamorous ingenue. Consequently, in the 2000 Wimbledon tournament she received considerable TV coverage even though she had never won a major tournament.

The Organization of the Scoring/Competition. In football's sudden-death overtime and tennis's tiebreaker we can see instances in which the structure of a sports' scoring has been modified to suit television's structure. In more general terms, a sports' scoring, the structure of its competition, suits television best when it echoes the conflicts of narrative (individual protagonist vs. individual antagonist) and poses enigmas as television narratives do. The most important sports enigma is, naturally, who will win? If a game becomes so lopsided that the outcome is obvious, then the game runs the risk of television death—either from our switching channels or the network turning to a concurrent, more suspenseful game. Sports programs must maintain that quasi-narrative enigma if they are to succeed on television.

The conclusion of each game determines the winner for that day. But, like the soap opera, the closure is incomplete. Most professional sports on U.S. television are predicated on a season that leads to a championship: for example, the Super Bowl, the World Series, or the NBA finals. The weekly games resolve the question of athletic superiority for a particular day, but they leave open the larger question of who will triumph over the course of the season. This season-long conflict is a significant part of what draws us back each week. It also contributes to the high ratings that championships such as the Super Bowl earn as they bring to a climax months of conflict. (The lack of a definite season and a final championship may contribute to the comparatively modest draw of sports such as tennis.) Thus TV sports shares a fundamental structural principle with other TV series: Each individual program offers a small amount of closure within the ongoing TV schedule. Full closure would mean the death of the series. Sports championships provide that closure, and effectively kill off the sport for that specific year—only to be regenerated the following year.

Game Shows

Game shows, like sports programs, are based on competition, on winning a contest. But from there they mostly part ways. College and professional sports, though heavily dependent on TV money, do still have an existence outside of television. They preserve a presence in historical reality. Game shows do not. Furthermore, most televised sports existed before television came into being, and thus evolved their structure before being telecast. Television has had to adapt to their structure more than they have had to adapt to TV. Game shows, even though they draw on previous gaming traditions, do not possess this pretelevision history. *Who Wants to Be a Millionaire*, for instance, did not exist before it appeared on TV. It was designed for television (first in the U.K. and then in the U.S.) and could not survive without it.

In sum, the game show does not re-present a preexisting historical reality to us. It does not originate in the historical world. Rather, it originates in television. It constructs a television reality and brings social actors, representatives from the historical world, into it. The television world clearly interacts with the historical one here, rather than constructing an argument about it (as in the expository mode) or observing it from a distance. The announcer on *The Price Is Right* urges contestants to "Come on down!" And as they do, they travel from the historical world of the audience/viewers to the television world of the stage (Fig. 4.4). Once on stage, their movement and speech are shaped by the rules of the game, which of course are administered by Bob Barker, a typical game show host. It is indicative of the game show's control over social actors that they must come to a television sound stage, the space of a television reality, rather than television going into historical reality to interact with social actors.

The host is comparable in function to the news anchor and the sports play-by-play announcer. All three are authorized by TV to place some order on the chaos of historical reality. In this regard, the host is a much more powerful figure than either the anchor or the sports announcer. For hosts can totally and directly control the behavior of social actors (stand here, answer this question, leave the stage), while anchors and sports announcers can only interpret and partially shape (through interviewing techniques, editing, etc.) that behavior in the historical world. The hosts, moreover, know all of the answers to the questions they pose—whether it's the price of a toaster oven or the 14th president of the U.S. Even the most skillful news interviewer is not as all-knowing.

To use an odd-sounding adjective, it may be said that game shows are very televisual. Though they bring together components from reality with those of television, it is clear which is the dominant force.

Game shows borrow elements from other aspects of television to create their basic structure. As in television fiction, game shows rely on a narrative-like enigma to provide the engine that drives the show forward. "Who will win this game?" is the central question, which obviously links game shows with sports programs. Even though the game show is something of a hybrid genre, drawing on narrative and sports conventions, it is important to seek the ways that it is unique, to distinguish its form from other television programs. This should become evident as we consider its address, textual organization (of time and space), and competition.

Semidirect Address. There are parts of any game show where the host speaks and looks directly at us. Like a news anchor or sports play-by-play announcer, the game show host welcomes us at the start of the show, guides us in and out of commercial breaks, and bids us farewell at the end. The address of the game show becomes more complicated than that of the news program, however. During most of the game show, the host does not speak directly to us, but instead directly addresses the contestants—as when Alex Trebek poses an "answer" to contestants on *Jeopardy!* (1964–75, 1978–79, 1984–). At this point, the game show's address resembles that of narrative, where we are generally unacknowledged, rather than news or sports. In game shows, host and contestants speak to one another without noticing us; in narrative programs, characters do the same thing. But contestants and narrative characters do not bear the same relationship to the viewer. Game show contestants are drawn from the ranks of TV viewers. They are social actors. Characters are not.

This crucial distinction changes the address of the game show. In a somewhat schizophrenic manner, we are invited to see ourselves as *contestants*, but at the same time we are also invited to *compete with the contestants*. The connection between contestants and viewers is particularly evident when contestants are stumped by a question in *Who Wants to Be a Millionaire*. At that point they may poll the audience or call a friend for help. Additional social actors (the audience members, the friend) are drawn into the game and encouraged to try to answer the question—just as, implicitly, the viewer at home is. The alliance between spectators and participants is here affirmed. We not only root for the contestants, we also directly assist them and the host's questions are addressed toward us as much as toward the contestants.

However, the majority of game shows do not permit this collaboration between contestants and other social actors. Instead, most programs present the questions to the contestants and the television viewer in a timed fashion that encourages us to try to beat the contestant to the answer. While contestants are positioned as identification figures for the viewers, they are also presented as our antagonists, competitors for prizes. The address of game shows is thus direct (the host's greeting of the viewer), indirect (the host's conversation with the contestants), and a blurry mixture of the two (the host's posing questions to the contestants to which we may also respond).

The Organization of Time and Space. Unlike sports and news, which must adapt historical world time and space to the demands of television, game shows create their own from scratch. Game shows are specially designed to suit television's structures of time and space.

The time of a game show divides the contest into increasingly intense segments—thereby managing the flow and interruption of television time. On *Jeopardy!*, for instance, the competition is split roughly into regular jeopardy, double jeopardy, and final jeopardy. Each segment is separated by commercial breaks. The competition escalates until the climactic final moment, when the outcome is decided. Time is strictly regimented. Game shows, unlike sports programs, never run overtime. The space of a game show is determined by its set, which is wholly designed for television and has no historical world counterpart. It exists completely within television's rarefied realm. The implications of this style of set design are discussed later (see chapter 5).

Competition. The main thing separating game shows from sports programs is the form of their competition. In sports it takes the form of physical prowess; in game shows it is different types of knowledge. Certainly, professional sports require a knowledge of the game and the ability to implement successful strategies, but these qualities would mean little if the players were not athletically superior. Game shows involve little physical ability. Instead, they rely on their contestants' knowledge of the world and human nature.

According to John Fiske, the knowledge tested in game shows may be grouped by type:

- Factual knowledge
  1. "Academic" knowledge
     - *Mastermind*
     - *The $64,000 Question*
     - *Sale of the Century*
     - *Jeopardy!*
  2. "Everyday" knowledge
     - *The Price Is Right*
     - *Wheel of Fortune*
- Human knowledge
  1. Knowledge of people in general
     - *Family Feud*
     - *Play Your Cards Right*
  2. Knowledge of specific individual
     - *The Newlywed Game*
     - *Mr. and Mrs.*
     - *Perfect Match*[16]

As Fiske proposes with his "factual knowledge" category, the type of knowledge that is most prized on game shows is a warehousing of facts, of individual bits of information. Even "intelligent" game shows such as *Jeopardy!* and *The $64,000 Question* do not require contestants to synthesize, analyze, interpret, or otherwise *process* information. What is required instead is a lightning-fast retrieval of data. These data may be obscure "academic" information taught in school, such as this *Jeopardy!* answer: "The first of these Roman waterways was the Aqua Appia, built about 312 B.C. by Appius Claudius." (The question was, "What is an aqueduct?") Or they may be more common, everyday data learned through interaction with other humans in social situations. Familiar phrases (e.g., "Don't put your foot in your mouth," as on *Wheel of Fortune* [1975–]) and the prices of household appliances (as on *The Price Is Right*) are part of our everyday knowledge about the world.

Fiske's "human knowledge" category pertains to less clear areas of human behavior. As Fiske comments, "This is a knowledge that resides in the human or social rather than in the factual. It has no absolute right and wrong answers and thus cannot be possessed or guarded by an elite [as teachers guard academic knowledge]. It depends instead upon the ability to understand or 'see into' people, either in general or as specific individuals."[17] In *Family Feud* (1976–85, 1988–95, 1999–), for example, contestants (grouped by families) answer questions hoping to match their responses with those of a surveyed audience. The family that best approximates the survey results—in other words, the contestants with the greatest knowledge of the average, the norm—are the winners. Other programs in the human knowledge category include ones that demand detailed knowledge of one person: a spouse or a lover or even just a date. On *The Newlywed Game* (1966–74, 1977–80, 1984–89, 1996–) husbands and wives compete through their knowledge of each other. In *Studs* (1991–93), *The Dating Game* (1965–73, 1986–88, 1997–) and other programs related to dating and romance, the contestants display their knowledge of each other's emotional-sexual experiences.

The competition on many game shows is not entirely based on knowledge. Much of the contestant's success in programs such as *Wheel of Fortune* depends on luck or good fortune—the spin of the wheel. The element of chance is fore-grounded in game shows. It serves to further complicate the show's progression. Each spin of the wheel raises new enigmas. Chance also serves as a leveling agent. All contestants are equal when they grab the wheel. Consequently, the most knowledgeable contestant is not necessarily the one who will march straight to victory. Basically, devices that bring chance into the game show function to delay the game's outcome and to keep it from becoming too obvious. As in sports and narrative programs, the conclusion must be kept in doubt as long as possible. Otherwise, the program ends prematurely.

In summary, the game show is a non-narrative program supremely suited to the demands of television. Its rhythms are televisual rhythms. Its space is televisual space. And its form of address is uniquely designed to captivate the television viewer. It is a genre that interacts with the historical world, but does so on its own terms.

S U M M A R Y

This chapter has sought to make sense out of television's perplexing and contradictory relationship to reality. To this end we have incorporated the terms historical world (or historical reality) and social actor to describe that reality more accurately. Non-narrative television, in this terminology, draws on the actions of social actors in the historical world. It depicts those actions through four principal modes of representation: expository (argumentation), interactive (interaction between the historical world and that of television), observational (TV watching historical reality and minimizing its intrusive effect), and reflexive (emphasizing self-reference and intertextuality).

To see these modes in action, we considered three types of non-narrative material: newscasts, sports programs, and game shows. As we have dealt with each, we have considered four aspects:

1. The realm of historical reality it depicts: Since TV cannot present everything, it must select certain aspects of historical reality and neglect others. Which technological, economic, and aesthetic reasons explain why one incident is chosen and another is not?

2. The implied relationship between the television world and the historical world: Do they appear to interact? Do the TV producers appear to influence the social actors? Does the television world affect the historical world?

3. The implied relationship between the text and the viewer: Is the viewer addressed directly or through a representative in the text?

4. The textual organization (or logic): What principles dictate how the information will be presented? For example, is it organized according to the principles of argumentation?

Our consideration of non-narrative genres is necessarily incomplete. A comprehensive study would need to be another full book, at least. However, the preceding discussion does lay the groundwork for analyzing non-narrative television.

FURTHER READINGS

The most comprehensive attempt to theorize non-narrative television, and the book that has guided our analysis here, is Bill Nichols, *Representing Reality: Issues and Concepts in Documentary* (Bloomington: Indiana University Press, 1991). This approach to documentary is also pursued in Bill Nichols, *Ideology and the Image: Social Representation in the Cinema and Other Media* (Bloomington: Indiana University Press, 1981) and Julianne Burton, "Toward a History of Social Documentary in Latin America," in *The Social Documentary in Latin America*, ed. by Julianne Burton (Pittsburgh: University of Pittsburgh Press, 1990). The standard historical/critical study of the documentary is Erik Barnouw, *Documentary: A History of the Non-Fiction Film*, 2nd ed. (New York: Oxford University Press, 1993), which places the television documentary in the context of film documentaries made for theatrical distribution. The impact and structure of the groundbreaking "reality television" program, *An American Family*, is discussed in detail in Jeffrey K. Ruoff, *Family Programming: The Televisual Life of An American Family* (Minneapolis: University of Minnesota Press, 2001). Nichols extends his commentary on television in *Blurred Boundaries: Questions of Meaning in Contemporary Culture* (Bloomington: Indiana University Press, 1994)—discussing the permeable boundary between narrative and non-narrative TV and the implications of reality television programs such as *Cops*. The impact of feminism on documentary is assayed in the anthology, *Feminism and Documentary*, ed. Diane Waldman and Janet Walker (Minneapolis: University of Minnesota Press, 1999).

The television newscast is often studied separately from the fully developed documentary. Short summaries of the evolution and the structure of television news can be found in Raymond Carroll, "Television News," in *TV Genres: A Handbook and Reference Guide*, ed. Brian G. Rose (Westport, CT: Greenwood Press, 1985) and Stuart Kaminsky, *American Television Genres* (Chicago: Nelson-Hall, 1985). The Radio-Television News Directors Association's "Code of Ethics and Standards"(www.rtnda.org/ethics/coe.shtml) has itself evolved over the decades.

Television news is presumed by many to be a major purveyor of ideology. Not surprisingly, several authors analyze the ideological function of the news: Charlotte Brunsdon and David Morley, *Everyday Television: "Nationwide"* (London: British Film Institute, 1978); William Gibson, "Network News: Elements of a Theory," *Social Text* 3 (Fall 1980): 88–111; Andrew Goodwin, "TV News: Striking the Right Balance," in *Understanding Television*, eds. Andrew Goodwin and Garry Whannel (New York: Routledge, 1990); Patricia Holland, "When a Woman Reads the News," in *Boxed In: Women and Television*, eds. Helen Baehr and Gillian Dyer (New York: Pandora, 1987); Margaret Morse, "The Television News Personality and Credibility: Reflections on the News in Transition," in *Studies in Entertainment: Critical Approaches to Mass Culture*, ed. Tania Modleski (Bloomington: Indiana University Press, 1986); Gaye Tuchman, "Representation and the News Narrative: The Web of Facticity," in *American Media and Mass Culture: Left Perspectives*, ed. Donald Lazere (Berkeley: University of California Press, 1987).

Interviews and talk on television are obviously not limited to newscasts and news magazines. The daytime talk show ("chat show," in the U.K.) has developed its own interview format, which is discussed at length in Wayne Munson, *All Talk: The Talkshow in Media Culture* (Philadelphia: Temple University Press, 1993).

The significance of television sports is the topic of several essays in Lawrence A. Wenner, ed., *Media, Sports, and Society* (Newbury Park, CA: Sage, 1989). Steven Barnett, *Games and Sets: The Changing Face of Sport on Television* (London: British Film Institute, 1990) offers a mostly historical consideration of TV sports, focusing primarily on the U.K. Analyses of how television represents sports include John Hoberman, *Sport and Political Ideology* (Austin: University of Texas Press, 1984); Margaret Morse, "Sport on Television: Replay and Display," in *Regarding Television: Critical Approaches*, ed. E. Ann Kaplan (Frederick, MD: University Publications of America, 1983); Geoffrey Nowell-Smith, "Television—Football—The World," *Screen* 19, no. 4 (Winter 1978–79): 45–59; and Jimmie L. Reeves, "TV's World of Sports: Presenting and Playing the Game," in *Television Studies: Textual Analysis*, eds. Gary Burns and Robert J. Thompson (New York: Praeger, 1989).

Critical analyses of game shows are not nearly as numerous as those of documentary/news and sports. There have, however, been a few attempts to deal with these issues. The game show of the 1950s is the subject of William Boddy, "The Seven Dwarfs and the Money Grubbers," in *Logics of Television: Essays in Cultural Criticism*, ed. Patricia Mellencamp (Bloomington: Indiana University Press, 1990). Michael Skovmand uses four different international versions of *Wheel of Fortune* to investigate how the game show functions as a "cultural practice"—"Barbarous TV International: Syndicated *Wheels of Fortune*," in *Television: The Critical View*, ed. Horace Newcomb (New York: Oxford University Press, 2000). John Fiske's short chapter on game shows, "Quizzical Pleasures," in *Television Culture* is alluded to in chapter 4. Morris B. Holbrook takes issue with Fiske's approach and provides his own interpretation of *The Price is Right* in *Daytime Television Game Shows and the Celebration of Merchandise: The Price is Right*" (Bowling Green, OH: Bowling Green State University Popular Press, 1993).

E N D N O T E S

[1] Considering that *American High* was canceled by Fox after only four airings, it appears that they did not find the drama they wanted. The program was subsequently picked up by PBS. Dan Snierson, "Taking the High Road," *Entertainment Weekly* 553 (August 4, 2000): 43.

[2] Bill Nichols, *Representing Reality: Issues and Concepts in Documentary* (Bloomington, IN: Indiana University Press, 1991), 105–198.

[3] John Fiske, *Television Culture* (New York: Methuen, 1987), 283.

[4] Dennis K. Mumby and Carole Spitzack, "Ideology and Television News: A Metaphoric Analysis of Political Stories," in *Television Criticism: Approaches and Applications*, eds. Leah R. Vande Berg, Lawrence A. Wenner (New York: Longman, 1991), 316.

[5] Nichols, 42.

[6] These modes draw on the "documentary modes of representation" developed in the work of Bill Nichols and Julianne Burton. See Bill Nichols, *Ideology and the Image: Social Representation in the Cinema and Other Media* (Bloomington, IN: Indiana University Press, 1981); Julianne Burton, "Toward a History of Social Documentary in Latin America," in *The Social Documentary in Latin America*, ed. Julianne Burton (Pittsburgh: University of Pittsburgh Press, 1990), 3–6; and Bill Nichols, *Representing Reality*.

[7] Mike Budd, Steve Craig, and Clay Steinman, *Consuming Environments: Television and Commercial Culture* (New Brunswick, NJ: Rutgers University Press, 1999), 126.

[8] The premiere dates for these two programs are for their original versions. *The Oprah Winfrey Show* began as a regional program (in Chicago) in 1984 and was nationally syndicated in 1986. *Nightline* started out as *The Iran Crisis: America Held Hostage* in 1979 and assumed its present format and name on 24 March 1980.

[9] These categories derive from ones developed by Nichols, but they modify his concepts. Nichols, *Representing Reality*, 51–54.

[10] Sut Jhally, "Cultural Studies and the Sports/Media Complex," in *Media, Sports, and Society*, ed. Lawrence A. Wenner (Newbury, CA: Sage, 1989), 77.

[11] The television time-out was instituted on a trial basis in 1955 and adopted permanently in 1958. Steven Barnett, *Games and Sets: The Changing Face of Sport on Television* (London: British Film Institute, 1990), 122.

[12] There have been exceptions to this. In 1969, for instance, the pitching mound in professional baseball was lowered in order to make it tougher for pitchers to strike out batters. The goal was fewer defensive battles, which are not visually interesting. Barnett, 124.

[13] A team must make a shot at the basket within 24 seconds of receiving the ball. This rule was instituted in 1954.

[14] As noted by Margaret Morse. Margaret Morse, "Sport on Television: Replay and Display," in *Regarding Television: Critical Approaches—An Anthology*, ed. E. Ann Kaplan (Frederick, MD: University Publications of America, 1983), 47–48.

[15] Jimmie L. Reeves, "TV's World of Sports: Presenting and Playing the Game," in *Television Studies: Textual Analysis*, eds. Gary Burns and Robert J. Thompson (New York: Praeger, 1989), 214.

[16] Fiske, *Television Culture*, 269.

[17] Fiske, 268.

PART TWO

TELEVISION'S STYLE: IMAGE AND SOUND

CHAPTER 5

Style and Setting: Mise-en-Scene

In the theater, the director positions actors on a carefully designed set, organizing the on-stage space. This staging of the action was dubbed, in French, **mise-en-scene**. The mise-en-scene of a play, then, is all the physical objects on the stage (props, furniture, walls, actors) and the arrangement of those objects to present effectively the play's narrative and themes. "Mise-en-scene," the phrase, was adopted by film studies in the 1960s and broadly used and sometimes misused. For some film critics the term carried almost mystical connotations, while for others it vaguely described any component of visual style. For our purposes, we will adopt a much narrower understanding of the term. Mise-en-scene will here refer to the staging of the action for the camera. Mise-en-scene thus includes all the objects in front of the camera and their arrangement by directors and their minions. In short, mise-en-scene is the organization of *setting, costuming, lighting,* and *actor movement.*

Mise-en-scene is a powerful component of the television apparatus. It forms the basic building block of narrative in fiction programs, influencing our perception of characters before the first line of dialogue is spoken. It directs and shapes our understanding of information in news, game shows, and sports programs. And it forcefully channels our perception in advertisements and other persuasive TV material. To understand these narrative, informational, and commercial uses of mise-en-scene, we need to consider its basic materials.

SET DESIGN

The walls of a room, the concrete and asphalt of a city street, the trees of a tropical rain forest, the stylized desk of a TV newsroom: all are elements of a setting that must be either built or selected by the **set designer** or **scenic designer**, subject to the approval of the director or producer.

One initial distinction that may be made in television set design is between **studio sets** (constructed) and **location settings** (selected). Newscasts, game shows, talk shows, sitcoms, and soap operas all rely on sets erected on television **sound stages**. Prime-time dramas and MOWs shoot on studio sets, too, but they also make extensive use of location shooting.

The decision to stage a program on a studio set or on location is in equal parts economic, technological, and aesthetic. Studio shooting is more economically efficient because the production resources are centralized. Equipment, actors, and technicians are all conveniently close at hand. For programs such as game shows and sitcoms that incorporate a studio audience, it would obviously be impractical to bus the entire group to a distant location. Technologically speaking, it is certainly not impossible to set up cameras in a remote location (sports programs do it every day and soap operas do it on special occasions), but the equipment cannot be as easily controlled and manipulated when it is out of the studio. This leads to slower production time and increased costs. Aesthetic convention also encourages indoor, studio-based set design for some genres. Soap operas, for example, tend to tell "indoor" stories. Their aesthetic emphasis on tales of emotion necessitates indoor scenes: hospital rooms, restaurants, bedrooms, and so on. And even when soap opera narratives do go outdoors, such as swimming scenes at the Snyder pond in *As the World Turns*, they are still mostly shot on studio sets. In contrast, the aesthetics of crime dramas and other action genres demand exterior shooting to facilitate the fast-paced movement of people and cars around city streets. Moreover, location shooting adds a certain patina of "realism" to these programs, which is another aesthetic concern.

Studio Set Design

Studio sets fall into two broad categories: narrative and non-narrative.

Narrative Studio Set Design. The main function of narrative sets is, obviously enough, to house characters engaged in a story. But sets in fiction television are not just neutral backgrounds to the action; they also signify narrative meaning to the viewer. The bar in *Cheers*, for instance, conveys meaning about the characters who socialize and work there, especially Sam Malone, the bar's owner. The type of bar that it is (lots of polished wood, sports mementos on the walls) helps characterize Malone as a very masculine character and suggests a male camaraderie associated with a neighborhood bar ("where everybody knows your name"). Thus, these sets and props serve as objective correlatives of the characters who inhabit and use them. Or, to put it in different terms, they are narrative **icons**—objects that represent aspects of character. Remaining sensitive to the **iconography** of television programs can help the analyst understand just how characterizations are created.

Narrative significance is not the only thing governing the look of studio sets. Overriding economic, technological, and aesthetic considerations combine to determine how those sets will be designed.

There are no ceilings on most studio sets, for the simple technological/aesthetic reason that lighting is done from above (more on this later). The lights are hung on a grid where the ceiling would normally be. This lack of ceilings limits the shots that may be done with the camera down low, looking

FIGURE 5.1

upward at the characters; such an angle might reveal the tops of the sets and the lights. It also means that ceilings cannot be used within the frame to enclose the characters, creating a slightly claustrophobic sensation—as was popular in 1940s films following the lead of *Citizen Kane* (1941; Fig. 5.1). One exception to this is *ER*, which does indeed reveal the ceilings in its sets (Fig. 5.2). By so doing, it emulates a prestigious style of shooting not normally associated with television—helping to distinguish it from other TV medical programs such as *Chicago Hope* (1994–), which debuted at the same time.

Studio sets are normally wider than they are deep, rectangular rather than square. Generally speaking, studio sets are shallow. And, of course, they are constructed of three walls rather than four, with the side walls occasionally splayed outward. The lack of a fourth wall, an aesthetic holdover from the theater, is further necessitated by the technological need to position two or three (or more) bulky video or film cameras in front of the actors. The added width gives the camera operators room to maneuver sideways, allowing them

FIGURE 5.2

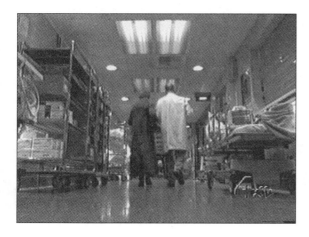

FIGURE 5.3

Frasier Set Design

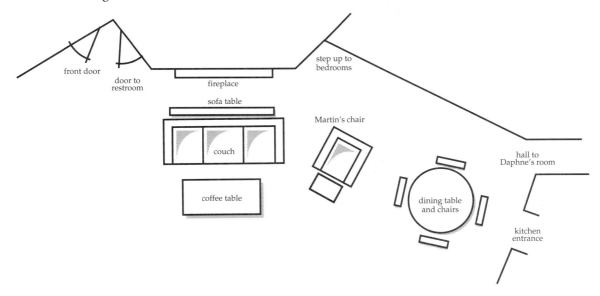

to vary their camera positions, mostly along a line that, in a sense, forms the invisible fourth wall. In studio production the cameras do not move forward or backwards very much because the closer they get to the actors, the more likely they will be within range of another camera behind them. As with the cameras, the actors also tend to move side-to-side, rather than up-and-back because of the limited depth of the sets.

Figure 5.3 diagrams the main apartment in *Frasier* (1993–)—as is shown in Figs. 5.4 and 5.5. The lateral orientation of the set is quite evident. To the left is the door through which family and friends enter. From there we encounter the living room furniture (Fig. 5.4). The dining table, kitchen, and a hallway are on the right (Fig. 5.5). The function of this set is to permit free interaction among

FIGURE 5.4   **FIGURE 5.5**

the main characters—three of whom live together. Although the movement on this set is predominantly side-to-side, there is a hallway to the bedroom on the left and a balcony in the back of the set that are occasionally incorporated.

The positioning of doors on the sides facilitates actors entering and exiting the room without blocking or being blocked by other actors. Aesthetic convention also holds that doors not be located "behind" the cameras on the invisible fourth wall. On television, characters never exit toward the cameras or enter from behind them. This shows, once again, the aesthetic influence of the theater, where such an entrance or exit would mean walking into or out of the audience. Television maintains the sense of our being behind the cameras, and does not want to draw attention to us by having the characters walk directly toward us.

The quick and easy entering/exiting of characters is important to all narrative programs, but it is especially significant to ones in which the narrative is segmented and interruptible. Soap opera is the pinnacle of this trend. Soap opera characters are constantly coming, going, and being interrupted by other characters' entrances and exits. This is necessitated by the genre's frequently interrupted narrative structure. (Just when the two young lovers are about to consummate their romance, someone knocks on the door or the phone rings; more instances of coitus interruptus have appeared on soap opera than any other genre in narrative history.) Thus, a seemingly small detail like the position of the doors in a set's design fits into the overall narrative scheme of a genre. Set design follows narrative function.

These three-sided rectangular boxes are arrayed in specific fashion in television sound stages, depending on whether an audience is present at the filming or taping. This economic/technological concern influences the size and shape of the sets, as well as the number of settings an episode will have. Narrative programs with studio audiences, such as *Frasier*, typically have room for only three (or at most four) sets, which are arranged next to one another, facing the audience (Fig. 5.6). The program's main location, such as the *Frasier* living

FIGURE 5.6

Studio Setup for Programs with Studio Audiences

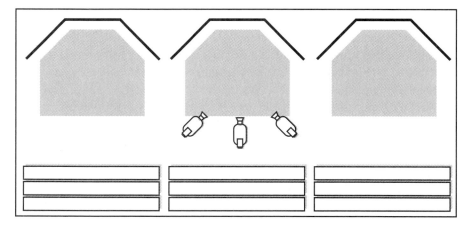

FIGURE 5.7

Studio Setup for Live-on-Tape Programs Without An Audience

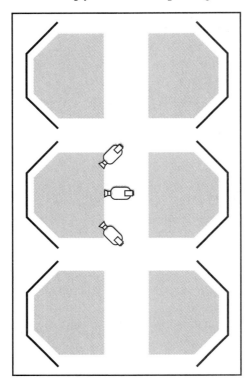

room, is usually placed in the center, so that most of the audience can see it well. In contrast, programs without audiences are produced on sets parallel to one another, leaving the middle space open for cameras and other equipment. In the CBS studios in New York, two separate studios are dedicated to videotaping *As the World Turns*. Six to ten sets are put together every single day, although some of the more elaborate sets are left standing from one day to the next. They are positioned against the walls (Fig. 5.7), with the videotape control room located right next door.

The economic reliance on studio sets has the aesthetic repercussion of limiting the stories to a very few locations: just three or four in a weekly sitcom, and seven or eight in the more narratively complicated daily soap opera. In a sense, stories must be written for the sets. Characters must be brought together in locations that are as much economically required as they are aesthetically determined. (This is also why when characters die or leave a soap opera other characters often move in to their houses and apartments.) And a large part of what they may do and what themes are presented is determined by where they are. Hospital sets are used to deal with issues of life, death, paternity, and maternity. Courtrooms house questions of justice. Private homes are the sites of intense personal and interpersonal emotions. In television programs, setting often determines story and theme, rather than vice versa.

Non-narrative Studio Sets. Most non-narrative genres (e.g., news, sports programs, and game shows) make a very different use of space than

FIGURE 5.8

narrative programs do. This use of space aligns with a different way of addressing the viewer. Non-narrative programs seldom create the illusion of an everyday room, preferring instead to construct a space that more resembles that of non-narrative theater (that is, music and dance performances): a stylized presentational space that *directly* addresses the performance to us. Non-narrative programs do not create the illusion that we do not exist, but instead acknowledge us by performing toward us. The direct address of non-narrative television is evident in the way that the set design positions the spectacle for our entertainment. News desks face the cameras straight on (Fig. 5.8). Game show hosts stand behind podiums that are aimed at the cameras (Fig. 5.9). The furniture on talk show sets positions guest and host at 45-degree angles to one another so they face the camera as much as each other (Fig. 5.10). In short, the set design of non-narrative programs is emblematic of the form of address they use.

The studio sets we see on newscasts, game shows, talk shows, musical variety programs, and the like follow different conventions than those of narrative

FIGURE 5.9

FIGURE 5.10

television. Within each non-narrative genre the conventions of set design are often quite rigid. What follows is a sampling of the various non-narrative set designs and is not meant to be exhaustive.

The sets of network and local news broadcasts invariably include some form of desk behind which the anchors sit. The desk implies that these are busy, working journalists, pausing briefly from tracking down leads to pass a few tidbits on to the viewer. Behind them, on many news sets, is a newsroom (actual or fabricated) that reemphasizes the earnestness of their journalistic mission (Fig. 5.8). These newsroom sets stress the up-to-the-minute nature of TV news, as if one of the worker drones in the background might hand the anchor a news flash at any moment. Adding to the illusion of immediacy are monitors into which reporters on location may insert remote segments at that moment.

The mise-en-scene of game shows is one of the few that regularly incorporates into it social actors (see chapter 4), members of the audience. Consequently, the sets of many game shows play up the audience's presence by incorporating the audience area into what still might be called the performance area. As the difference between spectator and performer blurs, so does the demarcation between audience space and performance space. This is particularly evident in *Who Wants to Be a Millionaire*, where host Regis Philbin conducts the competition on a stage surrounded by the audience, from which the contestants are drawn through a competitive process (Fig. 5.11). These audience members function as our surrogates, pulling us into the action in a way that few other television genres can. The program's set design confirms this alliance.

Other conventions of the game show set include some form of scoreboard, a space for contestants, and a podium for the host. Beyond that, each program must develop some distinctive contest, which may be represented in visual terms: for example, *Wheel of Fortune* (1975–) contestants spin an oversized roulette wheel and a woman in evening wear reveals letters forming a phrase by turning blocks suspended on a frame (Fig. 5.12). Surrounding the game itself may be a broad assortment of neon-bright colors and on-stage lights—unlike most other

FIGURE 5.11

FIGURE 5.12

genres where the studio lights are hidden from view. Note the evident lighting grid in Fig. 5.13, above the set of *The Newlywed Game*. In this shot, the lights cause a minor distortion, a flare, diagonally across the image—drawing attention to themselves. Similarly, the set design of *Who Wants to Be a Millionaire* emphasizes lights above and below the host and the contestants, and even reveals part of the structure that appears to support the lights (Fig. 5.14). Obviously, these swirls of light and color signify excitement and heighten competitive tension. They also reemphasize the value of winning and the glamorous validity of competition.

Many talk show sets have inherited the desk from television news. NBC's venerable *The Tonight Show* has had a desk since 1954 (Fig. 5.10). In this instance the desk provides a boundary between guest and host and, further, establishes the authority of the host over the guests, who do not get their own desks and must eventually share the couch with other guests. Additional areas of the set

FIGURE 5.13

FIGURE 5.14

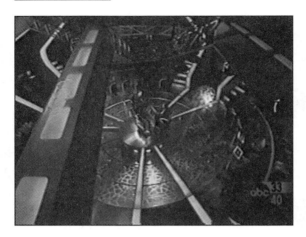

establish separate, *theatrical* spaces for performances by Jay Leno and visiting musicians and comics (Fig. 5.15). Thus, set design facilitates the talk show's two main functions: conversation and performance.

Location Set Selection

Most sports programs and news events (or **actualities**) are videotaped on location. The reason for this is obvious enough: Sports and news activities occur out in historical reality, where the newscasters "capture" them for us. Not all parts of historical reality are equally significant, however. Some settings are invisible to television. Why? Either they are taken for granted and are not considered important enough for TV (e.g., the inside of a factory, unless there's a strike or an industrial accident); or they are officially banned by the government (e.g., the battlefields of the Gulf War); or they are censured by television itself (e.g., a gay bar). Missing from television's location settings are the ideologically safe (that which is so "normal" it has no meaning) and the ideologically dangerous (that which is so "abnormal" or threatening it must be contained and censured).

There are certain television sports and news settings, or types of settings, that recur over and over again and acquire meaning from this repetition. In sports, for example, the center court stadium at Wimbledon carries specific connotations of British royalty, wealth, and class status, in addition to the tennis competition. The mud-and-crushed-cars setting of a monster truck competition carries a whole separate set of connotations.

Television news also makes pointed use of iconography. Figure 5.16 is a shot of a reporter standing before some significant news scene. This denotes first that "she is really there," and second that the information she is giving us must be true because she is at the scene and has witnessed something personally. Thus, setting is typically used in TV news to validate the authenticity of the report. Further, when local newscasters present themselves standing on the site of a murder or car

FIGURE 5.15

FIGURE 5.16

crash or the like, it is usually hours after the event has taken place. The event itself cannot be shown, so its setting is used to stand in for it, to certify that it really took place and that it really happened as the reporter is telling us it happened. Setting thus becomes a guarantor of television's **verisimilitude**—its illusion of truth and reality—and it helps authenticate the reporter's interpretation of the event.

Sports and news programs are not the only television shows that shoot on location, however. Many narrative programs also use location settings. Although most sitcoms and soap operas do not usually tape on location (except during **sweeps** weeks when ratings are taken), prime-time dramas and MOWs frequently shoot outside the studio walls. Mostly, this location shooting is used for outdoor, **exterior** scenes. Indoor, **interior** scenes are still shot on studio sets, except in rare circumstances. Location setting in narrative programs is used, as in news, to heighten television's sense of verisimilitude, of being "true to reality." Police and crime programs, for instance, are prone to location shooting to authenticate the realism of the show. *NYPD Blue* (1993–) would strike us as "phony" if the exterior scenes were shot on a studio lot and not the streets of New York City. However, verisimilitude isn't the only motivating factor in the use of location settings in narrative programs. Narrative, like the news, makes extensive use of the preestablished iconography of the real world. *Miami Vice* is a particularly good example of this. The program's opening credits consist of a collage of Miami sights (and sites) and thus play on our associations with the city: Cuban culture, money, power, overheated sexuality, potential violence, and so on (Figs. 5.17–5.19). *Ironside* (1967–75); *Hawaii Five-O* (1968–80); *The Streets of San Francisco* (1972–77); and *Magnum, P.I.* (1980–88) are among the other police/detective programs that draw on the iconography of a particular location. Thus, setting—whether constructed or selected—is not iconographically neutral. It always has the potential to contribute meaning to the narrative or the program's theme.

FIGURE 5.17

COSTUME DESIGN

In narrative television, costume design is closely allied with set design. Just as props and backgrounds are objective correlatives or icons designed to establish character, so are the clothes a character wears. Dr. Mark Greene's scrubs and glasses (*ER*), Columbo's distinctively rumpled trenchcoat (Peter Falk on *Columbo* [1971–77]), B.A.'s copious jewelry (Mr. T on *The A-Team* [1983–87]), and even Kenny's cartoon snow parka (*South Park* [1997–]) help construct the characters who wear them (Figs. 3.2, 5.20, 5.21, 5.22). Costume is one of the first aspects of a character that we notice and on which we build expectations. It is a significant part of the program's narrative system. Columbo's rumpled overcoat expresses the sort of detective he is—suggesting that doesn't care about superficial things like appearance and also misleading murder suspects into thinking he doesn't notice details. He was so clearly identified by his iconography

FIGURE 5.18

FIGURE 5.19

that ads for a Columbo MOW needed only ask rhetorically: "How many detectives can catch a killer with nothing but a trenchcoat and a cigar? Only one. Peter Falk in the role he made famous . . . *Columbo: Ashes to Ashes* [2000] on ABC."

Costume design is not limited to narrative television. News and sports have their own coded conventions of appropriate dress. Sports teams are the most regimented, with their uniforms identifying both which side of the conflict they are on and what their position within that conflict is (e.g., football players' uniforms are numbered according to the positions they play). The dress of sportscasters is practically as regimented as the players' uniforms is, with men wearing the inevitable blazer and women dressed in modified blazers or some variation on the businesswoman's suit. In news there is a sharp demarcation between the formal business dresses and suits of the anchorwomen and men, and the less formal dress of the reporters in the field. The studied "informality" of the field reporters (appearing in their suspenders or wearing fatigues while

FIGURE 5.20

FIGURE 5.21

covering international incidents) signifies that they are the ones in the trenches, digging stories out by any means necessary.

LIGHTING DESIGN

In the early years of television, camera technology dictated that sets be broadly and brightly lit. Because the early TV cameras were not very sensitive to light, a huge amount of illumination was necessary to transmit the simplest image. Consequently, TV cameras could only broadcast images of outdoor scenes in direct sunlight or indoor scenes under powerful studio lights. Today, however, cameras are much more sensitive, which presents videographers and cinematographers with the ability to manipulate lighting for a variety of effects. No longer is it a matter of simply getting enough light on the set; now lighting may be used to develop mood or tone and contribute to characterization.

FIGURE 5.22

FIGURE 5.23

The Characteristics of Light

There are four basic properties of light in television: *direction, intensity, color,* and *diffusion* (or *dispersion*).

Lighting Direction and Intensity. Probably the most significant lighting characteristic is the direction in which the light is shining. Lighting direction has long been used to imply aspects of a character. Underlighting (the light source below the subject) has suggested a rather sinister character in hundreds of horror and suspense television programs. In Fig. 5.23, from the "Lane Change" episode of *Amazing Stories* (1985–87), the joy of a bridal couple is undermined by the eerie lighting. Backlighting may be used to mask a killer's identity or imply an angelic state. In the case of the music video for Low Pop Suicide's "Disengaged" (Fig. 5.24), backlighting may heighten the enigmatic character of the lead singer. The variation of camera position derives much of its significance from its deviation from a conventional norm of lighting known as **three-point lighting**.

Three-point lighting is yet another part of the legacy that television inherited from the cinema. According to this aesthetic convention an actor (or object) should be lit from three points or sources of light of varying intensity: the **key light**, the **fill light**, and the **back light** (Fig. 5.25). The key light is the main source of illumination, the most intense light on the set. Normally, it is positioned at an oblique angle to the actor's faces—not directly in front or directly to the side. And, as in all three points of light, it is above the actor's head and several feet in front. If this is the only light on the set—as in Fig. 5.26—there will be deep shadows beneath the actor's nose and chin; and these, in conventional television, are thought to be unsightly. Consequently, a second source of illumination is provided to fill the shadows. This fill light is directed obliquely toward the actor from the opposite side of the key light, at approximately the same height (or a little lower), and is roughly half as bright as the key light. The third point, the back light, is placed behind and above the actor. Its main function is to cast light on actors' heads and shoulders, creating an outline of light around them. This outline helps to distinguish the actors from backgrounds. In

FIGURE 5.24

Fig. 5.27, for instance, fill and back lights have been added to a shot of the actor from Fig. 5.26.

On any particular studio set, three-point lighting is achieved with more than just three lights. But the basic principle of one main source of illumination, one

FIGURE 5.25

Three-Point Lighting

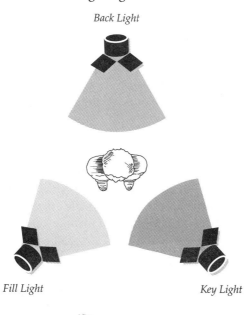

Back Light

Fill Light   *Key Light*

Camera

FIGURE 5.26

FIGURE 5.27

source filling in shadows, and one source backlighting the actors dominates all television production. Indeed, this lighting principle prevails in programs as diverse as prime-time dramas, daytime soap operas, and local news broadcasts. This norm is so accepted, so taken for granted, that any deviation from it—such as underlighting or sidelighting—seems odd and, more important, communicates meaning to us about the characters.

Two related lighting styles earn their names from the key light: **high-key lighting** and **low-key lighting**.

High-key lighting means that the set is very evenly lit, as in most scenes from 1960s sitcoms such as *The Dick Van Dyke Show* (1961–66). Even though Fig. 5.28 is from a shot that occurs at night, the lighting is still bright and even. In other words, the difference between the bright areas of the set and the dark areas is very little; there is a low contrast between bright and dark. High-key lighting is achieved by pumping up the fill light(s) so that the key light is comparatively less strong. Most talk shows, game shows, soap operas, and

FIGURE 5.28

FIGURE 5.29

sitcoms use high-key lighting. The economic decision to shoot these programs with two or three cameras simultaneously (which is cheaper than film-style single-camera shooting) leads to the technological necessity of high-key lighting. When several cameras are shooting at the same time, the lighting needs to be fairly even so that different camera angles are fully illuminated. In addition, such programs as sports and game shows, which allow for unpredictable figure movements by social actors, need a broadly lit stage so that people do not disappear into the darkness.

These economic and technological imperatives result in an aesthetics of high-key. As the norm, high-key lighting comes to signify normalcy, stasis, equilibrium. Variations on high-key lighting result in deviate meanings.

Low-key lighting means that there is a high contrast between bright and dark areas, that the bright areas are very bright and the dark areas are very dark (Fig. 5.29). To achieve low-key lighting, the key light must be comparatively stronger than the fill light, so that the bright areas are especially bright. This lighting style often has shafts of light cutting through dark backgrounds—a style that also goes by the name of **chiaroscuro** when applied to theatrical productions or the dark paintings of Rembrandt. If high-key lighting is associated with normalcy, then low-key represents oppositional values: deviance, disequilibrium, even social rupture. On TV, it is linked to criminal elements or the supernatural and is frequently used in detective, suspense, and mystery programs, as can be seen in *Buffy the Vampire Slayer* (1997–; Fig. 5.30).

Lighting Color. Light may be colored by placing a **filter** or **gel** (short for "gelatin") in front of a light source. Colored light is used to convey different moods (say, blue light for sorrow) and times of day (orange tints for morning, blue for twilight) in narrative television, but principally it is used in stylized set designs for game shows and music videos. Otherwise, colored light is too great a deviation from the norm for use in conventional programs.

Lighting Diffusion. On an overcast day, when the sun's rays are diffused through the clouds, the shadows that are cast have indistinct, blurred outlines. In television, this form of illumination is called **soft light**. It is often

FIGURE 5.30

used to make actors look younger or more vulnerable. **Hard light**, in contrast, is illustrated by direct, undiffused sunlight and the harsh, distinct shadows it casts. In television, hard light is best exemplified by television news footage that is illuminated by a single light mounted on the camera (Fig. 5.31, from *Cops*, which is shot in that same style). Narrative TV finds uses for hard light to emphasize characters' toughness and invulnerability—turning their faces into impenetrable masks (Fig. 5.32; the lead singer from Manic Street Preachers).

ACTOR MOVEMENT

Chapter 3 discussed the basics of performance in television. Now let's add a few thoughts about how actors are incorporated as part of the mise-en-scene, how they are moved around the set by the director. In the theater, this pattern of movement around a set is known as **blocking**.

In blocking a scene, the director must first take into consideration the position of the cameras and the layout of the set. How can the actors be moved around the set in such a fashion as to best reveal them to the camera(s) filming or taping them?

Since the sets are usually fairly shallow in most TV studio productions, the actors usually move side to side, rather than up and back (see Fig. 5.3). The cameras are positioned where the fourth wall would be, pointed obliquely at the set. Consequently, actors' movements tend to be at angles to the cameras as they move laterally in this **shallow space**.

Deep space blocking, in contrast, is not commonly used on television. This type of blocking underscores the depth of the set by positioning one actor near the camera and another far away. In Fig. 5.33, from *My So-Called Life* (1994–95), Graham Chase watches ballroom dancers, unaware that his wife, Patty, has entered the room behind him. She is slightly out of focus, but when Graham turns his head to look at her, the focus shifts back to her (Fig. 5.34).

FIGURE 5.31

FIGURE 5.32

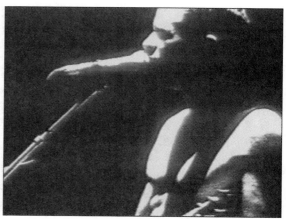

FIGURE 5.33

FIGURE 5.34

Graham is hesitant about dancing. Patty, who persuaded him to go dancing, is in a flamboyant red dress and is about to surprise him with a new haircut. The moods of the characters in the foreground and background counterpoint one another in this scene.

Deep space blocking normally uses **deep focus** (see chapter 6), where the entire image is in focus. Occasionally, however, deep space will be used without deep focus, and one of the actors will be out of focus—as in this shot. Thus, deep space and deep focus, though often confused, are independent of one another.

SUMMARY

Every television program has a mise-en-scene that communicates meaning to the viewer—meaning that may be understood before a single line of dialogue or news copy is spoken. Mise-en-scene contributes to the narrative system of fiction programs and the informational system of news and sports programs. It is shaped by the needs of these systems and by other economic, technological, and aesthetic concerns.

The frugality of studio shooting has led to a specific style of setting that caters to the technological demands of multiple-camera production. Three-walled, ceilingless studio sets form the backdrop for game shows, soap operas, news programs, sitcoms, and the like. In each of these types of programs, the studio setting performs a slightly different function—heightening competition in game shows, signifying journalistic ethics in news programs, and helping construct characters in narrative programs. Location settings play the additional role of signifying verisimilitude—the illusion of reality—in both news and narrative programs.

Costuming is closely linked with set design. Both are aspects of the program's iconography—the objects that signify character and theme.

Most of television's settings and costumes are illuminated in high-key, three-point lighting. But there are important deviations from that style. Each of the main properties of light (its direction, intensity, color, and diffusion) can be manipulated in order to contribute to the narrative or the mood of a program. In low-key or chiaroscuro lighting, for instance, the relative intensities of the light sources are varied to create a high-contrast image of bright light and dark shadow.

Mise-en-scene was originally a theatrical term. Converting it for use in television studies, we must keep in mind that the mise-en-scene of TV is experienced only through the camera; hence it must be designed explicitly for that purpose. This technological parameter thus governs all aesthetic designs of setting, costuming, lighting, and actor movement, as we shall see in the following chapter.

FURTHER READINGS

The conventions of televisual style are described in many handbooks for television production. See Gerald Millerson, *The Technique of Television Production*, 13th ed. (Boston: Focal Press, 1999) and Herbert Zettl, *Television Production Handbook*, 6th ed. (Belmont, CA: Wadsworth, 1996). Chuck Gloman and Tom LeTourneau detail the specifics of lighting design in *Placing Shadows: Lighting Techniques for Video Production*, 2nd ed. (Boston: Focal Press, 2000). A more ambitiously theoretical approach is taken in Gorham Kindem, *The Moving Image: Production Principles and Practices* (Glenview, IL: Scott, Foresman, 1987). Kindem endeavors not just to describe television's common practices, but also to articulate the aesthetic rationales of those practices.

The sole attempt to create an entire stylistics of television production is Herbert Zettl, *Sight Sound Motion: Applied Media Aesthetics*, 3rd ed. (Belmont, CA: Wadsworth, 1999). Zettl's ambitious undertaking is occasionally idiosyncratic and quirky—and also quite provocative.

The most thorough guide to interpreting audial-visual style is not a television book at all: David Bordwell and Kristin Thompson, *Film Art: An Introduction*, 6th ed. (New York: McGraw-Hill, 2000). Although Bordwell and Thompson have nothing to offer on some crucial aspects of television (e.g., multiple-camera editing or the characteristics of videotape), they provide an extensive introduction to understanding cinema production.

CHAPTER 6

Style and the Camera: Videography and Cinematography

When we look at television, our gaze is controlled by the "look" of the camera. What the camera "saw" on the set or on location during a production, we now see on our television screens. The camera's distance from the scene and the direction in which it is pointed, among other factors, determine what we will see in a television image. In essence, our look becomes the camera's look and is confined by the frame around the image. To understand the camera's look, it becomes necessary to understand the aesthetic, economic, and technological factors that underpin the camera's perfunctory gaze.

The camera, although a mechanical recording device, does not neutrally record images. The camera fundamentally changes the objects it records: three dimensions become two; the colors of nature become the colors of video or film; the perimeter of the camera frame delimits the view. The recording process of film and video could more accurately be thought of as one of translation, where the three-dimensional historical world is translated into the two-dimensional "language" of televisual images. This camera language is a major part of the visual style of a television program. It works in conjunction with mise-en-scene (chapter 5) and editing (chapter 7) to create a program's overall visual design.

Almost everything we see on television began its trip to our homes by being recorded by a camera. It would be wrong, however, to assume that this camera is always a video camera. Indeed, many television images were originally created by a film camera (although everything on TV these days is edited digitally if not done live). Soap operas, game shows, some sitcoms, musical variety programs and specials, news programs, talk shows, and most locally produced commercials are shot on videotape or broadcast live using video cameras. In contrast, prime-time dramas, some other sitcoms, MOWs, music videos, and large-budget, nationally broadcast commercials are all currently recorded originally on film. The distinction is not merely technological. Even though these images all come to us through the television tube, there are still discrete visual differences between material that was originally filmed and that which was videotaped. Each technology affects the visual style of television in different ways. Each might be thought of as a separate dialect within the language of televisual style.

This chapter concerns the components of video and film camera style, the elements of **videography** and **cinematography** that record an image and affect our understanding of it. In simplest terms, videography designates the characteristics of the video camera while cinematography refers to those of the film camera. The person overseeing the video camera is the **videographer**; the corresponding person in charge of the film camera is the **cinematographer**. Typically, in contemporary production, videographers and cinematographers leave the actual handling of the camera to the **camera operator**, who is not credited as a full-fledged cinematographer/videographer. Videographers, cinematographers, and camera operators, all operate under the guidance of the program's **director**. The director designs the program's overall style, with the videographers and cinematographers working within the specific province of camera style.

On the most basic level, camera-style characteristics are shaped by technological considerations. For instance, one could not have recorded videographic images in the 1890s, before video was invented. But we should be wary of overemphasizing the importance of technology to videography and cinematography. As we have seen in our discussion of mise-en-scene in the previous chapter, the ways that video and film technologies have been used are always shaped by aesthetic convention and economic determinants. The aesthetic conventions of composition in European oil painting, for example, greatly influence the composition of TV images. And economics principally determines whether a program will be shot in film or video—with less expensive (and less prestigious) programs being shot on video. Thus, technology, aesthetics, and economics merge together in determining camera style. To fully understand videography and cinematography we must remain alert to each of these three counterbalancing elements.

In many respects, video and film share basic camera principles. In U.S. television today the two formats have begun to resemble one another more and more—especially as **high-definition television (HDTV)** is more and more widely implemented. It is with these shared principles that we begin our study of videography and cinematography. Even so, there do remain some important distinctions between video and film, and they will be considered toward the latter part of this chapter.

THE FUNDAMENTALS OF CAMERA STYLE: SHARED VIDEO AND FILM CHARACTERISTICS

The Camera Lens

The earliest "camera," the **camera obscura** of the eighteenth century, had no lens at all. It was merely a large, darkened room with a hole in one wall. Light entered through that hole and created an image of the outdoors on the wall opposite the hole. Very little could be done by way of manipulating that image. Today's camera lens, the descendent of the camera obscura's hole-in-a-wall, permits a variety of manipulations—a catalogue of optical controls that the camera operator may exercise.

Chief among these optical controls is **focal length**. One need not be a physicist to understand focal length, although sometimes it seems like it. The focal

FIGURE 6.1

The Physics of Focal Length

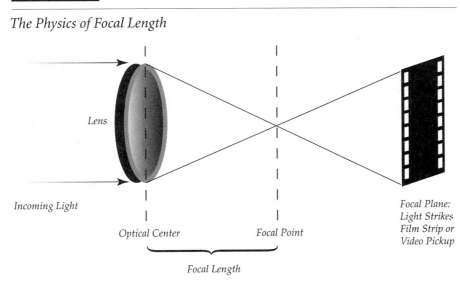

Lens

Incoming Light

Optical Center

Focal Point

Focal Plane: Light Strikes Film Strip or Video Pickup

Focal Length

length of a lens, usually measured in millimeters, is the distance from the lens' optical center to its **focal point**, which is that spot where the light rays bent by the lens converge before expanding again and striking the film or electronic pickup at the **focal plane** (Fig. 6.1). This definition, however, tells us very little about the images that result from lenses of different focal lengths. In more familiar terms, the three conventional types of focal length are:

1. Wide angle (or short)

2. "Normal" (or medium)

3. Telephoto (or long or narrow)

The reader may already know these terms, but it is important to recognize the different and sometimes subtle effects these focal lengths have on the image.

The **wide angle lens** gives the viewer a wide view of the scene, and it also heightens the **illusion of depth** in the image. All television images are two-dimensional, of course; there is no true depth to them. They have dimensions along only two axes: horizontal and vertical (left and right, up and down). Using principles of perspective developed in the Renaissance, however, the television image creates an illusion of depth (back and forth). Because of this illusion, some objects seem to be in front of other objects; the space seems to recede into the image. A wide angle lens increases that illusion of depth. Objects filmed with a wide angle lens seem to be farther apart from one another than they do with normal or telephoto lenses. In Fig. 6.2, which was shot with a wide angle lens, the distance between the front and the rear of the piano is elongated, giving the image an illusion of great depth.

The **telephoto lens** gives a narrower view of the scene than a wide angle lens, but magnifies the scene (brings it closer). In Fig. 6.3 the same piano as in Fig. 6.2 has been shot with a telephoto lens. Compare how the distance between the front and the rear of the piano appears. Telephoto lenses are widely used in

FIGURE 6.2

FIGURE 6.3

sports coverage, to get a "closer" view of the action (Fig. 6.4). Just as the wide angle lens heightens the illusion of depth, the telephoto lens diminishes it. Thus, the illusion of depth appears to be compressed in telephoto shots. The pitcher in Fig. 6.4 appears to be much closer to the batter than he would to someone sitting in the bleachers because of the compression of depth by the telephoto lens. The longer the lens, the more compressed the depth will appear.

The so-called normal focal length lens is medium-sized in comparison to both wide angle and telephoto. This is the lens that has come to be accepted as "natural." However, the normal focal length does not actually approximate the human eye's range of vision (it's narrower) or illusion of depth (it's shallower). Rather, it creates an image that, to the Western world, seems correct because it duplicates that style of perspective developed during the Renaissance of the 1500s. Camera lenses that create images suggesting Renaissance perspective have come to be accepted as the norm, while wide angle and telephoto lenses are defined as deviations from that norm.

FIGURE 6.4

FIGURE 6.5

FIGURE 6.6

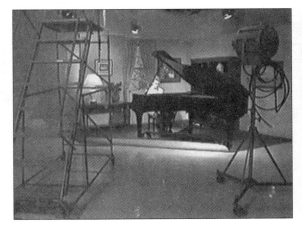

FIGURE 6.7

Film and video cameras may be supplied with individual lenses of different focal lengths. More commonly, today's cameras come equipped with a **zoom lens**, which in optical terms is a *variable focal length* lens. With a zoom, one can shift immediately and continuously from wide angle to telephoto without switching lenses. To **zoom in** is to vary the focal length from wide angle to telephoto, getting increasingly "closer" to the object and narrowing your angle of view (Figs. 6.5–6.6). To **zoom out**, in contrast, is to vary the focal length from telephoto to wide angle—thereby getting "farther" from the object as the angle of view widens. *Closer* and *farther* are misleading terms when referring to the zoom lens, however, because the camera does not get physically closer to or farther from the object it is recording. Thus, to be accurate, the zoom really just magnifies and de-magnifies the object. The point-of-view from which we see the object does not change.

A characteristic of the camera lens even more fundamental than focal length is its **focus**. On television, the image is nearly always in focus. Only perhaps in

FIGURE 6.8

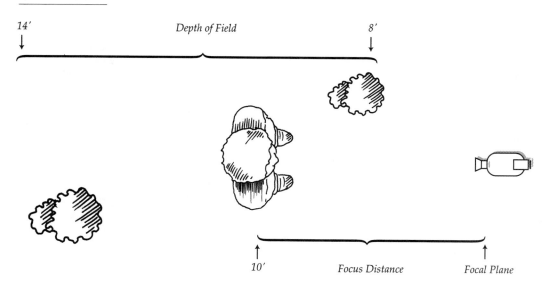

sports events do we see occasional out-of-focus images as the camera operator struggles to follow a fast-moving athlete. However, in most televisual images there are areas of the image that are not in focus, parts that have been left out of focus to de-emphasize them. Camera operators can selectively focus parts of the image and unfocus other parts. In other words, they can use focus for specific effect.

The selective use of focus is facilitated by the photographic phenomenon of **depth of field** (Fig. 6.8). (Care should be taken not to confuse depth of field with the *illusion* of depth previously discussed.) Depth of field is the distance in front and behind the **focus distance** that is also in focus (the focus distance being the distance from the camera to the object being focused on). If a lens is focused at 10 feet, as in Fig. 6.8, some objects nearer to and farther from the camera will also be in focus. This range (say, 8–14 feet in this instance) is the depth of field. Typically, the range is approximately one third in front of the focus distance and two thirds behind it. The camera operator can manipulate depth of field to influence our perception of an image—decreasing the visual impact of parts of the frame by rendering them out of focus and indistinct. A small depth of field—so that just one plane (foreground, middle ground, or background) is sharply focused—is termed **shallow focus**. In Fig. 6.9, the director has chosen to emphasize the foreground leaves by blurring the background. The shallow focus of this shot is further manipulated by shifting the focus from foreground to background, which is known as **racking** or **pulling focus** (Figs. 6.9–6.10). Rack focus is frequently used in inexpensive television productions to add some visual interest to a shot without changing to a new camera position and revising the lighting setup.

Shallow focus sounds confusingly similar to **soft focus**. However, in a soft focus shot the entire image, not just a single plane within it, is slightly out of focus. Soft focus is often used in conjunction with special filters and lighting—and even Vaseline on the lens—to create an image that conventionally signifies

FIGURE 6.9

FIGURE 6.10

romantic attraction, vulnerability, sweetness, or youthfulness (concealing wrinkles in an actor's face) in a character. In *Moonlighting* (1985–89), for example, Cybill Shepherd was frequently shot in this fashion.

Focus does not have to be shallow or soft, however. In **deep focus** shots, all planes of the image are in focus.[1] In one shot from a commercial for GEICO insurance, deep focus enables the viewer to see a pregnant woman in a wheelchair in the background while a young man speaks on the phone in the foreground (Fig. 6.11). The background establishes that he's in a maternity ward even though, in the phone conversation, he's pretending not to be talking about his wife giving birth. Deep focus is often used in conjunction with deep-space blocking, where background and foreground interact with one another. Deep focus is not absolutely necessary for deep space, however. In the *My So-Called Life* illustration previously discussed, the space is deep, but the focus is shallow (Figs. 5.33–5.34).

Deep focus has been heralded by film critic André Bazin as a major advance in the realism of the cinema.[2] He argues that:

FIGURE 6.11

- Deep focus is more like the human perception of reality (we mostly see the world in deep focus).
- Deep focus preserves the continuity of space by maintaining the visual connections between objects in their environments.

Bazinian realism could also be applied to television (although his theories have had minimal impact on television aesthetics), but with caution. The smaller size of the television screen is a major impediment to deep focus staging of action. The background actors/objects can become so small as to have negligible impact on the shot's meaning.

Camera Framing

The **framing** of a shot, at a most rudimentary level, determines what we can and cannot see. In the early years of television (the 1940s), camera operators tended to choose a distant view of the action, which showed the entire setting. This framing was based on an aesthetic assumption (inherited from the theater) that the "best seat in the house" would be in the center, about seven or eight rows back, where one could see all of the action at once. Also, early television cameras were large and cumbersome, which made it difficult to move them around a set to achieve a variety of camera positions. Soon, however, camera technology improved. Television directors discovered the impact of a variety of framing and began incorporating the **close-up** in their television programs.

Since the "invention" of the close-up, television directors have developed conventions of framing. It is possible to chart television's conventional framing with the human body as a standard, since that is the most common object before the camera. (The conventional abbreviation of each framing is included in parentheses.)

1. Extreme long shot (XLS). The human form is small, perhaps barely visible. The point of view is extremely distant, as in aerial shots or other distant views (Fig. 6.12).

2. Long shot (LS). The actor's entire body is visible, as is some of the surrounding space (Fig. 6.13).

3. Medium long shot (MLS). Most, if not all, of the actor's body is included, but less of the surrounding space is visible than in the LS (Fig. 6.14).

4. Medium shot (MS). The actor is framed from the thigh or waist up (Fig. 6.15).

5. Medium close-up (MCU). The lower chest of the actor is still visible (Fig. 6.16).

6. Close-up (CU). The actor is framed from his or her chest to just above his or her head (Fig. 6.17).

7. Extreme close-up (XCU). Any framing closer than a close-up is considered an XCU (Fig. 6.18).

In actual video and film production, these terms are imprecise. There is some variation between shooting for television and theatrical film shooting, with the former tending toward closer framing to compensate for the smaller screen. What one director considers a medium close-up, another might term a close-up. Even so, the above terminology does provide some guidelines for discussing framing.

In fiction television, the long shot is—among other things—used for positioning characters within their environment and can thereby construct aspects of those characters. A long shot of a woman in a newspaper office, a prison cell, or a convent could establish her as a journalist, a convict, or a nun, respectively. The GEICO ad contrasts the man's phone conversation with the setting behind him (Fig. 6.11). Environment feeds our understanding of character, and the long shot facilitates that understanding. A long shot that helps to establish character or setting is known as an **establishing shot**. It often inaugurates a scene.

The medium shot is frequently used for conversation scenes. The framing of two characters from about the knees up as they begin a dialogue is so often used that it has been designated with the term **two-shot** (Fig. 6.15). (Similarly, a

FIGURE 6.12

FIGURE 6.13

FIGURE 6.14

three-shot frames three characters). The medium shot can establish relationships between characters by bringing them into fairly close proximity.

For some, the close-up provides the "window to the soul" of the actors/characters, a gateway to their innermost emotions. Romantic hyperbole such as this aside, the close-up functions both to emphasize details and to exclude surrounding actions, channeling viewer perception. It thus exercises the most extreme control over the viewer's gaze.

The aesthetics of framing follows certain conventions of function. The close-up is the dominant framing in television programs such as the soap opera, where the emotional states signified by the actors' faces are stressed. Television soap opera's reliance on the close-up has coincided with the evolution of its acting style, which favors the human face over larger gestures. Television sports and action genres, in contrast, place more emphasis on medium and long shots—to facilitate the movement of automobiles, planes, and human bodies through space.

FIGURE 6.15

FIGURE 6.16

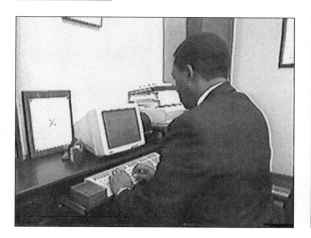

FIGURE 6.17

FIGURE 6.18

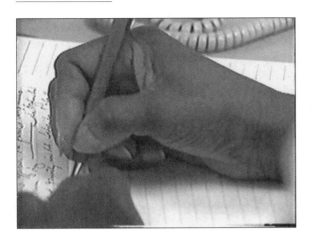

Camera Height and Angle

In most television shots the height of the camera matches that of the actors' faces. This camera height is so ingrained in our understanding of camera style that eye level has become synonymous with "normal" height. It becomes transparent to the viewer, taken for granted. Variations on this height consequently become important, apparently signifying something about the characters. The two principal variations on eye-level camera height are:

1. Low angle—in which the camera is lower than the filmed object (Fig. 6.19).

2. High angle—in which the camera is higher than the filmed object (Fig. 6.20).

It has become a truism in television production manuals to observe that a low angle—where we look up at an actor—makes a character appear stronger and more powerful, while a high angle—looking down on an actor—weakens the

FIGURE 6.19

FIGURE 6.20

FIGURE 6.21

character's impact. We can see the commonsensical basis for this assumption: When looking up at an object, it tends to appear large; and when looking down at it, small. But in actual television programs this use of low and high angles is much less systematic. In Fig. 6.21, from *thirtysomething* (1987–91), Bree Ann Pratt is shot from a low, supposedly empowering angle; yet she is crying and vulnerable at this point in the story. (In addition, the mise-en-scene traps her within the staircase.) Obviously, the low camera angle is not enough to make her a strong figure.

Stylistic elements such as camera angle do have meaning, but those meanings are always set within the context of the program and general aesthetic practice. Consequently, it's impossible to generalize about the "vocabulary" of television technique, where technique A = meaning B. Technique A does indeed have meanings, but only when considered within the entire textual system of a program.

Camera Movement

Film cameras had been around for 20 years or more before tripods and dollies and other mechanical devices were developed that permitted the movement of the camera. Early films initially had little or no camera movement because of this technological limitation and because the camera operator had to hand crank the cameras, thus making their turning or movement awkward. When cameras finally did begin to move, they were limited by the practical aesthetics of early directors. Little use was seen for camera movement beyond following character action and panoramic views. Filmmakers gradually expanded the use of camera movement, and by the time television arrived, film camera movement was smooth and relatively frequent. Early television cameras, because of their enormous bulk, were as stationary as the first film cameras. Also, initial studio-based television was constricted in its camera movement by lack of space. Before long, however, television developed its own uses for the moving camera.

Principal among the functions of the moving camera are:

- To establish a space, a particular area.
- To establish a relationship between objects/actors in a certain space.
- To follow action.
- To emphasize/de-emphasize one portion of a space, or an object/actor within that portion.

To achieve these functions, a variety of camera movements have evolved.

Panning and Tilting. The most rudimentary camera movement derives its name from the affection for broad, "panoramic" views in early motion pictures. The **pan** is when the camera twists left and right, on an imaginary axis stuck vertically through the camera. The camera support—the legs of the tripod—does not move in a pan; only the tripod head turns. Similarly, in a tilt the camera twists up and down on an axis stuck horizontally through the camera. The camera height does not change; only its angle of vision.

Several other camera movements depend on the movement of the *entire* camera support rather than just the tripod head: dollying/tracking/trucking; craning/pedestaling; hand-held; and Steadicam. Camera technology provides the names for these movements, rather than the actual direction of the movement (as in "tilting") or what is represented (as in "panning" over panoramic views). Thus, the conventionalized method for viewers to describe these movements is to refer to presumptions of the technology used to create them.

Dollying, Tracking, and Trucking. In television there are several terms used to describe the sideways and backward/forward movement of the camera. Principal among these are **dollying**, **tracking**, and **trucking**. Each of these differs from the pan in that the entire camera support moves, rather than just the tripod head. It's like the difference between twisting one's head left and right—the human equivalent of panning—and walking in one direction or the other—human dollying.

The dolly shot is named for the device that creates it, the camera dolly— a wheeled camera support that can be rolled left and right or forward and backward. Similarly, the tracking shot earns its name from small tracks that are laid over rough surfaces, along which the dolly then rolls. In practice, "tracking" is such a broadly applied term that it may be used to refer to any sideways or backward/forward movement, even if actual dolly tracks are not involved. In addition, in television studio production sideways movement is sometimes called trucking or crabbing, and a semicircular sideways movement is usually called **arcing**. Many of these terms are used interchangeably. Also, dollying need not be in straight lines that are either perpendicular or parallel to the action; dolly shots may move in curves, figure eights, and any other direction a dolly can be pushed or pulled.

To most viewers, dollying in or out is indistinguishable from zooming in or out. There are, however, important visual differences between the two techniques. Even though it takes a practiced eye to recognize them, the differences may generate disparate perceptions of the objects and humans that are presented.

When camera operators zoom in or out, they change the focal length of the camera and magnify or demagnify the object, but the position from which the object is viewed remains the same. The point of view of the camera is thus constant. In contrast, when camera operators dolly forward or backward, the position from which the object is viewed shifts. And because the point of view changes in the dolly shot, we see the object from a different angle. Parts of it are revealed that were previously concealed, and vice versa (see Fig. 6.7, taken from the ending of a dolly-in shot that begins at the same position as the zoom in of Fig. 6.5). In Fig. 6.7 we see the entire picture on the wall behind the pianist, where at the start of the dolly (Fig. 6.5) it is partially blocked. Contrast this with the zoom in on the same subject matter (Fig. 6.6). At the end of the zoom in, the picture is still obscured and the piano-top strut still crosses the actor's face. Even though the subject matter is enlarged, it is still seen from the same point of view; the camera is still in the same position as at the start of the zoom. Moreover, because we have changed the focal length, we also change the image's illusion of depth. Everything looks flatter, more compressed as we zoom in. In Fig. 6.6, the actor looks squeezed between the piano and the wall—especially when compared with Fig. 6.7.

Thus, although the zoom and the dolly share the quality of enlarging or reducing an object before our eyes, they differ in how they represent point of view and the illusion of depth. Consequently, they serve different functions on television. For example, camera movement—not zooming—is conventionally used when the viewer is supposed to be seeing through the eyes of characters as they move through space—say, as killers approach their prey. Zoom shots do not conventionally serve this function, because they do not mimic human movement as convincingly as dollying does. Zooming, in turn, is more common in contemporary television production as a punctuation for extreme emotion. In soap operas, camera movement is fairly limited and zooms-in function to underline character emotions. In this case economics blends with aesthetics. Zoom shots are less time-consuming to set up than dolly shots are and thus are less expensive. Consequently, the modestly budgeted soap operas favor the zoom.

Craning and Pedestaling. A camera crane or boom looks just like a crane on a construction site, except that there is a camera mounted on one end. A camera pedestal is the vertical post of the camera support. Cranes and pedestals are the technology that permit the upward/downward movement of the camera, and those movements—**craning** and **pedestaling**—take their names from that technology. Thus, in a crane shot, the camera is swept upward or downward. Additionally, since the crane is mounted on wheels, like a dolly, it can also be moved in all the directions a dolly can. A pedestal shot is one in which the camera is raised or lowered. The crane or pedestal movement is different from the tilt: in a tilt, the tripod head is twisted up or down—as if the camera were nodding—while in craning and pedestaling the entire camera body is moved higher or lower.

Crane shots serve a variety of functions. Typically, a crane down may be used first to establish a location with a wide angle shot from up high, and then particularize one element of that location by craning down to it. And cranes up are often used to end sequences or programs. Craning up and back from characters at the end of a program, we are literally distanced from them at a point when we are about to leave the characters' story.

Hand-held and Steadicam. A **hand-held** shot is one that was filmed just as the name implies: with the camera held in the operator's hands instead of being placed on a camera mount. As a consequence, the hand-held shot is noticeably unsteady—especially during quick movements when the camera operator is running. A large percentage of news and sports videotaping is done with hand-held cameras: shots from the field of play in sports shows (e.g., courtside shots at basketball games); documentary footage of automobile crashes; murder suspects leaving a courtroom; and so on.

We might think that hand-held shots would be avoided entirely in the more controlled camera style of fiction television. Even though the majority of camera movement in fictional programs is not hand-held, hand-held shots do serve several narrative functions. First, hand-held work is used to create a documentary feel, to signify "documentary-ness," within works of fiction. Many episodes of *NYPD Blue* include noticeable hand-held camerawork—signifying the program's "realism." Second, hand-held movement is often used when we are seeing through a character's eyes—as was mentioned above regarding dolly shots. Indeed, hand-held camera is more frequently used in this situation than dollying because hand-held is thought to more closely approximate human movement. After all, we all have legs like a camera operator, not wheels like a dolly.

The **Steadicam** is a registered trademark for a piece of technology that has come to identify a style of camera movement that closely resembles hand-held. The Steadicam is a gyroscopically balanced device that straps to the operator's body. The resulting motion is as smooth as that produced with a dolly. It is conventionally used in situations where stability is desired but economic and technical practicalities dictate that dolly tracks cannot be laid. *ER* (1994–) was among the first TV programs to use a Steadicam on a daily basis. Its camera operators move through the sets in ways previously reserved for feature films.

DISTINGUISHING VIDEO AND FILM

As we have seen, video and film utilize many similar techniques: photographic technology that originated in still photography (focal length, depth of field, etc.) and aesthetic presumptions about framing, height, and movement of the camera. As a result of digital convergence the two media are becoming closer and closer. In the near future, convergence will be complete and the differences between film and video will be erased. For now, however, important distinguishing characteristics remain.

Aspect Ratio

After World War II, the TV frame stabilized at a size of 4 units wide by 3 units high—the same dimensions as movie screens of the time. That is to say, a screen 4 feet wide would be 3 feet high; a screen 16 inches wide would be 9 inches high; a screen 40 feet wide would be 30 feet high; and so on. Its width compared to its height is thus 4:3, which may be reduced to 1.33:1 or simply 1.33. In technical

FIGURE 6.22

Aspect Ratio

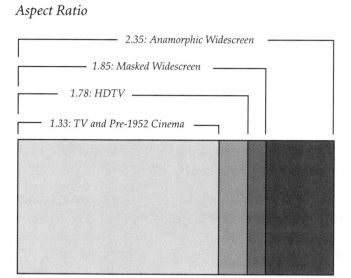

terms, this is TV's **aspect ratio**. The recently established standard for **high-definition television (HDTV)** requires a wider image. Its standard width is 1.78 to 1, although it is normally identified as 16 to 9. Theatrical film's aspect ratio is wider still and consequently when theatrical films are shown on television, the video frame cuts off portions of the cinematic image. In other words, when we watch a theatrical movie on television, we see only a part of the image that the viewer in the theater sees. Since theatrical films still form a significant portion of television programming and since more viewers experience theatrical films on videocassette and DVD than in theaters, it is important to understand just how the video frame modifies the film frame. The major TV and film aspect ratios are diagramed in Fig. 6.22.

The elongation of the film frame was originally realized as a response to the perceived threat of television in the decade after World War II. Film producers reasoned that theatrical films must provide viewers with something they cannot get from television. How else could they coax customers away from their television sets? Thus, in the 1950s film studios attempted a variety of technological lures: color, 3D, stereo sound, and wider screens. Widescreen, its advocates maintained, presented the viewer with a larger and grander and more overwhelming image. (Its detractors claimed that it was only suitable for filming snakes and dachshunds.) These new, wider screens had aspect ratios of 2.35:1 and 2.55:1, almost twice as wide as the standard ratio of 1.33:1. At first, widescreen was used principally for travelogues such as *This Is Cinerama* (1952) and lavish productions on the order of *The Robe* (1953). But by the 1960s widescreen films had become quite commonplace.

The first commonly used widescreen process was based on an **anamorphic lens** and is best known by its trademark labels: **CinemaScope** and **Panavision**. During the shooting of the film, the anamorphic process uses a special lens that squeezes the image. If we were to look at a frame of the film

FIGURE 6.23

itself, everyone and everything would appear skinny (Fig. 6.23). When this film is projected, the process is reversed; it is projected through an anamorphic lens, which unsqueezes the image and presents a broad, wide view (Fig. 6.24). The 'Scope frame thus achieves an expanded aspect ratio—specifically, a 2.35:1 ratio.

The second, more common, widescreen process is created through **masking** and does not involve the use of a special lens while shooting or projecting. Masked widescreen is created during the projection of the film, not the actual filming. A regular 1.33 frame is used, but horizontal bands across the top and the bottom of the frame are "masked" (blackened). As is evident in Fig. 6.25, the frame *within* the frame is wider than the old 1.33 ratio. This widescreen frame-within-the-frame—with a ratio of 1.85:1—is enlarged to fill the screen. Thus, masked widescreen (1.85) is not as wide as anamorphic widescreen (2.35), but it is still wider than the pre-1952 film standard (1.33); more important, it is also wider than the old television and the HDTV standards (1.33 and 1.78, respectively), as illustrated in Fig. 6.22. Currently, masked widescreen is the predominant format

FIGURE 6.24

FIGURE 6.25

FIGURE 6.25

Masked Widescreen

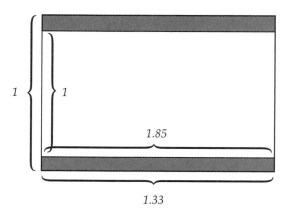

for theatrical films. Approximately 90% of contemporary films are presented in the 1.85 aspect ratio.

Television has adopted a variety of strategies to present widescreen theatrical movies with a minimum of viewer annoyance. The greatest widescreen challenge to TV's ratio is the anamorphic frame's 2.35 width. In other words, television has had to find a way to fit an anamorphic film's extra-wide image into the skinnier television screen. Two processes have emerged to deal with the conversion from 2.35 to 1.33 (or 1.78): **letterbox** and **pan-and-scan** or **scanning**.

Letterboxing, the less frequently applied option for converting anamorphic films to video, preserves most of the original image, but shrinks it. This process closely resembles widescreen masking for the theater, in that the tops and bottoms of the video frame are blackened. In letterboxing, the anamorphic film frame is reduced and fit into the frame-within-the-television-frame. A small amount of the left and right sides of the anamorphic frame is sacrificed, but it is considerably more similar to the original framing than is a pan-and-scan version. In Figs. 6.26 and 6.27, from a letterboxed version of *He Said, She Said*

FIGURE 6.26

FIGURE 6.27

FIGURE 6.28

FIGURE 6.29

(1991), the reader may see how the anamorphic frame from the original film has been shrunk and placed within the television frame. Most of the width of the original composition has been maintained (see Fig. 6.24). We can see both Dan Hanson and Lorie Bryer on opposite sides of the frame as she bounces a coffee mug off his head.

The pan-and-scan process, in contrast, reduces the 2.35 anamorphic frame to television's 1.33 by selecting the most "significant" part of the frame and eliminating the rest. Figs. 6.28 through 6.30 present a pan-and-scan version of the same *He Said, She Said* shot discussed above. Compare the pan-and-scan Fig. 6.28 with the letterbox Fig. 6.26. In the pan-and-scan version, Dan fills most of the frame and Lorie cannot be seen at all—quite a difference from the original film!

In addition, pan-and-scan can affect both camera movement and editing. The pan-and-scan frame need not remain fixed on one portion of the original frame. It can slide or "scan" left or right across the original. For example, in the

FIGURE 6.30

original *He Said, She Said* shot above, the camera stays still as the coffee mug sails across the frame (Figs. 6.26–6.27). In the pan-and-scan version, however, the pan-and-scan frame quickly scans across the image *with the mug* as it moves through the original frame, thus keeping the mug centered in the pan-and-scan frame. That is, the frame scans from Fig. 6.29 to Fig. 6.30, coming to rest on Dan as the mug beans him. What was achieved with a stationary camera in the original is now presented through the "movement" of scanning.

Further, in terms of editing, the pan-and-scan version can alter the rhythms of the original edit by cutting between portions of a shot—even if there had been no cutting in the film version. Returning to *He Said, She Said,* we can see how the shot has been edited for the pan-and-scan release. In the letterbox rendering, the mug-tossing shot begins with Dan talking on the left side of the frame, with Lorie visible on the right (as in Fig. 6.26). For pan-and-scan the shot starts with Bacon large in the frame and Perkins completely cut out (Fig. 6.28). Then, the camera *cuts* to Perkins (Fig. 6.29) as she prepares to pitch the mug. What was one shot in the original has now become two. Thus, the rhythm of the original version's editing is completely altered.

In broadcast television, there is an overriding compulsion to fill the image, to leave nothing blank. The visual voids at the top and bottom of letterboxed films thus do not suit the medium, where almost all anamorphic films are panned-and-scanned. In this fashion, anamorphic films are made to conform to the norms of television. Their images are processed until they fully load the TV screen, regardless of the injury done to the original images. However, it should be noted that DVD releases of films frequently feature both letterbox *and* pan-and-scan versions—allowing consumers to decide whether or not they wish to see the entire frame of the original.

There have been a few, rare attempts by televisual texts to reshape the frame within the standard 1.33 rectangle. In a MicroStrategy consulting commercial discussed later the top and bottom of the frame have been blacked out (Fig. 12.24), as in a letterboxed version of a film. This effect, which can also be observed in some music videos (e.g., Hal Ketchum's *Mama Knows the Highway*; Fig. 6.31), alters the image's aspect ratio without actually changing the dimensions of the picture tube. Commercials and music videos can also be found that blacken the sides of the image (creating a tall, narrow rectangle), or darken all but a small rectangular or circular portion of the image. Each of these manipulations of the frame leaves blank areas in the image that would not be tolerated in conventional television. The result is an image that looks oddly distinct, that distinguishes itself from "normal" television and thereby captures our attention—which is precisely the effect needed in commercials and music videos.

The differences between film and television aspect ratios are most apparent in anamorphic films, but they are also evident in the transfer of masked widescreen films to video. When masked widescreen films—with an aspect ratio of 1.85—make the transition to 1.33 TV, they lose a little from the edges, but not much because of the technique used to create this form of widescreen. Recall that masked widescreen films use the entire 1.33 frame when shooting, but blacken the tops and bottoms when projected in a theater. On the actual frames of film, however, the areas to be masked are still visible. When transferred

FIGURE 6.31

to video, the TV frame—which is a rounded rectangle—trims all four edges of the film frame. This maintains most of the width of a masked widescreen image and, coincidentally, it also reveals portions of the film image that are masked out in the theater. Normally this has no major effect, for today's camera operators compose their images with television in mind. Indeed, marked in their cameras' viewfinders is the area that is "safe for television." But sometimes film directors are less cautious about the use of the areas to be masked, in which things such as boom microphones, lights, and the tops of sets may be visible. In *Pee-wee's Big Adventure* (1985), a car is driving past traffic signs at night—or so it appears in the widescreen theatrical film version. In the television version, the bottoms of the traffic signs—hidden in the masking of the original—are visible, and it is revealed that they are actually on wheels (Fig. 6.32). Pee-wee's car is not moving; the signs are rolling toward the camera.

As viewers, we need to be aware of film's and television's differing aspect ratios to understand anomalies such as the wheeled signposts in *Pee-wee's Big*

FIGURE 6.32

Adventure and *He Said, She Said's* bizarre framing. These odd occurrences are becoming less and less common, however, as the television and film industries become more and more intertwined. HDTV's ratio of 1.78 is not all that different from masked widescreen's 1.85. And many widescreen films—both anamorphic and masked—are now composed with television's aspect ratio in mind. For this reason, even widescreen films tend to position the actors in the center of the frame—for fear of losing them when the film is transferred to video. Thus, the technological and economic necessities of converting widescreen film images to television images generate aesthetic results in the way the image finally appears on TV.

Image Quality: Definition

The more clearly details in an image appear or are defined, the higher that image's **definition**. Film, standard video, and high-definition video have different levels of clarity. To understand the differences between these media, we must consider some of the technological bases of both film and video.

Definition in film is primarily determined by the size of the **grain** of the **film stock**, the specific type of film. The grains are the silver halide crystals that swim around in the chemical soup, or **emulsion**, that is attached to the celluloid backing, or **base**, of a piece of film. In **fine-grain** film stocks the grain is smaller, less noticeable, and the definition is higher. Just how noticeable a film stock's grain is depends principally on two factors.

First, film stocks that are very sensitive to light and thus may be used in dark, low-light situations are grainier than those that are less sensitive to light. These kinds of film stocks are often used in documentary shooting, for example, where the light level cannot always be controlled.

Second, smaller **format** film stocks are grainier than larger format stocks. (Format here refers to film width and is measured in millimeters.) Thus, of the three most common film formats—**super-8, 16mm**, and **35mm**—the largest also has the finest grain, the highest definition. One might think therefore that 35mm's high definition would mean that it is the only film stock used in production for television. This has not been the case. Both economic and aesthetic factors have created specific niches for each of the formats. Inexpensive super-8 (and its immediate predecessor, "regular" 8mm) was the size of choice for home movie makers for over three decades, until the 1980s when low-cost video cameras virtually destroyed the super-8 market. For documentary work and low-budget films 16mm film is used. And 35mm film dominates filmmaking for theatrical movies, MOWs, prime-time television programs, national commercials, and music videos. Super-8 and 16mm—with their noticeably higher grain levels—are still used within 35mm programs to achieve particular effects. For example, the fuzzy, high-grain images of a 1960s family that are used in the credit sequence for *The Wonder Years* (1988–93) denote "home movies" and connote nostalgia for a bygone era. (Those scenes have been shot in super-8 or 16mm, while the rest of the program is shot in 35mm.) High grain images—particularly black and white images—are also used to connote "documentariness" in fiction programs and have appeared in many music videos and commercials.

Definition in video is not a factor of graininess, since video images are not composed of chemical crystals or grains. Moreover, although video image quality is defined somewhat by the material used to record that image—as do film stocks in the cinema—it is not exclusively so defined. This is because, unlike film, the video image can exist *without being recorded in any fashion*. Indeed, video images existed long before there was videotape to record them. Film's existence, in contrast, depends on an elaborate mechanical-chemical process that fabricates a piece of film that runs through a projector. It cannot exist without that recording medium. In contrast, all that television needs to create an image is a camera to produce an image and a television set to receive it. An immediate image may be instantaneously generated on a video screen, even if it is never stored on a recording medium such as videotape. What this means in terms of understanding image quality is that we may separate the quality of the video image from the quality of the video image as it *appears on videotape*. This distinction would be impossible to make in regard to the cinema because the medium does not exist separate from its presence on a physical strip of film.

At the most basic level, the video image is made up of phosphorescent dots that are arranged in horizontal lines on the TV screen. To be precise, these "dots" are really three tiny colored rectangles—one red, one green, and one blue—clustered together to form a single picture element, or **pixel**. An **electron gun** (three electron guns, in most color TVs) in the rear of the picture tube, or **cathode ray tube (CRT)**, fires an electron beam at these pixels, scanning line by line across the horizontal lines of the TV image. The number of **scan lines** varies in countries that use different broadcasting systems. The U.S. standard was set at 525 lines by the **National Television System Committee (NTSC)** decades ago. In the European system, the image consists of 100 more scan lines than it does in North America. And HDTV increases the NTSC number by several hundred lines, depending on which HDTV system is used.

When struck by the beam, the pixels glow and thereby create the television image. The pixels in NTSC television are so large that the scan lines are visible to the naked eye—if one should care to sit so close to the TV. Because the video pixels in these scan lines are much larger than the grain in 35mm film stocks, the video image is less clear—has a lower definition—than the 35mm film image (although it is roughly equivalent to the 16mm film image). And, though it may seem somewhat strange, when film images are converted to video signals, they still retain a higher degree of definition than do images originally shot with a video camera. Thus, filmed images on television are clearer and more sharply defined than are standard, non-HDTV video images.

What all of this boils down to is that—until recently—filmed images have held much more visual information than video images. If you took a video camera and a film camera to a football game and recorded the crowd from exactly the same angle, the film shot would contain details that would be blurry or impossible to see in video. Film's higher definition equals more details visible in the image. The aesthetic result of this technological aspect is that TV videographers

TABLE 6.1

North American TV and Film Resolution

CHARACTERISTICS	NTSC	HDTV(ATSC)	FILM
Total lines	525	1,125	
Active lines	486	1,080	3,000
Pixels per line	720	1,920	4,000
Aspect ratio (to 1)	1.33	1.78	1.33, 1.85, or 2.35
Total pixels	349,920	2,073,600	12,000,000

and directors tend to use more close-ups and fewer long shots—fearing that otherwise viewers will not be able to see important elements within the frame. The lower resolution of video is one reason why TV tends to be a more "close-up" medium than is theatrical film.

However, the long-standing supremacy of 35mm film is now being surpassed by new developments in video. By increasing the number of scan lines in the video image and decreasing the size and shape of the pixels, the video image may be made much clearer, more highly defined. This is the intent of high-definition television (HDTV). The **Advanced Television Systems Committee (ATSC)** was formed in the early 1990s to set a standard for HDTV—much as the NTSC had set the standards for the North American TV system decades before. In 1996, the FCC accepted ATSC recommendations for **digital television (DTV)**, of which HDTV is one part. As of this writing, the conversion to DTV is proceeding slowly and erratically. Wrangling over the **multicasting** and **enhanced TV** issues is delaying its implementation. Even so, the FCC has given U.S. stations and networks the deadline of 2002 to start digital broadcasting. And by 2006, analog NTSC television is scheduled to be eliminated entirely and replaced with some form of digital television. It seems likely, however, that these deadlines will be extended.

As we consider these new technical developments, the numbers start to get really confusing. But if you look closely at Table 6.1, you'll see that the old (NTSC) television standard contains 525 scan lines, but only 486 of them are visible—due to reasons best understood by broadcast engineers. On each of these 486 scan lines reside 720 rectangles of colored light, the pixels that make up the image. If we multiply 486 pixels times 720 lines, we find that the (North American) TV image consists of 349,920 pixels, which seems like a lot. But it really isn't when you compare it to film, which has the equivalent of 12,000,000 pixels (if, indeed, film had pixels instead of grain).

How much closer to 35mm film is high-definition TV? First, the ATSC HDTV standard more than doubles the old NTSC standard of lines of pixels—to 1,125, of which 1,080 are active. Second, it also changes the *shape* of the pixels. By modifying the NTSC rectangular pixel into a square one, HDTV is able to fit more pixels on each line—1,920 square pixels instead of 704 rectangular ones. If we multiply HDTV's 1,920 pixels times its 1,080 lines, we find that its image is made of 2,073,600 pixels—many times more than NTSC's 349,920 pixels. Consequently, HDTV's image definition is noticeably better than conventional broadcast television, but it still falls well short of film. Remember also that HDTV stretches the screen's aspect ratio from the NTSC width of 1.33 to 1.78, which is quite close to the theatrical film standard of masked widescreen (1.85).

Not only is the HDTV image clearer and more detailed than the NTSC image, it's also wider so there's more to see on the left and right.

As digitally recorded and transmitted video evolves, the visual differences between film and video will evaporate. By 2010 it seems likely that everything from TV productions to theatrical films will be recorded digitally and the question of "film or video?" will be rendered moot. Until then, however, the differences among film, NTSC video, and HD video will continue to influence the style of television.

When the video recording process is factored into the image-quality equation, we may see that the different video formats can have a marked impact on image definition. The situation is particularly confusing just now as we are in the midst of a transition to digital formats. Older video formats such as 8mm, 1/2″, 3/4″, 1″, and 2″ tape are being phased out in favor of digital recordings on tape of varying sizes. The burgeoning popularity of **digital video (DV)** is evident in the increasing number of theatrical films (e.g., *Star Wars: Episode II*), TV programs (especially news and documentary shows), and home "movies" (using digital camcorders) that are being recorded in digital formats. Home videographers, however, are probably most familiar with 1/2″ VHS and 8mm videocassette formats. These formats find very limited use in broadcast television. Like super-8 film, 1/2″ VHS tape and 8mm videocassette recordings are sometimes used in videotaped narrative programs to denote home movie-style videotaping. And, parallel to 16mm film, the video formats used in television news are sometimes used in videotaped/filmed fiction programs to signify "news style."

Home videotaping formats also make occasional appearances on television news when "amateur" videotapes of news events (e.g., tornadoes, earthquakes, police brutality) or surveillance videotapes of crimes are broadcast. The poorer resolution of these tapes—their difference from broadcast-quality tapes—becomes significant in these instances. It marks the tapes as "authentic," as unposed and spontaneous and supposedly a pure piece of the historical world. Regardless of how that footage was obtained, it appears to be part of reality because we consciously or unconsciously link it with other amateur videotapes we have seen. Thus, the technology (1/2″ VHS videotape) creates a visual style (poor resolution images) that carries certain significations based on our association with other videotaped images.

Image Quality: Color and Black and White

There are a few basic color characteristics that are described the same in both video and film: **hue**, **saturation** and **brightness**. Hue designates a specific color from within the visible spectrum of white light: for example, red, green, blue. The level of saturation defines a color's purity—how much or little grayness is mixed with the color. Deep, rich, vibrant colors such as those in a brand-new U.S. flag are said to be heavily saturated. They become less saturated as the weatherbeaten flag's colors fade. Saturation is also termed **chroma** or **chrominance** in video color. Brightness or luminance in video indicates how bright or dark a color is.

Despite these similarities, video and film take different approaches to creating color images. Video constructs colors by adding them together (**additive**

color). A single phosphor on the TV screen is colored red, green, or blue. The electron gun (or guns) ignite three nearby phosphors and combine their individual colors, thus generating a broad variety of colors. Film, in contrast, is a **subtractive color** process. As white light from a projector lamp passes through a piece of motion picture film, yellow, magenta (reddish), and cyan (bluish) colors are filtered out of the light. The colors that are not filtered out form the many colors of the spectrum.

Thus, both video and film rely on three-color systems to generate color images. Different video systems and film stocks **balance** these three colors in different ways. Some are more sensitive to red, others to blue; some appear more naturalistic under sunlight, others under tungsten light (as in household light bulbs). No video system or film stock captures color exactly as it exists in nature, but this is not necessarily a drawback. Rather, it presents a wide range of color options to the camera operator. Color may be manipulated through the choice of video system and film stock, as well as through lens filters and colored gels on the lights.

In the 1980s, long after television had been a strictly color medium, black-and-white video and film began to be reintroduced. Although black-and-white images are uncommon in narrative programs, they have been used to indicate dream sequences or events that occurred in the past. In these cases, black-and-white's contrast from color has been used to communicate narrative information. It becomes diegetically significant—significant in the world the characters inhabit. Black-and-white is also used in non-narrative television such as commercials and music videos. In these situations the colorless images cannot always be anchored in specific meanings beyond product differentiation. Yes, there have been several commercials in which everything is black-and-white except for the product advertised (a rather obvious use of black-and-white); but there are also black-and-white music videos in which the significance of the lack of color is ephemeral or elusive. In any event, black-and-white video/film is still another option that the camera operator may use to affect the viewer.

Special Effects

Special effects are not, strictly speaking, part of the style of the camera. Very few special effects are achieved solely by using a camera. Rather, most are accomplished by computers transforming the video images created by the camera. In the animation chapter we expand on the techniques of **computer-generated imagery (CGI)** and its manipulation that are available in television production. Still, a few comments on special effects seem in order at this point so that we do not innocently presume that the images we see on television could not have been somehow processed and manipulated.

Among the first special effects to be developed for television was **keying**, which is an electronic process, but not a digital one. That is, a computer is not required. In keying a portion of a video image is cut out and another image is placed in that video "hole." The simplest form of keying is the insertion of letters and numbers into an image, as can be seen in Figures 5.8 and 5.16, discussed in

FIGURE 6.33

terms of mise-en-scene. The text in each case—"NBC Nightly News with Tom Brokaw" and "13 Fran Curry"—has been keyed into the image using a special effects generator. The process is instantaneous and can be done while a program is broadcast live.

Chroma key is a special type of keying in which a particular color (blue or green, usually) is subtracted from an image and a new image is inserted in its place. Weather forecasters, for example, stand in front of a blue screen, which is transformed into map or radar images. The Weather Channel forecaster in the background of Fig. 6.33 is in a studio gesturing toward a blue screen. As can be seen in the monitors on the lower left and far right, a map has been created by a computer and inserted into the image behind him, taking the place of the blue screen.[3]

SUMMARY

This chapter has been filled with more technological information—mechanical, chemical, electronic and digital—than have the other chapters. This is because camera style is inevitably described in technological terms—words borrowing from technological roots for their meanings: dolly shot, anamorphic framing, telephoto shot. To discuss television style, then, it becomes necessary to understand television technology. Technology does not exist in a vacuum, however. The use of specific technological inventions—videotape, camera dollies, etc.—depends on the TV program's budget and the aesthetic conventions of the time. Moreover, many elements of camera style are not at all determined by technology. Framing and camera height decisions, for example, do not depend on specific technological devices. Instead, they result from shifting aesthetic conventions.

Technology, economics, and aesthetic convention blend together in the videographer's, cinematographer's, and/or director's manipulation of camera style. The people responsible for visual style choose initially between video (analog and digital) and film, and thereby determine much about the definition and color of the final product. But—regardless of the originating medium—focal lengths, depths of field, framings, camera heights, and movements will be selected to maximize narrative, informational, or commercial effect. Each of these camera-style aspects serves many functions on television, affecting our understanding of a program. As critical viewers, we need to remain alert to the significance of camera-style techniques. We can then understand their function within television and their impact on television's construction of meaning.

FURTHER READINGS

Video and film camera style is discussed in many of the readings suggested at the end of chapter 5. Peter Ward, *Picture Composition for Film and Television* (Woburn, MA: Focal Press, 1996) addresses the specific principles behind the framing of images with the camera and the positioning of objects and humans within that frame.

The nuts and bolts of digital video production are well covered in Michael Rubin, *Nonlinear 4: A Field Guide to Digital Video and Film Editing* (Gainesville, FL: Triad, 2000). The convoluted story behind the evolution of DTV is chronicled in entertaining fashion in Joel Brinkley, *Defining Vision: The Battle for the Future of Television* (New York: Harcourt Brace, 1997). Joan Van Tassel, *Digital TV Over Broadband: Harvesting Bandwidth* (Boston: Focal, 2001) accounts for both technological and economic convergence in contemporary television and related electronic media.

Readers interested in the specifics of *film* camera technology should consult J. Kris Malkiewicz, *Cinematography: A Guide for Film Makers and Film Teachers*, 2nd ed. (New York: Simon & Schuster, 1989).

ENDNOTES

[1] In the cinema deep focus was not used much until the 1940s, when directors such as Orson Welles and cinematographers such as Gregg Toland began incorporating it. In *Citizen Kane* (1941) and *The Magnificent Ambersons* (1942), Welles uses deep focus to coordinate simultaneous action on several planes: for example, while a young boy's mother and father discuss the boy's future he (the boy) is visible through a window, playing in the snow in the far background (*Citizen Kane*).

[2] André Bazin, *What Is Cinema?*, ed. and trans. Hugh Gray (Berkeley: University of California Press, 1967.

[3] On the issue of whether to use blue or green for chroma key, Greg Stroud, senior brand manager and on-air promotions of the Weather Channel, comments, "Most places switched to green walls long ago because talent kept complaining that they couldn't wear blue in their wardrobe. A legit complaint, since blue is a very common wardrobe element. However, the green used in a green wall is very reflective. Because of that, the talent cannot stand very close to the wall or the green reflects back on them, not only giving them an odd skin tone but then keying them out. So to use green, you have to have a very deep studio with proper lighting."

CHAPTER 7

Style and Editing

Editing is at once the most frequently overlooked and the most powerful component of television style. We are seldom conscious of a program's arrangement of shots, and yet it is through editing that television producers most directly control our sense of space and time, the medium's building blocks. For many theorists of television, editing is the engine that powers the medium.

At its most basic, editing is deceptively simple. Shot one ends. Cut. Shot two begins. But in that instantaneous shot-to-shot transition, we make a rather radical shift. We go from looking at one piece of space from one point of view to another piece of space from a different perspective. Perspective and the representation of space suddenly become totally malleable. Time, too, can be equally malleable. Shot two need not be from a time following shot one; it could be from hours or years before. The potential for creative manipulation is obvious.

Within broadcast television, however, editing is not completely free of conventions—far from it. Most television editing is done according to the "rules" of two predominant **modes of production: single-camera** and **multiple-camera**. By mode of production we mean an aesthetic style of shooting that often relies on a particular technology and is governed by certain economic systems. As we have seen before, television forever blends aesthetics, technology, and economics. Single-camera productions are filmed with just one camera operating at a time. The shots are not done in the order in which they will appear in the final product, but instead are shot in the sequence that is most efficient in order to get the production done on time and under budget. Consider, for example, a scene between two characters named Eugene and Lydia, in which shots 1, 3, 5, 7, and 9 are of Eugene and shots 2, 4, 6, 8, and 10 are of Lydia. The single-camera approach to this scene would be to set up the lighting on Eugene, get the camera positioned, and then shoot the odd-numbered shots one after another. Then Lydia's lighting would be set up and the camera would shoot all the even-numbered shots of her. Later, the shots would be edited into their proper order.

Multiple-camera productions have two or more cameras trained on the set while the scene is acted out. In our hypothetical 10-shot scene, one camera would be pointed at Eugene while the other would simultaneously be pointed at Lydia. The scene could be edited while it transpires or it could be cut later, depending on time constraints. Sequences in daily soap operas and game shows tend to be edited while they are shot, but weekly sitcoms are generally edited after shooting.

These modes of production are more than just a matter of how many cameras are brought to the set. They define two distinct approaches, whose differences cut through

- **Pre-production**—the written plan for the shoot.
- **Production**—the shoot itself.
- **Post-production**—everything after.

And yet, both modes rely on similar principles of editing.

Historically, the single-camera mode of production came first. It developed initially in the cinema and has remained the preeminent way of making theatrical motion pictures. On television, it is the main mode used to create prime-time dramas, MOWs, music videos, and nationally telecast commercials. As it is also the site for the development of most editing principles, we will begin our discussion of editing there. Subsequently we will consider the multiple-camera mode of production, which is virtually unique to television and is only rarely used in theatrical films. Sitcoms, soap operas, game shows, sports programs, and newscasts are shot using several cameras at once. Although multiple-camera shooting has developed its own conventions, its underlying premises are still rooted in certain single-camera conceptualizations of how space and time should be represented on television.

Before discussing the particulars of these modes of production, it should be noted that the choice of single-camera or multiple-camera mode is separate from that of the recording medium (film or video). While most single-camera productions today are still shot on film and not on video, this is becoming less true as high-definition digital video evolves. One notable convert to digital video is George Lucas, who is shooting *Star Wars: Episode II* in that format. Multiple-camera productions are also not tied to one specific medium. They have a long history of being shot on both film and video. As we shall see, these modes of production are not determined by their technological underpinning—although that is certainly a consideration. Rather, they depend as much on certain economic and aesthetic principles as they do on technology.

SINGLE-CAMERA MODE OF PRODUCTION

Initially it might seem that single-camera production is a cumbersome, lengthy, and needlessly expensive way to create television images, and that television producers would shy away from it for those reasons. But television is not a machine driven solely by the profit motive. Just as we must be cautious of technological determinism (i.e., that television producers will use new technology as soon as it becomes available), we must also be wary of slipping into an economic determinism. That is, we must avoid the mistaken belief that television producers' aesthetic decisions and technological choices will always be determined by economic imperatives. In a study of how and why the Hollywood film industry adopted the single-camera mode of production, David Bordwell, Janet Staiger, and Kristin Thompson contend that technological change has three basic explanations:

1. Production efficiency—does this innovation allow films to be made more quickly or more cheaply?

2. Product differentiation—does this innovation help distinguish this film from other, similar films, and thus make it more attractive to the consumer?

3. Standards of quality—does this innovation fit a conventionalized aesthetic sense of how the medium should "evolve"? Does it adhere to a specific sense of "progress" or improvement?[1]

Although single-camera production is more expensive and less efficient than multiple-camera, it compensates for its inefficiency by providing greater product differentiation and adhering to conventionalized aesthetic standards. Because single-camera mode offers more control over the image and the editing, it allows directors to maximize the impact of every single image. Consequently, it is the mode of choice for short televisual pieces such as commercials and music videos, which rely on their visuals to communicate as powerfully as possible and need a distinctive style to distinguish them from surrounding messages that compete for our attention.

Stages of Production

Pre-production. To make single-camera production economically feasible, there must be extensive pre-production planning. Chance events and improvisation are expensive distractions in a single-camera production. The planning of any production—whether an MOW or a Pepsi commercial—begins with a script. Actually, there are several increasingly detailed stages of scripting:

- **Treatment**—a basic outline.
- **Screenplay**—a scene-by-scene description of the action, including dialogue.
- **Shooting script**—a *shot-by-shot* description of each scene.
- **Storyboard**—small drawings of individual shots (Fig. 7.1).

For our purposes it is not important to go into the differences among these written planning stages, but it may be helpful to consider the storyboard, which consists of drawings of images for each shot (with more than one image for complicated shots). Storyboards indicate the precision with which some directors conceptualize their visual design ahead of time. Alfred Hitchcock, for example, was well known for devising elaborate storyboards. For him, the filmmaking process itself was simply a matter of creating those images on film. Commercials and music videos are also heavily storyboarded. Each frame is carefully plotted into a particular aesthetic, informational, or commercial system.

Production. A single camera is used on the set and the shots are done out of order. Actors typically rehearse their scenes in entirety, but the filming is disjointed and filled with stops and starts. Because the final product is assembled

FIGURE 7.1

1. Car speeds recklessly down a tree-lined road.

2. Woman and man in front seat. He drives.

3. The road; his point of view.

4. Front seat, same scene as in #2.

5. Woman looks toward man.

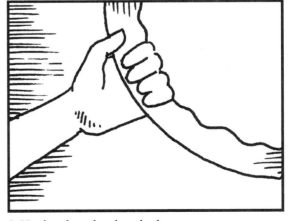

6. Her hand reaches for wheel.

from these fragments, a **continuity person** must keep track of all the details from one shot to the next—for example, in which hand the actor was holding a cigarette and how far down the cigarette had burned. Nonetheless, small errors do sneak through, illustrating just how disjointed the whole process is. For instance, in Fig. 7.9, a frame enlargement from a *Northern Exposure* (1990–95) scene that is analyzed later, a dishcloth is on actor Janine Turner's shoulder. At the very beginning of the next shot, Fig. 7.10, the dishcloth has disappeared.

The "production" stage of making television is under the immediate control of directors. They choose the camera positions, coach the actors, and approve the mise-en-scene. Most television directors do not write the scripts they direct (which is done in pre-production), and most do not have control over the editing (post-production). However, the actual recording process is their direct responsibility.

Post-production. The task of the technicians in post-production is to form the disjointed fragments into a unified whole. Ideally the parts will fit together so well that we will not even notice the seams joining them. At this point in narrative television production, the **sound editor** and **musical director** are called on to further smooth over the cuts between shots with music, dubbed-in dialogue, and sound effects. Of course, in music videos and many commercials the music provides the piece's main unifying force and is developed well before the visuals. Indeed, the music determines the visuals, not vice versa, and becomes part of the pre-production planning.

The post-production process was revolutionized in the 1990s by computer-based **nonlinear editing (NLE)**, on systems such as the Avid Media Composer and Media 100 (Fig. 9.6). Virtually everything in television and film today, with the exception of nightly newscasts, is edited on NLE systems. To understand what makes these systems "nonlinear" and why that is significant, a bit of history is required (see chapter 9 for further details).

Early video editing systems were strictly *linear*. To assemble shots A, B, and C, you first put shot A on the master tape and then shot B and then shot C. If you decided later that you wanted to insert shot X between A and B, you were out of luck. You had to start all over and put down shot A, followed by X, and then B, and so on. One shot had to follow the other (there were exceptions to this, but we are simplifying for clarity). In contrast to this linear system for video, film editing was always *nonlinear*. If film editors wish to insert a shot X between shots A and B, they just pull strips of film apart and tape them together again. Digital editors changed video's reliance on linear systems.

NLE systems typically use two computer monitors—as is illustrated by editor Niklas Vollmer's project, *Fit to Be Tied*, which was edited on the Media 100 (Figs. 7.2–7.4). In Fig. 7.2 (taken from the left-side monitor) you see lists of available image and sound clips and a preview window that shows what the finished project will look like. In Fig. 7.3 (taken from the right-side monitor) is the project's **timeline**. All NLE systems use timelines to structure the editing. In the detail for the *Fit to Be Tied* timeline (Fig. 7.4), each shot is signified by a rectangle, with a label such as "Monster sings" and "Big Al walk by." Unlike linear video editing, Vollmer may place any shot anywhere on the timeline—inserting shots between other shots if he wishes. NLE also permits fancy transitions from one shot to the next. In the Media 100 timeline, the editor may specify two simultaneous

FIGURE 7.2

FIGURE 7.3

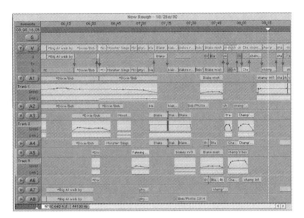

image tracks (labeled "a" and "b" in Fig. 7.4) and create special effects between shots—as is signified by the small arrows between tracks a and b. In this manner, the NLE editor may create fades, dissolves, and more elaborate transitions. Also visible in this detail of the timeline is one audio track (labeled "A1"), with the relative loudness of the audio indicated by the graph-like line. Several other overlapping audio tracks can also be added—allowing editors to create sound mixes.

NLE is a big part of the digital overhaul of the television industry. Its computers are cheaper than old-fashioned video editing equipment, and it provides television editors with much greater aesthetic flexibility. Moreover, it is part of the motivation behind the move to digital video (DV). Analog video and film must be converted to a digital format before they can be sucked into an NLE computer, but images shot in digital video can skip this process since they are already digital. The ease and relative lack of expense of DV and NLE are changing the face of post-production and facilitating work by independent video producers—such as the people behind *The Blair Witch Project* (1999) and *Time Code* (2000).

FIGURE 7.4

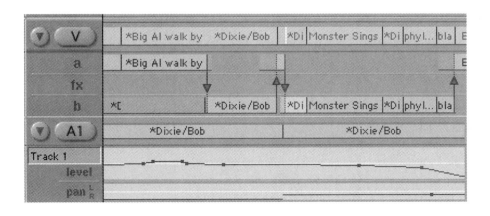

The Continuity Editing System

In chapter 2 we discussed Hollywood classicism as the major narrative system in theatrical film. Accompanying this narrative structure is a particular approach to editing that has come to be known as **continuity editing**. It operates to create a continuity of space and time out of the fragments of scenes that are contained in individual shots. It is also known as invisible editing because it does not call attention to itself. Cuts are not noticeable because the shots are arranged in an order that effectively supports the progression of the story. If the editing functions correctly, we concentrate on the story and don't notice the technique that is used to construct it. Thus, the editing is done according to the logic of the narrative.

There are many ways to edit a story, but Hollywood classicism evolved a set of conventions that constitute the continuity system. The continuity editing system matches classicism's narrative coherence with continuities of space and time. Shots are arranged so that the spectator always has a clear sense of where the characters are and when the shot is happening—excepting narratives that begin ambiguously (e.g., murder mysteries) and clarify the "where" and "when" later. This spatial and temporal coherence is particularly crucial in individual **scenes** of a movie.

A scene is the smallest piece of the narrative action. Usually it takes place in one location (continuous space), at one particular time (continuous time). When the location and/or time frame change, the scene is customarily over and a new one begins. To best understand the continuity system, we will examine how it constructs spatial and temporal continuity within individual scenes. How these scenes then fit together with one another in a narrative structure is discussed in chapter 2.

Spatial Continuity. In the classical scene the space is oriented around an **axis of action.** To understand how this axis functions, consider Fig. 7.5, an overhead view of a rudimentary two-character scene. Let's say that the action of this scene is Brent and Lilly talking to one another in a cafeteria. The axis, or line of action, then, runs through the two of them. The continuity system dictates that cameras remain on one side of that axis. Note the arc in Fig. 7.5 that defines the area in which the camera may be placed. If you recall your high school geometry, you'll recognize that this arc describes 180°. Since the cameras may be positioned only within the 180° arc, this editing principle has come to be known as the **180° rule.**

The 180° rule helps preserve spatial continuity because it ensures that there will be a similar background behind the actors while cutting from one to the other. The cafeteria setting that is behind Brent and Lilly recurs from shot to shot and helps confirm our sense of the space of the room. A shot from the other side of the axis (position X) would reveal a portion of the cafeteria that had not been seen before, and thus might contain spatial surprises or cause disorientation.

More important than similar backgrounds, however, is the way in which the 180° rule maintains **screen direction**. In the classical system, the conventional wisdom is that if characters are looking or moving to the right of the screen in shot one, then they should be looking or moving in the same direction

FIGURE 7.5

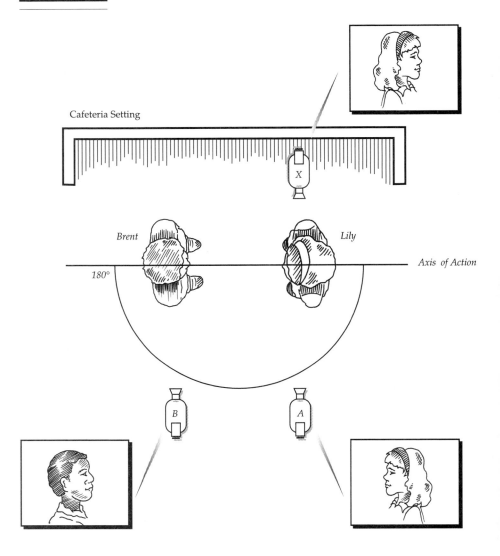

in shot two. To cut from camera A to camera X (Fig. 7.5) would break the 180° rule and violate screen direction. In a shot from camera A, Lilly is looking screen left. If the director had cut to a shot of her from position X, Lilly would suddenly be looking screen *right*. Even though the actor herself had not changed position, the change in camera angle would make her *seem* to have changed direction. This is further illustrated by camera position B. A cut from Brent (camera B) to Lilly from the hypothetical X position would make it appear as if they were both looking to the right, instead of toward one another. Breaking the 180° rule would confuse the spatial relationship between these two characters.

Maintaining screen direction is also important to action scenes filmed outdoors. If the directors are not careful about screen direction, they will wind up with car chases where the vehicles appear to be moving *toward* each other rather than following. And antagonists in confrontational scenes might appear to be running in the same direction rather than challenging one another.

There are, of course, ways of bending or getting around the 180° rule, but the basic principle of preserving screen direction remains fundamental to the classical construction of space. For this reason, the continuity system is also known as the **180° system**.

Built on the 180° rule is a set of conventions governing the editing of a scene. Although these conventions were more strictly adhered to in theatrical film during the 1930s and 1940s than they are on television today, there are several that still persist. Some of the most prevalent include:

- The **establishing shot**
- The **shot-counter shot** editing pattern
- The **re-establishing shot**
- The **match cut**—including the **match-on-action** and the **eyeline match**
- The prohibition against the **jump cut**

This may best be illustrated by breaking down a simple scene into individual shots. In Fig. 7.6, the basic camera positions of a *Northern Exposure* scene are diagramed. While examining the frame captures from this scene, keep in mind that this was a single-camera (film) production. That is, multiple cameras were not used. Just one camera was on the set at the time of filming.

FIGURE 7.6

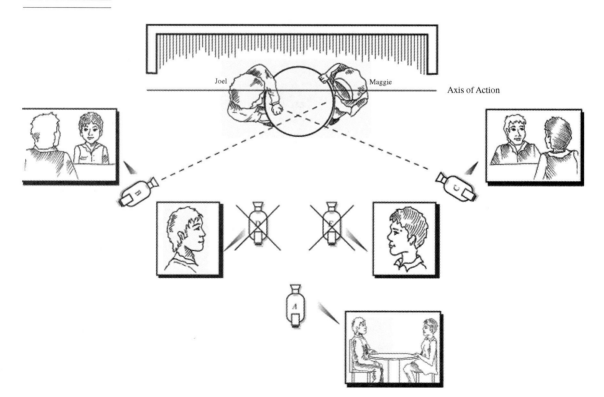

The first shot of a classical scene is typically a long shot that shows the entire area and the characters in it, as in the long shot of Maggie and Joel in Fig. 7.8. (camera position A), preceded by an exterior shot of her cabin (Fig. 7.7). This establishing shot introduces the space and the narrative components of the scene: Maggie, Joel, her cabin, a dinner cooked by her. In a sense, the establishing shot repeats the exposition of the narrative, presenting specific characters to us once again. If the establishing shot is from a very great distance, it may be followed by another establishing shot that shows the characters clearly in a medium shot or medium long shot.

From there the scene typically develops some sort of alternating pattern, especially if it is a conversation scene between two people. Thus, shots of Maggie are alternated with shots of Joel, depending on who is speaking or what their narrative importance is at a particular point (camera positions B and C, Figs. 7.11 and 7.12). Note that once again the 180° rule is adhered to, as the cameras remain on one side of the axis of action. Note also that the angles of positions B and C crisscross each other, rather than being aimed at Joel and Maggie from positions D or E. These latter two positions do not violate the 180° rule, but positions B and C are preferred in the continuity system for two reasons. First, these angles show more of the characters' faces, giving us a three-quarter view rather than a profile. We look into their faces without looking directly into their eyes and breaking the taboo against actors looking into the camera lens and at the viewer. Second, since we see Joel's shoulder in Maggie's shot (Fig. 7.11) and vice versa (Fig. 7.12), the space that the two share is reconfirmed. We know where Maggie is in relationship to Joel and where he is in relationship to her.

Since shots such as C in Fig. 7.6 are said to be the counter or reverse angle of shots such as B, this editing convention goes by the name shot-counter shot or shot-reverse shot. Shot-counter shot is probably the most common editing pattern in both single-camera (such as *Northern Exposure*) and multiple-camera productions (e.g., soap operas).

Once shot-counter shot has been used to detail the action of a scene, there is often a cut back to a longer view of the space. This re-establishing shot shows us once again which characters are involved and where they are located. It may also be used as a transitional device, showing us a broader area so that the characters may move into it or another character may join them. Often it is immediately followed by another series of shots-reverse shots.

The *Northern Exposure* scene does not contain this type of re-establishing shot, but provides a variation of it. After a series of 15 shots in fairly tight close-up (framed as in Figs. 7.13 and 7.14), the camera cuts back to a medium close-up (Fig. 7.17) as the tone of Joel and Maggie's conversation shifts. The scene is then played at medium close-up for seven shots (Figs. 7.17–7.23), as Joel and Maggie drift apart emotionally. Just when Maggie is most disenchanted with Joel (Fig. 7.24), he compliments her and their intimacy is regained. This is marked in the framing with a tighter shot of Joel (Fig. 7.25), as he raises his glass to toast her. She reciprocates his intimacy and is also framed tighter (Fig. 7.26). After one more close-up of Joel (Fig. 7.27), the camera cuts to the original medium shot of the two of them (Fig. 7.28, compare with Fig. 7.8), which tracks back and out the window (Fig. 7.29).

FIGURE 7.7

FIGURE 7.8

FIGURE 7.9

FIGURE 7.10

FIGURE 7.11

FIGURE 7.12

FIGURE 7.13

FIGURE 7.14

FIGURE 7.15

FIGURE 7.16

FIGURE 7.17

FIGURE 7.18

FIGURE 7.19

FIGURE 7.20

FIGURE 7.21

FIGURE 7.22

FIGURE 7.23

FIGURE 7.24

FIGURE 7.25

FIGURE 7.26

FIGURE 7.27

FIGURE 7.28

FIGURE 7.29

FIGURE 7.30

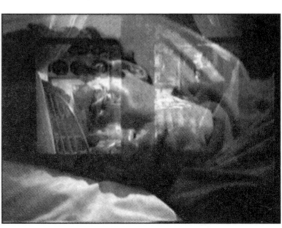

FIGURE 7.31

Thus the framing has gone from medium shot to medium close-up to close-up, coming closer to the characters as the scene intensifies. But it does not remain at close-up. The camera cuts back to medium close-up and then returns to close-up before ending the scene with a track backward from a medium shot. The key to any classically edited scene is variation, closer and farther as the narrative logic dictates.

Two other editing devices are among those used to maintain space in the continuity system: the match cut and the **point-of-view** or **subjective** shot.

In a match cut, the space and time of one shot fits that of the preceding shot. One shot "matches" the next and thereby makes the editing less noticeable. Matching may be achieved in several ways. Two of the most common are the match on action and the eyeline match.

In a match-on-action cut, an activity is continued from one shot to the next. At the end of shot two in the *Northern Exposure* scene, Maggie begins to sit down (Fig. 7.9); at the start of the next shot she continues that movement (Fig. 7.10). The editor matches the action from one shot to the next, placing the cut in the midst of it. This, in effect, conceals the cut because we are drawn from one shot to the next by the action. We concentrate on Maggie's movement, and the cut becomes "invisible." We probably don't even notice the vanishing dishcloth.

An eyeline match begins with a character looking in a direction that is motivated by the narrative. For instance, in *L.A. Law* (1986–94), legal boardroom scenes are edited based on the looks of the characters. Jonathan looks in a specific direction in one shot (Fig. 7.32) and the editor uses that look as a signal to cut to Leland (Fig. 7.33), toward whom Jonathan had glanced. Jonathan's *eyeline* provides the motivation for the cut and impels the viewer toward the new space. In an eyeline match such as this, the second shot is *not* from the perspective of the person who is looking, but rather merely shows the area of the room in the eyeline's general direction. The shot of Leland is from a camera position in the middle of the table, not from the chair where Jonathan was sitting, even though his glance cued the shot of Leland.

FIGURE 7.32

FIGURE 7.33

A shot made when the camera "looks" from a character's perspective is known as a point-of-view shot. A point-of-view shot is a type of framing in which the camera is positioned physically close to a character's point of view. The shots of Joel and Maggie in Figs. 7.17–7.23, for example, are all point-of-view shots. In each, we could see from Joel's or Maggie's point of view. If the camera were positioned as if it were inside the character's head, looking out his or her eyes, then it would be known as a subjective shot. Frequently, point-of-view and subjective shots are incorporated in a simple editing pattern: in shot one someone looks and in shot two we see what he or she is looking at from his or her perspective. In Fig. 7.34, from another *Northern Exposure* scene, Maggie draws Joel's attention to his brother, Jules. Joel turns and looks in the first shot. The camera cuts to a close-up of the brother in shot two that is taken from Joel's perspective (Fig. 7.35). Subjective shots such as this are very similar to eyeline matches, but the eyeline cut does not go to a shot that is the character's perspective.

FIGURE 7.34

FIGURE 7.35

FIGURE 7.36

FIGURE 7.37

The opposite of a match cut is a jump cut, which results in a disruptive gap in space and/or time, so that something seems to be missing. Jump cuts were regarded as mistakes in classical editing, but they were made fashionable in the 1960s films of Jean-Luc Godard and other European directors. Godard's first feature film, *Breathless* (1960), features numerous jump cuts, as is illustrated in Figs. 7.36 and 7.37. The camera maintains similar framing from one shot to the next while the woman's position shifts abruptly and a mirror appears in her hand. Today, jump cuts similar to this are quite common in music videos and commercials, and even find their way into more mainstream narrative productions. *Homicide: Life on the Street* (1993–99) is peppered with them (e.g., Figs. 7.38 and 7.39, which are taken from two shots that were edited together). But then, *Homicide* is not a conventionally edited show. In most narrative television programs, match cuts remain the norm and jump cuts are generally prohibited.

FIGURE 7.38

FIGURE 7.39

Sample Decoupage. The best way to understand editing is to take a scene and work backward toward the shooting script, thereby deconstructing the scene. The process of breaking down a scene into its constituent parts is known as decoupage, the French word for cutting things apart.

In our discussion of _Northern Exposure_ we have created a sample decoupage. You may want to perform a similar exercise with a videotape of a short scene of your own choosing. Watch the tape several times with the sound turned off. Try to diagram the set and each of the camera positions from a bird's-eye view. Draw a shot-by-shot storyboard of the scene. Ask yourself these questions:

1. How is the scene's space, the area in which the action takes place, introduced to the viewer? Does an establishing shot occur at the start of the scene (or later in it)?

2. What is the narrative purpose or function of each shot? What does each shot communicate to the viewer about the story?

3. Why was each shot taken from the camera position that it was? Do these angles adhere to the 180° rule? Is screen direction maintained? If not, why is the viewer not disoriented? Or if the space is ambiguous, what narrative purpose does that serve?

4. If the characters move around, how does the editing (or camera movement) create transitions from one area to another?

5. Is an alternating editing pattern used? Is shot-counter shot used?

6. How does the camera relate to the character's perspective? Are there point-of-view or subjective shots? If so, how are those shots cued or marked? That is, what tells us that they are subjective or point-of-view shots?

7. Is match-on-action used? Are there jump cuts?

8. How does the last shot of the scene bring it to a conclusion?

9. In sum, how does the organization of space by editing support the narrative?

Temporal Continuity. Within individual scenes, story time and screen time are often the same. Five minutes of story usually takes 5 minutes on screen. Time is continuous. Shot two is presumed to instantaneously follow shot one. Transitions from one scene to the next, however, need not be continuous. If the story time of one scene always immediately followed that of another's, then screen time would always be exactly the same as story time. A story that lasted 2 days would take 2 days to watch on the screen. Obviously, story time and screen time are seldom equivalent on television. The latter is most commonly much shorter than the former. There are many gaps, or ellipses, in screen time. In addition, screen time may not be in the same chronological order as story time. Through flashbacks, for example, an action from the story past is presented in the screen present. So, both time's _duration_ and its _order_ may be manipulated in the transition from one scene to the next.

To shorten story time or change its order without confusing the viewer, classical editing has developed a collection of scene-to-scene transitions that break the continuity of time in conventionalized ways, thus avoiding viewer disorientation. These transitions are marked by simple special effects that are used instead of a regular cut.

- **The fade**. A **fade-out** gradually darkens the image until the screen is black; a **fade-in** starts in black and gradually illuminates the image. The fade-out of one scene and fade-in to the next is often used to mark a substantial change in time.

- **The dissolve**. When one shot **dissolves** into the next, the first shot fades out at the same time the next shot fades in, so that the two images overlap one another briefly. The conclusion of the *Northern Exposure* scene illustrates this. The final shot is a long shot of Joel and Maggie, as seen through the window of her cabin (Fig. 7.29). From there it dissolves to a close-up of Joel's face in his own bed (Fig. 7.31). The two shots both appear on screen for short period of time, overlapping one another (Fig. 7.30). Here the dissolve serves to mark the transition from Joel's dream state to "reality." Dissolves are more conventionally used to signal a passage in time; and the slower the dissolve, the more time has passed.

- **The wipe**. Imagine a windshield wiper moving across the frame. As it moves, it wipes one image off the screen and another on to take its place. This is the simplest form of a wipe, but wipes can be done in a huge variety of patterns. Wipes may indicate a change in time, but they are also used for an instantaneous change in space.

In addition to these transitional devices, classical editors also use special effects to indicate flashbacks. In films of the 1930s and 1940s, the image may become blurry or wavy as the story slips into the past (or into a dream). The special effect signals to the viewer, "We're moving into the past now." During the prime of the classical era, changes in time were inevitably clearly marked, and these techniques continue to be used (as is suggested by the dissolve in *Northern Exposure*).

Fades, dissolves, and wipes were part of the stock-in-trade of the film editor during the cinema's classical era, and they are still evident in today's single-camera productions. Historically, however, narrative filmmakers have used these devices less and less. Initially, this was due in large part to the influence of 1960s European filmmakers, who accelerated the pace of their films through jump cuts and ambiguous straight cuts (no special effects) when shifting into the past or into dream states. The jump cuts in Godard's *Breathless* revolutionized classical editing, breaking many of its most fundamental "rules." And Luis Buñuel's films enter and exit dream states and flashbacks without signaling them to the viewer in any way, creating a bizarre, unstable world.

Classical editing is not a static phenomenon. It changes according to technological developments, aesthetic fashions, and economic imperatives. Current fashion favors straight cuts in narrative, single-camera productions; but fades, dissolves, and wipes are still in evidence. Indeed, the fade-out and fade-in are television's favorite transition from narrative segment to commercial break and back. In this case, the fade-out and fade-in signal the transition from one type of television material (fiction) to another (commercial).

Non-narrative Editing

Not all television material that is shot with one camera tells a story. There are single-camera commercials, music videos, and news segments that do not present a narrative in the conventional sense of the term. They have developed different editing systems for their particular functions. Some bear the legacy of continuity editing, while others depart from it. The specifics of editing for music videos and commercials are discussed in chapters 10 and 12, respectively, but we will here consider some aspects of editing for television news.

News Editing. Although the in-studio portion of the nightly newscast is shot using multiple cameras, most stories filed by individual reporters are shot in the field with a single video camera. The editing of these stories, or **packages** (ranging in length from 80 to 105 seconds), follows conventions particular to the way that the news translates events of historical reality into television material (see chapter 4). The conventional news story contains:

- The reporter's opening **lead**.

- A first **sound bite**, consisting of a short piece of audio, usually synchronized to image, that was recorded on the scene: for example, the mayor's comment on a new zoning regulation or a bereaved father's sobbing.

- The reporter's transition or **bridge** between story elements.

- A second sound bite, often one that presents an opinion contrasting with that in the first sound bite.

- The reporter's concluding **stand-up**, where he or she stands before a site significant to the story and summarizes it.

This editing scheme was inherited, with variations, from print journalism and a specific concept of how information from historical reality should be organized. The reporter typically begins by piquing our interest, implicitly posing questions about a topic or event. The sound bites provide answers and fill in information. And, to comply with conventional structures of journalistic "balance"(inscribed in official codes of ethics), two sound bites are usually provided. One argues pro, the other con, especially on controversial issues. The news often structures information in this binary fashion: us/them, pro/con, yes/no, left/right, on/off. The reporters then come to represent the middle ground, with their concluding stand-ups serving to synthesize the opposing perspectives. Thus, the editing pattern reflects the ideological structure of news reporting.

MULTIPLE-CAMERA MODE OF PRODUCTION

Although a good deal of what we see on television has been produced using single-camera production, it would be wrong to assume that this mode dominates TV in the same way that it dominates theatrical film. The opposite is true. It would be impossible to calculate exactly, but roughly three quarters of today's television shows are produced using the multiple-camera mode. Of the top 10 most popular prime-time shows in the 1998–99 season, only three were shot in single-camera mode (Table 7.1). This doesn't even take into consideration non-prime-time programs such as daytime soap operas, game shows, and late-night talk shows—all of which are also done in multiple-camera. Obviously, multiple-camera production is the norm on broadcast television, as it has been

TABLE 7.1

Top 10 Prime-Time Shows: 1998–99

All of the following are multiple-camera productions except for *ER*, *Touched By an Angel*, and *CBS Sunday Movie*.

1. *ER*	5. *Veronica's Closet*
2. *Friends*	7. *60 Minutes*
3. *Frasier*	8. *Touched By an Angel*
4. *NFL Monday Night Football*	9. *CBS Sunday Movie*
5. *Jesse*	10. *20/20*

Note: Source: Nielson Media Research.

since the days of television's live broadcasts–virtually all of which were also multiple-camera productions (Table 7.2).

It is tempting to assume that since multiple-camera shooting is less expensive and faster to produce than single-camera, it must therefore be a cheap, slipshod imitation of single-camera shooting. This is the aesthetic hierarchy of style that television producers, critics, and even some viewers themselves presume. In this view, multiple-camera is an inferior mode, a necessary evil. However, ranking one mode of production over another is essentially a futile exercise. One mode is not so much better or worse than another as it is just different. Clearly, there have been outstanding, even "artistic," achievements in both modes. Instead of getting snarled in aesthetic snobbery, it is more important to discuss the differences between the two and understand how those differences may affect television's production of meaning. In short, how do the different modes of production influence the meanings that TV conveys to the viewer? And what principles of space and time construction do they share?

Stages of Production

Pre-production. Narrative programs such as soap operas and sitcoms that utilize multiple-camera production start from scripts much as single-camera productions do, but these scripts are less image-oriented and initially indicate no camera directions at all. Sitcom and soap opera scripts consist almost

TABLE 7.2

Top 10 Prime-Time Shows: 1950–51

Of the following, all but the Westerns (*The Lone Ranger* and *Hopalong Cassidy*) and *Fireside Theatre* were telecast live using multiple camera technology.

1. *Texaco Star Theater*	6. *Gillette Cavalcade of Sports*
2. *Fireside Theatre*	7. *The Lone Ranger*
3. *Philco TV Playhouse*	8. *Arthur Godfrey's Talent Scouts*
4. *Your Show of Shows*	9. *Hopalong Cassidy*
5. *The Colgate Comedy Hour*	10. *Mama*

Note: (1950–51 was the first season during which the A.C. Nielsen Company [which became Nielsen Media Research] rated programs.)

entirely of dialogue, with wide margins so that the director may write in camera directions; a page from a script for *No Business of Yours* (an unproduced sitcom) is shown in Fig. 7.40. Storyboards are seldom, if ever, created for these programs. This type of scripting is emblematic of the emphasis on dialogue in multiple-camera programs. The words come first; the images are tailored to fit them.

Non-narrative programs (game shows, talk shows, etc.) have even less written preparation. Instead, they rely on a specific structure and a formalized opening and closing. Although the hosts may have lists of questions or other prepared materials, they and the participants are presumed to be speaking in their own voices, rather than the voice of a scriptwriter. This adds to the program's impression of improvisation.

Production. A multiple-camera production is not dependent on a specific technological medium. That is, it may be shot on film, on video, or even broadcast live. *Seinfeld* was filmed; *Roseanne* was videotaped. All talk shows and game shows are videotaped. Some local news programs and *Saturday Night Live* are telecast live. If a program is filmed, the editing and the addition of music and sound effects must necessarily come later, after the film stock has been digitized and imported into a nonlinear editor (NLE). If a program is videotaped, there are the options of editing later on NLE or while it is being recorded **live-on-tape**. (Obviously, a live program must be edited while it is telecast.) Time constraints play a factor here. Programs that are broadcast daily, such as soap operas and game shows, seldom have the time for extensive editing in post-production. Weekly programs, however, may have that luxury.

The choice of film or video is, once again, dependent in part on technology, economics, and aesthetics. Since the technology of videotape was not made available until 1956, there were originally only two technological choices for recording a multiple-camera program: either film live broadcasts on **kinescope** by pointing a motion-picture camera at a TV screen; or originally shoot the program on film (and then broadcast the edited film later). Early-1950s programs such as *Your Show of Shows* (1950–54) and *The Jack Benny Show* (1950–65, 1977) were recorded as kinescopes. In 1951, the producers of *I Love Lucy* (1951–59, 1961) made the technological choice to shoot on film instead of broadcasting live. Although this involved more expense up front than kinescopes did, it made economic sense when it came time to syndicate the program. A filmed original has several benefits over kinescope in the syndication process. A filmed original looks appreciably better than a kinescope and is easier and quicker to prepare since all the shooting, processing, and editing of the film has already been done for the first broadcast. Since producers make much more money from syndication than they do from a program's original run, it made good economic sense for *I Love Lucy* to choose film over live broadcasting and kinescope. Moreover, its enormous success in syndication encouraged other sitcoms in the 1950s to record on film.

After the introduction of videotape, the economic incentive for multiple-camera productions to shoot on film no longer held true. A videotape record of a live broadcast may be made and that videotape may be used in syndication. This videotape—unlike kinescopes—looks just as good as the original broadcast. Today, producers who shoot film in a multiple-camera setup do so primarily

FIGURE 7.40

NO BUSINESS OF YOURS   Revision #3   13.
                            Sep 13 1993   (2/J)

(George, Allen, Mr. Franklin)

<u>ACT TWO</u>

<u>SCENE J</u>

<u>INT. BARBER SHOP - DAY</u>

GEORGE CUTS MR. FRANKLIN'S HAIR. <u>ALLEN ENTERS</u>.

                    GEORGE

        Well, now, what do you know?

        Look who's here!

                    ALLEN

        Hi, Mr. Shearer.

                    GEORGE

        (LOUDLY) Mr. Franklin, you

        remember Allen Scott? Used

        to work summers next door at

        the grocery?

MR. FRANKLIN IS STARTLED AWAKE. GEORGE INTER-

PRETS THIS TO BE A NOD.

                    GEORGE

        (CONT., TO ALLEN) Out of

        school and everything. Did

        you get the graduation present

        from Winnie and me?

                    ALLEN

        Sure did. Thanks. I appreciate it.

for aesthetic reasons. Images in live broadcasts and on videotape are certainly better than the old kinescopes, but film still holds a slight edge over video in terms of visual quality. However, the introduction of high-definition TV may spell the end for film's visual superiority.

Narrative programs that are filmed and those videotaped narrative programs that are edited in post-production follow a similar production procedure. The actors rehearse individual scenes off the set, then continue rehearsing on the set, with the cameras. The director maps out the positions for the actors and the two to four cameras that will record a scene. The camera operators are often given lists of their positions relative to the scene's dialogue. Finally, an audience (if any) is brought into the studio (see Figs. 5.6, 5.7).

The episode is performed one scene at a time, with 15- to 20-minute breaks between the scenes—during which, at sitcom filmings/tapings, a comedian keeps the audience amused. One major difference between single-camera and multiple-camera shooting is that, in multiple-camera, the actors always perform the scenes straight through, without interruption, unless a mistake is made. Their performance is not fragmented, as it is in single-camera production. Each scene is recorded at least twice and, if a single line or camera position is missed, they may shoot that individual shot in isolation afterwards.

Further, in multiple-camera sitcoms, the scenes are normally recorded in the order in which they will appear in the finished program—in contrast, once again, to single-camera productions, which are frequently shot out of story order. This is done largely to help the studio audience follow the story and respond to it appropriately. The audience's laughter and applause is recorded by placing microphones above them. Their applause is manipulated through flashing "applause" signs that channel their response, which is recorded for the program's **laugh track**. The laugh track is augmented in post-production with additional recorded laughter and applause, a process known as **sweetening** in the industry.

The entire process of recording one episode of a half-hour sitcom takes about 3 to 4 hours—if all goes as planned.

Live-on-tape productions, such as soap operas, are similar in their preparation to those edited in post-production, but the recording process differs in a few ways. Once the videotape starts rolling on a live-on-tape production, it seldom stops. Directors use a **switcher** to change between cameras as the scene is performed. The shots are all planned in advance, but the practice of switching shots is a bit loose. The cuts don't always occur at the conventionally appropriate moment. In addition to the switching/cutting executed concurrently with the actors' performance, the scene's music and sound effects are often laid on at the same time, though they may be fine-tuned later. Sound technicians prepare the appropriate door bells and phone rings and thunderclaps and then insert them when called for by the director. All of this heightens the impression that the scene presented is occurring "live" before the cameras, that the cameras just happened to be there to capture this event-hence the term **live-on-tape**. The resulting performance is quite similar to that in live theater.

In soap operas, individual scenes are not shot like sitcoms, in the order of appearance in the final program. Since soap operas have no studio audience to consider, their scenes are shot in the fashion most efficient for the production. Normally this means that the order is determined by which sets are being used on a particular day. First, all the scenes that appear on one set will be shot—regardless of where they appear in the final program. Next, all the scenes on another set will be done, and so on. This allows the technicians to light and prepare one set at a time, which is faster and cheaper than going back and forth between sets.

As we have seen, narrative programs made with multiple cameras may be either filmed or videotaped and, if taped, may either be switched during the production or edited afterward, in post-production. Non-narrative programs, however, have fewer production options. Studio news programs, game shows, and talk shows are always broadcast live or shot live-on-tape, and never shot on film. This is because of their need for immediacy (in the news) and/or economic efficiency (in game and talk shows). Participants in the latter do not speak from scripts, they extemporize. And, since these "actors" in non-narrative programs are improvising, the director must also improvise, editing on the fly. This further heightens the illusion of being broadcast live, even though most, if not all such programs, are on videotape.

Post-production. In multiple-camera programs, post-production (often simply called "post") varies from the minimal touch-ups to full-scale assembly. Live-on-tape productions are virtually completed before they get to the post-production stage. But similar programs that have been recorded live, but *not* switched at the time of recording must be compiled shot by shot. For instance, sitcoms often record whatever the three or four cameras are aimed at without editing it during the actual shoot. The editor of these programs, like the editor of single-camera productions, must create a continuity out of various discontinuous fragments—using an NLE system.

It might appear that sitcoms and the like would have a ready-made continuity, since the scenes were performed without interruption (except to correct mistakes) and the cameras rolled throughout. What we must recall, however, is that there are always several takes of each scene. The editor must choose the best version of each individual shot when assembling the final episode. Thus, shot one might be from the first take and shot two from the second or third. The dialogue is usually the same from one take to the next, but actors' positions and expressions are not. Inevitably, this results in small discontinuities. In one *Murphy Brown* scene, for instance, TV producer Miles argues with his girlfriend, Audrey, and her former boyfriend, Colin. In one shot, Colin, on the far left of the frame, is holding a sandwich in his right hand (Fig. 7.41). The camera cuts to a reverse angle and instantaneously the sandwich has moved to his left hand (Fig. 7.42). Evidently, the editor selected these two shots from alternative takes of the same scene.

To hide continuity errors from the viewer, the editor of a multiple-camera production relies on editing principles derived from the single-camera 180° editing system (e.g., match cuts, eyeline matches, etc.). Also, the soundtrack that is created in post-production incorporates music, dubbed-in dialogue, sound effects, and laugh tracks to further smooth over discontinuities and channel our attention.

FIGURE 7.41   **FIGURE 7.42**

Narrative Editing: The Legacy of the Continuity System

It is striking how much multiple-camera editing of narrative scenes resembles that of single-camera editing. In particular, the 180° principle has always dominated the multiple-camera editing of fiction television. This is true in part because of the aesthetic precedent of the theatrical film. But it is also true for the simple, technologically based reason that, to break the 180° rule and place the camera on the "wrong" side of the axis of action would reveal the other cameras, the technicians, and the bare studio walls (position X in Fig. 7.5). Obviously, violating this aspect of the 180° system is not even an option in television studio production.

However, acceptance of the continuity editing system in multiple-camera production goes beyond maintaining screen direction due to an ad hoc adherence to the 180° rule. It extends to the single-camera mode's organization of screen space. As you read through the following description of a typical scene development, you might refer back to the description of single-camera space. Note also that the following applies to all narrative programs shot in multiple-camera, whether they are filmed or videotaped (or recorded live-on-tape).

A scene commonly begins by introducing the space and the characters through an establishing shot that is either a long shot of the entire set and actors, or a camera movement that reveals them. On weekly or daily programs, however, establishing shots may be minimized or even eliminated because of the repetitive use of sets and our established familiarity with them. In any event, from there a conventionalized alternating pattern begins—back and forth between two characters. In conversation scenes—the foundation of narrative television—directors rely on close-ups in shot-counter shot to develop the main narrative action of a scene. After a shot-counter shot series, the scene often cuts to a slightly longer view as a transition to another space or to allow for the entrance of another character. Standard, single-camera devices for motivating space (match on action, eyeline matches, point-of-view shots, etc.) are included in the multiple-camera spatial orientation. Try watching a scene from your favorite soap opera with the sound turned off and see if it doesn't adhere to these conventions.

The differences between multiple-camera programs and single-camera ones are very subtle and may not be immediately noticeable to viewers. But these differences do occur, and they do inform our experience of television. The main difference between the two modes is how action is represented. Although multiple-camera shooting arranges space similarly to the space of single-camera productions, the action within that space—the physical movement of the actors—is presented somewhat differently. In multiple-camera shooting, some action may be missed by the camera and wind up occurring out of sight, off-frame, because the camera cannot control the action to the degree that it does in single-camera shooting. For example, in one scene from the multiple-camera production, *All My Children*, the following two shots occur:

1. Medium close-up of Erica, over Adam's shoulder (Fig. 7.43). She pushes him down (Fig. 7.44) and is left standing alone in the frame at the end of the shot (Fig. 7.45).

2. Medium close-up of Adam, seated, stationary at the very beginning of the shot (Fig. 7.46).

Here, the camera operators had trouble keeping up with Adam's actions and consequently his fall happens off-screen. If this scene had been shot in single-camera mode, the fall would have been carefully staged and tightly controlled so that all the significant action was on-screen. Multiple-camera editing frequently leaves out "significant" action that single-camera editing would include. Single-camera continuity editing might have used a match-on-action cut in this instance—editing these shots in the middle of Adam's fall, showing his action fully, and establishing his new position in the chair.

Small visual gaps such as this and other departures from the continuity editing system occur frequently in multiple-camera editing. What significance do they have? They contribute to the programs' illusion of "liveness." They make it seem as if the actors were making it up as they went along, and the camera operators were struggling to keep up with their movements, as if the camera operators didn't know where the actors were going to go next. Of course, in reality they do know the actors' planned positions, and yet they cannot know

FIGURE 7.43

FIGURE 7.44

FIGURE 7.45

FIGURE 7.46

exactly where the actors will move. In single-camera shooting the action is controlled precisely by the camera, bound by the limits of the frame. In multiple-camera shooting that control is subtly undermined. As a result, in their editing, multiple-camera narrative programs (soap operas and sitcoms, principally) come to resemble talk shows and game shows. The visual "looseness" of multiple-camera editing comes to signify "liveness" when compared to the controlled imagery of single-camera productions. The spatial orientation of the two modes is quite similar, but the movement of actors through that space is presented a bit differently.

Non-narrative Editing: Functional Principles

The non–narrative programs that are shot with several cameras in a television studio include, principally, game shows, talk shows, and the portions of news programs shot in the studio. (Sports programs and other outdoor events such as parades also use several cameras at once, but that is a specialized use of multiple-camera production.) These programs do not share the need of narrative programs to tell a story, but their approach to space is remarkably similar to that of narrative programs. Typically, their sets are introduced with establishing long shots, which are followed by closer framings and inevitably (in conversation-oriented genres such as talk shows) wind up in shot-counter shot patterns. Game shows also follow this pattern of alternation, crosscutting between the space of the contestants and that of the host (Fig. 4.5–4.6). The mise-en-scene of non-narrative programs is quite distinct from narrative settings (see chapter 5), but the shot-to-shot organization of that mise-en-scene follows principles grounded in the continuity editing system.

S U M M A R Y

In our consideration of editing on television, we have witnessed the pervasiveness of the continuity system. Although originally a method for editing theatrical films, its principles also underpin both of the major modes of production for television: single-camera and multiple-camera.

The continuity system functions, in a sense, to deceive us—to make us believe that the images passing before us compose one continuous flow, when actually they consist of many disruptions. Or, in other terms, one could say this system constructs a continuity of space and time. Many techniques are used to construct this continuity. The 180° rule maintains our sense of space and screen direction by keeping cameras on one side of an axis of action. Shot-reverse shot conventionally develops the action of a scene in alternating close-ups. Match cuts (especially matches-on-action and eyeline matches) and the basic point-of-view editing pattern motivate cuts and help prevent viewer disorientation.

Time on television is not always continuous. Indeed, gaps and ellipses are essential to narrative television if stories that take place over days or months are to be presented in half-hour, hour, or 2-hour time slots. Through editing, the duration and order of time may be manipulated. Within the continuity system, however, our understanding of time must always be consistent. We must be guided through any alteration of chronological order. Fades, for instance, are used to signal the passage of time from one scene to the next.

These principles and techniques of the continuity system are created in both single-camera and multiple-camera modes of production. An understanding of the stages of production—pre-production, production and post-production— helps us see their subtle differences. The key distinction is that single-camera productions shoot scenes in discontinuous chunks, while multiple-camera ones (especially live-on-tape productions) allow scenes to be played out in entirety while the cameras "capture" them. Even so, both modes of production must find ways to cope with discontinuity and disruption, and it is here that the continuity system's principles come into play, regardless of the actual production method used to create the images.

Non-narrative television is not as closely tied to the continuity system as narrative programs are, yet it does bear the legacy of continuity-style editing. Establishing shots, shot-reverse shot editing patterns, and the like are as evident on talk shows and game shows as they are on narrative programs.

The power of editing, the ability to alter and rearrange space and time, is a component of television that is taken for granted. Its "invisibility" should not blind us, however, to its potency.

FURTHER READINGS

Editing style and mode of production are discussed in many of the readings suggested at the end of chapter 5.

The evolution of single-camera production is comprehensively described in David Bordwell, Janet Staiger, and Kristin Thompson, *The Classical Hollywood Cinema: Film Style and Mode of Production to 1960* (New York: Columbia University Press, 1985). John Ellis, *Visible Fictions* (New York: Routlegde, 1992) is not as exhaustive, but it does begin the work of analyzing the multiple-camera mode of production. Few other sources make such an attempt.

In the cinema, the principles of editing have long been argued. This stems from the desire to define film in terms of editing, which was at the heart of the very first theories of the cinema. These initial forays into film theory were carried out in the 1920s by filmmakers Eisenstein, Kuleshov, and Pudovkin. See, for example, Sergei Eisenstein, *Film Form: Essays in Film Theory*, edited and translated by Jay Leyda (New York: Harcourt, Brace & World, 1949); Lev Kuleshov, *Kuleshov on Film*, edited and translated by Ronald Levaco (Berkeley: University of California Press, 1974); and V. I. Pudovkin, *Film Technique and Film Acting*, translated by Ivor Montagu (New York: Bonanza, 1949).

Editing has also been a central component of debates within film studies over the position of the spectator, as can be seen in Jean-Louis Baudry, "Ideological Effects of the Basic Cinematographic Apparatus," in *Narrative, Apparatus, Ideology*, ed. Philip Rosen (New York: Columbia University Press, 1986), 286–98; Nick Browne, "The Spectator-in-the-Text: The Rhetoric of *Stagecoach*," in Rosen, 102–19; and Daniel Dayan, "The Tutor-Code of Classical Cinema," in *Movies and Methods*, ed. Bill Nichols (Berkeley: University of California Press, 1976). Kaja Silverman, *The Subject of Semiotics* (New York: Oxford University Press, 1983) reviews this debate.

Thomas A. Ohanian, *Digital Nonlinear Editing: Editing Film and Video on the Desktop* (Boston: Focal Press, 1998); Thomas A. Ohanian and Michael E. Phillips, *Digital Filmmaking, The Changing Art and Craft of Making Motion Pictures* (Boston: Focal Press, 2000); and Michael Silbergleid and Mark J. Pescatore, eds., *Guide to Digital Television* (New York: Miller Freeman PSN, 2000) approach television editing from a hands-on perspective—explaining editing principles and the operation of editing systems. Ken Dancyger, *The Technique of Film and Video Editing*, 2nd ed. (Boston: Focal Press, 1996) offers a broad historical and critical overview of film editing that includes a limited section on editing for television.

Despite the obvious impact of editing on television style, television criticism has been slow to articulate its significance. However, this work has been begun in Jeremy G. Butler, "Notes on the Soap Opera Apparatus: Televisual Style and *As the World Turns*,"*Cinema Journal* 25, no. 3 (Spring 1986): 53–70; and the previously cited Herbert Zettl, *Sight Sound Motion*.

ENDNOTES

[1] David Bordwell, Janet Staiger, and Kristin Thompson, *The Classical Hollywood Cinema: Film Style and Mode of Production to 1960* (New York: Columbia University Press, 1985), 243–244.

[2] Many people use "point-of-view"and "subjective"interchangeably. Here, however, we will distinguish between subjective shots from within the head of the character and point-of-view shots that are nearby, but not through the character's eyes.

CHAPTER 8

Style and Sound

Up to this point our discussion of television style has dealt primarily with visual elements: mise-en-scene, the camera, and editing. But television is not solely a visual medium. Sound has always been a crucial component of television's style. This is not surprising when one remembers that, in economic and technological terms, television's predecessor and closest relation is *radio*—not film, literature, or the theater. Economically, television networks replicated and often grew out of radio networks. Technologically, TV broadcasting has always relied on much of the same equipment as radio broadcasting (microphones, transmitters, and so on). With these close economic and technological ties to radio—a *sound-only* medium—it is almost inevitable that television's aesthetics would rely heavily on sound. The experience of *watching* television is equally an experience of *listening* to television.

Sound's importance to the medium becomes obvious if one performs a simple experiment. Turn the sound off and watch 15 minutes of a program. Then "watch" the next 15 minutes with the sound on, but do not look at the picture. Which 15 minute segment made more sense? Which communicated the most narrative (or other) information? Which had the greatest impact? Typically, sound without image is more self-sufficient than image without sound. Sound affects the viewer and conveys televisual meaning just as much, and possibly more, than the image does. Indeed, so little is communicated in the visuals of some genres—talk shows, game shows, soap operas—that they would cease to exist without sound.

In approaching television sound, we need to understand:

- The different types of televisual sound.
- The functions that sound serves on television.
- Sound's basic acoustic properties and how they are rendered through televisual sound technology.
- The significance of sound to television's structuring of space, time, and narrative.

TYPES OF TELEVISION SOUND

The types of sound that are heard on television can be divided into three main categories:

1. **Speech**
2. **Music**
3. **Sound effects**

In television's more expensive productions, each of these components is given to a separate sound technician to create and shape. That is, one person does speech, one does music, and one does the rest. Each sound category is separately edited on different **tracks** of a sound editor, or **digital audio workstation** (**DAW**). DAWs are the audio-only version of digital video editing and are configured much like the Media 100 editor discussed in chapter 7. Digital sound editors typically divide the audio into numerous discrete tracks—marked A1 through A8 in Figs. 7.3 and 7.4. In the Media 100, each sound element is labeled and the line beneath the label shows the volume (or level) of that element. A single sound source can be placed in each of these tracks and thereby is separated from the other sounds. Typically, certain tracks would only contain speech, while others would be limited to music and sound effects. This allows the sound editor to manipulate individual sound components before combining them together into the finished, composite soundtrack. The use of multi-track technology and the assignment of labor to the sound technicians indicates how the industry categorizes sound. This will serve as our starting point.

Speech. Without doubt, talk is the most conspicuous aspect of television sound. Soap operas thrive on it, and talk shows are defined by it. Even sports programs, which one would think would provide enough visual interest to get along without commentary, rely heavily on discussion of the game. Once, during the 1980s, a network experimented with broadcasting a football game without announcers, providing only the sights and sounds of the game and on-screen statistics. Sports fans were not comfortable with this, and it hasn't been tried since. Apparently, television visuals are lost without speech. Sometimes it appears as if the images were superfluous, as if TV were, as one critic put it, a "lava lamp" with sound.

Speech in narrative television most commonly takes the form of **dialogue** among characters. Dialogue does not typically address viewers. It is as if they were eavesdropping on a conversation. In some comic situations, however, a character (e.g., George Burns, Dobie Gillis, Malcolm) will break this convention of the "fourth wall" and speak directly to the camera. Additionally, **narration** or **voice-over**, in which a character's or omniscient narrator's voice is heard over an image, can sometimes speak directly to the viewer, as when the adult Kevin Arnold talks to the viewer about his younger self in *The Wonder Years* (1988–93). (Note the difference between "narra*tion*," which refers to a voice speaking over an image, and "narra*tive*," which we use more generally to refer to a some sort of story or fiction.)

Speech in non-narrative television, in contrast, is often directly addressed to the viewer (see chapters 4 and 12). News anchors look at and speak toward the viewer. David Letterman directs his monologue right at the camera.

The announcers in advertisements cajole viewers directly, imploring them to try their products. Other programs are more ambiguous in the way they address the viewer. Game shows pose questions to the social actors on screen, but these questions are also meant for viewers so that they can play along. Needless to say, the way that speech is addressed can be quite complicated, and even contradictory.

In terms of standard production practice, speech is most often recorded live on the set, during the "production" phase, rather than during pre-production or post-production (see chapter 7). This means that speech is usually recorded at the same time that the image is, but not always. Post-production sound work can modify the dialogue or, indeed, can even add to it or replace it altogether—as occurs when sound is **dubbed** or dialogue is changed using **Automatic Dialogue Replacement** (**ADR**, also known as **looping**).

In dubbing and ADR, one voice is substituted for another, as is illustrated in the backstage film *Singin' in the Rain* (1952), where one woman's voice is dubbed in for another's in the movie within that movie. ADR is conventionally used in several instances in television. First, when an actor's reading of a line is not considered satisfactory, it may be replaced with an alternative reading by that same actor. Second, if an actor's voice is not considered appropriate to the character it may be replaced by a different actor's. For example, when Andie McDowell played Jane, a British character, in *Greystoke: The Legend of Tarzan, Lord of the Apes* (1984), the producers felt that her natural Louisiana dialect did not suit the role. Subsequently, Glenn Close's voice was dubbed in for all of McDowell's dialogue. Third, dubbing is used in puppetry (e.g., Alf) and animation, as when Nancy Cartwright's voice is used for Bart Simpson's. Fourth and finally, in the rare instances in which foreign-language films or television programs are shown on U.S. television they are frequently dubbed into English, although they can be **subtitled** instead of dubbed. (In subtitling, the English translation is printed on the bottom of the screen and the original dialogue is retained.)

Music. Music and speech go hand-in-hand on television. Customarily, dialogue will be accompanied by music throughout narrative programs. Indeed, it is the rare line of dialogue that has no music beneath it. And portions of a program—say, a car chase—that have no dialogue will almost always increase the presence of the music. Television is seldom devoid of both music and speech. It is not a quiet medium.

Television music comes in many different genres—from the rock soundtrack of *That '70s Show* (1998–), to the country tunes of *The Dukes of Hazard* (1979–85), to the rap music of *In Living Color* (1990–94). Television absorbs a fairly broad spectrum of popular music, although it seldom presents avant-garde performances, and classical music appears infrequently (and is relegated to its own "highbrow" ghetto on PBS). Until relatively recently narrative programs did not use much music by well-known popular performers. If a scene required rock music, then studio musicians were used to create the rock sound, rather than using a well-known performer's work. When *WKRP in Cincinnati* premiered in 1978, it was thought to be groundbreaking because it featured music by original performers rather than sound-alikes.

Television's reticence to use popular music is partially an economic decision and partially an aesthetic one. As far as economics goes, if one uses a song that has been **copyrighted** then one must pay **royalties** for its use. If there is no current copyright on a piece of music, then it is said to be in the **public domain**, and may be used without charge. This provides an obvious economic incentive to avoid copyrighted music, and encourages producers to either use public domain music or generate new, original music. Copyright issues have become particularly complicated in this digital age—where an MP3 copy of a Metallica song sounds identical to the original and may be easily distributed across the Internet. The U.S. Congress has attempted to pass laws protecting the corporations that own copyrights, but this often leads to the abridgement of free speech. In addition to facilitating copying, digital technology also expedites rap music's **sampling** of bits of older tunes, which has occasionally resulted in lawsuits over the ownership of this music. As you can see, television producers face numerous new challenges in the legal use of copyrighted music.

One other, principally aesthetic, reason that some TV genres have shied away from popular music in the past is because rock music during the 1950s and 1960s was associated with subversive or countercultural elements. Soap operas and sports programs, for instance, avoided rock music until the 1980s because it was perceived as too decadent for those historically conservative genres. The fact that both sports and soaps now regularly incorporate rock tunes indicates both a change in rock's position in U.S. culture (it has now become mainstream) and a change in these genres themselves, an attempt on their part to attract younger viewers.

Music fits into television's mode of production slightly differently than speech does. Unlike speech, very little music is recorded live on the set during the production phase—excepting, of course, videotapings/broadcasts of live musical performances (e.g., the musical segments of *Saturday Night Live* [1975–], the Boston Pops Orchestra broadcasts). Instead, most music is either prepared before the production or after. In music videos, the music is recorded ahead of time (with a few, very rare exceptions). The performers then mouth the words to the song while they are filmed or videotaped. This form of synchronization of image to music is known as **lip sync** (see chapter 10 for more on music videos).

Aside from musical productions, however, it is more common to add music to the image later, in post-production, than before shooting begins. Most scenes are shot without music, even ones in which music is supposed to be in the background—for example, a nightclub or dance. Music is laid on later so that the sound technician can get a clear recording of the dialogue and the director can tightly control the music's impact.

Live-on-tape productions have a fairly unique approach to music. In both narrative (principally, soap operas) and non-narrative programs (talk shows and game shows) that are recorded live-on-tape, the music is inserted while the scene is being videotaped rather than during post-production. In narrative programs, sound technicians record the theme song and several generic musical themes ahead of time. When the cameras start to roll, they insert the appropriate music when cued by the director—much like a musical cue in the theater. Non-narrative programs follow the same procedure for their theme music. Other non-narrative programs such as late-night talk shows include a live band (e.g., Paul Shaffer's on *Late Show With David Letterman*) and live performances by guests. The principle remains the same, however. The music is inserted while the program is being videotaped—the only difference being that the music is performed rather than played back on an audio device.

Sound Effects. All the elements of television's sound that are not speech or music fall into the catch-all category of sound effects. This includes gunshots, doorbell rings, footsteps on the pavement, the crunch of a fist into a jaw, and so on. It also includes the background sound of a particular room or other space—in other words, the room's **ambient sound**. In live-on-tape productions, most of these sound effects are whatever is picked up on the set or inserted by the sound editor during videotaping, but in programs that are edited in post-production, sound effects can be fabricated and manipulated in seemingly infinite ways.

During the actual videotaping/filming, sound technicians will record the background noise and various other sound effects elements, but they will try, as much as possible, to isolate those sounds from the dialogue. This gives them the greatest flexibility in post-production sound editing. Footsteps may be heightened to increase suspense, or the background sound of a jet chancing to pass by during videotaping/filming may be eliminated. Sound effects, like speech and music, are endlessly malleable—especially through the use of sound processing software.

Commonly, sound effects are created in post-production work using the **Foley** process. Foley artists view a segment of video/film in a sound studio, a Foley stage, that is equipped with different floor surfaces (rug, tile, wood, etc.), a variety of doors (car doors, screen doors, house doors, etc.), and many other sound effects contraptions. While the segment is projected on a screen, the Foley artists recreate the appropriate sounds. When a character walks up to a door, the Foley artist is recorded walking along the studio floor. When the character opens the door, the Foley artist is recorded opening a door in the studio, and so on. Some programs have only occasional Foley work in them, but others, especially complicated mini-series and MOWs, might create all of the sound effects in this manner.

PURPOSES OF SOUND ON TELEVISION

Among the many purposes that sound serves on television, four will concern us here:

    1. Capturing viewer attention.

    2. Manipulating viewer understanding of the image.

    3. Maintaining televisual flow.

    4. Maintaining continuity within individual scenes.

Regardless of the production techniques used to create sound, these are the essential functions that it serves on television.

Capturing Viewer Attention. The first and perhaps most significant function of television sound is to snare the attention of the viewer. Television, unlike cinema and the theater, exists in an environment of competing distractions. Most people watch television in a brightly lit room, with the TV set positioned amid a variety of visual stimuli (unlike the darkened room of a theater). While the television is on, conversations continue, a phone rings, a tea kettle may start boiling, a cat may rub against a viewer's leg. In sum, television viewing is an inattentive pastime. The viewer's gaze may be riveted to the set for brief, intense intervals, but the overall experience is one of the distracted glance.

In this setting, visuals alone are not captivating enough to grab the viewer's attention. Sound is a much more effective stimulus in this regard. This is not just the case of the loud, abrasive commercial demanding your attention. It's also the sports announcer's excited comments and the cheers of the crowd that cause one to look up from folding laundry to see an instant replay; or the soap opera character posing the question, "So, April, are you ready to reveal the true father of your child?" that brings one running back from the kitchen. Sound invokes viewers' attention, cuing them to significant visual action or a major narrative twist. In other words, sound may be used to hail viewers—much as one hails a cab.

Manipulating Viewer Understanding. The second function sound serves is to shape our understanding of the image. The sound-image relationship is a complex one that we will return to several times in this chapter. In the most general terms, this relationship manifests itself in three ways:

1. Sound and image support one another.

2. Sound and image contradict one another.

3. Sound helps to emphasize select elements within the image.

Sound and image can support each other in a variety of fashions. In Fig. 7.8, from our discussion of editing in *Northern Exposure*, we see a medium shot of Maggie and Joel and a table laden with food. Her lips are moving. On the soundtrack is the sound of a woman's voice, coordinated to the moving lips, and classical music in the background. The viewer presumes that that voice originates from those lips; the acoustic properties (discussed later) of the voice help characterize Maggie and her attitude toward Joel: slightly flirtatious, inquisitive, probing. Classical music plays in the background, signifying a certain romantic potential in this context. In this simple example, sound supports and heightens the impact of the image.

One of the most blunt ways in which television sound underscores the image and directly attempts to affect viewer response is the **laugh track**. The laugh track fabricates an audience and inveigles the viewer into responding as the ersatz audience is responding. Television is one of the few, if not the only, media that includes its implied audience response within texts themselves. And, in this case, sound is the vehicle by which this response is presented.

Sound does not always reinforce the image, however. Contrasting sound-image would be exemplified if, in the scene between Joel and Maggie above, Joel's voice accompanied the image of Maggie's moving lips, or funereal music were played over the flirtatious dialogue. Obviously this stark contradiction between sound and image occurs infrequently on television. When sound does contrast with image it's normally to make some sort of narrative or editorial point. For example, obvious political commentary was made by contrasting the image of

President Clinton hugging a beret-wearing Monica Lewinsky (during a White House lawn party in 1996) with the audio of his angry declaration: "I want to say one thing to the American people. I did not have sexual relations with that woman."

The sound-image relationship need not simply be one of either support or contrast. Often sound emphasizes part of the image while negating or de-emphasizing other parts. In Fig. 8.1, the first shot in a scene from *The Wonder Years*, Haley sits in a high school cafeteria, eating lunch. In the background are the program's central figure, Kevin, and two friends of his. Sound is used in this shot to draw our attention from her to Kevin's table at the back of the image, as we hear what they say about her. Although Kevin and the others are in the background, their voices are louder than the ambient sound. It might seem strange, but Haley does not hear their voices even though we do and we are closer to her than we are to them. That is, if we were standing where the camera was positioned then we could hear Kevin only if Haley could, too. (See the following discussion of sound perspective.) Even though this use of sound is implausible it would likely not be noticed by most viewers. Why? Because this use of sound fits the narrative logic of the scene; it helps to tell the story of Haley's interaction with Kevin and his friends.

One could imagine other uses of sound in Fig. 8.1. The wall clock's ticking might be heard above everything else, suggesting the rushed nature of high school lunches. The sound of Haley eating might dominate the soundtrack, signifying that she is a glutton. Or, in contrast, an eerie foreboding could be represented by the lunchroom being totally, unnaturally silent. If the soundtrack were filled with sounds of wind howling and hail pelting the ground (off camera) it would direct our attention in another fashion, and spark other meanings: nice weather for werewolves. Each of these uses of sound and silence would move the story in a different direction. Each is an example of how, in subtle ways, the viewer's attention and comprehension may be channeled by the sounds accompanying the image.

Maintaining Televisual Flow. The third function sound serves on television is the maintenance of television's pulsion, its forward drive. As is

FIGURE 8.1

discussed in chapter 1, television pulls the viewer along in a flow of segments leading from one to the next. Sound plays a major role in this segment-to-segment flow.

Audio transitions between scenes parallel the visual transitions described in chapter 7. One may **fade out** or **fade in** sound just as one may fade out/in image—although the two fades are often not quite simultaneous. Image frequently fades out just a bit earlier than sound. Additionally, the sound equivalent of a dissolve is the **cross-fade**, in which one sound fades out while the other fades in and the two overlap briefly. Another term for the transition from one sound to another—especially one song to another in music video presentations—is **segue** (pronounced "seg-way"), which may be a cross-fade or a fade out/in.

There are several ways in which sound aids televisual flow, working to keep the viewer watching. First, the speech of television announcers and the dialogue of characters are frequently used to pose questions and enigmas in order to lure the viewer into staying around to see what happens next. Station promotional announcements promise uncommon sights to come, and narrative dialogue frames questions that the viewer may hope to see answered. In either case, speech plays on our curiosity to pull us into the television flow.

But speech is not the only sound device that pulls the viewer into the flow. Music is another common hook. Within programs it is especially common that the music does not end at the same time as the scene. Rather, the music continues—if only for just a few seconds. This continuity of music helps to soften the disruption inherent in the transition from one scene to the next. It is seldom used, however, between one program and the next. Here it is more important for television to differentiate slightly between the shows, to signal that one show is ending but that another follows immediately.

Audience applause is one final aspect of sound that plays an important role in television transitions. Applause is commonly used as the marker of the end or beginning of a segment. However, in contrast to its traditional meaning as a sign of audience respect or appreciation or enjoyment, television applause more often simply means: "This is the beginning" or "This is the end." As everyone knows, studio audiences of sitcoms and talk shows are *told* when to applaud. Moreover, if the actual audience does not provide enough applause the sound editor can easily add more, in a process often called **sweetening**. This is particularly important toward the end of sitcoms' taping/filming sessions when, commonly, much of the audience has become bored and left the studio and, thus, the level of real applause is diminished. Also, sitcoms usually splice together alternative takes of scenes. Artificial applause and laughter help to conceal the transition between the shots.

Maintaining Continuity Within Scenes. A fourth and final function of sound is its use within each individual scene to help construct the continuity of space and time. As explained in chapter 7, each television scene is made up of a variety of shots that are strung together according to the continuity editing system. The main purpose of this continuity system is to smooth over the potential disruptions that are caused by cutting from one shot to another. In this way the space and time of a particular setting and scene are made to appear continuous, even though they may have been recorded out of order. Dialogue, music, and ambient sound all play parts in maintaining this continuity.

Dialogue scenes, especially in the single-camera mode of production, are edited so that the cuts do not coincide with vocal pauses or the ends of sentences. (This is less true in live-on-tape productions that are switched much more approximately.) Instead, the dialogue usually continues across a cut, helping to ease the transition from one shot to the next. In the scene from the single-camera production *Northern Exposure* analyzed in chapter 7 (see Figs. 7.7–7.29), most cuts come in the midst of a phrase—creating, in a sense, a verbal match-on-action as the words continue across the cut. The phrasing serves as the glue holding the cut together.

Similarly, music and ambient sound unify the shots. The forward movement of a melody helps to propel the story onward. The temporal continuum of the music, its ability to flow through time, overrides the discontinuous time of the editing. Music helps to draw the viewer's attention from jump cuts, continuity errors, or other disruptions in the visuals. Ambient sound serves the same function, though even less noticeably. Ambient sound signifies a specific space and time to the viewer. A particular room, for example, has a particular sound associated with it at a particular time. Even slight shifts in that ambient sound can disrupt the viewer by making it appear that the space and/or time has changed. This is why sound technicians will record ambient or wild sound to lay down over shots that were originally done silent, or to make consistent the sound behind dialogue that was shot at different times or locations. Consistent background sound, in a sense, certifies that the action took place in the same location at the same time, even though the shots are from different angles and may have been taken hours or days or weeks apart.

Laugh tracks also function in the background to underscore the continuity of a scene. For example, *The Andy Griffith Show* (1960–68), an unusual, *single-camera* sitcom, incorporated a laugh track even though there was no studio audience. In each episode, the laughter continues across the cuts within a scene and thereby diminishes their disruptive potential. Viewers, in theory, don't notice the cut because they are too busy laughing along with the laugh track. In addition, multiple-camera programs such as *Rowan & Martin's Laugh-In* (1968–1973) are videotaped in short segments, with a laugh track tying all the segments together in post-production.

ACOUSTIC PROPERTIES AND SOUND TECHNOLOGY

Sound on television appears deceptively simple. This is largely due to the fact that the sounds emanating from the TV speaker closely resemble the sounds that surround us in our everyday lives—unlike television's two-dimensional images, which are fundamentally dissimilar from our visual experience of the three-dimensional world. A person's voice on TV is not that different from a person's voice coming from someone sharing the living room with you. A person's image on TV is flat and two-dimensional compared to your 3D viewing companion. The aesthetic techniques and digital/mechanical technology that are used to create sound are much less intrusive than are those used to create image. It sometimes seems as if television sound were merely an exact copy of the sounds of reality. This makes television's manipulation of sound even more difficult to detect than its manipulation of image. One aim of this chapter is to alert the reader to the ways that the makers of television shape our perception and our understanding by controlling acoustic properties and sound technology.

General Acoustic Properties

Even though we are mostly concerned here with the differences between television sound and real-life sound, it would be foolish to presume that there are not rudimentary similarities between the two. Any television sound shares three basic characteristics with the sounds we hear in reality:

1. **Loudness**, or **volume**
2. **Pitch**
3. **Timbre** (pronounced "tam-burr"), or **tone**

Loudness. How loud or soft a sound is plays an obvious role in our perception of it. The more amplified a sound is, the greater its impact. Loudness is used for more than just emphasis in television, however. It can also, among other things, signify distance. The louder a sound is, the closer we assume the person or thing causing the sound must be. Further, the variation of loudness can be used for different effects. A sudden loud noise after a quiet segment, needless to say, causes shock or surprise. In contrast, soft sounds after a loud segment can force viewers to focus their attention in order to hear what's going on.

Pitch. Pitch is how high or low a sound is. On television, pitch is especially important to the meanings that voices convey (see chapter 3). For example, higher pitched voices carry conventionalized connotations of femininity, and lower pitches of masculinity. Pitch is significant to the impact of television music as well as its speech. In narrative scenes, higher notes are often used to accompany suspenseful situations, while lower notes can imply an ominous presence. These examples should not be taken proscriptively (high notes don't *always* mean suspense), but they do indicate how television conventionalizes pitch to signify meanings and establish atmosphere. As with all stylistic conventions, the meanings associated with pitch shift over time and from culture to culture.

Timbre. Timbre is a term borrowed from music theory. It signifies the particular harmonic mix that gives a note its "color" or tonal quality. A violin has a different tone than a cello even when they play the same note. A saxophone's tone can be distinguished from a piano's.

The human voice also has timbre, and that tonal quality can be used by actors and directors to convey meaning. A nasal timbre can make a character into an annoying toady. A throaty timbre in a woman can signify a certain androgynous sexuality. In particular contexts, timbre communicates particular meanings.

TV-Specific Acoustic Properties

The sounds that the viewer hears on television are altered as they journey from sound stage to living room. The technology of various audio machines affects those sounds and provides the sound technicians with opportunities to manipulate volume, pitch, and timbre. Their use of this technology is guided by aesthetic conventions, by "rules" regulating the function of sound on television.

Digital Versus Analog. Before **digital** technology changed our concept of sound recording in the 1980s, audio and video tapes were based on **analog** principles. The presence of analog sound (and image, too) is rapidly decreasing in the consumer marketplace. However, it is still important to understand how analog recording works and how digital recording differs from it because the remnants of analog technology will be with us for some time to come.

First, let's consider the basic difference between all analog or digital phenomena. Anything labeled "digital" is rooted in digits or, put more simply, in numbers. An analog replica of something, in contrast, is a model that reproduces that thing in a different form from the original. The concept is a slippery one, but may become clearer if we consider the differences between analog and digital representations of temperature. An analog thermometer is one in which the mercury appears as a line within a tube. When the line gets up to a certain area it signifies "warm," when it goes farther, it signifies "hot." There are numbers calibrating the heat, but they aren't entirely necessary because the length of the line represents, in analog fashion, the amount of heat. The line's length is, in a sense, a model of the amount of heat. When it's long, it's hot. A digital thermometer, one that just displays numbers (e.g., 32 degrees), converts the amount of heat into digits. It doesn't tell us "warm" or "hot" or show us a model of the heat; it only gives us numbers. Further, as you can see in this example, all digital information is packaged in discrete units (e.g., a single degree), while analog models are unbroken continua (e.g., the continuous length of a mercury line in a tube).

Now, let's apply this principal to sound recording. Analog sound technology creates replicas of sound waves on audio tape (or, earlier, on vinyl records and wax cylinders). That is, the sound wave is converted into an electronic replica that is recorded on a piece of **magnetic tape**—a ribbon of plastic with a coating on it that is sensitive to magnetic impulses created by electricity. These magnetic impulses are modulated on the tape in a fashion that parallels the sound wave's modulation.

In contrast to analog recording, digital technology transforms the sound wave into numbers. The process is called **sampling**, but it's not the same as the rap-music sampling mentioned above. Digital recording takes a tiny snippet from a sound—a fraction of a second—and measures the characteristics of the sound at that very instant. The characteristics of this sample are then converted into a set of binary numbers—just strings of zeros and ones—and recorded on magnetic tape or a hard drive (i.e., a magnetic disk). Thousands of samples are taken each second and then combined to create a digital representation of the sound. Much like our digital thermometer, this digital recording contains no information other than groups of digits—lots and lots of zeros and ones.

That, then, is the difference between analog and digital recording. But what is the significance of digital recording to television sound as it is played back in our living rooms?

Currently, the sound technology in our television sets is analog, but this is quickly changing. For the home user, the digital audio revolution began in the 1980s with compact discs (CDs), which are little more than a collection of numbers that have been pressed into aluminum (or occasionally gold) and coated with plastic. DVDs, which debuted commercially in 1997, use a similar process to marry digital sound to a digital image. By 2006, the FCC has required that U.S. broadcasters completely phase in **digital television** (**DTV**) and other countries are taking similar initiatives to launch DTV. At that point, most sounds emanating from our stereos and TVs will be fully digital—excepting those old audio/video cassettes and vinyl LPs with which we refuse to part!

What does the difference between analog and digital really mean to the listener? If you compare the sound of a digital recording with that of a comparable analog one you'll notice three aspects of the digital recording: (1) less background noise (hiss and the like caused by analog recording), (2) a larger **dynamic range** (reproducing softer sounds without noise obscuring them and louder sounds without distortion), and (3) a greater **frequency response** (reproducing a wider range of low-to-high tones). Today's analog TVs lose much of these digital advantages, because the digitally recorded sound is still passing through analog technology. A certain additional amount of noise is added in the broadcast process as well. Consequently, much of the value of digital sound quality is lost on analog TV. DTV, in contrast, will not degrade the quality of the digitally recorded original sound—unless the DTV signal has been severely compressed.

Perhaps more significant than the digital recording process and its high quality are the abilities of digital technology to both process existing sounds and manufacture new sounds. A broad variety of sound effects are now achieved using DAWs (digital audio workstations), which may significantly alter the volume, pitch, and timbre of any recorded sound. There is virtually no way for the viewer to be able to tell when this sort of subtle manipulation has taken place. It is equally difficult to discern when sound, especially music, has been fabricated digitally. This manufactured music has become popular in live-on-tape productions where a variety of music is needed, particularly for narrative programs such as soap operas.

Just about any type of instrumentation—from lush orchestral sounds to jazz and rock quartets—can be digitally created, instantaneously and inexpensively. This has greatly changed the musical sound of many genres. Productions that previously could not afford a full orchestra may now synthesize that sound cheaply. Soap operas, for instance, always used to be accompanied by a lone organ. That organ sound was so identified with the genre that it was a prominent part of soap opera parodies such as "As the Stomach Turns" on *The Carol Burnett Show* (1967–79). Nowadays, however, the soaps have a wide-ranging variety of music, much of which is synthesized digitally. Economics and technology have worked to change television's aesthetics.

Sound Perspective and Directionality. The position of a microphone, like the position of a camera, sets up a relationship between the recording device and the person or object creating the sound. The point of view that this relationship implies is its sound perspective. Mike placement and the division of sound into stereo channels permit the manipulation of sound perspective—thus influencing the viewer's understanding of a scene. If a mike is placed close to someone's lips, then the sound recorded will be an intimate, "close-up" perspective. And if the mike is positioned far away, then the sound perspective will be distant, similar to a long shot. In a sense, then, mike position "frames" the sound for viewers, signaling to them how "close" they are to the sound-producing person or object.

In terms of distance from the mike to the recorded object or person, there are four conventional positions:

1. Overhead boom (which can also be beneath the actors)

2. Lavaliere

3. Hand-held

4. Close-miking

These positions incorporate different types of microphone technology based largely on the direction in which the mike is capable of picking up sound. That is, some mikes pick up sound from all directions *equally* and are thus **omnidirectional** (Fig. 8.2). Other mikes are more sensitive to sound coming from certain directions. These **unidirectional** mikes usually have somewhat heart-shaped pickup patterns, which have come to be labeled **cardioid** and **hypercardioid** (Fig. 8.2). A cardioid mike's pickup pattern looks like an inverted heart, with most of its sensitivity aimed toward the front. Similarly, hypercardioid mikes emphasize sound from the front, but they also allow sound from the rear to be recorded as well. The aesthetics of microphone positioning works with the technology of microphone directionality to determine how sound is picked up.

The overhead boom mike is held on a long arm that enables the **boom operator** to position it above the actors' heads, just out of the view of the camera. (It may also be placed below the camera frame.) It uses a hypercardioid, **shotgun** mike so that the operator may aim it directly at a specific person and minimize the surrounding ambient sound. Since the mike is 3 or 4 feet away from the actors' mouths, the sound perspective is roughly equivalent to the sound one hears when standing near a group of people and engaging in conversation. Boom miking helps position the viewer vis-a-vis the characters or performers.

FIGURE 8.2

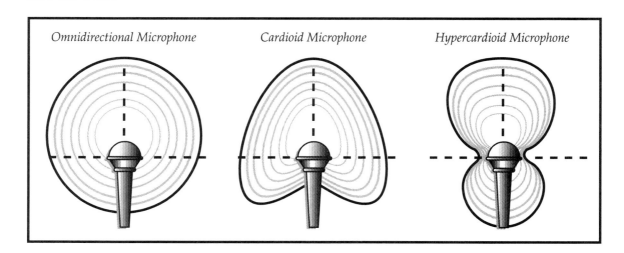

Omnidirectional Microphone   *Cardioid Microphone*   *Hypercardioid Microphone*

This particular position implies an objective point of view, of being slightly distanced from the characters—or, at least, of not hearing subjectively through a character's mind.

The boom mike position has become the conventionalized norm for most narrative programs, whether using single-camera or multiple-camera mode of production. Moreover, it is the principal way that multiple-camera sitcoms and soap operas are recorded. They are videotaped/filmed straight through and consequently the mikes must record several persons from one mike position. Thus the economic imperative of shooting these programs live-on-tape results in the technological necessity to use boom mikes, causing the aesthetic consequence of a certain "objective" sound perspective.

The omnidirectional **lavaliere mike** is attached to actors' chests, clipped to their clothing under which the microphone wire is concealed. Lavaliere miking is the norm for news broadcasters in the studio, though not for those out in the field who use a more directional mike to filter competing, incidental sounds. Although closer than boom miking, the lavaliere mike is still 1 or 2 feet from the broadcaster's mouth. The sound that it picks up is the audio equivalent to the medium close-up and close-up perspective that typify framing in contemporary news practice.

The **hand-held mike** sounds much like the lavaliere mike because it is also positioned around chest high, although it may also be held higher than that. Hand-held mikes are used in news and sports field production (e.g., in interviews with athletes) and in talk shows. These cardioid or hypercardioid mikes yield a sound perspective quite similar to the lavaliere mike, but, because they are directional microphones, the pickup may be aimed in one direction or another.

Hand-held mikes are never utilized in narrative programs. Unlike boom and lavaliere mikes, the hand-held mike is both visible and obvious to the viewer (the lavaliere mike is so small it can be overlooked or mistaken for a broach or a tie-clip). To use it in narrative programs would make evident the technology involved in creating television; it would be like having a camera appear on-screen. This violates conventions of repressing television devices in narrative programs; to see a mike would make the viewer conscious of the whole production apparatus, which is taboo unless you are avant-garde playwright Bertolt Brecht or comedian Garry Shandling (in *It's Garry Shandling's Show* [1988–90] and *The Larry Sanders Show* [1992–98]).

In news reporting, the hand-held mike is sometimes wielded like a club, intruding into the personal space of interviewees whether or not they wish to be spoken to. Thus, the hand-held mike has come to signify broadcast journalism in certain contexts. Occasionally, it means overly aggressive reporting.

In **close-miking**, the mike is positioned right next to a person's mouth—the "extreme close-up" of miking. This is how radio announcers are miked and it is also how television announcers—the ones that read promotional announcements and advertisements—are miked. Moreover, it is the miking technique used to record singers in a sound studio. This type of miking creates sound that has a full, rich timbre, a wide frequence response (often emphasizing bass pitch for male studio announcers), and very little ambient noise. Viewers have come to expect the close-miked sound in television announcements and music videos. For these elements of television, close-miking is the norm. However, close-miking can also prove to be disruptive when used in narrative programs. Dubbing and other ADR in narrative programs are often recorded in close-miking. This can clash with the viewer's expectations for the sound perspective created with boom-miking. To cut from a boom-miked piece of dialogue to one that is close-miked makes it sound as if the characters were suddenly right on top of you. To avoid this, sound technicians position the mike away from the ADR actors.

Sound perspective is not limited to a sense of closeness, of near or far. The widespread acceptance of stereo-TV sets and programs in the 1990s afforded sound editors with another tool for representing perspective. By altering the relative loudness of sounds in the right and left channels, they give us a sense of the lateral (i.e., sideways) position of a person or object. For example, a gun appears on the right side of the frame and when it is fired, the gunshot principally emanates from the right-hand speaker. This sound cue confirms our spatial sense of the position of the gun.

Sound mixing in theatrical films, DVDs, and DTV has seen the number of channels multiply in recent years. Dolby Digital, for instance, was introduced in film theaters in 1992 and DTV in 1998. It boasts 5.1 channels. The Dolby Web site explains their arrangement:

> Dolby Digital programs can deliver surround sound with five discrete full-range channels—left, center, right, left surround, and right surround—plus a sixth channel for those powerful low-frequency effects (LFE) that are felt more than heard in movie theaters. As it needs only about one-tenth the bandwidth of the others, the LFE channel is referred to as a '.1' channel (and sometimes erroneously as the "subwoofer" channel).[1]

Thus, Dolby Digital 5.1 is actually created with six speakers. Four speakers for the left, right, center, and LFE channels are in front of the viewer. The two so-called "surround" channels emanate from speakers placed *behind* the viewer. By literally surrounding viewers with six speakers, Dolby Digital creates a sound space in which sounds may come from behind and in front, and to the left and right—unlike the sound in original monaural TVs that only came from a single point in front of the viewer.

Dolby Digital and other multi-channel sound systems greatly enhance the potential for sound-perspective manipulation on TV, but the placement of sounds in particular channels is not without its "rules" and conventions. Almost all dialogue is placed in the center channel—even if actors are positioned to the far left or right of the frame. Left/right channels are reserved for music and sound effects only. The rear left/right ("surround") and the LFE channels contain only sound effects, no dialogue or music. Aside from the LFE channel, there is no technical reason for this assignment of channels to certain types of sound. Thus, the seemingly endless variety of sound perspective is constrained by aesthetic convention—with sound again being largely divided into speech, music, and effects.

To this point, we have suggested ways in which sound perspective may be roughly equivalent to image perspective. But directors and sound editors, especially in narrative programs, need not rely on that equivalence. Indeed, they may try to subvert it for specific narrative effect. In the scene from *The Wonder Years* discussed above (Fig. 8.1), for instance, Kevin is shown in the background in long shot, too far away for the viewer to hear, but his voice is presented at "normal," boom-miked level. Sound perspective contrasts with image perspective in order to achieve a specific narrative effect—in this case, Kevin's opinion of Haley is presented without her knowledge of it. This is a major plot point in the narrative. Only later in the episode will she learn of his and his friends' opinions of her.

SPACE, TIME, AND NARRATIVE

Much of what we hear on TV comes from a source that we can see on TV at the very same time. In other words, much TV sound originates in onscreen space and is synchronized with the time of the image. But this is not true of all sound on television. What, then, is the relationship of a sound to the space and the time of the image that it accompanies? And if it does not match them, then what effect does that disjuncture cause?

Sound and Space. In chapter 6 we discussed how the aesthetic/technological fact of the camera frame can be used by the director and videographer/cinematographer to achieve a variety of framing effects. The frame is also important to our consideration of sound. It forms the division between offscreen space and onscreen space, between what is within the frame and what is presumed to be outside it. Often the source of a sound will be situated offscreen. This is quite common in non-narrative, live-on-tape productions when a voice is heard from an actor who is not currently onscreen—for example, Paul Shaffer's chortle following one of David Letterman's jokes. And, of course, the laughter and applause of the studio audience normally comes from offscreen, too.

Our commonsensical understanding of offscreen space is also used in narrative programs. A voice or sound from offscreen helps to create the illusion that life is going on all around the characters that we see onscreen. Offscreen space thus aids the construction of the continuity of space—that is, the sense that the onscreen space *continues* out beyond the camera frame. This can be as simple as the sound of traffic inserted in the background of a scene in an apartment, or it can involve the more complicated manipulation of sounds and framing that create the illusion of a killer following a victim in a shadowy alley. In short, sound draws the viewer's mind out past the frame into a fictional world that has been created for this narrative.

Sound and Time. The time of a sound, in relation to the image it accompanies, can be:

1. Earlier than the image.

2. Simultaneous with the image.

3. Later than the image.

Obviously, the vast majority of sound falls into the second category, but there are also many instances of sound being displaced from the time of the image.

In a sound flashback we hear speech, music, or sound effects from an earlier time than the image currently on the screen. This occurs frequently in narrative programs. A boy, for example, may be trying to make up his mind about whether or not to shoplift. As we see his face in close up we might hear repeated the words of his mother about being honest. Those words come from a much earlier time in the story. The reverse—that is, sound later than the image—can also occur. When a sound flash-forward is used, the viewer hears sound from a future part of the story. The time frame of a sound is similarly displaced when a character's voice in the "present" speaks over images of the past, as in *The Wonder Years* when we see an image from the 1970s and hear the voice of Kevin in the 1990s commenting on it.

Diegetic and Nondiegetic Sound. Recall that "diegesis" has been used in TV/film studies to refer to the story itself, the narrative action. The physical world in which this narrative action takes place is the **diegetic space**. In *Seinfeld* (1990–98), for example, this would be Jerry's apartment and the New York City locations the characters frequent (e.g., Monk's Cafe). Diegetic sound, then, consists of speech, music, and sound effects whose source is in the world of the story: the dialogue of Jerry, Elaine, George, and Kramer; the noises and ambient sound in the apartment; and so on.

Diegetic sound may be either **objective** or **subjective**. Objective diegetic sound originates in the external world of the narrative and would include, for example, Jerry and George's conversations. Subjective diegetic sound comes from inside a character's head and cannot be heard by other characters at the same location. When characters' voiceovers are used to signify their thoughts, then diegetic sound is being used subjectively. One strange example of this is *Hennesy* (1959–62), in which the thoughts of a dog are frequently presented in voiceover.

Not all of the sound on narrative TV programs, however, originates in the diegesis. Most notably, this **nondiegetic sound** includes the so-called "mood" music that accompanies each scene. The viewer hears it, but the characters do not because it is not part of their world. They also do not hear the narration of an omniscient announcer (one who is not a character). Nondiegetic music and narration are commonly used to guide the viewer's perception of the narrative.

SUMMARY

The importance of sound to television is easy to overlook, because it is often difficult to detect how sound has been manipulated by the makers of television programs. When watching television, however, it is important to recognize how the different types of sound (speech, music, and sound effects), have been molded in order to achieve particular purposes. As always, these manipulations, these purposes, are ruled by television's aesthetics, economics, and technology.

The essential function of sound on TV is to hail the viewer to watch TV. This purpose cannot be overstated. The producers of commercials have long understood the significance of sound in capturing viewer interest. Once we have been hooked, sound channels our perception of an image by either reinforcing the meaning of that image or directing us toward select elements of the image. In less common instances, it may subvert what the image seems to be saying.

Sound also functions to propel television forward. Within individual scenes, the illusion of continuity is preserved through the mix of music, speech, and sound effects. Sound, thus, becomes an integral part of the continuity system. On a larger scale, sound also helps maintain the flow between one televisual segment and the next. Speech is especially significant in its construction of enigmas to pull the viewer into the televisual current.

Sound on television is in some ways identical to the sounds of life. In both, sound may be characterized in terms of its volume, pitch, and timbre, but it would be wrong to assume that TV sound is not manipulated in its transition from historical world to TV speaker. Digital and analog technologies present sound editors with a broad audial palette from which to choose. They may orchestrate pre-existing sounds or even create them, synthesize them, from scratch. One of the simplest components of sound technology is the positioning of the microphone and the effect that this has on sound perspective. Different types of microphone technology, in different locations, give the viewer an audial point-of-view from which to hear the action.

Most of the sound we hear on television is synchronized with the space and time of the images we are watching, but it need not always be so. Sounds can be offscreen as easily as they are onscreen. Offscreen sound draws the viewer out beyond the frame, further constructing spatial continuity. And the time of a sound may be displaced from that of the image. Sound of an earlier or later time can be laid over an image to various effect.

Thus television sound, which so often appears to be the "simple" recording of life's speech, music, and sound effects, is actually another manipulated and/or fabricated component of the television medium.

FURTHER READINGS

Sound style is discussed in many of the readings suggested at the end of chapter 5.

The critical study of television sound is just beginning. Rick Altman, "Television/Sound," in *Studies in Entertainment: Critical Approaches to Mass Culture*, ed. Tania Modleski (Bloomington: Indiana University Press, 1986), 39–54 builds on his work on sound in the neighboring medium of the cinema. Stephen Heath and Gillian Skirrow, "Television: A World in Action," *Screen* 18, no. 2 (Summer 1977): 7–59 is not wholly devoted to sound, but it does make some keen observations on the sound-image relationship. Also important for their considerations of sound's significance are the previously cited John Ellis, *Visible Fictions* and Herbert Zettl, *Sight Sound Motion*.

The principal essays on cinema sound are collected in Elisabeth Weis and John Belton, *Film Sound: Theory and Practice* (New York: Columbia University Press, 1985) and two journal issues on the topic: *Yale French Studies* 60 (1980) and *Screen* 25, no. 3 (May–June 1984).

ENDNOTES

[1] "Frequently Asked Questions about Dolby Digital in the Home," *Dolby Laboratories, Inc.* 2000, http://www.dolby.co.uk/tech/l.br.0007.FullDDFAQ.html.

CHAPTER 9

A History of Television Style

GARY A. COPELAND

Radio comedian Fred Allen once observed, "Imitation is the sincerest form of television." Allen never made the successful transition to television, so his remark may have been seen as sour grapes. But, as with many jokes, the humor in the statement comes from its ring of truth. Television has borrowed its visual and aural style from other entertainment forms. Where necessary, it co-opted and transformed these other media to produce the look and sound of the television we see.

Television did not develop a style in isolation from other entertainment traditions. Just as television networks borrowed many of their early programs from parent radio networks, TV also borrowed its style from such diverse entertainment forms as movies, theater, and vaudeville. Each of these contributed in some fashion to television style, but motion pictures and radio—the media most closely associated with television—provided its strongest influences.

The lifting of stylistic elements from the various forms of entertainment was often a matter of technological, economic, or aesthetic requirements. Each of these areas was important in the selection of elements from the precursors of television, and each has continued to influence the evolution of television style.

It is difficult to talk about one element—technology, economics, or aesthetics—without also discussing the other two. For example, original 60- and 90-minute live dramas were weekly staples of television in the 1950s. Such TV plays as *Requiem for a Heavyweight*, *Twelve Angry Men*, and *Days of Wine and Roses*, which were later made into movies, were telecast live. They were broadcast in this format for reasons that were technological (videotape was not in use at the time), economic (to film the plays would have been prohibitively expensive), and aesthetic (many of the actors and crew members came from Broadway productions and brought to television some methods and goals of the New York theater).

This chapter explores how style has changed in television and discusses the influence of these three key elements on style, mainly in narrative television. Non-narrative televisual forms have their own important stylistic histories, but they are so varied and wide-ranging that they extend beyond the scope of this chapter. Elements of non-narrative television style enter the discussion, however, when they pertain to the stylistics of narrative television under examination.

TECHNOLOGICAL MANIFEST DESTINY

When we think of changes in television style, the first that come to mind are usually technological: color, stereo sound, computer-generated imagery (CGI), high-definition television (HDTV). According to such a view, technology drives change. There is a sense of a manifest destiny within technological developments—a technological determinism. New breakthroughs, it is presumed, will instantly be adopted by the industry and accepted by the public.

This view is, at best, only occasionally correct. For a technology to become accepted it must find an acceptance among consumers/audiences and producers/directors. In fact, technological changes occur only within economic constraints and according to aesthetic convention, which translates into consumer acceptance.

You may have experienced the fallacy of the technological determinism argument yourself. If you are the owner of a Divx player, you have experienced how new technologies may not survive. Assuming that you are one of the lucky ones who didn't purchase a Divx player from a Circuit City or a Good Guys store, let us explain. Divx was designed as a rentable DVD system and was aggressively marketed during the 1990s. The Divx player was about $200 more than the cost of a low-end DVD player. The Divx player plugged into the owner's telephone line so that information about playing the Divx software and subsequent billing could be made to the owner's credit card. (The Divx name may be confusing because these Divx disc players are not related to the DivX video compression format—also known as MPEG-4.)

The owner of a Divx player could purchase movies or other programming on a Divx disc for about $4.50. However, the disc was viewable for only 48 hours from the time that it was originally played. (It could be watched as many times as one wanted in that 48 hours.) Once that 48 hours was up it was necessary to pay again for any additional viewing. These additional views cost about $3.50 for another 48 hours or, for a much larger fee, one could purchase unlimited viewing.

The system was sold based on certain advantages—primarily over the rental of videotapes or DVDs from video stores. The *audio and video qualities* of Divx were superior to videotape, though it was not better than DVD as Divx used the DVD format for its discs. It provided *freedom* from late fees and returning tapes or DVDs to the video store as one purchased the Divx medium. It also claimed *flexibility* of when to view the purchased Divx medium. The 48-hour viewing period began when the viewer first pushed the play button. Actually, the flexibility advantage is just a redressing of the freedom advantage since it has to do with problems of rental periods. *Availability* of new releases was one of the suggested advantages. Stores would stock the number of Divx copies that the store believed could be sold versus a video rental store with a set number of copies available. *Convenience* was promoted through the ability to build a home library of Divx and only pay about $3.25 to watch the programming again.

If you have one of these devices, you know that the system ceased operation in 1999. Training materials suggested sales people answer skeptical customers' questions about the viability of the system with an answer of "It's almost impossible to believe that Divx could go under. Divx is supported by major studios like Disney, Universal, Fox, Dream Works, Paramount and MGM." But the purported reason for Divx's demise—according to the company that created the system, Digital Video Express, LP—was that the company was unable to get sufficient commitments from the movie studios for content and other manufacturers declined to produce the Divx hardware. The economic model for such a format was not right even though the technology was available and its aesthetic qualities were superior (to videotape).

There are many such technological innovations that are introduced but are not viable. Sometimes, nonviable technology will reappear when it is repositioned in the market or a new, desirable use can be found. In other words, when the technology can be shown to be economically viable in a new configuration and at a new time it may resurrect itself.

The early 1970s saw the introduction of quadraphonic sound. Rather than the two speakers of stereo this system—as the name implies—had four speakers. In addition to front left and right speakers, the quadraphonic audio system also included left and right rear speakers. Quadraphonic records were produced though not in the numbers that stereo records were. One of quadraphonic's problems was that there were five competing noncompatible systems—CBS's SQ, Sansui's QS, UHJ's Ambisonic, Electro-Voice's EV Stereo-4, and CD4's Quadradisc. Consumers were concerned that if they purchased the wrong system, they might get stuck with a very expensive stereo with a couple of extra speakers. Another problem was that unless one wanted to hear the Black Watch play bagpipes and sound as if they were marching about in your room, it wasn't seen as a very practical system. Most people expected musical performances to take place in front of them rather than sitting in the center of the music. Was there really an advantage to seemingly be sitting in the middle of the Atlanta Tuba Quartet as they played John Philip Sousa's "Stars and Stripes Forever"?

Quadraphonic systems lasted for a few years before record companies stopped making quad records. The systems were dropped—but the concept was not forgotten.

Home theatres now use the old quadraphonic idea but call it Surround Sound (also known by trademarked names such as Dolby Digital 5.1 and Dolby Surround Pro Logic). The growth of Surround Sound was encouraged by the introduction of the DVD (1997) and the marketing of the "Home Theater" concept. This time the technology, aesthetics, and economics are aligned. Technologically, the DVD facilitates additional, high-quality sound channels because it easily accommodates more electronic information than a VHS videotape does. And Surround Sound systems also don't suffer from the incompatibility problem. The Surround Sound signal, unlike its Quadraphonic progenitor, is encoded so that it is compatible with systems that are only two-channel stereo or—dare we mention it—one-channel monaural. There is also aesthetic justification for Surround Sound from motion pictures with sound tracks that emanate from speakers on the sides and in the rear of movie theaters. Cinephiles want TV equipment that allows them to experience the movie just as they do in theaters—sound from the sides or the rear—in their homes. Economics also steps in to make the system viable. As the cost of the equipment continually reduces, a greater number of people are purchasing Surround Sound systems. The amount of programming available for Surround Sound, and the number of releases and broadcasts that contain Surround Sound information also continues to increase.

These examples illustrate that technological determinism, or a manifest destiny driven only by technological improvements, grossly oversimplifies the process of change in the media. In addition to knowledge and the ability to build a device, there must be a supportive economic climate, an aesthetic motivation, and consumer interest for such technologies to be meaningful.

The two most obvious components of television are its sights and its sounds. Each has its own stylistic elements, which have evolved at varying rates since television became a viable narrative medium in the mid-1940s. To discuss how style has changed, this chapter is divided into elements of visual style and aural style.

Visual Elements of Television Style

The Birth of Video

The development of an all-electronic television system replaced earlier attempts, which used a combination of mechanical and electronic technologies. A German named Paul Nipkow devised the earliest patented device in 1884. His television system used a rotating disk with holes arranged in a spiral between the outside of the wheel and the hub. A motor turned the wheel and the spinning wheel broke the picture into bits (a process called *scanning*). Light coming through the hole hit a light-sensitive cell, which converted light into electricity. The television set receiving this signal had a similar wheel, which turned in sync with the camera. Nipkow himself never made his device work, but later inventors were able to develop this electro-mechanical system.

Boris Rosing was the first to develop an all-electronic system using the cathode ray tube (CRT). Rosing, a Russian scientist, successfully transmitted an all-electronic picture by 1911. It was a relative of Rosing's CRT system that eventually developed into the electronic television system. The two inventors most responsible for television technology as we know it are Vladimir Zworykin, a Russian émigré and a student of Rosing's, and Philo Farnsworth, an American inventor. Both Zworykin and Farnsworth invented a workable all-electronic television pickup tube—the piece of technology that actually changes light into an electronic video image.

Farnsworth's conceptual design for his "image dissector" was done while still a farm boy. He presented his idea for television to his high school class. It was fortunate for him that he made this presentation, as his school teacher was able to produce notes taken from it to later prove, for patent purposes, that the idea was Farnsworth's before Zworykin's.

The Influence of Radio on Television

The development of television was undertaken primarily by private industry rather than government. Electronics firms that had profited from the development of radio saw television as another potentially large profit center. One key player in the economic development of television was the Radio Corporation of America (RCA), owner of the NBC radio network.

The corporate strategy for television was the same as the one that had worked so successfully for the development of commercial radio. Radio-set manufacturers became the pioneer broadcasters as a means of creating a market for their products. RCA's strategy was to begin broadcasting television signals so there would be a demand for the television sets rolling off the company's assembly lines.

The end of the 1920s found the new medium of television promoted by NBC, CBS, and a California based, West Coast regional radio network, the Don Lee Broadcasting System. The influence of existing radio-set manufacturers, their broadcasting divisions, and existing radio networks in the creation of television had far-reaching impact on the organization, and ultimately the style, of television. From an economic perspective, it was assumed that television, like radio, would be a commercial venture licensed by government but controlled by private enterprise. The configuration of a national broadcasting system designed around commercial networks and their affiliates was hardly questioned, because television was assumed by broadcasters and government to follow radio's pattern of networks and affiliates.

The creative processes, and thus the aesthetics, of television were also heavily influenced by radio. Much of the creative talent for television programming, for instance, came from the networks' radio divisions. This crossover from radio to television ensured that programming on television would be very similar to radio—except with pictures.

In the Beginning: Video

Early experimental television programming was produced exclusively in live video— that is, for immediate transmission. Neither film nor videotape (which was not introduced until the latter half of the 1950s) was used in the programs of the experimental period. The need for bright light to achieve a clear picture, the bulkiness of the camera equipment, and the general vulnerability of the video apparatus required that programs be broadcast almost exclusively from a studio. Thus, the primitive technology and the economic reliance on radio professionals and their specific aesthetic resulted in a visual style delimited by the television studio. In 1931 experimental television programming consisted of such in-studio shows as *Doris Sharp, The Television Crooner* and *Roger Kinney, Baritone,* along with *The Art of Bookbinding.* Television's reliance on live, studio-based programming mirrored how radio was produced.

The importance of programming live rather than recorded telecasts carried over from radio, whose programmers preferred live broadcasts to electrical transcriptions, or recordings on acetate disks. This preference for live over recorded radio programs would even require some programs to be done twice—once for the East Coast and hours later for the West Coast.

Part of the preference for live television programming was technological. The means for cheaply and efficiently recording television programs had not been developed. The **kinescope** process (16mm motion pictures created by filming the program off a television receiver) permitted television programs to be recorded on film, but the images were blurry and of generally lower quality.

Part of the preference for live programming was economic. During the early development in the late 1940s and the beginning of the 1950s, the television audience sizes were small and did not justify large expenditures for programming material. In the beginning the major movie companies were generally leery of "free" television and hoped to develop their own pay television systems. They had no interest in providing what seemed to be a potentially major competitor with programming help.

The influence of live radio on television was generally pervasive, but is most strongly indicated by the early network use of **simulcasts** of such programs as *Arthur Godfrey's Talent Scouts* (1948–58) on CBS, *The Voice of Firestone* (1949–63) on NBC, and DuMont's *The Original Amateur Hour* (1948–60). Simulcasts, which began on the networks in 1948 and continued until the mid-1950s, were regularly scheduled network radio shows simultaneously broadcast both on radio and television. As a result, people with television sets saw the radio program being produced.

Even television stations not connected by cable to the networks provided the aesthetic of live programming, because of the method by which they received program material. These outlying stations were sent 16mm kinescopes by the networks as a means of broadening the program's audience. The distribution of kinescopes to nonwired affiliates served as some protection against the television station changing affiliations when wired access was available. This use of kinescopes of live productions also provided a transition from the live network television presentations to prerecorded (filmed) programming.

One of the earliest network television programs to use films made specifically for television was *Fireside Theatre* (1949–63). First airing in April 1949, the program began as a mixture of live and filmed episodes. By September 1949, however, the program used filmed stories exclusively. A dramatic anthology filmed mostly at the Hal Roach Studios in Southern California, the series featured a different story and usually a different cast each week. *Fireside Theatre* and William Boyd's *Hopalong Cassidy* (1949–51) led the field in bringing film to serial television. Other, smaller, independent producers started producing filmed series for television and were joined by the major Hollywood companies in 1953.

How was the move to film and away from live productions greeted? A 1952 *New York Times* article, titled "A Plea for Live Video," argued:

> The decision of television to put many of its programs on film has turned out to be the colossal boner of the year. On every account—technically and qualitatively—the films cannot compare with "live" shows and they are hurting video, not helping it.[1]

Despite the popularity of the increasing number of filmed network shows, a prejudice against filmed television remained. Notwithstanding this aesthetic preference, the amount of live programming steadily decreased during the 1950s. First film and then videotape were used to record television programs. The television program that did the most to shake television free of the myth of live programming and fix the elements of a television genre to this day concerned a Cuban bandleader and his (supposedly, for the program was produced in black and white) redheaded wife.

I Love Lucy

Programs with a studio audience were always performed live on the networks until 1951. That year, however, a breakthrough show appeared. The show was to have a significance to television that no one at the time could have imagined. One of the most successful television programs—perhaps *the* most successful— in the world, its popularity over 5 decades is not the main reason for its pivotal status. *I Love Lucy* is important because it encapsulated what television would become (Fig. 9.1).

I Love Lucy was the first network TV series shot on film before a studio audience. CBS had wanted the show to be produced live, but Lucille Ball and Desi Arnaz believed that it should be filmed, even though, to help their comic timing, the two actors wanted a studio audience as well. Ball and Arnaz were the producers as well as the stars of the show; they spent $5,000 of their own money to film the pilot episode and subsequent shows. This $5,000 was the additional cost of filming the show before a live audience, and neither the sponsor, Philip Morris, nor the network wanted to spend the extra money for film. Arnaz agreed that he and Ball would pick up the extra cost but in consideration for their expenditure they would own the program. This investment netted Arnaz and Ball millions and created Desilu Studios.

The advantages of filming a television series instead of broadcasting the show live were numerous. First and principally, film facilitated **syndication** of *I Love Lucy* to local stations after the network's license period for showing the programs had expired. Programs that were broadcast live were difficult to reuse

FIGURE 9.1

later. Some live programs, such as the early episodes of "The Honeymooners" on *The Jackie Gleason Show* (1952–59, 1962–70), were recorded on kinescopes, but kinescopes have poor resolution compared to programs originally shot on film. The production on film of *I Love Lucy* meant that any subsequent broadcast of an episode could look as good as the initial network broadcast.

Several film cameras shot the program while the audience watched from bleachers. The cast performed the show as they would a play, running the scenes in the order that they would appear for the home viewer. This was not the first use of multiple cameras to film an event, however. Multiple-film camera techniques had been developed about a half-decade earlier, when Jerry Fairbanks created the multicam system to shoot films for NBC newscasts. The camera technique may not have been new, but using it to record a performance before a studio audience was. Hence, Desi Arnaz has been credited with developing the multiple-camera technique for shooting television programs in front of a live audience.

I Love Lucy introduced the visual style of multiple-camera sitcoms that survives today (see chapter 7 for a full description of multiple-camera production). Lighting is broad and even, to cover all of the actors in a scene. Camera movement is kept to a minimum. Action has to be limited to a restricted number of sets because of the audience. All sets reside on the same stage and should be visible to the audience (though that isn't always so); in most cases, sitcoms recorded before a live audience have one main set, with no more than three additional sets per episode (Fig. 5.6).

In many sitcoms the living room or the kitchen serves as the main set. For example, *I Love Lucy, The Odd Couple* (1970–75), *The Cosby Show* (1984–92), and *Frasier* (1993–) used living rooms as their main sets (see Figs. 5.3–5.5). Main sets can also be a garage, as in *Taxi* (1978–83); a hotel lobby, as in *Newhart* (1982–1990), or even a bar, as in *Cheers* (1982–93). Most of a sitcom's action, which may be quite diverse, takes place on the main set. In *Cheers*, for example, the barroom has served as the site for wedding ceremonies, radio broadcasts, and even Diane's rendition of Shakespeare (Fig. 9.2).

FIGURE 9.2

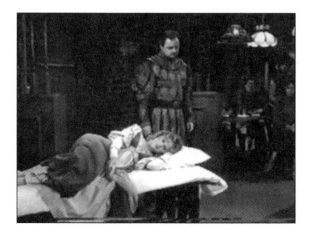

Filming before an audience does introduce some limits on the production, but many comic actors feel that an audience is essential for the success of their performance. *I Love Lucy* is thus further significant for introducing a studio audience to narrative television series. Although studio audiences had commonly been used for radio comedy, in television they had been restricted primarily to variety and game shows. The radio precursors had been produced on a theater-style stage, with a proscenium arch framing the action. By contrast, *I Love Lucy* was shot on a cinema sound stage, with the audience seated in bleachers.

Independent and Major Studios

I Love Lucy was the product of one of the many independent Hollywood production companies established to produce television programs in the absence of the major studios. Desilu was formed by Desi Arnaz and Lucille Ball to produce *I Love Lucy* and other shows. Other contemporary independent producers included Bing Crosby Productions, Flying-A Productions (Roy Rogers's company), General Service Studios, Mark VII (Jack Webb's company), and Ziv, which specialized in syndicated programs. The company that started with *I Love Lucy* lasted about 15 years as a production company and provided shows for all three commercial networks; at the time Paramount bought it, Desilu was turning out episodes of *Star Trek* (1966–69), *Mannix* (1967–75), and *Mission: Impossible* (1966–73) for network broadcast.

Independent producers could make an impact in television in the early 1950s because the major motion picture studios were trying to ignore or impede the progress of television. The motion picture industry feared television would keep people at home rather than buying tickets at motion picture theaters. The fear was well founded; television did affect the attendance at U.S. movie theaters, which declined steadily for years after reaching its all-time high in 1948.

The major motion picture companies continued to ignore television until Walt Disney Studios signed with ABC to produce *Disneyland* in 1954. Disney originally agreed to the deal as a means to promote the new theme park he had carved out of some orange groves in Southern California. The show proved to be immensely popular and profitable for both ABC and Disney. Later, the television network and the movie producer signed an agreement to produce *The Mickey Mouse Club*. After Disney broke the ice, other motion picture production companies began to produce programming for the networks. By 1957 the big Hollywood motion picture corporations were the largest suppliers of television programming in the U.S.

The increasing participation of Hollywood meant a greater volume of production in California and a concomitant reduction in New York City. Approximately two thirds of the network's programming was being shot on film in Hollywood by the late 1950s. The migration to the West Coast continued through the 1960s, and by the beginning of 1970, 90% of television's entertainment programming originated in Los Angeles.

A comparable geographical shift in television production would not occur again until the 1980s, when many independent TV producers began to move their operations to Canada. Stephen J. Cannell, who produced such shows as *21 Jump Street* (1987–90), *Stingray* (1986–87), and *The A Team* (1983–87) found that he could take advantage of reduced production costs and more elastic regulations in Canada. Basing his productions in British Columbia, he found locations that could represent U.S. cities, and established a large production facility in Vancouver.

In the 1980s, such Hollywood majors as Disney and Universal also began to produce television shows in their own newly constructed facilities in Florida. They had moved from California because of cheaper production, fewer state regulations of the television and movie industries, and as a means to use and publicize facilities that doubled as theme parks and tourist attractions.

Such migration from Hollywood, however, has not affected the style of production. Most shows look similar, no matter where they are shot. The look of television programs had been set in the early days of television, when independent producers filmed shows using the single-camera technique that is also used to make theatrical motion pictures.

Television and Single-Camera Technique

The introduction of the Hollywood film companies into the creation of network programming introduced the aesthetic standards and conventions of theatrical film production to television. The standard mode of production in Hollywood was to use a single film camera and utilize a master-scene technique of production: First, shoot the master long shot of the entire scene; next, shoot the medium shots (e.g., two-shots); and finally, shoot the close-ups. Then let the editor put it all together. (See chapter 7 for more on the single-camera mode of production.)

It was not until programs were filmed without an audience that the look of sitcoms changed. The use of a single camera without an audience provided a new freedom to the look of a comedy. A show no longer had to be limited to three or four sets; and exteriors, though more expensive, were as easy to shoot as interiors. To see the difference between multiple-camera, live-audience programs and single-camera productions shot without an audience, compare *Friends* (1994–) as an example of the former and *Malcolm in the Middle* (2000–) as an example of the latter.

Perhaps more important, the use of film opened up a range of genres to producers and audiences. Police dramas were difficult or impossible to produce without using the single-camera system, and such popular police shows as Desilu's *The Untouchables* (1959–63) or Jack Webb's *Dragnet* (1952–59, 1967–70) relied on Hollywood-style film techniques as do current productions such as *N.Y.P.D Blue* (1993–).

Film production had at least one advantage over live video or early videotape in that film could be edited in post-production. The immediate broadcast of live video offered no opportunity to correct either performance or technical flaws. A live production might have at most one or two complex shots, because such shots take relatively long to rehearse and block. Thus, live production necessitated a Spartan visual style.

Film provided creative directors a means to gain greater control of the images and the performance than did live video. A scene might be shot several times until the desired performance is captured on film. The editor would then select the best, the most interesting, or at least the most suitable work of the creative team for the finished program. Through the editing process, film also allowed for a more quickly paced program than was generally possible through a live production. In sum, filmed programs could be more effectively manipulated.

Introduction of Videotape

The first videotape recorder (VTR) available to television stations was introduced in 1956 by the Ampex Corporation, which had established a reputation for manufacturing superior audio recording equipment. (The company name is an acronym of the initials of founder Alexander M. Poniatoff and the first two letters of the word *excellence*.) Fig. 9.3 shows an early working model with the engineering team that designed and built it— including a young Ray Dolby who would later create the Dolby noise reduction system. Ampex started delivering VTR equipment to networks and stations in 1957. Larger and heavier than an upright piano, these machines made it possible to record programs and replay them immediately. Programs that once had to be broadcast live or from film could now be replayed at any time. The quality of the first videotaped images was not as sharp as current pictures, but they were much better than the competing kinescope technology. Image quality quickly improved to the point where viewers could not tell if the show was live or on tape. Videotape significantly changed the appearance of network television for people living in the western regions of North America. Before videotape, television shows broadcast live by the networks to the East were recorded on kinescopes for rebroadcast to the western time zones. Recording live programs from New York on videotape provided the West with images as good as those seen by a live audience. NBC's *Saturday Night*

FIGURE 9.3

Live (1975–) provides a current example of what was being experienced for the first time in the late 1950s. While the program is live for viewers in the Eastern and Central time zones, audiences in Mountain and Pacific zones see a live-on-tape version. Live-on-tape also allows the network to make changes for the replay—such as the deletion of Paul Schaffer's 1980, Charles Rocket's 1981, and Norm McDonald's 1997 accidental use of profanity on *Saturday Night Live*. The expletive was heard in the East and Central time zones but not in the Mountain and Pacific time zones.

There is, however, a difference in appearance between filmed and videotaped images—although the introduction of HDTV threatens to erase that difference. To compare film and videotape, you might find a copy of the television program *Max Headroom* (1987) at a video store; it contains segments originally shot in both media. So did the HBO series *The Larry Sanders Show* (1992–98), for which the talk show sequences were produced on tape, while all the backstage stories were shot on film. A *Monty Python's Flying Circus* (1969–74) episode also provides a good example of the visual difference between film and tape; because of union labor rules everything recorded outside the studio was shot on film, and everything in the studio was shot on tape. One episode includes a brief sketch dealing with the difference, in which one of the Pythons is seen looking out a window from the exterior (film) and from the interior (videotape), and commenting anxiously that the outside is film but the inside is videotape.

Television movies have been almost exclusively shot on film. One major exception is NBC's *Special Bulletin* (1983). This Emmy-winning made-for-TV movie tells the story of nuclear terrorism using fictional news reports. The exclusive use of videotape provides the program with the look of a newscast (Fig. 9.4).

The nearly exclusive use of film for television movies is one convention that is likely to change over the next few years. The introduction of HDTV equipment produces an image that is the near equal of 35mm film. Shooting with video in terms both of **production** and **post-production** will become easier and cheaper as more of high-definition equipment comes into day-to-day use.

FIGURE 9.4

FIGURE 9.5

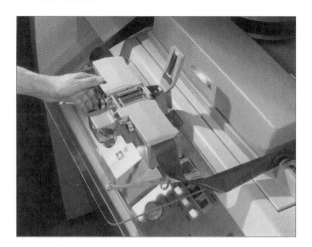

The introduction of videotape did not initially make video the equal to film in terms of artistic control. Many of the early videotaped programs were simply live shows recorded on tape, and post-production work on videotape was difficult, if not impossible, in the beginning. The earliest forms of videotape editing required that the tape be physically cut in the same manner as audiotape or film. The videotape was edited by cutting and gluing the pieces together, using a specially constructed videotape splicer as seen in Fig. 9.5. To prevent the television image from rolling at each splice, the cut and reassembly had to be made between frames, and to find those frames a chemical solution was applied to the bottom of the videotape, revealing the spikes that indicated frame changes. This method of editing was cumbersome, inaccurate, and time consuming. Added to these limitations, tape sometimes broke at the splices, damaging the expensive video record/playback heads of the VTR.

The medium took a leap forward when Ampex introduced the first electronic means of editing videotape: a system called **Editech**. The ability to edit electronically, rather than physically, made videotape a much more useful medium. Editing systems became increasingly sophisticated while simultaneously becoming easier to use. Editors could make more edits in less time; they had greater flexibility in pacing and the capacity for complex organization of a program. For example, *Rowan and Martin's Laugh-In* (1968–73)—the first network series to make extensive use of electronic videotape editing—changed the pace of television thanks largely to the opportunities that evolving editing techniques offered. Its quick cuts, blackout sketches, and fast pace required electronic methods of editing, and the editors were awarded an Emmy for their stylistic innovation.

The style of video editing introduced by the Editech has now been replaced by **nonlinear editing (NLE)** on a computer. Figure 9.6 shows an example of an NLE system and Figures 7.2–7.4 illustrate the discussion of computer-based editing in chapter 7.[2] Most television shows—regardless of whether they were shot on film or video—are now digitized for NLE, which is faster and cheaper than conventional, analog video editing or film-as-film editing on a Steenbeck

FIGURE 9.6

or Moviola (two brands of film-editing machines). Such developments blur the line between film and video. While the show you are watching may have been shot on film, it probably has been edited on computer to produce a videotape as a final product and may never exist as a film that could be projected in a conventional movie theater. This combination of technologies opens up a number of possibilities that film or video alone could not easily accomplish. Computer-generated special effects (SFX), for example, can digitally manipulate an image. Moreover, digital **compositing** (the merging of two or more video, film, and/or digital sources) has reduced the cost of special effects for television programs.

The conversion from analog images (created on video or film) to digital for editing and compositing also means that the computer may be used for image manipulation to create digital SFX. Digital technology is not limited to network or major productions. You probably have seen digital SFX on your local television station's weather reports. The insertion of the reporter into a map of weather information in Fig. 6.33 is accomplished with a computer.

Star Trek: The Next Generation (1987–1994), *Babylon 5* (1994–1998), and more recent science fiction programs make extensive use of digital special effects. These special effects are produced more quickly, more cheaply, and more convincingly than if they were done using older, film-based processes, which results in more special effects per episode. This increased use of digital SFX has allowed television programs to mimic the visual style of more expensive motion pictures. And, to blur the line between film and video even more, expensive motion pictures such as *Independence Day* (1996) have incorporated the creative possibilities of high-tech, computer-generated effects, which can be transferred from high-definition video to motion picture film for theatrical exhibition.

Color Television

The date of the introduction of color television sets to U.S. homes is a little complicated. As will be explained, there were two introductions of color broadcasting in the U.S. The first, which was initiated by CBS, took place in 1951, but production of those sets ceased in the same year. The second introduction, from which today's color televisions trace their lineage, was in 1954. In that year, RCA introduced its home color television sets. RCA followed the pattern it had developed with radio by using its broadcasting arm, NBC, to create a market for RCA color receivers.

Color television took more than a decade to reach a significant number of households and to enrich RCA by sales of its color TV sets. Color came to predominate in 1966, when CBS converted from all-black-and-white to all-color broadcasting. Ironically, CBS had been both the last and the first of the commercial networks to transmit regularly scheduled programs in color. The irony stems from the way color television was developed.

CBS had proposed a hybrid electronic-mechanical color television system as early as 1946. The pickup tube of the camera and picture tube of the television were electronic and black-and-white, but placed before each was a spinning color wheel. The color wheel would spin so rapidly that through persistence of vision the eye would put the three separate colors together to form a properly colored image. In 1950, after a series of hearings and test demonstrations, the Federal Communications Commission (FCC) approved the hybrid as the official U.S. color system.

The FCC approved the CBS system over the protests of RCA, which was scrambling to perfect an all-electronic version. The system RCA proposed, but had not yet perfected, would provide color pictures, but would also be compatible with the existing black-and-white television sets. (The approved CBS system was not compatible with the existing sets). This lack of compatibility upset all the current television set manufacturers, who, along with RCA, protested the FCC decision. They vowed that they would not produce color television sets using the CBS hybrid system, but CBS promised that they would build the color sets themselves.

CBS began programming in color on June 25, 1951. The total potential audience for its kickoff broadcast was small; the number of color sets capable of receiving the broadcast was estimated at fewer than 100. CBS began regularly scheduled network color broadcasts between 4:00 and 5:00 in the afternoon—the hour of the smallest television audience. Transmitting color programs receivable only by CBS color sets when the audience was smallest, network executives believed, would be least offensive to the overwhelming majority of viewers, who had black-and-white sets. CBS hoped that the hour would not hurt the network's audience figures for its prime-time schedule.

When the government issued an order to stop production of the color sets in November 1951, CBS ceased color broadcasting. The federal government ruled that color set manufacture used strategic materials necessary for the Korean War effort. (The order to conserve strategic materials, however, was not applied to manufacturers of black-and-white sets. This led some to suspect that CBS may have maneuvered the order so they could suspend broadcasting color programs and manufacturing color sets, which were losing the company millions of dollars.) After the CBS system had been accepted by the FCC, RCA and most of the other manufacturers of television sets formed the **National Television System Committee (NTSC)** to develop specifications for black-and-white-compatible color transmission and reception. The NTSC used RCA's all-electronic color system as its basis for development and standards.

The FCC accepted the NTSC color television system as the official standard on December 17, 1953. They authorized commencement of commercial broadcasting in color for January 1954, and the NTSC standard is used in the U.S., as well as Canada, Japan and about 45 other countries, to this day. It is only now being challenged in some of these countries by the switch to HDTV. So, CBS had been the first network to broadcast regularly scheduled color programming—but eventually, the last of the networks to begin color broadcasting.

Color and Style

The initial introduction of color did little to affect the overall style of broadcasting. Early color programs were specials rather than series or serial television, but these specials did not necessarily exploit the abilities of color television by presenting particularly colorful events. One of the early color broadcasts in 1954 was that year's World Series. The World Series coverage was exceptional because it was the first time color television cameras were taken outdoors for a network broadcast. Early color video cameras were very large and cumbersome, weighing around 400 pounds, and their color registration (alignment of the camera's pick-up tubes) was easily knocked out of alignment. Their size was due to almost three times the number of parts as the black-and-white cameras of the time. While black-and-white cameras had been shrinking in size, color cameras returned television to earlier days of enormous, unwieldy technology.

The standard black-and-white camera of the 1950s had four lenses of different focal lengths mounted on a rotating turret (see the discussion of focal length in chapter 6). The introduction of the color camera resulted in the elimination of lens turrets and the subsequent adoption of the zoom lens as the standard. Before the zoom lens, the camera operator selected the proper lens for a given scene, but since each lens was of a fixed focal length, physical movement of the camera was often necessary to achieve the proper framing.

Zoom lenses replaced turrets on color cameras because each lens on the turret had slightly different color properties. With turret lenses, it would have been necessary to readjust the camera after each lens change; a zoom lens required only a single adjustment. The introduction of the color camera thus changed the visual style of television by substituting the zoom lens for a series of fixed focal-length lenses. And focal length has a major impact on the visual style of a shot.

In narrative television, black and white is virtually no longer an option. According to industry wisdom, viewers will not watch programs presented entirely in black and white. During the initial planning of *Hill Street Blues* (1981–87), it was suggested to the network that the show be shot in black-and-white with hand-held cameras as a means to emphasize its documentary, gritty quality. This notion was quickly axed by NBC, who felt that the audience wouldn't watch a black-and-white television show. However, black-and-white currently finds frequent use in commercials and music videos and in segments of narrative programs. Its difference from the norm of color is used for various commercial, narrative, or expressive effects, as in "The Dream Sequence Always Rings Twice," an episode of *Moonlighting* (1985–89) that parodied film noir. Black-and-white images are thought to cut through the continuous clutter of color images that makes up so much of the current television fare.

Logo-mania

Network or station logos that appear in the corners of the screen are near ubiquitous in television. These logos are called **bugs** by the industry.

They were introduced in the early 1980s as a means of combating the confusion caused by the proliferation of channels provided by cable systems. Because of the growing number of programming choices, it was discovered that many people were unaware to which network they were tuned. This could have a significant impact in the days when the diary method was used for television ratings in many markets. The diary method requires that the person write in the diary what program on which channel is being viewed. Cable networks such as USA were worried that people would not know or remember which programming service was being watched.

While bugs caused some outcry from viewers, the strongest complaints came from the subscribers to the premium movie channels such as Showtime and HBO. Thinking that one movie channel looks like another when a movie is showing, the premiums began using bugs to reinforce their name recognition with viewers. Needless to say, people who subscribed to movie channels did not like their movies being marred by these corporate reminders. Most premium channels no longer use bugs during their theatrically released motion pictures but commercial networks continue to use their bugs to remind people of what they are viewing.

Networks generally justify the use of these bugs in terms of network recognition both for knowing to which station a person is tuned and for being able to find the channel while a viewer channel surfs. Bugs also help fend off video piracy. These electronic watermarks clearly identify the original source of stolen material and make it difficult for illegal duplicators to pretend that the tape was properly acquired. This is particular true of the broadcast of sports events—the images of which are jealously guarded by their copyright and trademark holders.

Information that moves across the bottom of the screen—such as sports scores, weather updates or promotional announcements—is called a **ticker**. Tickers are particularly common on such cable networks as ESPN, CNN, and CNBC. The all-time winner for the most graphic information on the television screen at one time is probably Bloomberg Television (Fig. 9.7). This financial news cable channel uses at least half of its screen for ticker information.

While a static bug will generally come to be ignored, the moving ticker information continues to draw viewers' attention. This is due to the human eye's photoreceptors. The eye contains both rods and cones. The rods are motion sensitive. When the brain detects motion it will reorient attention to the movement. This is a survival trick that was probably particularly useful when humans

FIGURE 9.7

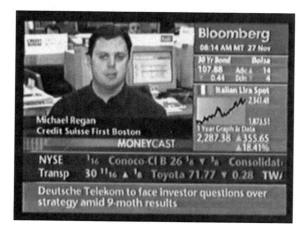

were hunting and being hunted. Some networks, such as the SciFi network have animated bugs, which draw the viewer's attention back to it. Stationary bugs can be ignored but the movement catches both the eye's and the brain's attention.

The increasing use of these text and symbols on-screen creates a competitive environment for the programming. You may have seen the *Saturday Night Live* "Newsforce" skit where the newscasters find themselves unable to continue because the screen has become filled with bugs and tickers. While it is an exaggeration, the humor of the skit comes from our understanding that the problem of on-screen information continues to increase.

Remote Control

The history of the remote control for electronic mass media appears to start with the Kolster Radio Corporation who developed a wired remote control for their radios in the late 1920s. The majority of these early radio remote controls had wires that ran from the shoe box-sized remote control to the radio. The remote push of a button would engage an electric motor inside the radio that would turn the tuner to specific stops. The system wasn't very reliable, the wire was a nuisance, and the remote was big and bulky. Radio remote controls were not very popular.

Remote control devices (RCD) for television began in the 1950s. Some of the earliest had names such as Tune-O-Magic and Remot-O-Matic. The company that pioneered in the research and marketing of TV RCDs was the Zenith Corporation.

Zenith developed a number of remote controls for television using various technologies. The Zenith Lazy Bones was the first wired remote produced by the company in 1950. The wire running across the floor turned out to be both unsightly and a potential hazard.

Zenith introduced their Flash-Matic remote control in 1955. The brainchild of Zenith engineer Eugene Polley, it was the first of the wireless remote controls and used four photocells in the corners of the television set. One aimed the remote (more or less a flashlight) at one corner to turn the set on or off, another to change channels in ascending order, another for descending, and finally a fourth corner to mute the audio. One problem with this system was that sunshine falling inopportunely on the set could turn the set off or on, mute the sound or send the channels rotating.

The first alternative that Zenith investigated to replace the Flash-Matic was radio waves. This system worked but the problem was that if you had a nearby neighbor with a similar remote control you could suddenly find your television being hijacked by the neighbor's remote. This system was abandoned without ever being marketed.

Zenith engineer Robert Adler led the team that developed the breakthrough remote. He created the Space Command remote control (so called as a salute to Zenith head and the man demanding the development of a TV remote control, Commander Eugene F. McDonald). This remote operated using ultrasonic sounds created by pressing one of its four buttons. When the button was depressed a hammer would strike one of four short aluminum rods producing a sound too high for the human ear. Each rod produced a different frequency— one for each of the four functions identical to those on the outmoded Flash-Matic. A receiver in the television set would detect which tones had been produced and carry out the appropriate function. The Space Commander met all the requirements of Commander McDonald for a remote: it was wireless, hand-held, and required no power source. The ultrasonic Space Command technology was the industry standard in wireless remote controls until the introduction of infrared remotes in the 1980s.

The first infrared (IR) remote control device—today's standard remote— was developed by General Electric. The infrared light is supplied by three light emitting diodes (LED) that blink off and on to transmit a particular binary-coded decimal. A receiving unit in the television, VCR, or other device receives the coded message and, if it is one that is recognized, will carry out the preprogrammed instruction.

The IR remote is very common in today's households. It has been estimated that 99% of all television sets and 100% of VCRs currently sold come with an IR remote. The penetration rate for IR remotes is beyond 90% of all households in the U.S.

The remote control has contributed new concepts with which television programmers must deal. The new broadcaster or cablecaster "problems" or viewer "opportunities" of zapping (using the remote to tune to another station to avoid commercials—called zipping when the remote is used to speed past commercials on time-shifted video taped programs) and grazing (the switching between programs) face programming executives. This severely affects the audience flow—the movement of the audience from one program to another—that used to be a given in the television industry. Without an RCD, a person had to get out of the chair and change the channel or at least give instructions to one of the children to make the change. It was assumed that viewer inertia would deliver a good proportion of the audience from one program on a given network to the next. The RCD device changed that.

One result has been a change in how television programs begin and end. A decade ago programs began with a "teaser" segment to hook the audience,

FIGURE 9.8

Ally McBeal

Supervising Sound
Editor
DAVID RAWLINSON
Re-Recording Mixers
NELLO TORRI
PETER R. KELSEY
Music Editor
MICDI PROD /
SHARYN TYLK
Visual EFX Supervisor
MICHAEL D. MOST
Colorist
KEVIN KIRWAN
Assistant Editor
JOHN KERIS

FOX.COM

a theme song with the first set of opening credits and then a commercial break. Programs would end with the close of narrative, a commercial break, and then the program's theme song played under the end credits. At the conclusion of network programming, networks scheduled time for local stations to broadcast their local commercials. Usually these times were at 28 and 58 minutes after the hour. This meant that from the end of one program's narrative to the beginning of the next program's narrative 3 or 4 minutes could pass. In pre-remote control days, this was not considered a problem. The diffusion of the RCD into over 90% of the households made it one.

Current network programs are now scheduled to directly abut one another. Immediately after the end of one program's credits another program starts. Producers of programs may squeeze credits into boxes while post-dénouement dialogue, promotions of future episodes or other visual bits are seen on screen (Fig.9.8). Theme songs have been shortened. In the early 1990s, the head of ABC programming ruled that none of the shows on ABC would have theme songs because theme songs with credits provided time for viewers to switch to see what was showing on other channels. This particular edict didn't last very long, but, nonetheless, the beginnings of most television programs have changed under the influence of the remote control device. In this instance, a piece of technology has had major impact on television aesthetics.

AURAL ELEMENTS OF TELEVISION STYLE

Dialogue

Most of the early writing and performing talent in television came from radio rather than from motion pictures. Television performers and, particularly, writers who came from radio tended to emphasize the aural rather than the visual. As a consequence, radio conventions strongly affected the way television sounds.

Most television genres rely heavily on dialogue to drive the narrative. Sitcoms, dramas, and soap operas are usually very dialogue dependent. Action/adventure shows tend to be less dialogue centered, because, as the name suggests, the show's pleasures derive from action that must be seen. Compare, for example, the use of dialogue in *The Young and the Restless* (1973–) to that in *Walker, Texas Ranger* (1993–).

This reliance on the soundtrack has been especially exemplified in cartoons made specifically for television. Hanna-Barbera, the pioneer in made-for-television cartoons, was able to create and market affordable cartoons for television by reducing the quantity of animation (the number of pictures used to create the animated image), along with some innovations in animation techniques that reduced some of their labor requirements. The reduction in the amount of animation corresponded with an increased investment in the soundtrack to carry the story line (see chapter 11).

Reliance on audio allows people to do other things while they "watch" television. Research has shown that many people are engaged in a simultaneous activity while they experience television. For instance, viewers may eat dinner, read the paper, do homework, or fold laundry while they "watch" television.

Music

Television's use of music has changed over the years (see chapter 10). Early live programs with small budgets were often forced to use organ music (also performed live, of course) as their sole form of incidental, or nondiegetic, music. This device was adopted directly from radio programming. Producers of early, filmed shows could purchase the rights to production music libraries for use as incidental music. When the major film studios entered into television production, however, they had their own music libraries, as well as composers who could write original scores for a series.

Soap operas are an excellent example of the changes in incidental music in television. When soaps began on television in the 1950s, organ music was used exclusively for incidental music, as it had been in radio soap opera. This association between organ music and daytime dramas became so ingrained that organ music continues to be a cliche associated with soap operas, even though no soap has used a solo organ in decades. Electronic pianos and organs and audio synthesizers, which provide a diverse range of musical sounds and styles, replaced the standard organ as the source of music for soaps. Moreover, the music is no longer performed live while the program is shot, but added to the soundtrack using recorded selections.

Today, soap operas and other network series have also licensed the rights to copyrighted popular music for occasional use in their episodes. Several soap opera episodes, for example, will accompany a visual montage of a young couple's romance with a currently popular pop song. (And there have even been cases where a tune written as a soap opera theme has found its way onto the pop charts.)

In this way, soap opera music resembles the music of the style-setting police drama *Miami Vice*. Most of the incidental music that accompanied the

FIGURE 9.9   **FIGURE 9.10**

adventures of Crockett and Tubbs was created on a synthesizer by the composer Jan Hammer, but the producers also budgeted enough money for each show to include recognizable rock music by the original performers. The show licensed music from Glenn Frey, Phil Collins, Tina Turner, and others. They were to evoke, in former NBC executive Brandon Tartikoff's words, "MTV Cops."

The use of rock and roll music on TV sound tracks has become more acceptable over the years, but this was not always the case. A classic example is *Dragnet.* Whenever "teen" themes were part of the narrative in the 1960s–1970s incarnation of Jack Webb's "realistic" police series, the "rock" bore a closer resemblance to Muzak than to Hendrix. For many adults, of that time rock music did not have favorable connotations. Since the majority of prime-time programming was aimed at adults or at the nuclear, middle-class family, rock music was relatively rare.

Perhaps ironically in this context, the first nonmusical television show to use rock music regularly was a family-oriented sitcom, *The Adventures of Ozzie and Harriet* (1953–66). Starting in 1957, Ozzie and Harriet's younger son Ricky (or, Rick, as he was later called) Nelson would perform a musical number at the end of each episode as seen in Fig. 9.9. The presence of Ricky's music caused some controversy. Was rock and roll too decadent, too animalistic for a good, clean family like the Nelsons? To dispel criticism about the music, in one episode Ricky asks his mother what she thinks of rock and roll. The real audience for Harriet's response is fairly clear; she tells us (Fig. 9.10) that this music may be different from what she is used to (in real life, Harriet was once a singer in husband's Ozzie's and other bands), but there is nothing really wrong with it. She likes the energy of the music, she says.

Other family-oriented, domestic sitcoms of the period occasionally included a rock/pop tune within the diegesis. Shelley Fabares, who played daughter Mary on *The Donna Reed Show*, was ordered by the show's producer to cut the single "Johnny Angel." Fabares didn't want to record, because she felt she had no voice for singing. The producer suggested that if she liked her employment with the show she should record the song. The song was recorded and performed by

Fabares on *The Donna Reed Show*, and the 1962 single "Johnny Angel" became a hit. At best, however, early television's attitude toward rock was ambivalent.

While rock/pop music would occasionally invade family sitcoms, 1966 saw the introduction on NBC of a television show whose entire raison d'être was the marketing of pop music. *The Monkees* (1966–1968) was inspired by the success of the Beatles and other British Invasion pop groups and the Beatles' film *A Hard Day's Night* (1964). Each episode featured at least two musical numbers—most of which would go on to become a marketing success as singles or as part of an album. The show was sufficiently "safe" that adults would tolerate their children watching it even though it featured mildly risque pop music.

Two years after *The Monkees* debut, ABC offered *That's Life* (1968–69), which included original music and dance numbers similar to a Broadway show with, generally, show-tune (and not rock) sensibilities. Pop/rock would also find its way into this show, however, and the first episode did include a pop group, the Turtles, playing in a "discotheque." *That's Life* was the first to be an original episodic program with the musical numbers fully integrated into the narrative. Musical series that followed all used rock-n-roll beats for their music; for example, *Fame* (1982–87), *Hull High* (1990), and *Cop Rock* (1990).

Rock beats did not invade the nondiegetic music of television until much later. Producers in the 1970s realized that a significant portion of their viewers grew up listening to rock music, and that most still listened. The decision to incorporate a more "modern" sound into television programs resulted not so much from the producers' and networks' discovery of rock, but from the reduction of the threat they felt the music posed. Even shows skewed to an older audience, such as *The Equalizer* (1985–89), have incidental music with distinctive rock stylings.

Laugh Tracks

Another device carried over from radio to television was the use of laughter on the soundtrack. Two forms of television laugh tracks have evolved: (1) those labeled as coming from a studio audience, and (2) those incorporating recorded laughter, the show not having been recorded before a studio audience. Network executives say that canned laughter, as recorded laughter is sometimes called, is placed on a show's soundtrack to make us feel better about laughing at the program. One network executive claimed that people didn't like to laugh alone. Laugh tracks, according to this view, give us permission to laugh. The laugh track also serves as a signpost pointing to the jokes, which may be less than obvious. Moreover, laugh tracks serve to engage us in the television situation, enticing us to join the responding audience that we hear on the soundtrack, but never see (in narrative programs, although, obviously, they're quite evident in non-narrative shows such as *Late Show With David Letterman*).

During the 1950s and 1960s, one man was responsible for creating every TV laugh track. He had a box containing tape loops of various kinds of laughter–for example, titters, guffaws–with each type of laughter activated by a switch. He pushed what he considered the appropriate button on his box to elicit the correct demonstration of amusement for that part of the program. A particularly morbid commonplace in the business noted that the canned laughter heard on shows was the mirth of the dead. This was probably very true, because the laughs on the tape loops inside the box had been lifted from old, live radio shows.

Producers Gene Reynolds and Larry Gelbart tried to convince CBS to allow *M*A*S*H* (1972–83) to be run without a laugh track, but network executives became nervous at the thought of a sitcom without some type of laughter on the audio track. Tests were run to measure enjoyment of *M*A*S*H* with and without a laugh track, and there appeared to be no difference in terms of enjoyment between the laugh track audience and the nonlaugh track audience. Despite these test findings, the network executives remained uncomfortable without a laugh track. Subsequently, the producers and network reached a compromise: No laugh track in operating room scenes, but all other scenes would have the off-screen chuckles and chortles. This distinction was not kept in the exported show, as *M*A*S*H* was shown in Great Britain without any laugh track.

More recently, it seems network executives are beginning to relax about sitcoms without laugh tracks. Fox's *Parker Lewis Can't Lose* (1990–92), ABC's *The Wonder Years* (1988–1993), and Fox's *Malcolm in the Middle* are examples of comedies (and their audiences) that survived without laugh tracks. Not incidentally, all are, like *M*A*S*H*, single-camera productions.

Even shows with live studio audiences may **sweeten** the laughter. Programs performed before audiences are often taped twice in front of two different groups. The first time is usually called the dress rehearsal, and the second time the actual performance. Both performances are recorded, however, and the laughter from the dress rehearsal may be used to augment the laughter in the final production. Another way to augment the studio audience's laughter is to revert to the canned laugh track. The recorded track can be used to make the audience sound larger than it was, or to fill in spots where the production team thinks there should be a laugh, even though the audience didn't.

S U M M A R Y

The history of television style intertwines issues of technology, economics, and aesthetics. No single element explains sufficiently why television looks and sounds the way it does today. Though technology, primarily in video, continues to provide a number of evident opportunities for changes in style, technology alone is not sufficient to cause change. There must also be a perceived aesthetic need, and the change must not lose money for a network or a station.

Television drew from radio, motion pictures, and theater for its style. Radio was one of the biggest influences, because control of the television industry rested with those who controlled the radio industry.

Television began as a live medium, and live broadcasting was seen as more appropriate to the medium than recorded performance, and consequently superior. Filmed programs gradually began to replace live ones, and then videotape was introduced, both to replace kinescopes for recording live programs for later playback and to serve as an original recording medium. The introduction and development of electronic videotape editing made videotape even more viable. Today analog-style electronic editing has been replaced by computer-based non-linear editing.

Some have argued that television is primarily an aural medium. Despite and in conjunction with the presence of pictures, television audio plays an important role in building both narrative and mood. Musical styles for background and incidental music have changed over the years; the use of laugh tracks has not changed in any significant way. Networks seem to be comfortable with the conventional use of recorded laughter in comedies, although some recent television comedies—a small minority—have done without.

FURTHER READINGS

Historical development of the electronic media in general receive excellent treatments in most introductory broadcasting books. See Joseph R. Dominick, Barry L. Sherman, and Gary A. Copeland, *Broadcasting/Cable and Beyond: An Introduction to Modern Electronic Media*, 3rd ed. (New York: McGraw-Hill, 1996). These treatments are usually chapter-long highlights of how the technologies evolved and were implemented. Greater depth can be found in Christopher H. Sterling and John M. Kittross, *Stay Tuned: A Concise History of American Broadcasting*, 3rd ed. (Mahweh, NJ: Lawrence Erlbavm, 2001).

For insights as well as interesting stories from the period when many of television's finest dramas were being broadcast live from New York, there is Frank Sturcken, *Live Television: The Golden Age of 1946–1958 in New York* (Jefferson, NC: McFarland, 1990).

Those more interested in the technical development of electronic broadcasting might want to read Thomas S. W. Lewis, *Empire of the Air: The Men Who Made Radio* (New York: Edward Burlington, 1991). This was designed as a companion for the PBS series of the same name but holds up well by itself. See also Joseph H. Udelson, *The Great Television Race: A History of the American Television Industry 1925–1941* (University: University of Alabama Press, 1982).

ENDNOTES

[1] Jack Gould, "A Plea for Live Video" *New York Times*, December 7, 1952, sec. 2, 17.

[2] The nonlinear editor shown here is a media 100 system at the University of Alabama Center for Public Television and Radio.

PART THREE

SPECIAL TOPICS IN TELEVISION FORM

CHAPTER 10

Music Television

BLAINE ALLAN

MTV, the United States' first round-the-clock television service devoted to popular music, went on the air in 1981. The first video broadcast featured a song by the forgettable British band the Buggles, titled "Video Killed the Radio Star." Recalling the Hollywood myth about stars of the silent period who because of their voices could not survive the transition to sound cinema, the title seemed to predict that television would supplant radio as the more important medium to the pop music industry. It suggested that video and the exposure of television might destroy some musical careers.

Changes in the world of pop music occur quickly. Styles and fads regularly appear and fade away. Whether music television has by its form proved detrimental to any popular musician is questionable, but many have certainly benefited. The apparent importance of music television and videos may change as other forms of advertising and promotion or other methods of delivering music to consumers develop. Since MTV went on the air, for example, computers have proliferated as means of communication about popular music and for the exchange of recorded music. The Internet competes with television for the time and attention of young audiences, yet also complements TV. While music television once seemed the young, brash intruder of television, a dedicated channel has existed for a significant portion of the total history of the medium, and music TV has become part of the mainstream.

MUSIC TELEVISION AND MUSIC VIDEO

For the sake of clarity, we should differentiate between **music television** and **music videos**. Music television is a general term used to refer to a system through which programming is delivered. Music TV may be a cable or satellite service for which the broadcast material is musical, such as MTV (which stands for Music Television), MTV2, or VH-1 (Video Hits-1) in the United States (or in the countries where the MTV format is licensed), CMT (Country Music Television, which originates in Nashville), or the Canadian English-language MuchMusic and MuchMoreMusic and their French-language counterpart, MusiquePlus, as well as the Canadian version of CMT. Alternately, music television may refer to programs and segments broadcast on television services that are devoted to music, mainly those that program videos. Coinciding with the introduction of MTV, other telecasters introduced programs to compete for viewers interested in pop music; probably the most prominent was NBC's *Friday Night Videos* (1983–1993), although appetite for music videos on network television diminished, and dedicated programs disappeared. BET (Black Entertainment Television), another cable channel, devotes a considerable portion of its schedule to music videos featuring African–American artists. Individual programs and series, such as the PBS broadcast *Austin City Limits* (1976–) and the independent *Sessions at West 54th* (1997–), may also qualify as music television.

Music television arose as a distinctive form at the end of the 1970s, however, as satellite communications and cable television services grew. MTV and comparable services arose alongside other specialized channels, directed at audiences that were more narrowly defined than the mass audiences sought by broadcast networks. Youth was quite clearly MTV's target audience, and popular music was the means to deliver that audience to advertisers.

Popular music has formed part of TV programming since television itself began, but the period of music television marked a shift due to the proliferation of music videos. Music television, a system, offers music videos, a specific form of production, as the mainstay of its programming. A music video is a visual representation of or accompaniment to a song or other musical selection that usually also exists independently as a recording. That the recording is generally available for purchase as a tape or disc underlines the role of the video as promotion for recorded music. One of the elegant paradoxes of music television is that much of its programming material is also advertising. Videos that record companies provided constituted free advertising for them and free program material for the broadcaster, until MTV was challenged to pay fees comparable to those charged to radio stations for playing music on the air.

Although performers and record companies package music in albums (in whatever tape or disc formats), videos are most often produced for individual songs. The videos themselves may be collected and released for sale or rental on home video, though often as retrospective anthologies of diverse clips.

Music video, a simple term, incorporates two elements that merit brief exploration. For one, in common usage music video and rock video are generally interchangeable. Employing the former term simply suggests that rock is not the only form of music to lend itself to video. Nothing precludes the production and broadcast of videos of any type of music, from heavy metal to grand opera. In fact, a British term for music video is pop promo, which suggests not only the range of pop music, beyond rock, but also the status of the clip as a promotional tool.

Second, most music videos are not shot on videotape at all, but on film. Early videos, such as Queen's groundbreaking *Bohemian Rhapsody* (1975), were shot on tape, but following the example of clips such as *Vienna* (1980), directed by Russell Mulcahy for Ultravox, more directors used film. A video shot on video for the particular qualities of the electronic image—for example, Stone Temple

Pilots' *Big Bang Baby* (1996)—marks itself as distinctive. The relation of film and videotape in the production of music videos illustrates the trade-offs between the two. Film offers an image with higher resolution than standard video, but video presents a vast range of possibilities for manipulating the picture with electronic, computer-controlled visual effects. As a consequence, while the raw image may be made on film, the film image is usually transferred to videotape or digital format for editing. Moreover, because the ultimate destination for most music video is a television set, a video may be completed on tape and never exist as a finished film at all. Some videos have been produced with high-definition television (HDTV) technology, which produces a more detailed image than any previously existing video standard. As HDTV is rolled out into the marketplace, and as more viewers buy high-definition receivers, we can expect to see the results in music television and all other formats.

ANTECEDENTS AND INFLUENCES

Music videos and music television can be seen as an amalgamation of parts of the cinema, of radio, and of television. The music video draws from the cinema its defining feature, the synchronization of sound and image of musical performance. As far as the cinema is concerned, that feature goes back to the earliest presentations of sound cinema. The Hollywood feature film that popularized "talking pictures," *The Jazz Singer* (1927), was also a singing picture. Hollywood musicals are characterized by the alternation of dramatic sequences, which outline a story, and musical sequences in which characters break into song and dance. The musical sequences punctuate the narrative, but they also suggest that the act of performance has value of its own, that singing and dancing have significance. In Hollywood nowadays musicals are rare, apart from animated films, although some videos have modeled themselves on productions of the past. The writhing choreography in Paula Abdul's *Cold Hearted* (1989) resembles dances Bob Fosse designed for his film *All That Jazz* (1979), a connection the video makes explicit from the start, when a character calls the number "a Bob Fosse kind of thing." Director Spike Jonze staged Björk's *It's Oh So Quiet* (1995) as a full-scale musical production on a sunlit street set (Fig. 10.1), like a Gene Kelly picture of the 1950s or, more precisely, the French musical *The Umbrellas of Cherbourg* (1964).

The method of producing music videos is also essentially the same as that used to produce musical numbers for a film. Filmed musical numbers, whether for feature films or music videos, are usually **lip-synced**, or sung to playback. The camera rolls while the existing recording plays over speakers on the set. This allows the performers to sing along with their own voices and move to the beat of the music, knowing that from one take to the next the musical quality will be consistent. On occasion a video may present a song filmed "live," though it is usually a filmed or videotaped record of a concert appearance, made with more than one camera. This, of course, is the case when performances are extracted from *MTV Unplugged* and aired as videos. Bruce Springsteen's *Rosalita* (1978), shot with several cameras at a Phoenix, Arizona, concert, is also a good example.

By contrast, his *Dancing in the Dark* (1984), which was supposed to take place at a concert appearance, was actually shot to playback, in part in the middle of a St. Paul, Minnesota, show.

The video takes from the Hollywood musical not only the form of visualized, recorded, musical performance and the methods of realizing it, but also the importance of the properties of musical performance in determining the form. For instance, musical properties—particularly rhythm and song structure—or physical qualities of the performers may well take precedence over the coherent depiction of space. Probably the best-known examples in classical Hollywood are the Depression-era musicals choreographed or directed by Busby Berkeley, such as *42nd Street* (1933) and *Gold Diggers of 1933* (1933), in which musical sequences arise in the story as stage shows. With vast arrangements of bodies and objects framed at unusual angles (overhead shots of chorus girls organized in circles, like human floral arrangements, were a Berkeley trademark), they would have been impossible to stage, and certainly would have been impossible for a theater audience to see. *It's Oh So Quiet*, already noted as indebted to the Hollywood musical, features overhead shots of dancers and umbrellas resembling Berkeley's patterns (Fig. 10.2), but such elaborate production numbers are rare in videos. Spatial incoherence abounds in video, however. From one shot to the next, the musicians may appear in different costumes, different lighting and visual styles, different hairstyles, or totally different locations, yet they continue to appear to be performing the same song, without any corresponding aural changes. In fact, the music video has made such extreme visual discontinuity, married to the aural continuity of the music itself, one of the most characteristic parts of its stylistic stock-in-trade.

If the precedents of music television and music video can be found partly in the Hollywood musical, they can also be found in other forms of movies and television. These include such films as *Jazz on a Summer's Day* (1959), *Monterey Pop* (1969), and *Woodstock* (1970), filmed records of music festivals from the 1950s and 1960s, and celebrity profiles, such as *Don't Look Back* (1967), about Bob Dylan, and Madonna's *Truth or Dare* (1991). They have made the filmed representation of pop music and its performers part of the history of documentary film. Avant-garde filmmakers, too, have frequently married innovative combinations of images to music tracks. Bruce Conner's *Cosmic Ray*, made in black and white in 1961, matches a frenetic arrangement of short fragments of film to a recording of Ray Charles's "What'd I Say?" Using a similar technique, he recombined diverse shots from educational and promotional films to illustrate a recording by Devo in *Mongoloid* (1978). By way of contrast, Bruce Baillie's *All My Life* (1966) matches Ella Fitzgerald's recording of the title tune with a single shot, a 3-minute pan and tilt across a fence and a row of flowers under a brilliant blue sky. Music documentaries provide impressions of performers and events, and access to them, to some degree, while the avant-garde films indicate the expressive possibilities in combining images and popular music.

Films such as these were not necessarily produced to promote the performers and their recordings, and avant-garde productions typically do not depict the performers. **Soundies**, **Scopitones**, and **Telescriptions** did represent the musicians, and were different types of predecessor for music videos and music television. Soundies and Scopitones, produced in the 1940s and 1960s, respectively, were short films of performances by popular musicians that were found in coin-operated machines, like jukeboxes. Telescriptions, produced by Louis Snader in the early 1950s, similarly packaged musical performances on film, marketed to television stations, which used them as filler or in variety shows. In fact, the earliest format of *American Bandstand* (1957–87, 1989) on television, in 1952 (before Dick Clark and then called simply *Bandstand* [1952–57]), featured an on-camera announcer who introduced Telescriptions—essentially a version of music television in its present form.

This example suggests that pop music formed part of what television had to offer long before MTV. For many years, variety shows were responsible for introducing the new pop sensations to the broadly based television audience. Elvis Presley, for example, made his first national U.S. television appearances on *Stage Show* (1954–56) in 1956, with subsequent dates later that year on *The Milton Berle Show* (1948–67) and *The Ed Sullivan Show* (1948–71, see Fig. 4.9). Until its cancellation, the latter program was probably U.S. television's most prominent showcase for pop music, underlined by the successful repackaging of performances in half-hour shows called *Ed Sullivan's Rock 'n' Roll Classics* (1999–). Television followed the growth of rock culture in the 1960s, even if it did so at a measured pace. U.S. television venues dedicated to pop, with young target audiences, included *Shindig* (1964–66) and *Hullabaloo* (1965–66) and, later, *The Midnight Special* (1973–81) and *Don Kirshner's Rock Concert* (1973–82), which presented concert performances. The BBC series *Top of the Pops* (1964–) has been especially significant for fostering and presenting talent to British television viewers.

Among the most appropriate predecessors of contemporary music television were *American Bandstand* and *Soul Train* (1971–), both dance party programs. Their studios fill with teenagers, who dance to current hit records and act as an audience for guest performers who lip-sync their latest hits. Mouthing a song to the recording as it is played back, rather than actually singing it, the performers also guarantee viewers a flawless vocal performance, the same as the one the viewer can purchase. The dance party shows consequently function as showcases for both performers and recordings. They also serve as direct prede-cessors for such programs as *Electric Circus*, a weekly dance-music show staged in MuchMusic's Toronto studio.

Such variety programs acted as one general source for music television, but the other significant marriage of pop music and television preceding the MTV era was the NBC series *The Monkees* (1966–68). One of the few television programs to dramatize the growth of pop music culture in the 1960s, it was a parody along comic lines established by the Beatles, films, *A Hard Day's Night* (1964) and *Help!* (1965). It combined situation comedy with musical numbers, several of which became chart hits, as it followed the adventures of a pop group. The initially fictional Monkees, with the exposure of a weekly television series, quickly became an actual hit of the music industry. Mickey Dolenz, Davy Jones, Michael Nesmith, and Peter Tork, the actors who were cast as (and ultimately became) the Monkees, initially lip-synced their own voice tracks, in the manner customary to filmed musical numbers, but played instruments along with tracks that had already been recorded by session musicians. Later, in a widely publicized dispute with record producer Don Kirshner, they won their right to play music themselves, effectively forming themselves as a band, and subsequently played concerts.

The Monkees appealed to young viewers, many likely female, like the audi-ences so visible for the Beatles' shows (as did the Monkees' rare successors on television, such as *The Partridge Family* [1970–74], which made a teen idol of David Cassidy). Despite the anarchic slapstick or subversive humor frequently in the show (in one episode, for example, at a perplexing part of the story, Mickey Dolenz broke character and walked through the set to the writers' room for a solution), the situations that *The Monkees* presented were innocuous. Their music was catchy, rock-oriented pop, but distinctly polished and safe. The in-fluence that the series had on music television was as an early example of the creative combination of television and popular music. Television exposed Elvis Presley and the Beatles to mass audiences, but the television industry created the Monkees to be exposed to the medium's broad audience. Incidentally, for-mer Monkee Michael Nesmith was a pioneer producer of music videos, and his work was influential in the design of MTV and its format. Although accounts suggest that there was no love lost between him and the builders of the music television service, MTV paid homage to *The Monkees* in February 1986, by de-voting almost all of one programming day to air 45 episodes of the series. The program has continued to have a presence in contemporary music television. In the 1990s, MuchMusic made *The Monkees* a weekly broadcast and a staple of its schedule, and in 2000 VH-1 produced *Daydream Believers*, a biographical TV movie.

HOW MUSIC TELEVISION ORGANIZES TIME

In addition to movies and television variety, radio also preceded modern music television as a means of delivering popular, recorded music to mass audiences. Music television originally adapted from radio a format, or pattern of orga-nization, for broadcast. The format has changed over time, and differs from one broadcaster to another, but some features remain. Both music television services and programs have tended to emulate the model of popular radio. It involves the serial presentation of individual units (recorded singles in the case of radio, videos for television), clustered and punctuated by commercials, promotional messages, news, and other segments. Generally a person introduces the individual song or cluster (or "pack," the MuchMusic term) of two or three. On the dedicated pop services, such as MTV and MuchMusic, the regular hosts are called VJs (or veejays), meaning video jockeys, adapting the radio term disc jockey (or DJ). Each takes a shift lasting a certain time or hosts a program, and introduces videos, makes announcements, and provides patter. Like other broadcasters' official voices, such as news readers, commercial pitchmakers, or game show hosts, they are authorized to speak directly to the camera, and hence to the viewer. In addition, they may speak to other people—to audiences in the studio, for example, or to a guest as an interviewer. They act as the viewers' mediator, on the one hand speaking to us, on the other speaking for us.

Videos on music television are subject to a system that determines the frequency with which they appear on the air. That system, in which the broadcaster's programming authorities determine how often a video is played, was adapted from radio formats, and shares radio's name for it, "rotation". MTV and other broadcasters have different ways of dividing the range, but the simple categories light, medium, and heavy or high suggest the range. A popular artist's video of a new release, which the recording company is promoting heavily, may be put in heavy rotation and played several times a day. A lesser-known performer's video, or a clip that has been out for some time may appear only once or twice a week, in light rotation. Of course, music television forms part of the promotional apparatus of the recording industry, so the level of rotation can play a role in the exposure of the public to the tune and in its sales. Other forces—an appearance on another TV show, for instance—may propel an unknown musician or recording into unexpected popularity and cause music television services to move a video from light rotation to heavy.[1]

Like all broadcast media, music television services organize not only the materials they transmit, such as recorded music, speech, and advertising, but also time. Many radio stations operate around the clock, offering a continuous stream of sound that is available to listeners to switch on at any time, like water from a tap. MTV and other music television systems operate similarly. News reports, weather forecasts, and traffic updates—all of which must change regularly—act as markers of the "live" nature of much radio broadcasting. Music television may be similarly immediate, although in many cases it simply gives the impression of being broadcast live. With some exceptions, such as *TRL (Total Request Live)* [1998–], which is broadcast live from MTV's Times Square studio, the segments in which MTV's VJs talk between videos are prerecorded and dropped in amid the clusters of videos and commercials. In Canada, MuchMusic's and MusiquePlus's VJs generally broadcast live once during the day, but entire shows may be rebroadcast later in the day. Repeat broadcasts offer the viewer more opportunities to see a specific program; for the broadcaster they mean more time filled with fewer hours of original programming, and consequently lower costs.

Through much of the 1980s, music television services tended to be organized primarily around VJ shifts, lasting a couple of hours, but increasingly their time has been segmented like other forms of television. Andrew Goodwin has pointed out that in 1988 MTV began two particular practices. "Dayparting" refers to the practice of presenting distinct types of music in blocks at different times of day, and effectively it means the growth of specialized programs. "Stripping"—as many comedy and drama programs are scheduled when they are syndicated—involves presenting those programs at the same time each day.[2] Increasingly, then, MTV organized itself around a predictable schedule and programs, which might be an hour long or even a half-hour rather than the longer VJ shifts that characterized the broadcaster in its earlier years.

Although most music television broadcasters have common traits, each has its own specific and continually evolving approach to scheduling. (Table 10.1 presents MTV's schedule for a single day in 2000.) Among other differences between the two, the Canadian service has retained more of the longer shifts of programming in which VJs introduce an eclectic range of videos. Whether or not anyone was aware of Raymond Williams, MuchMusic calls these blocks "Video-Flow" (although there are no introductory titles to identify these segments as a program). Like MTV, Much also groups videos by type within titled programs,

TABLE 10.1

MTV Programming, 8 November 2000

TIME	PROGRAM
6:00AM	MTV Video Wake-Up
7:30AM	MTV Jams
8:00AM	TRL
9:00AM	Best Sports Moments on MTV
9:30AM	Music Videos
10:00AM	Music Videos
11:00AM	Music Videos
11:30AM	Hot Zone
1:00PM	Behind the Scenes of MTV's Campus Invasion Tour
1:30PM	Adam Sandler's Hell of a Movie Special
2:00PM	Diary
2:30PM	TRL Presents: Christina's Greatest MTV Moments
3:30PM	TRL
4:30PM	Real World New Orleans
5:30PM	Direct Effect
6:30PM	Jackass
7:00PM	Adam Sandler's Hell of a Movie Special
7:30PM	Diary
8:00PM	Say What? Karaoke Moments
10:00PM	Jim Carrey Uncensored
11:00PM	MTV's Truth
11:30PM	Undressed
12:00AM	Undressed
12:30AM	Adam Sandler's Hell of a Movie Special
1:00AM	Limp Bizkit's Playboy Bash
2:30AM	Diary
3:00AM	Hot Zone (From Campus Invasion 2000)
4:30AM	The Return of the Rock

such as *DaMix*, which presents black music, or *French Kiss*, a set of music by Francophone artists. Programs may also present a variety of videos organized around a structuring concept, in such series as the *MuchMusic Countdown*, a "Top 10" list, or *Much OnDemand*, a request show. A number of programs, such as *French Kiss* and the *Spotlight*, a half-hour of videos by a single artist or band, as well as the larger VideoFlow blocks, are stripped horizontally across the week—the work or school week, usually—while other programs are scattered throughout the schedule. Vertically, program material first broadcast in the afternoon may also show up in the evening or in the overnight hours.

Like radio, music television is organized in relatively small segments. Radio is often used as background to everyday activities at home or work. Apart from, say, public-radio documentaries or sportscasts it rarely gains a listener's exclusive attention, though it periodically attracts the listener to the radio for a moment, with the comments of a DJ, with a catchy commercial or piece of music or with a familiar record. Table 10.2 charts MuchMusic programming for one half-hour, and illustrates the size of the segments into which the time is divided. The longest, the Janet Jackson video, is just over four and one-half minutes, and the shortest is two seconds, a station logo that appears to run continually to be dropped into the broadcast at any time. The actual videos constitute just seconds under

TABLE 10.2

MuchMusic Programming, 7 August 2000, 1:00-1:30 P.M.

MIN.SEC.	PROGRAM
00.00	VJ: Rachel Perry
03.45	Video: Nelly, *Country Grammar*
06.25	MuchMusic logo
06.27	Video: Wyclef Jean and The Rock, *It Doesn't Matter*
10.25	Feature: *Much Stylin'* (on fashion)
12.00	VJ: Rachel Perry
13.12	Station Promo: "Janet Next on Much"
13.22	Station Promo: *Electric Circus* at Paramount Canada's Wonderland
13.52	Ad: Soft drink, Pepsi-Cola
14.22	Ad: CD, *Planet Pop 2000*
14.32	Promo: *MTV Video Music Awards* Contest
15.02	Ad: Movie, *Bless the Child*
15.32	Ad: Candy, Jolly Rancher
15.48	Ad: CD, *Dance Hits 2000*
16.20	MuchMusic logo
16.25	Video: Janet Jackson: *Doesn't Really Matter*
21.00	Video: 11:30, *Ole Ole*
24.22	MuchMusic logo
24.24	Promo: Canada Concert Listings
24.55	Ad: Game, *Who Wants to Be a Millionaire?* Playstation
25.25	Ad: Cosmetics, Neutrogena cleanser
25.40	Ad: Phone line, *Mind and Spirit* Tarot Readings
26.40	Ad: Movie, *Bless the Child*
27.10	Ad: Food service, Burger King
27.40	Ad: Candy, Skittles
27.55	Feature: *Speaker's Corner* (vox pop)
29.25	Station ID: MuchMusic
29.55	VJ: Rachel Perry

half the half-hour, and the VJ segments add considerably more time to what might be considered the broadcaster's program materials, by comparison with advertising, whether for paying advertisers or MuchMusic itself. This fragment of the broadcast day contains 28 segments, however, just over one per minute. The momentary structure of such broadcasting suggests that we are invited to join and drop out at will (or to pass over the station while grazing the channels with a remote control), or to let the television play like a radio until a piece of music or other sound might attract us to pay attention and watch.

HOW MUSIC TELEVISION RELATES TO ITS AUDIENCE

Music television drew for its format and structure in part from radio and its precedents in television variety, and it addresses its audience in ways drawn from those ancestors. Each format has its own type of person who speaks for the broadcaster, but there is little difference between a DJ introducing a record, a TV host introducing a performer, and a VJ introducing a video. There may be distinct differences in personality between stiff, older hosts—squares such as Ed Sullivan (Fig. 4.9)—and a young, relaxed, articulate, cool, and attractive VJs who presents themselves as part of the community and culture of the music. These are differences in specific cases, however. The VJ who mediates music television at least in part speaks for the viewer, and the viewer of pop-music television is typically young. Similarly, VJs have tended to be young adults who at least appear to be part of the audience for pop music, and a few are musicians themselves.

The VJ speaks for the broadcaster, but other forms of address are also expressed in music television, including additional graphic or verbal information. For example, music television helped set a model for many other broadcasters who decided to mark entire programs with a corporate logo or bug discreetly tucked in a corner of the screen throughout or appearing periodically during a show. Specialized programs might have their own logos. In addition, titles and graphics identify each video clip (see Fig. 10.1). Superimposed over the start or end of the video, they graphically name it, usually by song title, artist, album title, and recording company. All this information helps viewers to negotiate their way around the broadcast. If music television is organized in such a way that viewers may tune in and out or attend to the broadcast with only partial or distracted attention, then the broadcaster has devised ways for viewers to be continually regrounded. A viewer may switch on or hear an enticing tune. Within a few minutes, that viewer can know the name of the artist, the title of the song, and the name of the album on which it is found. Of course, such information also makes it possible for viewers to identify and buy a copy of an appealing tune, and underlines the status of the television service as an advertiser.

It also tends to attribute authorship for the video to the performer and responsibility to the recording company that underwrote the production. Unlike films or other television programs—but not unlike commercials—music video telecasts tend not to name the companies that produced the videos themselves. Propaganda Films became well-known when its logo was affixed to the end of each episode of David Lynch's *Twin Peaks* (1990–91) or his feature film *Wild at*

Heart (1990), but, creditless, it had little opportunity to advertise publicly its prolific volume (approximately 150 videos in 1990 alone), and its production of a string of distinctive videos in the late 1980s, including Steve Winwood's *Roll with It* (1988), Paula Abdul's *Straight Up* (1989), and Don Henley's *End of the Innocence* (1989). Similarly, the director of those videos also directed Madonna's expensive and elaborately designed *Express Yourself* (1989), as well as *Oh Father* (1989) and *Vogue* (1990), but they are identified less with David Fincher of Propaganda Films than they are with Madonna herself. (Fincher later used his considerable style in his feature films, including *Alien*[3] [1992] and *Se7en* [1995].) Some music television broadcasters include a director's credit as a matter of course, which probably has helped to generate some new creative pantheons and to propel some feature film careers. Perhaps the most notable example at the end of the 1990s was Spike Jonze. In a July 2000 MuchMusic marathon of the "100 Most Eye-Popping Videos of All Time," Jonze placed 2 in the top 10, Daft Punk's *Da Funk* (1997) and Weezer's *Buddy Holly* (1994), and two more, Fatboy Slim's *Praise You* (1999) and Björk's *It's Oh So Quiet*, at the 25th and 26th spots. Admittedly a nonscientific and highly subjective list, it nonetheless suggests the mark Jonze made in only a few years as an imaginative visual stylist, just as evident in his first feature, *Being John Malkovich* (1999). While there are a few stars behind the cameras, nonetheless much of the credit, authorship, and responsibility for music videos is attributed to the musicians, and credit invariably also goes to the recording company that distributes and promotes the sound recording, its product, and underwrites the video as a promotional tool.

Music television employs direct address in a number of forms to engage its viewers: by the VJ, by the use of informative graphics, by the musicians in the videos, who typically direct their performance to the camera and hence to the viewer. Even more than that, however, music television frequently invites viewers to respond or participate by holding contests and by staging competitions, including game shows, such as MTV's *Say What? MTV Karaoke* and *Sisqo's Shakedown*, a dance contest. VJs also solicit viewers' requests or dedications, as DJs have done of radio listeners for many years, and implore viewers to vote in order to rank new releases.

Both MTV and its Canadian counterparts have taken measures to make this virtual contact more real. In the late 1990s, MTV moved into its second-floor studio in the recently refurbished Times Square, where *Total Request Live* is produced. The show combines the interaction of viewer requests with the immediacy of a live telecast, but the location of the studio puts it out of the view of the people on the street. Still, fans turn up during the program, hoping to be invited into the studio during the broadcast, or perhaps to glimpse VJ Carson Daly and his guests, or maybe just to be on TV as one of the people outside. Each year, moreover, MTV goes to meet some of its audience, when during the summer months it relocates some production from New York City to a locale that suggests holidays. In 2000, it was "SoCal Summer" on the beaches of San Diego, where the VJs and hosts apparently mixed among the locals and visitors to Southern California at the beach.

MuchMusic makes the evidence of interactivity even more apparent and part of its daily routine. Its production center is located in the trendy commercial district of Toronto's Queen Street West, in a large building extensively renovated for Much and the other television operations of its owner ChumCity (named for the radio station CHUM and CITY-TV). Many of its production operations are at street level and visible through large display windows. VJs sometimes conduct their shows from the street, and the windows open for greater access. On Friday nights a crowd invariably gathers during the *Electric Circus* dance party, and when stars make personal appearances, fans crowd the streets.

If part of the purpose of commercial television is to provide advertisers with viewers, then some of the practical reasons for these devices should be quite clear. Evidence of audience response supplements ratings as markers of who exactly is watching. A goal of music television, however, seems to be to generate a heightened relation with its audience, by comparison with that of audiences for much other television. MuchMusic produces an irregularly scheduled show titled *Intimate and Interactive*, with an artist or band in performance and interview in front of a small audience in the studio and whoever collects on the street outside. Telecast live, the program also provides telephone and fax numbers and an e-mail address, inviting viewers to provide questions for the guests. This particular case illustrates the bond that music television strives to generate between viewer and television service, trying to appear both "intimate and interactive."

TYPES OF MUSIC VIDEO

Attempts to pin down a finite number of types of music video generally fall short. The vast number that have been produced in the history of the medium, and the differences among them, tend to confound easy categorization. There are always examples that defiantly cross lines marking one type from another.

Of course, videos are generally associated with each other according to the type of music they employ, not by forms or conventions that might define other types of television. On the basis of content or intent, for example, television might be subdivided into drama; news and public affairs; commercials; games; sports; and other such forms, of which music television would be one. As a narrative form, dramatic television might break down into such genres as police shows, medical shows, soaps, or family dramas, among others. News and public affairs might branch out with morning shows, nightly news, news magazines, and so-called tabloid television. With content as the basis for division, music videos are most likely to be identified through types of music: rock, rap, hiphop, country, alternative, heavy metal, classical, middle-of-the-road, jazz, and so forth. The television services themselves have organized along these lines, with MTV devoted to current music for young audiences (rock, pop, dance, rap, metal, alternative); VH-1 to other types of pop music, as well as programs about music and music videos, such as *Behind the Music* and *Pop-Up Video*; CMT to country. Segments or programs within the broadcast days are even more specialized and exclusive.

Videos can also be read according to categories that cut across their musical affiliations. As expressive forms, videos are poetic, and like poetry or other art forms, different means have been used to construct different types of expression. Most videos arguably incorporate to varying degrees elements of all the following categories: performance, narrative, non-narrative, and graphic. They all include musical performance, of course. In that they define characters enacting incidents, they invoke narrative, even if the characters are a musician or musicians and the incident is the performance of a song. Moreover, in most cases, the song itself has narrative facets, describing characters (who may be just "I" and "you") who interact. Many videos incorporate non-narrative elements and imagery that may be related by associative, rather than narrative, principles. The look of the video in itself, defined by cinematography, art direction, costume, and other crafts, is moreover a very important part of production, suggesting the significance of the graphic, although in some cases graphic properties characterize a video to particularly high degrees, even removing the action from the conventionally photographic and situating it more in animation or other pictorial forms.

Performance

The basis of the music video is musical performance. All videos concern musical performance, some exclusively so. Performance videos are often shot at a public concert. (Many videos incorporate concert footage with other visuals; some are shot at a concert, as *Dancing in the Dark* was, to use the fans as unpaid extras.) In some cases, performance film or videotape that has been shot for other purposes is repackaged for television and transformed into videos. A number from a concert film, such as *Monterey Pop*, or a television show, such as *Shindig*, may find itself on an oldies video broadcast. That a video is concerned principally with documenting a performance makes it no less meaningful than any other type of video. A performance video frequently has something to say about the audience's relations to the music and the performance itself.

Although they may take place somewhere other than a conventional entertainment venue, some videos still mainly concern the performance of a musical number. In Limp Bizkit's *Break Stuff* (1999), for example, the band and a variety of other people lip-sync the tune as they mug and otherwise heave themselves in front of the camera. Throughout much of the first part, the camera remains static, so different individuals appear and disappear to take a line or phrase of the song. In the last minute or so, the soundtrack includes the sound of other people, and the camera angles change to reveal fans outside the space to which the action has been restricted, and then the action moves outside, where the music continues and the band is surrounded by the rock fans.

Few music videos do not depict the musicians in action. In *Being Boring* (1990), the two Pet Shop Boys may be visible among the revelers at the wild party the video describes, but only momentarily, and Neil Tennant is not lip-syncing the song he sings on the soundtrack. Enigma's *Return to Innnocence* (1994) unfolds as a series of actions run in reverse, suggesting the sentiment of the title, but without any musicians represented in the video. In a few cases, the musicians may simply refuse to participate in video production. In some others the musical style—such as techno, where the action of the musicians may be visually less vivid than rock or rap artists', for example—may be consistent with the musicians' nonappearance in a video.

Narrative

Many videos are narrative in form. They outline a story, or at least the trace of a story or incident, and they delineate fictional characters, or make fictional characters of the musical performers who themselves have public personas. Unless they just play music, in videos musicians play roles and function as actors. They have already developed roles as musicians through their songs and performances, but the parts they play in videos may add to or alter their character images.

Experienced in club performance, Madonna became well-known to a wide audience through her videos before she had established her skills as a concert artist. Her videos seemed to describe her talents as a musical actor, as much as a musician. She took on a range of roles, from the original "boy toy" figure of *Like a Virgin* (1984) to the Marilyn Monroe-styled movie star of *Material Girl* (1985). She has portrayed a teenage waif who angers and disappoints her father in *Papa Don't Preach* (1986); salvation hunter in *Like a Prayer* (1989); and a sex slave in the futuristic industrial society of *Express Yourself*, with several other stops in between and since, including *Beautiful Stranger* (1998), in which she is a club performer—like the one she herself once was—who beguiles and ultimately rides off with "International Man of Mystery" Austin Powers.

Except for the last, in all these cases the video outlines a story in which Madonna plays the central character. In *Live to Tell* (1986), however, she portrays a figure whose song comments on the story. This video is a specialized case, but quite a common one, because the publicity campaigns for many movies include a video for a song on the soundtrack, as the release of *Beautiful Stranger* preceded and paved the way for *Austin Powers: The Spy Who Shagged Me* (1998). "Live to Tell" was a theme featured in *At Close Range* (1986). Like a "Coming Attractions" trailer, the video borrows footage from the film, presenting visual and narrative highlights that, even though the scenes are brief and out of order, clearly indicate the conflict the young man played by Sean Penn feels. Separated visually from the locations of the movie by the limbo lighting of a darkened studio, Madonna's song addresses his problems, seeming to speak for him—"If I live to tell the secret,/ It will burn inside of me"—like the chorus of a classical tragedy.

Many such videos position the musicians as narrator and the song as narrative, and the image track as a complement that may have a relation to the music that rewards close examination. The band or the singer frequently appears in shots completely separate from the narrative action, as, for example, Aerosmith does in *Janie's Got a Gun* (1989), but the relation of the song's narrative to that of the visuals may be less than direct, as in their *Crazy* (1993). The narrative sequences convey a story about two teenage girls (played by Alicia Silverstone and lead singer Steven Tyler's daughter Liv) on the road and on a tear, shoplifting, stripping in a bar, and enticing a farmboy out of his pants, then ditching him, all providing a particular story and characters to the more generalized lyrics.

The ways that such videos fragment the narrative suggest that the flouting of conventions of continuity typical of videos in general persists even in those that are recognizably narrative in form. Understandably for productions that run an average 5 minutes or so, the stories in videos are very condensed.

Non-narrative

Narrative suggests a story that is to some degree coherent, with characters who have definable relationships and situations that are recognizable, but many videos appear simply to be strings of images. The images themselves may be recognizable, and have associations with each other that accumulate to express a theme. They may come together less through a story than through ideas, impressions, or feelings. If we think of poetry as a literary form corresponding to the music video, and narrative videos comparable to narrative poetry, then perhaps non-narrative videos are the counterpart to lyric verse. The voice and visual presence of the performer act as a source for the impressions and images that unfold over the course of the video.

Perhaps the most self-evident case of this type is the video without images of the performer. Springsteen's *Atlantic City* (1982) stands as a short observation on contemporary social depression, represented by an assortment of barren, gray shots of the resort on the New Jersey shore, which in turn illustrate economic and social failure as they are felt by a man who clings to the last trace of hope. Because of its social theme and documentary imagery, this example may at first seem more like an essay or a speech than poetry, but poetry communicates as wide a range of ideas as any expressive form.

More often, the video incorporates the performer as a visual presence who is both involved with the imagery and, as a writer and speaker, separate from it. *Streets of Philadelphia* (1993) drew from the opening title sequence of the feature film, *Philadelphia* (1993), adding shots of Springsteen, apparently a witness singing while walking purposefully through the inner city. Paula Abdul's *(It's Just) The Way That You Love Me* (1989) organizes diverse images that illustrate wealth and power defined by brand names—Dom Perignon champagne, Visa Gold Card, Mercedes-Benz—associating them with a romantic and sexual connection between the singer and a young businessman. This suggests, on the one hand, that material goods are unimportant by comparison with the way that he loves her, and on the other, that she is one among his many possessions. Shania Twain's *Whose Bed Have Your Boots Been Under?* (1995) intercuts the performer in two situations. Dressed in casual clothes, she sits on the porch of a country house, simply singing and playing the tune to the camera. Wrapped in a form-hugging dress, she is also depicted in a diner, singing the song to the male patrons, oblivious as she nuzzles them or sashays around. In these sequences, she is something of a magical figure, unseen and unheard by the men in the restaurant as she presumably accuses them all of infidelity, the subject of the song, while showing us what they have been missing. In both cases, the images illustrate overtly or obliquely what the performer onscreen is singing about, and amplify the commentary.

Graphic

Some producers use image-making or image-processing techniques to make videos that are pictorially highly imaginative. Techniques may include forms of animation or computer-generated graphics, or may employ video processes

FIGURE 10.3

that drastically change a conventionally shot film or video image. Often the net result is the creation of an unusual or alien space for human figures. As an early example, *You Might Think* (1984), with the Cars, uses video techniques to set the action against a black background, and to manipulate the image of band leader Ric Ocasek—flattening him, or putting his head on the body of an animated housefly—as he relentlessly pursues a young woman. *Kiss* (1988), a cover version of Prince's song, sets Tom Jones against a constantly changing grid of suggestive animated drawings (Fig. 10.3). In some cases, a capacity to synthesize images and backgrounds makes it possible to create settings that have more concrete roots; the first two videos with the dance band Deee-Lite, for example, are set within bright colors and swirling and geometrical patterns that suggest the psychedelic era of the 1960s. In their *Californication* (2000), the Red Hot Chili Peppers are reconstituted as action figures racing through the video terrain of a video game, earning points as they go.

Among the most best-known examples is the animated *Sledgehammer* (1986). In simple terms, the video pixilates (pixilation is a term for frame-by-frame animation of human figures) Peter Gabriel in a close-up as he sings his hit. Starting with microscopic images of sperm, ovum, and fertilization, and ending with a human figure covered in black and strung with lights blending into a starscape, the video could be said to have a life-to-death theme culminating in union with the cosmos. What that human goes through between conception and cosmic end, however, is just as important, and the graphic treatment of Gabriel probably provides the stronger impression. His image continually transforms itself into something different, with more and more elaborate animation: designs swirl around him, moving pieces of fruit cover his face and adopt its shape, an ice sculpture of his head appears and quickly melts (Fig. 10.4).

In form, music videos are aurally restrictive but visually widely variable. Contained by the musical recording that they illustrate, the visuals have exceptionally wide possibilities. They have attracted much attention and appeared to some as an entirely new art form. This is due to visual invention, the abundance of rapidly edited, fragmentary images, and the range of image-making

FIGURE 10.4

techniques—from photography to animation to video processing to computer graphics—that producers mobilized to visualize familiar and evolving forms of popular music.

THE SOUND OF VIDEO

The most prominent formal trait of the sound of a music video is its featured musical selection. Usually it was recorded prior to the production of the video and exists independently as a recording. More often than not, it is also a song. Instrumental videos are rare, although some popular jazz artists have merited the investment, and some classical pieces have been given video treatment. Like the recording industry, however, video is ruled by popular music, in which vocals predominate.

A video is usually devoted to a single song. The song may form part of an album, and the album may yield a number of video releases. For example, Michael Jackson's album *Thriller* (1983)—a landmark for its success in sales— also produced three important videos in the formative years of MTV: *Beat It* (1983), *Billie Jean* (1983), and *Thriller* (1983). His follow-up recording *Bad* (1988) generated even more: *Bad* (1988); *The Way You Make Me Feel* (1988); *Dirty Diana* (1988); *The Man in the Mirror* (1988); and *Smooth Criminal* (1988). Within the video, the song may be introduced or framed by nonmusical material; the full version of *Bad*, for example, sets up the song with a narrative prologue much longer than the song itself. But once the song starts, it takes the most prominent role on the soundtrack, and almost invariably runs uninterrupted.

As with any type of television production, a number of elements combine on the soundtrack, principally the speaking voice, sound effects (which may include sounds recorded synchronously with dialogue, or effects added afterward), and music. Music is of course the defining element of music video, so it adopts an understandably important role in relation to speech or other sounds. In movies or television, however, voice and sound effects play important roles in constructing an impression of the reality of the depicted scene. They define a sound perspective that shapes distances and the space we see on a screen—someone or something that appears far away usually sounds far away. The sound perspective and ambience for a musical recording are uniform and consistent, however, unlike the shifting visual settings of a video. Most performance videos shot at concerts, for example, include camera angles that change from close shots to wide views of the venue, but the sound perspective remains consistent. In terms of physical space, then, the relations between music and image may seem disjointed, or the sound may not suggest the dimensions of the visual space at all.

Sound effects may add to the realism of a video, keeping the music from entirely taking over the soundtrack, or they may have an expressive impact beyond realism. Throughout *Bad*, the dozens of metal buckles on Michael Jackson's leather outfit clank and jingle as he moves. The noise underlines the musical score and reinforces at least one layer of realism in the scene. However, the soundtrack accentuates other movements with effects that are expressive—the gunshot-like beats when Michael Jackson snaps his arms, for example—but inexplicable in any realistic terms. ("Weird Al" Yankovic calls attention to this device in *Fat* (1988), his parody of *Bad*; when he notices that his arm seems to make these gunshot noises, he stops and tries it out a couple of times before he shrugs and goes on with the musical number.)

Voice in music video is mostly musical, whether singing or the rhythms of rap, but many videos also include some dialogue or other spoken voice. In many cases, dialogue is restricted to a prologue or to scenes at beginning and end that frame the musical number with narrative. *California Love* (1996), with 2Pac and Dr. Dre, for example, sets up its futuristic Thunderdome-style motif with a narrative prologue before the song starts. At the start of *Buddy Holly*, which emulates the sitcom *Happy Days* (1974–84), Al, the cook, introduces the 1990s band Weezer, who are playing Al's diner, also imploring his patrons, "Try the fish." At the end of the video, when Al asks whether anyone has taken his food recommendation, one of the band members comments, "Ah, that's not so good, Al," rounding out the situation and setting up the catchphrase that serves as a punch line.

Extensive dialogue in music videos, when they are programmed, may be entirely dispensable. After the first few weeks of its release, for example, broadcasters of *Bad* tended to drop the long sequence in which Michael Jackson's character returns from an exclusive school to the city, where his former buddies challenge him, and picked up the action near the end of their taunting, just before the song starts. In such cases, however, once again a form of nonmusical sound—voice—serves both realistic and expressive purposes.

Knowledge of the history and conventions of pop music aids any discussion of videos, because it helps illuminate the song itself. It is far beyond the scope of this discussion to outline a history of popular music, or to do more than suggest the range of current musical forms and styles that have affected the shape of music television. Nevertheless, analysis of music videos cannot justifiably ignore the music any more than analysis of narrative television can disregard exposition. The literature of music criticism has a wide range. However, videos feature songs with lyrics that can be read, quoted, and discussed for what they say and how they are arranged in relation to the images. Similarly, the songs have musical structures—whether the alternating verse/chorus pattern typical of popular song or another, more complex organization—and properties that contribute to the effects and meanings of the video. A video that might at first seem less creative or innovative than many others can serve to illustrate this point.

Bruce Springsteen's video *Born to Run* (1987) serves as a concise document and something of a souvenir of his worldwide tour in the mid-1980s, and follows the song's structure closely. It alternates between sequences drawn from a single performance in Los Angeles, at which the audio recording was made, and montages of diverse images from different concert appearances. In the montage sequences, from one shot to the next, the performers may be costumed differently, on obviously different stages, or in the daytime or under stage lights at night. The video starts with a brief montage, but the first two verses make up a coherent sequence from the Los Angeles show. It returns to a montage only at a saxophone break, then later at Springsteen's guitar break, which leads into the last verse. Instead of returning to the Los Angeles show, the video continues the montage sequence through the verse to the end of the number. The performance of the song builds to its climax through the second instrumental break to the final verse; by following its pattern, then adjusting to change that pattern slightly, the visuals both gain from the force of the music and add to it. By blending images of the many performances of "Born to Run" given by the band on its monumental tour and the single performance that, selected to be issued as a recording and video, gains status as an exemplary performance, the video also implies that all the performances were as special, as exciting, and as rewarding as that one.

THE LOOK OF VIDEO

Music video has many different looks. Along with commercials and graphic title sequences, videos have been a site for technical and artistic exploration beyond the conventions of everyday television. Lots of money and extensive resources can be concentrated into producing a 5-minute music video, such as *Scream* (1995), Michael and Janet Jackson's starkly futuristic, black-and-white clip, which cost a reported $7 million. Alternatively, a new and unknown act or an independent label might produce a successful video for only a couple of thousand dollars, although they still face the challenge of getting such a clip on the air, since most videos programmed on music television come from the major labels.

Visually, there are few requirements or strict conventions in videos. In fact, part of the force of music videos resides in their capacity to flout conventions and run contrary to expectations. This is because video producers acknowledge the status of the television as image, not exclusively a representation of the real world. They use and adapt properties of the film and video image that producers of television drama or news are likely not to touch in the body of their programs.

Since the 1960s, for example, color has been a standard for broadcasting. Almost no programs are regularly produced in black and white, and the very few black-and-white sequences or episodes that might appear are usually

FIGURE 10.5

bracketed as a character's memories, as historical images, as fantasy, or otherwise different. In music video production, however, the black-and-white image has been adopted as part of the expressive palette. The Red Hot Chili Peppers' *Give it Away* (1991), for example, combines black-and-white imagery with expressive makeup and costuming to produce imagery with a disarmingly alien sheen. Sheryl Crow's *Leaving Las Vegas* (1993) uses similar techniques to similar ends. Video processing also permits the alteration of tones and color within the image. The overall look of Michelle Shocked's *On the Greener Side* (1989) is black and white, except that in each shot some objects or items of clothing are colored green.

Some video producers have mimicked existing visual styles of black-and-white photography or cinema. Madonna's *Vogue* recalls the rich glamour photography of George Hurrell, and the close-up portraits that constitute Lyle Lovett's *Pontiac* (1987) might bring to mind some of Walker Evans's Depression-era photos, while Don Henley's *The End of the Innocence* (1989; Fig. 10.5) imitates both the snapshot style and roadside imagery of Robert Frank.[3] Smashing Pumpkins' *Tonight Tonight* (1996) imitates Georges Méliès's 1902 film *A Trip to the Moon*, for example; Stone Temple Pilots' *Interstate Love Song* (1994) opens with a prologue that emulates silent-era melodrama; and the Red Hot Chili Peppers' *Otherside* (2000) poaches the visual style and imagery of the German Expressionist *The Cabinet of Dr. Caligari* (1920). In general, video producers who choose black and white likely do so precisely because it is different from the conventional television image, and consequently stands out as distinctive among the predominating television images made in naturalistic color.

In addition, of course, color photography provides a wide range of possibilities for distinctive looks, from the rich saturation of Madonna's *Express Yourself* (Fig. 10.6), its story and elaborate design modeled on Fritz Lang's *Metropolis* (1927), to the muddy brown tones of Nirvana's slow-motion pep rally, which conveys anything but pep, *Smells Like Teen Spirit* (1991). In some cases, again, the look of the video may echo or refer to a specific, other style. One of the best

FIGURE 10.6

examples, because its concept required the meticulous matching of new images with old, is Weezer's *Buddy Holly*, which intercuts shots from *Happy Days* with images of the band, shot as if they were actually appearing on an episode. The video reproduces not only the setting of Al's place and the personal styles of the characters, but also the flat lighting and washed-out color of the 1970s sitcom in order to be able to edit reactions by Richie, Joanie, and other characters, as well as a concluding dance by the Fonz, clearly seen from the front in older shots and from the back in newer ones, into the clip.

Content involves a wide range of possibilities, but a music video typically does depict the performer. If the aural function of the video is to present recorded music, the main visual function is to present the performers—to attract fans not only by their sound, but also by the way they look, act, move, and dress.

Since the musical number exists prior to the video, the images are edited to correspond to properties of the recording. As the *Born to Run* example suggests, such connections can be made on the relatively large level of structure, where sequences in the video might correspond to entire stanzas or instrumental breaks in the song. Videos are also edited according to the beat of the recording. This does not mean that every cut or movement happens on a beat of music, but the changes between a loose correspondence and a more rigid one can create a very strong impact.

As with all television, one means by which videos position the viewer is through exchanges of looks by figures onscreen. Often performers look off-screen, toward a single listener or an audience. The listener or audience may be implied, or may be represented through a returned look. Such an exchange, alternating the looks of a performer and a listener, involves the viewer to some degree in the relationship. For most of *Dancing in the Dark*, Bruce Springsteen sings to a large, faceless audience of thousands. We see Springsteen from the perspective of a member of the audience, and we see the audience for whom he performs. As he reaches the end of the song, the view of the audience concentrates on the front row and several female fans, isolated from the crowd by lighting. What was a generalized exchange of looks between thousands of viewers and one performer becomes an exchange between two people, as Springsteen appears to make eye contact with a young woman (played by Courteney Cox), reaches out his hand, and pulls her onstage to dance with him as the song fades out.

This video illustrates the specifics of the relation between performer and fan that the exchange of looks implies, but often such exchanges are used to outline more general relations among characters or figures onscreen. Alanis Morissette's *Ironic* (1995) relies heavily on this editing figure, as she plays, apparently, four women in an automobile. Unlike Britney Spears's *Lucky* (2000), for which special visual effects created composite images allowing the singer to play two parts, Morissette's multiple figures result solely from the editing, and the characters never appear in the same frame. Editing creates a coherent space in the automobile, in which the four Alanises occupy different quarters of the car, and the vehicle always appears to be traveling in the same direction. When we see the Alanis in the driver's seat, for example, the landscape passes from screen right to left (Fig. 10.7), while the Alanis in the passenger seat, the reverse angle, sits in front of trees passing left to right (Figs. 10.10, 10.12). Eyeline matches generate the impression that they interact, and that they are singing together. Alanis 2 appears to sing a line in response to Alanis 1. Video form follows song form, to an extent, since the song starts with a slow and wistfully sung verse about different types of disappointing situations. The rear-view mirror discloses that Alanis 2 (Figs. 10.8, 10.10) is listening to Alanis 1 (Figs. 10.7, 10.9, 10.11). When the verse ends, the song slams into a shouted chorus, sung by Alanis 2 in the back seat, followed by a new verse sung by a third Alanis, also in the back (Figs. 10.12-10.13). As the video starts and ends, the Alanis who is driving is actually alone. Perhaps the video suggests diverse facets of the young woman Alanis Morissette portrays, but the impression of multiple characters generated by editing, within the world the video describes, is illusory, too.

Performers often look into the camera, implicitly to make eye contact with and sing directly to the viewer. Such a device underscores the address of a song to someone other than the performers or characters within the video, and generates a relation of identification for the viewer with the person to whom the song is addressed. However, it can be used to elicit different emotional reactions. Sinead O'Connor's extended gaze into the camera in *Nothing Compares 2 U* (1989) suggests a reflective appeal, as the title implies, though her looks off-camera are not evidently directed at anything or anyone, and seem to be moments of punctuation as she collects her thoughts before resuming her song (Figs. 10.14–10.15). Bruce Springsteen's unwavering gaze into the camera in the single-take *Brilliant Disguise* (1987) adds intensity and immediacy to the song, which recounts a troubled conversation with a lover. By contrast, the gaze into the camera of David Byrne's *Don't Fence Me In* (1990) removes personal emotion, depicting in quick succession close-ups of dozens of people lip-syncing the Cole Porter song.

Videos are frequently cited for the diversity of images they include and the rapid pace of their editing. To be sure, such qualities are typical of many rock videos, but they are not a requirement of the form. Some videos are frenetically paced, others have a slower rhythm. R.E.M.'s *Everybody Hurts* (1993) matches

FIGURE 10.7

FIGURE 10.8

FIGURE 10.9

FIGURE 10.10

FIGURE 10.11

FIGURE 10.12

FIGURE 10.13

the languorous tempo and keening lyrics of the song with measured traveling shots along a highway bumper-to-bumper with vehicles intercut with people caught in the traffic jam, as subtitles appear under the images, informing us of the individuals' thoughts. In the Verve's *Bittersweet Symphony (1998)*, singer Richard Ashcroft strides up a street, and people watch him as he walks by, sometimes brushing against a passer-by, pushing others out of the way, as the camera steadily follows his action, pulling back from his front or following him from the rear. Another example even more self-consciously runs against the grain of the typical music video: the wryly and subversively titled *This Song Don't Have a Video* (1989), in which, in a single take, Loudon Wainwright III sits in a chair, turns on a tape recorder, and listens to "This Song Don't Have a Video," until he gets up, leaves the frame, and lets the song finish and the tape run out.

Such a case, where the visuals are as continuous and unbroken as the music, are rare. Videos are typically discontinuous. A single video may use images

FIGURE 10.14

FIGURE 10.15

FIGURE 10.16

ranging from elaborately produced scenes to stock footage from a past production to actual home movie footage. Color and black-and-white images may adjoin each other, and pictures of widely varying quality and resolution may combine to illustrate a single song. They frequently isolate and depict in parts—of bodies, of objects, of actions, and of events. Even the screen itself may comprise parts, as in the Tragically Hip's *Ahead by a Century* (1996), in which several frames within the frame are arranged to depict the band members (by contrast with the more conventional image qualities of the allusive narrative with which the band images are intercut; Fig. 10.16). R.E.M.'s *Man in the Moon* (1993) uses a similar technique, situating screens within the screen. In effect, many videos fragment the visible world and recombine them with music.

One of the most important features of the video image is movement itself. Obviously, rhythmic movement is an integral part of dance and musical performance. Cutting on movement—making a splice while an object or figure onscreen is in motion, or while the camera is moving—is a convention of editing that can yield an enhanced sense of continuity and seamlessness from shot to shot in the organization of a sequence. Many videos employ a nearly constantly moving camera, permitting such continuity, as well as generating a visual rhythm corresponding to the rhythm of the music. The movement of objects or people onscreen, or the movement of the camera over objects, persons, or a scene, along with the continuity of the music track, acts as means of reintegrating the visual pieces.

SAMPLE ANALYSIS

Everything is Everything (1998) has a narrative component, in that it depicts a fantastical situation in which the people of New York City discover that Manhattan has become a long-playing record on a turntable. Lauryn Hill is the central character, although her role largely involves noting this phenomenon, and walking through the streets of New York while other people come to realize what is happening. Story of any complexity in the video remains subordinated to the computer-generated, visual conceit.

The video starts with a traveling shot, moving along a city street, accompanied by ambient sounds, but that realistic effect soon vanishes as a gigantic turntable arm drops into frame (Fig. 10.17). When the stylus touches the roadway, a click ends the street noise and replaces it with the surface noise of a vinyl record and the growing pitch of music as the record seems to be gathering speed. (That the steady traveling shot suggested the record might already be up to speed seems unimportant.) As the music of Lauryn Hill's recording starts, wider angles reveal Manhattan Island turning around a spindle represented by the Empire State Building, inflated in size to dwarf all the other skyscrapers, with the turntable arm resembling one of the bridges to the island (Fig. 10.18). One view presents the Empire State Building's shadow, static in the frame as it falls across the revolving city, seen from high above (Fig. 10.19).

Lauryn Hill appears first not as a performer, but in afuzzy, haloed image (Fig. 10.20). It turns out to be an shot made through distorting layers of glass, in a diner where she is served through a slot. She sings the opening chorus in this setting, in this style of image. The picture clears after she sits to eat, and she first sees the gigantic turntable arm pass by the restaurant window. From the restaurant, she watches a shakedown across the road, but then a massive hand reaches down to the ground, moving the disc—the whole island, actually—back and forth like a club DJ, in the process breaking up the bust (Fig. 10.21–10.22). Not only has the city been transformed into a record, but also someone is in control of the turntable.

Hill then leaves to walk through the city as the giant stylus also tracks through the streets (Fig. 10.23). As she does, the video depicts people engaged in events, such as loading clothes at a laundromat or taking out one's frustration on a public phone, everyday occurrences that contrast strongly with the bizarre transformation of a city into a long-playing record. Hill's character is the first to react to the weird sights, but while others discover the strange turn of events incredulously, although understated in their astonishment, she walks or runs with an apparent resolve, following the movement of the stereo cartridge toward the center of the record. Like many singers in music videos, she moves through the world while singing about it, both part of it and apart from it. This is consistent with her status as a narrator and commentator, in song, while New Yorkers gape upward as they see what's going on.

"What's going on" is significant, since the recording featured in the video recalls Motown recordings, including Stevie Wonder's work, but also Marvin Gaye's landmark 1971 hit of that title. In style, it recalls the rich, rhythmic, and orchestral soul of Gaye's recording, while also adding features of hiphop and contemporary dance music, a combination that characterizes Hill's first solo album, *The Miseducation of Lauryn Hill*, which includes "Everything is Everything." Where Gaye's arrangements are fluid, carried in part by a soaring soprano saxophone and wordless chorale, Hill's contains a forthright beat and the abrasive sounds of a scratch DJ playing the turntable. Hill's song also includes a rap, which maintains the beat of the music while considerably changing both the vocal style from singing to speech and the verbal, shifting from a more conventional lyric to the allusive and highly encoded language

FIGURE 10.17

FIGURE 10.18

FIGURE 10.19

FIGURE 10.20

FIGURE 10.21

FIGURE 10.22

FIGURE 10.23

FIGURE 10.24

FIGURE 10.25

FIGURE 10.26

FIGURE 10.27

of rap and hiphop. This passage creates a distinctive musical bridge. Gaye's recording predated rap by several years, although in addition to his luscious tenor singing voice, a responsive, spoken "Right on" or two punctuate the tune.

Both Hill and Gaye pose questions or set problems and posit conclusions or resolutions in answer. In his song Gaye asks, "What's going on?" about the decimating impact of the Vietnam War, racial strife, and social dissent on the United States, resolving, ". . . we've got to find a way/to bring some lovin' here today." Hill's lyric echoes Gaye's incomprehension about the current state of things, observing,

> It seems we lose the game
> Before we even start to play.
> Who made these rules?
> We're so confused,
> Easily led astray.

Later she observes, in a passage that clearly echoes Gaye's song,

> Let's love ourselves then we can't fail
> To make a better situation.

Gaye's chorus first asks, "What's going on?" but finally concludes, "I'll tell you/ What's going on." Hill's starts with a holistic "Everything is everything/After winter must come spring," finally concluding, "Change comes eventually."

The imaginative concept for the video may derive from the song's central rap. This passage alludes to religious myths and practices and builds a chain of images:

> I philosophy
> Possibly speak tongues
> Beat drum, Abyssinian, street Baptist
> Rap this in fine linen
> From the beginning
> My practice extending across the atlas
> I begat this

In part, it suggests the spiritual unity of the speaker with a higher being, a general tenet of Rastafarianism. With references to Abyssinia and the "tomb of Nefertiti," and "the Serengeti," this segment of the lyric suggests the "return to Africa" sentiments of the Jamaica-based movement, while also, with a mention of "cherubims [sic] in Nassau Coliseum," referring both to the Caribbean and to New York's suburban Long Island. Like the song as a whole, this section resolves in an image of hopeful change, as "Where hiphop meets scripture/Develop a negative into a positive picture."

Imagery in the video restates the connection with Rasta culture. Hill's own personal appearance, crowned with dreadlocks, suggests the culture, but so does the use of Jamaican colors, green, red, and yellow, and the image of the lion of Judah on the window of the restaurant where the action starts (Fig. 10.24).

The structure of the video matches the structure of the song, although generally not in lockstep. When the tune is scratched, like a turntable, the image may shift laterally to represent the disc-like, back-and-forth movement of the city, but video sequences do not rigorously coincide with the verses and chorus or with musical changes, with one significant exception. The first point at which Hill sings directly into the camera, in close-up, appears at the rap that serves as the song's bridge (Fig. 10.25). This new angle and direct visual and vocal address emphatically punctuate the video, as the rap does the song, providing an equally strong vocal and verbal change. Overall, the shape of the video can be said to follow that of the song, in that the clip starts with the stylus dropping into the groove of the roadway and ends when the needle reaches the center label. So does Lauryn Hill, whose destination on this trek through the city ends up the record label revolving around the spindle, the Empire State Building (Fig. 10.26).

Links between Hill's song, "Everything is Everything," and the video imagery are not rigid, however. The video does not simply illustrate the song, and it goes without saying that the song is not about an oversized stylus tracking the Manhattan streets, although the use of surface noise and scratching as features of the original recording may have suggested the visual conceit of the video. In fact, the video modifies the musical mix, also reinforcing connections between audio and video. The scratching rhythm so prominent on the CD is significantly reduced on the soundtrack of the video. Its audible presence rises when it is matched with the shifting of the image representing the manual movement of the turntable. At another point, the video actually adds an audio feature not in the original version of the song, explicitly connecting the audible qualities of the soundtrack to the action on screen. When the giant stylus catches a newspaper front page (with the headline, "WAR!") and drags it through the street, the sound quality thins, as a piece of dirt might diminish a stereo system's fidelity (Fig. 10.27). In both these cases, of course, the properties of the soundtrack underline the idea that the gigantic stereo system actually is playing "Everything is Everything," encoded in the streets of the city.

Like many videos, *Everything is Everything* has something of an open form that does not yield a single message. Lauryn Hill's song carries suggestions of a search for a holistic existence, and a resolve that it will come to pass. Although it refers to social distress and confusion, it also conveys ideas of evolutionary change, something that perhaps is also suggested by the image of a musical apparatus tracking irresistibly through the city streets, from the edge to the center, raising music all the way.

Although the image of a city magically transformed into such an object as an LP might at first seem disruptive or threatening, it also suggests that the world is subject to the DJ as deity. Although this characterization may seem a bit flip, it does suggest ideas of higher spiritual powers, or a being who oversees the everyday lives of people, and of the transformative values of music. That the overall structure follows that of a recorded song—from dropping the needle to its arrival at the label—and that the central character follows this same path strongly indicates the video's concern for the music itself. The musical style, which mixes the melodic qualities of soul with the rhythmic properties of hiphop, is conventionally associated with the city, one of the key subjects of the video. While the city is depicted as a place of some stress, a higher power can elicit the musical properties of an urban setting. In fact this 4-minute video, in that it imagines music encoded in the streets as it is imprinted in the groove of a record, figuratively depicts urban music as "music of the streets."

SUMMARY

After a prehistory in cinema, radio, and other forms of television, music television and music videos as they developed after the introduction of MTV have exerted tremendous impact. That it may be difficult to tell the difference between a commercial for jeans and a music video suggests that each has drawn from the other. Television dramas and situation comedies regularly use musical sequences. Beyond their influence on television itself, videos have been seen as detrimental to morality, as time-wasters, for some as evidence of postmodern culture, for others as evidence of social decay, but music television has persisted as a staple among the selections on the dial.

Music videos are a form of advertising for recorded music and promotion for the performers they feature, but they also make up the programming material for music television services and programs. They are intended to sell as well as to entertain. They have become one of television's main venues for the presentation of popular music and the representation of its performers. They consequently are affiliated with the music industry and share some of its interests.

Whether narrative, non-narrative, performance, or graphic (most likely combining elements of all these), a video generally revolves around a single musical number. Visually, it may be coherently organized by principles of continuity editing, but just as likely it has discontinuity, relying on associations of images to construct themes or evoke feelings that lend it unity for the viewer. The tools by which music television and music videos may be analyzed and discussed are essentially no different than those used for any other type of television, although rhythm and structure, which have as much to do with the music as the video, may seem more abstract than do the story and character that underpin narrative. By comparison with narrative television, music television is a more evidently open form.

FURTHER READINGS

The hit parade of music television changes constantly, making the selection of current examples to illustrate this discussion impossible. What is in high rotation on MTV as this is written will have fallen off the charts by the time you read this chapter. You may be able to find the examples discussed here in collections available on home video. As important, however, you should be able to measure these observations against other examples of music video and music television.

Several examples in my discussion of music television are drawn from MuchMusic, in Canada. In part that is because I am writing from Canada, where MTV and VH-1 are not carried on cable TV. (A version of MuchMusic, by the way, is available in the United States.) This offers you an opportunity to make comparisons. You should be able to measure these findings against MTV or whatever music television service is available to you, which may turn up some subtle and some not-so-subtle differences.

MTV's and MuchMusic's Websites (www.mtv.com and www.muchmusic. com) offer valuable adjuncts to examination of music television. They provide information about the broadcasters, programs, and VJs, but they also offer useful material for an examination of the ways music television tries to interact with its audiences. They suggest moreover the growth and breadth of the broadcasters' reach, not least in the links to international services the two corporations operate in Asia, Europe, and South America.

Video and music television have become important parts of the world of pop music. This change is reflected in contemporary writing on the music and its performers, such as the five articles Simon Frith commissioned for his anthology, *Facing the Music* (New York: Pantheon, 1988), including his own "Video Pop: Picking Up the Pieces." An early consideration of video by an authority on popular music is Dave Laing, "Music Video: Industrial Product, Cultural Form," *Screen* 26, no. 2 (March–April 1985): 78–83. One of the key sources for investigating music television is the popular press, in particular the segment of the press devoted to music or youth. *Rolling Stone*, for one, covered the innovation and development of MTV, and presented the first book-length assessment in Michael Shore, *The Rolling Stone Book of Rock Video* (New York: Rolling Stone Press, 1984). For institutional studies of the U.S. music television service, see R. Serge Denisoff, *Inside MTV* (New Brunswick, NJ: Transaction, 1988), and Jack Banks, *Monopoly Television: MTV's Quest to Control the Music* (Boulder, CO: Westview, 1996).

The impact of music videos and music television is reflected in the volume of criticism devoted to the form in the 1980s. One of the first substantial discussions is Marsha Kinder, "Music Video and the Spectator: Television, Ideology, and Dream," *Film Quarterly* 38, no. 1 (Fall 1984): 2–15. A later contribution to the same journal is my own "Musical Cinema, Music Video, Music Television," *Film Quarterly* 43, no. 3 (Spring 1990): 2–14. Several journals devoted entire issues to articles on music television, or relations of music, film, and TV. *Journal of Communication Inquiry* 10, no. 1 (Winter 1986) included a number of influential articles, such as Margaret Morse, "Post Synchronizing Rock Music and Television": 15–28, reprinted in *Television Criticism: Approaches and Applications*, eds. Leah R. Vande Berg and Lawrence A. Wenner (New York: Longman, 1991). *Wide Angle* 10, no. 2 (1988), titled "Film/Music/Video," contains articles not only on music videos and MTV, but also Japanese music video production and Spanish-language music television, as well as musical performance in feature films. A valuable, detailed analysis of a single video can be found in Kobena Mercer, "Monster Metaphors: Notes on Michael Jackson's *Thriller*," *Screen* 27, no. 1 (January–February 1986): 26–43.

MTV and the proliferation of music video on television coincided with the rise of postmodernism as an intellectual and historical frame for cultural studies. In fact, television and music television were frequently cited as evidence of the postmodern era. The first book-length, critical study of MTV appeared in this context: E. Ann Kaplan, *Rocking Around the Clock: Music Television, Postmodernism, and Consumer Culture* (New York: Methuen, 1987). Kaplan's analysis, from the perspective of a U.S.-based feminism, informed by psychoanalytic theory, and an approach deriving from film studies, opened itself up to rebuttal from the point of view of cultural studies, informed by Marxism and musical studies, notably Andrew Goodwin, "Music Video in the (Post)Modern World," *Screen* 28, no. 3 (Summer 1987): 36–55. Goodwin developed his discussion in his valuable book *Dancing in the Distraction Factory: Music Television and Popular Culture* (Minneapolis: University of Minnesota Press, 1992). Comparable positions appear in the anthology Goodwin edited with Simon Frith and Lawrence Grossberg, *Sound and Vision: The Music Video Reader* (London: Routledge, 1993), which also includes Mercer's article on *Thriller*. Furthermore, Kaplan's study caught MTV at a point of organizational transition, made clear in Lauren Rabinovitz, "Animation, Postmodernism, and MTV," *Velvet Light Trap* 24 (Fall 1989): 99–112. This augments the literature with a brief discussion of the political economy of MTV, as well as a consideration of the significance of animation techniques in music television. Among other valuable investigations of music television and its political and ideological implications are Deborah H. Holdstein, "Music Video: Messages and Structures," *Jump Cut* 29 (1984): 1, 13–14; and Pat Aufderheide, "Music Videos: The Look of the Sound," in *Watching Television*, ed. Todd Gitlin (New York: Pantheon, 1986), 111–35.

Robert C. Allen, ed. *Channels of Discourse* (Chapel Hill: University of North Carolina Press, 1987, revised in 1992, and retitled *Channels of Discourse, Reassembled*) is a collection of original essays that discuss television from different critical approaches, and music videos figure prominently in Kaplan's essay on feminism and John Fiske's on British cultural studies. Both use as examples Madonna, and *Material Girl* in particular. Fiske develops his analysis of music TV in his book *Television Culture* (New York: Methuen, 1987) and in the two-part chapter titled "Madonna" and "Romancing the Rock" in his *Reading the Popular* (Boston: Unwin Hyman, 1989), 95–132. Madonna is also a central character in Lisa A. Lewis's investigations of popular music, music TV, and female fans. See her book *Gender Politics and MTV* (Philadelphia: Temple University Press, 1990), which concentrates on four stars: Madonna, Cyndi Lauper, Tina Turner, and Pat Benatar.

ENDNOTES

[1] Jack Banks discusses some of the implications of the rotation system, and the changes in it over MTV's history, in his *Monopoly Television: MTV's Quest to Control the Music* (Boulder, CO: Westview, 1996), 184–85.

[2] Andrew Goodwin, *Dancing in the Distraction Factory: Music Television and Popular Culture* (Minneapolis: University of Minnesota Press, 1992), 142–43, reprinted in his "Fatal Distractions: MTV Meets Postmodern Theory," in Simon Frith, Andrew Goodwin, and Lawrence Grossberg, eds., *Sound and Vision: The Music Video Reader* (London: Routledge, 1993), 57.

[3] For examples of the photographic style that inspired Madonna's *Vogue*, see George Hurrell, *Portfolios of George Hurrell* (Santa Monica, CA: Graystone Books, 1991). Walker Evans's pictures are widely reproduced in collections concerning U.S. government sponsored photography of the 1930s, but probably the best source is the classic book in which they were first collected, James Agee and Evans's *Let Us Now Praise Famous Men* (Boston: Houghton Mifflin, 1941). The images of Don Henley's *The End of the Innocence* derive from Robert Frank's influential collection *The Americans* (New York: Grove Press, 1959).

CHAPTER 11

Animated Television:
The Narrative Cartoon

Animation has had a rather erratic presence on television. A mainstay of Saturday morning children's programming, small snippets of it appear regularly in commercials, credit sequences, music videos, news and sports, but there have been long stretches when there were no prime-time cartoon shows. After *The Flintstones* ended its original run in 1966 there wasn't another successful prime-time cartoon show until 23 years later, when *The Simpsons* debuted. Since 1989 there has been something of a Renaissance in television animation. Numerous prime-time cartoon programs have appeared and at least three cable channels have arisen that feature cartoons—the Cartoon Network, Nickleodeon, and Toon Disney. And, of course, cartoons continue to dominate the TV ghettos of Saturday morning and weekday afternoons.

Although numerous new animated programs are now being created, many of the cartoons regularly telecast today were produced 50, 60, or even 70 years ago. As much as any other aspect of television, cartoons illustrate the medium's ability to recycle old material. Thus, to understand animation we need to examine the evolution of narrative cartoons in both film and television. This will be the general purpose of this chapter. However, as we outline cartooning's history, we will also discuss its technology, aesthetics, and economics—each of which plays a significant part in determining how animation is created and presented on television. From *Gertie the Dinosaur* (1914) to *South Park* (1997–), cartoons have depended on technology to achieve aesthetic goals that are always restricted by cost (especially since cartoons mainly appeal to children, an audience without direct buying power). This chapter sketches how technology, aesthetics, and economics have intertwined to produce contemporary television animation as it has taken form in storytelling cartoons.

BEGINNINGS

Figures from cinematic animation were present at the various "births" of broadcast television. Among the very first experimental images transmitted by

RCA/NBC engineers in the late 1920s was a wooden doll of Felix the Cat, a cartoon star of the silent cinema. It was placed on a phonograph turntable and slowly rotated under painfully hot lights before the camera. A decade later, Disney's *Donald's Cousin Gus* was broadcast as part of NBC's first full evening of programming, on W2XBS, May 3, 1939. It would be many years, however, before cartoons as we know them would be created specifically for television. Early cartoon programming on television relied instead on short subjects initially exhibited in movie theaters and featuring now familiar characters such as Felix, Popeye, Bugs Bunny, Mickey Mouse, Donald Duck, Woody Woodpecker, Betty Boop, et al. As these shorts served to establish cartooning's basic mode of production, and since many of them still appear on television, a significant portion of our consideration of television animation will address the cartoon designed originally for the cinema.

Like live-action video and film, animation relies on the illusion of movement being created from a succession of still frames. But that is where their similarities end. Unlike other forms of video and film, a camera in an animation production is not pointed at real people in real settings. Rather, conventional animators aim their cameras at handmade drawings on paper or cels and computer-based animation generates images out of digital models. Animation's mode of production leads to unique economic imperatives, necessitates certain technologies, and raises distinct aesthetic issues that do not apply to other forms of video and film production.

The factors necessary for the creation of film cartoons came together soon after motion pictures were invented in the 1890s, but their initial development was slower than that of live-action cinema. Established newspaper cartoonists such as Winsor McCay became involved with the infant medium after the turn of the century, but their task was daunting: approximately 16–20 frames had to be drawn for every single second of film, 960 to 1200 per minute.[1] McCay's influential *Gertie the Dinosaur*, which ran about 7 minutes, comprised some 10,000 individual drawings (Fig. 11.1). It's small wonder that McCay's films often took years to prepare. The length of time involved in such cartoon productions discouraged film studio executives. If cartooning were to become a commercial reality, it would need a more cost-effective mode of production.

This economic imperative led to a simple technological refinement. McCay and other animators had been drawing and redrawing every detail of every frame to show movement, even when the action was occurring in a small part of the frame. In 1914 Earl Hurd applied for a patent on a process in which a transparent sheet of **celluloid**, commonly referred to as a **cel**, is placed before a background drawing (see Fig. 11.2, a detail from the patent application). The animator then needed only to draw the segment of the image that moves (which is transferred to the cel). The background stays constant and thus does not need to be redrawn. At the same time, John R. Bray had been aggressively patenting animation techniques and suing anyone who dared infringe on them. He united with Hurd to form the Bray-Hurd Process Company, and they began charging a fee for the use of cel technology—thus initially slowing its acceptance. Most animation studios of the 1910s and 1920s continued to painstakingly redraw every detail, to avoid the Bray-Hurd fees and Bray's litigious wrath. It wasn't until the early 1930s that animators converted to Hurd's system, and paid to use his cels. The shift to cel animation came close on the heels of another, more

FIGURE 11.1

significant technological invention (one that also had economic and aesthetic ramifications): the popularization of sound film in 1927.

During the silent era, cartoons had little more status than did parlor games, such as flip cards, the phenakistoscope (Fig. 11.3), and the zoetrope (Fig. 11.4), that had been popular during the 19th century.[2] Many of the studios that specialized in silent cartoon production went bankrupt before the coming of sound, because cartooning had not yet developed an efficient mode of production. With the arrival of sound, a major animation producer also arrived who would standardize and dominate theatrical cartooning and who was the first to take full advantage of the new sound technology. This was the impact of Walt Disney.

FIGURE 11.2

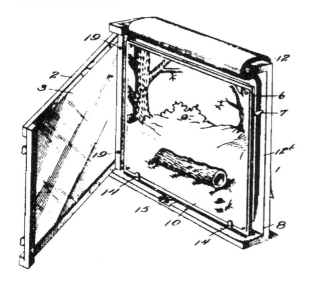

FIGURE 11.3

FIGURE 11.4

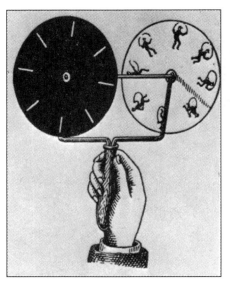

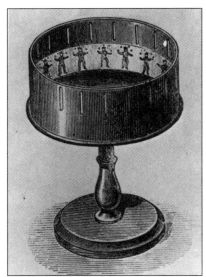

The Jazz Singer, the film that popularized sound in live-action cinema, was released in the Fall of 1927. On November 28 of the following year, Disney released the first significant sound cartoon, *Steamboat Willie*, featuring Mickey Mouse. The popularity of *Steamboat Willie* had three major repercussions on the animation industry.

First, it established Mickey Mouse as a major figure. At that time he had only appeared in two cartoons that had not been distributed to the public. He would go on, of course, to be possibly the most widely marketed cartoon character in the world and form a central component of Disney's theme parks, long-running, self-promoting television program, and cable channel.[3]

Second, *Steamboat Willie* positioned Disney as the 1930s' preeminent producer of cartoons. His studios in California (previously animation production had been based mostly in New York) attracted prominent cartoonists of the time, and he soon developed a cost-effective mode of production. To achieve this economy of production Disney divided his workers into specialized departments. Some focused on story development while others worked more on the animation. Disney's studio was also the first to use **storyboards** (Fig. 7.1), sketches that show the progression of the entire cartoon. With a precise outline of the full cartoon, Disney's animators were able to work more efficiently, the narrative structure was clearer, and Disney, the producer, was better able to control pre-production and minimize costs.

In addition to the stabilization of production budgets through Disney-pioneered methods, distribution costs were also standardized in the 1930s when major studios such as Paramount, Warner Brothers, Universal, and MGM signed distribution contracts with cartoon studios, or created their own cartoon departments whose product they distributed to theaters they themselves owned. Thus, by the mid-1930s animation producers had developed a cost-effective mode of production and distribution.

Third, with *Steamboat Willie*, Disney set the aesthetic standards for cartoons with sound. His approach to cartooning would continue to govern animation aesthetics throughout the 1930s—determining much of how cartoons looked and sounded.

THE AESTHETICS OF THE 1930S SOUND CARTOON: DISNEY'S DOMINATION

Naturalism Versus Abstraction

The aesthetics of animation has long been split between **naturalism** and **abstraction**. Naturalism advocates animation that replicates live-action film or videotape as much as possible. According to this aesthetic, cartoon characters should resemble objects in reality, and our view of cartoon figures should resemble a camera's view of real humans and objects. Abstraction, in contrast, maintains that the essence of cartooning is lines, shapes, and colors (or shades of gray)—*abstract* forms that animators may manipulate as they wish.

The extremes of these two positions seldom exist. Only now are computer-generated animations reaching a level of technical sophistication where a fabricated character might be mistaken for a real human—as can be seen in *Final Fantasy: The Spirits Within* (2001; Fig. 11.5)—but hand-drawn animation will probably never achieve this level of naturalism. And few cartoons are made that have no characters resembling real life objects, though there have been important exceptions to this, such as Norman McLaren's *Begone Dull Care* (Fig. 11.6; 1949). Most cartoons, especially ones that are broadcast on television, balance these two extremes. Drawn characters and objects bear enough correspondence with reality for us to recognize them, but animators do not draw every leaf on every tree.

The naturalist impulse began to dominate the Disney studio's productions in the 1930s as they aspired to feature-length theatrical cartoons such as *Snow White* (1937). Disney's naturalism has continued through its recent releases such as *Beauty and the Beast* (1991) and *The Lion King* (1994). Among the naturalistic changes Disney implemented during the 1930s were heightened rounding and shading of characters and objects. Silent-era characters such as Gertie

FIGURE 11.5

FIGURE 11.6

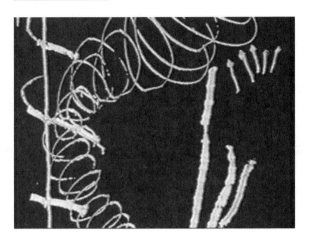

and Felix the Cat tend to appear flat, emphasizing their two-dimensionality (Fig. 11.1). Disney's animators used shading to create a more rounded appearance. Their characters, although two-dimensional, give a greater illusion of three-dimensionality. They seem almost bulbous.

Disney's Use of Sound and Other New Technologies

Disney's *Steamboat Willie* was more than a silent cartoon with music attached. After all, this would actually have been nothing new. "Silent" cartoons were hardly ever presented silently. When they were shown in theaters, they were nearly always accompanied by a pianist, band, or full orchestra. What is different about *Steamboat Willie* is that the movement in the image is precisely synchronized to the music, because *the music was planned before the images.* Linda Obalil explains: "Since music can be broken down mathematically, the animation was drawn to follow a musical pattern. For example, if the music had two beats per second, the animation would hit a beat every 12 frames (based on 24 frames per second)."[4] With this innovation, *Steamboat Willie* set an aesthetic standard for the synchronization of image and sound in animation. In the most highly regarded cartoons of the 1930s, sound does not merely overlay the image; instead, it dynamically interacts with character movement.

Music often forms the structuring principle for 1930s cartoons—as is evident in the titles of cartoon series such as Disney's "Silly Symphonies" and Warner Brothers' "Looney Tunes" (a rather direct parody of Disney's pretensions) and "Merrie Melodies." Because Max and Dave Fleischer—Disney's rivals—had access to Paramount's music library, their work, which was distributed through Paramount, also makes liberal use of songs. Their Betty Boop cartoons, *Minnie the Moocher* (1932) and *Snow White* (1933), for example, feature the Cab Calloway tunes "Minnie the Moocher" and "St. James Infirmary Blues," respectively. Other Fleischer shorts highlight music by Ethel Merman, the Mills Brothers, and Louis Armstrong (*I'll be Glad When You're Dead You Rascal You* [1932]). Many of these cartoons regularly appeared on television from the

1960s to the present—long after viewers would be familiar with Calloway, Merman, Armstrong, et al. In their interpretation of preexisting popular songs, these musical shorts anticipated the animated music videos of the 1980s and later. (The Fleischers also pioneered follow-the-bouncing-ball musical shorts, in which viewers were encouraged to sing along.)

Disney incorporated other new technologies during the 1930s, always with the goal of greater naturalism. The most influential of these technologies were:

- The **Technicolor** color process

- The **rotoscope**[5]

The history of color technology in film is long and complicated, but its end result was that three-color Technicolor—a process mixing yellow, magenta, and cyan dyes—would come to dominate color filmmaking in the late 1930s, 1940s, and early 1950s. Disney was among the first to experiment with the new three-color process, signing a contract with Technicolor that blocked any other cartoon studios from using it for 3 years. His first cartoon in three-color Technicolor, *Flowers and Trees*, was released in 1932, 3 years before the first live-action feature using the process (*Becky Sharp* [1935]). It was an instantaneous success and won the Academy Award for best animated short subject.

Although Disney's use of color in *Flowers and Trees* is somewhat stylized, the more routine "Silly Symphonies" use color in predictably naturalistic fashion. Color was mostly another way for Disney to make cartoons look more like reality (which, after all, is in color). Stylized experimentations with color were left to more avant-garde animators.

Rotoscoping was not invented by Disney's animators, but they used it to greatest naturalistic effect. The rotoscope was patented in the 1910s by Max Fleischer. It is a fairly simple device, still in use today, by which a single frame from a live-action film is rear-projected onto a light table (a table with a semiopaque glass in the center). The animator places paper on the light table and traces the image cast by the live-action film. Then the film is advanced to the next frame and the process is repeated. The tracings are rephotographed, and the end result is an animated film that is based on the live-action images.

In line with their naturalist aesthetic, Disney's animators put the rotoscope to work duplicating human movement. For their first full-length cartoon, *Snow White* (1937), the dancer Marge Champion's body and movements were filmed and then, through rotoscoping, converted into Snow White's. Thus, Snow White is actually a cartoon replica of Champion. Disney's naturalistic aesthetic peaked in *Snow White*. Cartoons were as close to live-action as they would come until the advent of computer animation.

Rotoscoping is not necessarily a tool for Disney-style animation or naturalism in general, however. Recent music videos have incorporated rotoscoping as a way of transforming performers into animated images, which may then be abstracted in a variety of ways. A-Ha's *Take On Me* video shifts effortlessly between live action and stylized, rotoscoped animation (Figs. 11.7–11.8). The technology of the rotoscope is open to various aesthetic uses, not all of them naturalistic.

As the 1930s came to an end and World War II began, cartoons were well established in the cinema. With Disney's move into features at the end of the decade, he became the most prominent cartoon producer. But there were many

FIGURE 11.7

FIGURE 11.8

other studios cranking out cartoon shorts with characters much more auda-cious than were Disney's: Warner Brothers' Bugs Bunny, Porky Pig, and Daffy Duck; Fleischer's Popeye and Betty Boop (officially censored by the Production Code); Walter Lantz's Woody Woodpecker; and MGM's Droopy, The Wolf, and Screwy Squirrel. Every major studio had a division for producing cartoons and, since they owned the major theaters, they also had assured exhibition for their cartoon product.

By this time animation found its own niche within the expanding film industry. Cartooning had developed an efficient mode of production through industrial specialization, the incorporation of cost-cutting technologies (e.g., the animation cel), and businesslike pre-production planning based on storyboards. It had also settled on the basic format that would prevail to the present day:

- 6–8 minutes long.

- In color.

- Structured around music and sound effects.

Cartoons' place in theatrical film exhibition seemed assured. At the time, movies were presented in double bills, and cartoons were a routine part of the short subjects (newsreels and the like) that were shown between feature films. Changes in film exhibition and the rise of television would change all this, absorbing and bringing to an end one form of the cartoon, but eventually spawning its own assortment of animation. We will detail these economic shifts below, but first we must consider an aesthetic change in cartooning that occurred just as television was beginning to make its presence felt.

UPA ABSTRACTION: THE CHALLENGE TO DISNEY NATURALISM

Disney and his naturalist aesthetic may have governed 1930s animation, but the early 1940s saw the disruption of his economic dominance and the rise of a new aesthetic of abstraction that has continued to have a major impact.

Disney's economic empire was briefly unsettled in 1941 when a strike against the studio resulted in the departure of several key animators. Among this group were John Hubley, Steve Bosustow, and Adrian Woolery, who would form the mainstays of United Productions of America (UPA). Obviously, the strike had little lasting economic impact on Disney as he went on to diversify his investments, founding Disneyland in 1954 and producing his long-running television program. But the eventual formation of UPA did provide the environment to nurture a new animation aesthetic. It contrasted markedly with Disney's work, which, after the 1930s, emphasized feature-length production, leaving the field open for other studios to produce animated shorts.

UPA's animators came to cartooning with a background in the fine arts and drawing. This nurtured an aesthetic that emphasized abstract line, shape, and pattern over naturalistic figures. UPA first achieved commercial success in 1949 with the Mr. Magoo series, but its aesthetic wasn't fully recognized until the Academy Award-winning *Gerald McBoing Boing* (1951). We can distinguish several characteristics of this aesthetic, each of which contrasts with Disney-style naturalism:

- Flattened perspective.
- Abstract backgrounds.
- Primary colors.
- Well-defined character outlines.
- Limited animation.

Flattened Perspective. Throughout the history of drawing, artists have been concerned with perspective, with the rendering of the three-dimensional world in two dimensions. Drawings and cartoons have horizontal and vertical dimensions, but they have no true depth. Hence, the illusion of depth must be fabricated. One of the principal artistic developments of the European Renaissance was **linear perspective**, a method for representing depth in which the parallel lines of "reality" are made to converge at a single point—the vanishing point—in a drawing. Naturalistic animation such as that produced by Disney used linear perspective and other visual cues (e.g., character shading) to heighten the sense of depth in their cartoons.

In a revolutionary move, the UPA animators rejected this illusion of depth. Instead, they flattened and distorted Renaissance perspective—as did avant-garde graphic designers and artists of the time. In one shot from *Gerald McBoing Boing*, for instance, a small boy, Gerald, walks up a flight of stairs (Fig. 11.9). There are four or five vanishing points, and none of them match. A doorway is askew and the side of the staircase is covered with an abstract design. The image resembles cubist paintings more than it does Disney's *Snow White*.

Abstract Backgrounds. Closely related to this flattening of perspective are the revolutionary backgrounds in UPA cartoons. The background in the shot from *Gerald McBoing Boing* consists of broad, abstract fields of color. In one respect, this returned animation to the earliest days when minimal backgrounds were used because animators were redrawing entire frames. After the animation cel was invented, backgrounds became quite elaborate, since they only had to be drawn once for each shot (only moving elements were redrawn). The Disney features in particular have intricate backgrounds in nearly every shot.

FIGURE 11.9

In striking contrast to Disney, the UPA films completely reject this naturalistic style.

Primary Colors. Coloring in cartoons has never been subtle. The technology of the three-color Technicolor process in the 1930s made muted colors tough to achieve because Technicolor's hues tended to be very rich and deep (i.e., highly **saturated**). That animators were able to get as much variation out of Technicolor as they did is a testament to their inventiveness. It is somewhat ironic, then, that in the early 1950s, when Kodak was introducing a more supple color technology (EASTMAN Color), cartoonists were experimenting with prominent, almost garish, primary colors in the abstract color fields of cartoons such as *Gerald McBoing Boing*.

Well-defined Character Outlines. In another "innovation" that actually made cartooning resemble its formative years, the UPA animators rejected the fully rounded, shaded, and molded look that Disney achieved (at great expense). Instead, they sharply outlined their characters and filled the outlines with single colors (i.e., little or no shading)—as had been done decades before in *Gertie the Dinosaur* (Fig. 11.1) and the Felix the Cat series. This contributed to the flattening of perspective by making the characters themselves appear two-dimensional.

Limited Animation. By far the most significant change inaugurated by UPA, at least as far as television is concerned, is so-called limited animation. There are three ways in which UPA animation is more "limited" than other animation of that time, especially compared to Disney animation such as *Snow White* and *Pinocchio* (1940).

First, in limited animation, the amount of movement within the frame is substantially reduced. Once animators began using cels, they stopped redrawing the entire image for each frame of film. But still, 1930s and 1940s animators typically redrew entire characters who were involved in any form of movement. Even if a character were just speaking and moving its mouth, the character's whole body would be redrawn. In the most extreme limited animation, in contrast, when a character speaks, only its mouth moves. Cels of the mouth drawings would be placed over one of the entire character, which, in turn, would be on top of the background. As the character speaks, only the mouth-drawing cels are changed. Thus, as animation has become more and more limited, less and less of the frame has been redrawn.

Second, in limited animation, eye blinks and arm, leg, and head motions are routinely repeated, using the same series of cels over and over. Consequently, the characters move in limited, repeatable directions. In full animation, characters make a large number of unique movements, which demand that a new set of frames be drawn.

Third, movements are constructed from fewer individual frames in limited animation. Consider a simple movement such as Bugs Bunny raising his hand, a movement that takes one second. Since sound film uses 24 frames per second, there must be 24 drawings for this movement. But even in full animation not all of the drawings will be *unique*. The movement might actually consist of only 12 cels, each of which is photographed twice. In limited animation the number of cels is reduced even below that of "full" animation, and the result is a less fluid movement.

The differences between naturalism (Disney) and abstraction (UPA) is summarized and parodied in a *Cow and Chicken* cartoon. In general, *Cow and Chicken* adopts the principles of UPA-style abstract animation and, further, is heavily influenced by the visual style of *Ren and Stimpy*, but in "The Bad News Plastic Surgeons" episode Chicken is turned into a naturalistic looking character, a "photo-realistic beaver." Its director, David Feiss, placed this naturalistic beaver into the program's abstract world—providing a sharp contrast between its naturalism and the stylized environment, including a very abstract character named Cow (Fig. 11.10). In Fig. 11.10, Cow and the background could have been done by UPA, while the photo-realistic beaver follows the Disney tradition.

There are obvious economic advantages to UPA's limited animation, flattened perspective, and abstract design (fewer, less-detailed frames mean faster production time); but there exists an aesthetic rationale independent of the financial advantages. Remember, *Gerald McBoing Boing* was a well-respected, Oscar-winning film of the time. One aesthetic justification is that this

FIGURE 11.10

FIGURE 11.11

herky-jerky animation style mirrors the frenetic pace of the modern world—just as jump cuts do in the French New Wave films of the late 1950s and early 1960s. One argument for the abstract design is that it is the cartoon equivalent of art movements such as abstract expressionism, which drew viewers' attention to the surface of the painting, making them aware of shape and formal patterns. In this sense, *Gerald McBoing Boing* may well be the only exercise in abstract expressionism that also won an Academy Award and was the model for its own television cartoon show (*The Gerald McBoing Boing Show,* [1956–58]).

UPA set the standard for theatrical animation during the gradual demise of cartoons in theaters. UPA's Mr. Magoo series incorporated the money-saving aspects of *Gerald McBoing Boing*'s animation, watered down its aesthetic of abstract stylization, and established what cartoons would be like during the 1950s and1960s. All of the major studios soon followed suit with stylized cartoons such as MGM's *Symphony in Slang* (1951) and Warners' *What's Opera, Doc?* (1957) (Fig. 11.11) and the Road Runner and Coyote series (Figs. 11.12–11.13). Even Disney finally recapitulated and released the UPA-esque *Pigs is Pigs* in 1954. The full and total victory of UPA animation style, however, would come in television.

FIGURE 11.12   **FIGURE 11.13**

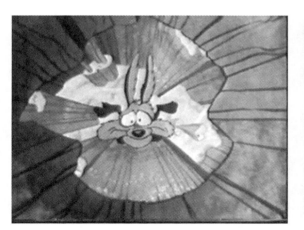

TELEVISION'S ARRIVAL: ECONOMIC REALIGNMENT

Television's ascent in the postwar years had direct and drastic economic effects on narrative cartoons.

First, it contributed to the demise of the theatrical exhibition of cartoons. As the film industry scrambled to economize during the 1950s and into the 1960s, the output of feature films tumbled to barely one fourth of what it had been during the 1930s—from a yearly norm of approximately 500 to an all-time low of 121 in 1963. Most troubling to cartoon studios was that the film exhibition patterns were changing as the production declined. The double bill, the cartoon's raison d'etre, was becoming extinct. With its passing, so did the need for short subjects to interject between the features. Shorts were shown before films on some single bills, but they were regarded by theater owners as an unnecessary expense. Perhaps most damaging to the theatrical exhibition of cartoons was a 1948 court ruling that forced studios to sell the theaters they owned, which meant that MGM, Warner Brothers, and the rest were no longer assured a venue for their product.[6] Suddenly, there was no guaranteed place to show cartoons theatrically. Since major studios regarded animation and other short film production as of secondary importance anyway and because cartoons are relatively more expensive to create than are live-action films, the cartoon divisions were soon abolished.

As cartoons were virtually eliminated from theaters, they found a new home on television. As discussed previously, the television and film industries have come to depend on one other in a variety of economic ways. For animation, this interdependence meant that theatrical cartoon stars such as Bugs Bunny, Popeye, and Woody Woodpecker became broadly known to children of the 1950s, 1960s, and 1970s through their appearance on television. Most often, these cartoons were packaged for television's use in locally produced, after-school children's shows, or grouped together for Saturday morning programming, beginning with *The Mighty Mouse Playhouse* (1955–66).

The initial move to television was led by smaller animation studios/distributors because the majors were locked in seemingly mortal combat with television over rights to their film libraries—which included cartoons. Consequently, the minor-league Van Beuren Studios, which had ceased production in 1936, was able to successfully market cartoons (e.g., Aesop's Fables) to early children's programs such as *Movies for Small Fry*, which was broadcast on the now-defunct DuMont network in 1947. Among the first of the majors, Disney came over to television in 1954 with *Disneyland*, and the following year premiered *The Mickey Mouse Club*. These programs maintained his exclusive control over the Disney animation library for decades to come. The other major cartoon studios began capitulating in 1955, when both Paramount-Fleischer-Famous Studios and Warner Brothers released their cartoons to television, and Terrytoons (from Paul Terry's Studio) was bought by CBS.[7] By 1960 most of the majors were releasing their cartoons to television, with the exception of the few cartoon series that were still running in movie theaters.

Bugs Bunny and the other Warner Brothers characters (Daffy Duck, Porky Pig, Tweety, Sylvester, and so on) made the most successful transition to television—starting in 1956 with *Bugs Bunny Theater*, which was syndicated to local stations. Then, in 1960, they premiered in a prime-time network series on ABC called *The Bugs Bunny Show* (1960–62). Most significant, the Warners characters found a permanent home on Saturday mornings, debuting in 1962 and remaining on the air ever since—the most long-lived of all Saturday morning cartoon shows. Virtually every child who has grown up watching television in the United States during the past 40-odd years is familiar with these cartoons.

Cartoon compilation programs such as *The Bugs Bunny Show* do not contain new cartoons but use theatrical releases from decades past. This can result in some odd cultural ruptures. For instance, when today's child viewers watch *The Goofy Gophers*, a Merrie Melodies cartoon from 1947 that is still occasionally broadcast on television, they will witness one scene in which two gophers pile fruit on their heads and say, "Toodle-oo, Carmen" and "See you tomorrow, Hedda." The first refers to Carmen Miranda, a 1940s movie star, and the second to Hedda Hopper, a gossip columnist from the same era. Both were known at the time for their outlandish headgear. To today's child viewers, plainly, the references can have little significance.

This disjunction between the text's discourse and that of the viewer is not just a matter of a changing frame of reference over the passage of time. It is also because these cartoons were originally designed for a general theatrical audience, an audience that was predominantly adult. Consequently, they were encoded with an adult discourse that even contemporary children could not have decoded. For example, in *My Artistical Temperature*, a Fleischer cartoon from 1937 that still appears occasionally on TV, Popeye and Bluto battle as rival artists. At one point Popeye has trouble arranging the arms on a statue of a woman. Finally, he tears them off, so that it resembles the Venus de Milo, and mumbles, "Oh! I think I got something here: a maskerpiece!" How many 10-year-olds in either 1937 or today would understand this joke? And yet, there is obviously much meaning and pleasure that children receive from cartoons such as this. Theatrical cartoons have often possessed a polysemy—a "double discourse" (child and adult)—that has facilitated their long-standing popularity on television.

Thus, the first cartoons on television, as well as many still being telecast, were drawn from the older libraries of theatrical product designed for general audiences (child and adult). The domination of television animation by theatrically exhibited cartoons could not continue once theatrical cartoon production declined. Television required more and more cartoon product, and the cartoon studios' archives were quickly being exhausted. An economically efficient mode of production was needed for the creation of cartoons specifically for use on television.

Made-for-Television Cartoons

The history of cartoons produced for television begins in syndication, rather than network programming. Around the time that UPA was first garnering attention for its new animation style, Jay Ward and Alexander Anderson were preparing to syndicate *Crusader Rabbit* (Fig. 11.14; 1948–51, 1957–69). Although never picked up by the networks, *Crusader Rabbit* was quite popular

FIGURE 11.14

in the major TV markets and established much of the made-for-TV cartoon's mode of production. The persons to benefit most from this format and to bring it to network television were Bill Hanna and Joe Barbera, the preeminent producers of made-for-TV cartoons. *The Ruff and Reddy Show* (1957–60, 1962–64) was Hanna-Barbera's first foray into network TV animation. It was also the first network cartoon series to use material designed specifically for TV—although it also mixed in older Columbia Pictures cartoons. Moreover, *The Ruff and Reddy Show* was the first such show to stake out the territory of Saturday morning children's programming, proving to the networks just how lucrative those time slots might be. Three years later, Hanna-Barbera introduced *The Flintstones* (1960–66) to prime-time network programming.

With *Crusader Rabbit, The Ruff and Reddy Show*, and *The Flintstones*, the blueprint for the made-for-TV cartoon was consolidated. Its format can be divided into four characteristics:

1. Program structure

2. Narrative structure

3. Limited animation

4. Emphasis on dialogue

Program Structure. Taking into account television's (commercial) interruptions and the need for segmentation, *Crusader Rabbit's* individual cartoons were even shorter than theatrical cartoons. They were compartmentalized into 4-minute segments that could be combined in a single day's program or run separately on subsequent days. Not all made-for-TV programs use such short segments. The average *Flintstones* segment lasts longer than 4 minutes, for example. The point is that cartoon segments on television are often shorter than are theatrical short subjects.

Since 1950s cartoon programs were made up of short individual cartoons, some structure was needed to unify and cohere the segments. Many programs solved this with a human host, sometimes accompanied by puppets. *The Ruff and Reddy Show*, for instance, was initially hosted by Jimmy Blaine, accompanied by the puppets Rhubarb the Parrot and Jose the Toucan. When revived in 1962, the program was hosted by Captain Bob Cottle and his puppets—Jasper, Gramps, and Mr. Answer. These hosts, both human and puppet, provided coherence to the disparate mix of material (old and new cartoons, live-action shorts, sketches performed by the hosts) presented in 1950s and 1960s children's programs. They also lured the viewer into staying tuned by introducing and promoting upcoming segments—much as a news or sports play-by-play announcer does. Since that time, hosted children's programs have gradually lost their hosts. The transitions between cartoons are now accomplished by voiceover narrators and visual material.

Narrative Structure. *Crusader Rabbit*'s and *Ruff and Reddy*'s segments are not self-contained narratives, as in theatrical cartoons. Rather, *Crusader Rabbit* and *Ruff and Reddy* are television's first cartoon serials—one segment picking up the action where the preceding episode left off. As Jay Ward commented, "We wanted to get the effect of an animated comic strip. The commercials would go in between the short segments."[8] In effect, each cartoon segment is like one panel in a comic strip. Incomplete on its own, it leads from one narrative segment (panel or animated cartoon) to the next. The effect, obviously enough, is to encourage us to remain tuned in, to impel us to continue watching through the commercials. Theatrical cartoons that have been packaged together for TV cannot provide this narrative propulsion, because they come to a explicit conclusion every 7 or 8 minutes. *Crusader Rabbit* established a form of narrative segmentation that would prevail in many subsequent television cartoons.

The Flintstones and other Hanna-Barbera programs modified this form of serialization. Like most live-action television series, the Hanna-Barbera programs come to a tentative conclusion at the end of the program. Each episode presents some dilemma that will be resolved. But the end of each segment *between the commercials* ends inconclusively, leading to the next segment—just as in *Crusader Rabbit* and unlike theatrical cartoons.

Limited Animation. *Crusader Rabbit* established that made-for-TV cartoons would use the limited animation style that had been pioneered by UPA. But made-for-TV animation does not use that style in exactly the same way. Made-for-TV animation rejects the *aesthetic* of abstraction that was embraced by UPA's theatrical animation, and for which it won honors such as the Academy Award. *Crusader Rabbit*'s limited animation was born of the necessity to produce an immense amount of animation in a short period of time and for a relatively small amount of money. In specific, while it cost approximately $60,000 to fully animate a 7-minute cartoon in the 1950s, a limited-animation cartoon could be created for $10,000 or less. Hanna-Barbera's *Ruff and Reddy* was produced for a paltry $2,700![9]

Do such stingy budgets make any difference in the texts themselves, in the way that these cartoons look? Do they differ, say, from award-winning shorts such as *Gerald McBoing Boing*? Yes, in small ways. UPA's style, at its most extreme, draws as much attention to the visual design itself as to the story being presented. Made-for-TV animation spurns that approach; the design of an image never intrudes into the storytelling, never impedes the progression of the narrative. Indeed, very little narrative information in contained in the images as early television's low resolution would not be able to show small visual details—even if money and time had been available to further develop the drawings. This

FIGURE 11.15

FIGURE 11.16

leads to a final narrative component of the made-for-TV cartoon: its reliance on dialogue.

Emphasis on Dialogue. Because of their limited animation and acknowledging TV's low resolution (compared to the cinema), the Hanna-Barbera cartoons do not rely on the visuals to convey narrative information or other meanings. Consequently, the visuals and the dialogue are often redundant. For example, in one episode of *The Flintstones*, we have the following five-shot sequence:

1. Medium long shot: Baby Pebbles' carriage speeds along, pulled by their pet dinosaur (Fig. 11.15).

2. Close-up: The leash breaks (Fig. 11.16).

3. Long shot: The carriage rolls out of control (Fig. 11.17).

4. Long shot: Fred and Barney chase the carriage (Fig. 11.18). Fred says, "Oh no, the leash broke! Pebbles, stop the carriage!"

FIGURE 11.17

FIGURE 11.18

FIGURE 11.19

5. Long shot: The carriage passes a sign pointing to the zoo (Fig. 11.19). Barney (in voiceover) says, "Ooooh, she's headed for the zoo!"

All of the dialogue in this segment reiterates what is already shown in the visuals. As in a soap opera, we could get most of the narrative information from a *Flintstones* episode by listening to it from another room. It has become what animator Chuck Jones called "radio with pictures." Contrast *The Flintstones* with one of Jones's Roadrunner cartoons to see the difference (Fig. 11.12–11.13). The Roadrunner cartoons are entirely dependent on visuals; the soundtrack consists almost solely of music, roadrunner beeps, and explosions. Dialogue never duplicates image, as it often does in limited-animation series.

The significance of the visuals is, of course, largely a matter of degree. Made-for-TV animation, even *The Flintstones*, does emphasize and derive humor from the visuals occasionally. And most theatrical cartoons are not as extreme as the Roadrunner series in their reliance on the visuals. Still, it is generally true that made-for-TV cartoons rely on dialogue and deemphasize the image more than do theatrical cartoons. This is in keeping with television's overall accent on sound, as discussed in chapter 8.

(*The Flintstones* also added a component of TV sound that has not been adopted by many other cartoon shows: the laugh track. This element of the program indicates *The Flintstones*' close relationship with the live-action genre of the sitcom. In fact, it has often been said that the program was an animated version of Jackie Gleason's *The Honeymooners*.)

By 1960, television cartooning had developed an efficient mode of production, a cost-effective aesthetic, and successful programming strategies (afternoons and Saturday mornings, but not prime time). The 1970s and 1980s saw very little change in the TV cartoon, but in the 1990s there was a revival of interest in prime-time cartoons and accelerated developments in the world of computer graphic technology—resulting in aesthetic and economic changes in made-for-TV animation, as well as in the theatrical, animated, feature film.

Contemporary TV Cartooning

Technology

As you might expect, the computer has had an enormous impact on contemporary animation. High-tech computer-graphics laboratories such as those at the California Institute of Technology, MIT, and the New York Institute of Technology, along with avant-garde computer-graphics visionaries have been experimenting with **computer-generated imagery** (**CGI**) since the 1960s. However, this activity didn't have much affect on television and feature film until Disney's *Tron* in 1982. A story of a computer programmer and video gamer who's sucked inside a computer, *Tron* features an animated world that was mostly computer-generated and set the standard for 1980s CGI. Throughout the 1980s and most of the 1990s, CGI was too expensive and time-consuming for narrative, serial/series television, but it found its way into commercials, credit sequences, and music videos—in addition, of course, to feature films and video games (see Table 11.1).

As prices on computer technology have come down and hardware capabilities have grown, we've seen an increase in the impact of computers on all aspects of television, but especially on animation. Essentially, the computer may be used in two ways in the animation process. First, in the **tweening** process it assists animators by drawing frames for them. Second, in three-dimensional CGI, it wholly fabricates the image based on a set of instructions from the animators. Let's examine each of these processes in more detail.

Tweening. In the mode of animation production that evolved in the 1930s, the work was highly specialized. To speed up the process, the top artists did not draw every single frame needed for a particular action. If, for example, Bugs Bunny were to raise his arm, the artists might draw two **keyframes**—the arm lowered and the arm raised. It would be the job of lower-paid animators to draw the in-between frames. This process thus came to be known as tweening, which, as you can imagine, was not a very glamorous job. Today's animation software has taken over the drudgery of tweening. For example, Macromedia Flash, a program commonly used to create compact Web animations, has a tweening function. If we wanted to have a robot hover from left to right we would begin by generating one instance of that robot and placing it on the left of a keyframe. Then we would make a copy of the robot and place it on the right side of another keyframe. Finally, we would have Flash tween from the robot on the left to the one on the right, from one keyframe to the other. The result would be an animation consisting of two keyframes and numerous tweened frames in between them. We can see the effect in static form in Fig. 11.20. The robot keyframes are superimposed on either side of the frame. In between them are **onion-skin** (slightly lighter) versions of the tweened frames so that you may see the progress of the robot across the frame. (See our companion Website, www.TVCrit.com, to witness the robot's hovering in action—with sound.)

In terms of how the final product looks, animation made with computer-based tweening is not all that different from Winsor McCay's *Gertie the Dinosaur*, Disney's *Snow White*, or Hanna-Barbera's *The Flintstones*. Computer tweening has made animation much less expensive and has counteracted some of the

TABLE 11.1

Notable Moments in Computer Animation (Since 1980)

DATE	EVENT
1980	Arcade video game features a three-dimensional world for the player to move through—*BattleZone*
1982	All-digital CG sequence in a feature film—the "Genesis Effect," in *Star Trek: Wrath of Khan* An elaborate CG virtual world, with a human inserted into it—*Tron*
1984	CG models (instead of physical ones) of spaceships in *The Last Starfighter*
1985	Wholly CG character, a stained-glass knight—*Young Sherlock Holmes* First widely distributed instance of morphing—the music video, *Cry*, by Godley and Creme CG world with three-dimensional CG characters moving through it—Dire Straits' *Money for Nothing* CG characters/objects begin appearing in commercials—e.g., "Sexy Robot" (Canned Food Informational Council), Listerine bottle, Life Saver candies
1986	Entirely CG short film—*Luxo Junior*
1988	Live-action morphing in a feature film—*Willow*
1989	CG television character, performing live on *The Jim Henson Hour* CG water-snake effect, with the face of actress, in *The Abyss* (director: James Cameron) Virtual reality demonstration at SIGGRAPH (Special Interest Group on Computer Graphics of the Association for Computing Machinery) conference
1991	Bulk of extensive, elaborate effects work for a feature film done on computer—including morphing between a human and a CG character, the T-1000 cyborg (who looks to be made of mercury)—*Terminator 2: Judgment Day* Morphing in a music video—Michael Jackson's *Black or White*
1992	Virtual reality in film—*The Lawnmower Man*
1993	Multi-user, "first-person shooter," personal-computer game—*Doom* Morphing in commercials—Exxon, Schick Plausible textures (fur, scales, etc.) on live CG creatures—*Jurassic Park* (sequel in 1997)
1994	Entirely CG cartoon show—*ReBoot* CG insertion of an actor into historical films, and the manipulation of historical figures—*Forrest Gump*
1995	CG feature-length film protagonist—*Casper* Entirely CG feature-length film—*Toy Story* (sequel in 1999) CG spaceship models in a TV show—*Babylon 5*
1996	Heightened detail in a three-dimensional gaming environment—*Quake*
1999	Mainstream interest in virtual reality—the success of *The Matrix*
2000	CG insertion of first-down line in live, televised football games
2001	Photo-realistic, CG, feature-length film—*Final Fantasy: The Spirits Within*.

FIGURE 11.20

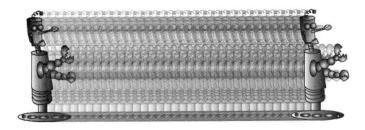

restrictions of limited animation. Now that some action may be quickly tweened, made-for-TV cartoons can afford to include more movement—although the details of the animation of specific characters still requires manual animation. Still, if you compare the amount of physical action in *The Flintstones* with what you see in a typical Saturday morning cartoon, you'll likely note much more activity in the recent program.

Three-dimensional CGI. Even more significant than digital tweening is the evolution of three-dimensional computer-generated animation, which is rapidly changing the look of animation. In 3D CGI, a schematic model is created in digital format. The model may then be controlled by the animator and made to move in a variety of ways. Animators do not draw frames as they did in traditional two-dimensional animation, where the characters and objects appear relatively flat on the screen (e.g., Homer in *The Simpsons*, Fig. 11.21). Three-dimensional animators direct the computer to generate frames based on the plotted movements of the model. In other words, the computer does the physical act of creating the individual frames based on instructions from the animator. The resulting images are still physically two-dimensional; they're still presented on a 2D television screen—but they create a greater illusion of three-dimensionality. To see the difference, examine the appearance of the 3D CGI Homer in Fig. 11.22—from a Halloween episode in which he transforms from 2D (Fig. 11.21) to 3D (Fig. 11.22). See how much more rounded and bulbous he appears in Fig. 11.22? That is the effect of 3D CGI work.

For further illustration, consider the image of an island with a huge sur-realistic ball, cube, and doughnut floating over it, which was created by Mark J. P. Wolf using Corel Bryce software (Fig. 11.23). The process he used to create this image is not unlike stop-motion animation—as in *King Kong* (1933), *The Gumby Show* (1957, 1966, 1988), or Nick Park's Wallace and Gromit series—where an object is made to move by shooting a frame of it, moving it slightly, shooting another frame, moving it again, and so on. Instead of using a puppet or pieces of clay, Wolf has created virtual objects that exist solely within the computer. He can position those objects where he will and he can illuminate

FIGURE 11.21

FIGURE 11.22

FIGURE 11.23

FIGURE 11.24

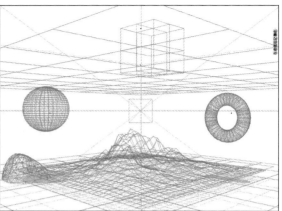

or shadow them as he wishes—with Bryce adding appropriate reflections. To generate movement, he repositions the objects in this virtual world and captures individual still frames (keyframes) of them—much as a stop-motion puppeteer would. The computer then tweens more images—generating frames to fill in between the keyframes. The result is animation created from original still frames of digital, virtual objects.

Wolf's first step in this process was to create a **wireframe** version of the objects—a virtual representation of their exteriors, which looks quite like a diagram of a Renaissance painting (Fig. 11.24). Another option to fabricating computer models from scratch is to digitally trace or "capture" a three-dimensional object or human. A **motion-capture device** was used to create, for example, Dash, one of the computer-generated hosts on the TechTV channel (Fig. 11.25, on left). Computers also captured the movement of humans to created the CG characters in the theatrical film, *Final Fantasy* (Fig. 11.5). In the motion-capture process, actors are recorded wearing suits with reflective

FIGURE 11.25

dots on them that computers can digitally trace. To the computer, these dots moving in three-dimensional space define the points from which a wireframe is constructed. It's quite similar to the decades-old rotoscope process, with the essential difference that in a motion-capture device it is a machine that is tracing a human's movement and not an artist. Just as Disney's use of a rotoscoped actor created the lifelike movement of Snow White in 1937, so did the digital motion-capture device produce the very plausible movements of Dash over 60 years later. Moreover, motion-capture systems can also be used to insert a CG figure into environments where the animated characters interact with real-world humans, as can be seen in Fig. 11.25 where Dash is interviewing a graphic designer. This resembles the rotoscoped interaction between animated figures and humans in 1930s Max Fleischer cartoons and A-Ha's "Take On Me" video (Fig. 11.7–11.8).

Wireframes are obviously not very realistic looking. They don't have substantial surfaces yet. The process by which different textures (water, rock, smooth surfaces, skin) are added to these frames is called **rendering**, which results in objects that appear strikingly three-dimensional on screen. The rendering stage requires the most resources and comes only at the end. The rendering of *Toy Story* (1995), the first entirely CG feature film, was particularly intense. Some 800,000 computer-hours were required to generate the 77-minute film. Each individual frame—consuming 300 megabytes of disk space—took from 2 to 15 hours to render and there are some 111,000 frames in the film!

Early computer 3D animation had its own distinct appearance that separated it from conventional 2D animation. *ReBoot* (the first CG TV program) typifies this look (Fig. 11.26—compare with *Final Fantasy*, Fig. 11.5), as do the ball, cube, and doughnut in Wolf's image. Much CG animation has coloring and movements that are mathematically precise, unlike those done by human hand. Their surface textures have a uniform sheen to them. The quirks of human animation are missing. The biggest challenge for computer animators is to be able to render irregular surfaces such as fur, hair, and skin. The island in Wolf's image illustrates the advances CGI is quickly making. Its surface is rough, craggy,

FIGURE 11.26

and quite photo-realistic. Three-dimensional CGI animation for video games is also becoming increasingly photo-realistic—as can be seen in games such as *Sega Sports NFL 2K1* (2000). *NFL 2K1* simulates many aspects of the look of TV coverage—including a game clock in the upper left corner. Moreover, a video game was also the source of *Final Fantasy*, the photo-realistic theatrical film. It's clear that the technology for wholly computer-generated actors is here today and that it goes way beyond any dream of true-to-life naturalism that Disney had in the 1930s.

Mode of Production

In the 1980s, production was internationalized. Much routine animation work, such as inking-in character outlines, began to be sent to firms outside the United States. Korean animators, for example, are largely responsible for creating *The Simpsons*—for which all of the tweening is still done by hand. The major conceptual work of most cartoons continues to be done in the United States, but the physical creation of the animation is often executed abroad. The reason for this change is clearly economic: Korean labor is less expensive than is U.S. labor. Further, it is part of a global economic shift whereby national boundaries are becoming less important than financial ones.

One less marked change in cartooning's mode of production has been the increase in merchandising of cartoon characters. Cartoon characters have been merchandised since at least 1904, when the Brown Shoe Company based an advertising campaign around the Buster Brown comic strip character. But the 1980s saw an intensification of the link between sponsors and cartoon programs as several already existing products were transformed into television characters: for example, Strawberry Shortcake, the Smurfs, and He-Man. The difference between the characters and the products became less and less clear, and the textual difference between the commercials and the narrative cartoons diminished correspondingly. It became difficult for (child) viewers to discern where one ended and the other began. Television network's ultimate goal, to advertise products, had become confusingly entwined with the medium's entertainment function.

Violence and Prosocial Messages

Concerns over violence and a discourse that is perceived as antisocial has led to modifications of cartoon stories. Made-for-television programs on broadcast networks are strictly monitored by the networks' **broadcast standards and practices** (**BSP**) units. For example, when *ReBoot* was airing on ABC, it repeatedly ran afoul of BSP. One of its producers, Gavin Blair, complains, ". . . we couldn't even have a punch-up [a fistfight] because that was violence. Also, we couldn't have jeopardy. Meaning we couldn't end an act with Bob [a central character] falling off a cliff and him yelling 'Aaaahh' as we cut to commercial—because that's jeopardy, and we'd upset the kiddies."[10] The brutality of older theatrical cartoons is also regularly censored by television networks and syndicators. In

FIGURE 11.27

Warners' *Duck, Rabbit, Duck* (1953), for example, Elmer Fudd blasts Daffy Duck in a variety of manners (Fig. 11.27). When it is broadcast today, most of those explosions are cut out. Generally, violence has become much less visual in today's cartoons, but the U.S. Congress is still concerned about violent imagery in television, film, video games, and other aspects of popular culture. In the 2000s, there have been repeated calls for Hollywood to curtail the violence in media designed for children.

In addition to taming the anarchic violence of cartoon visuals, animators have also added so-called prosocial meanings to the discourse of children's cartoons. For instance, in one episode of *He-Man and the Masters of the Universe*, He-Man runs around battling various villains. At the end of the program, he faces the camera and explains the value of cooperation to the (child) viewer. Theatrical cartoons, by virtue of their marginal existence and the distancing factor of drawings (compared to live action), were often permitted to violate social taboos against violence, sexuality, and general chaos. Contemporary Saturday morning cartoons are the enforcers of those taboos. They speak the language of the dominant discourse.

Not all television cartoons are so clearly under the sway of dominant discourse. The debut of *The Simpsons* in 1989 led the way for a series of controversial adult-oriented cartoons—namely, *Beavis and Butt-head* (1993–97) and *South Park* (1997–)—which appeared on cable channels and Fox, a then new network looking to disrupt the control of the Big Three. *The Simpsons* has satirized popular culture fads, organized religion, conservative politicians, consumerism, the merchandising of its own products, and the sanctity of the nuclear family. Its characters have said and done things that would have caused a scandal if they weren't cartoon characters. In these respects, it's quite ground-breaking, but we can also see that it fits within the tradition of theatrical cartoons such as those Warner Brothers, UPA, and Fleischer made in decades gone by. In those cartoons as well there was an anarchic spirit and a willingness to push the boundaries of acceptability.

SUMMARY

Television animation has appeared in many forms, from theatrical cartoons to computer-generated commercials. In this chapter we have focused on the types of narrative cartoons that have appeared on television. We have surveyed the counterbalancing forces of technology, aesthetics, and economics, which have determined the mode of production of those cartoons.

Initially, cartooning evolved a mode of production well-suited for creating films for movie theaters. Cel-and-background animation was coupled with new technologies of sound, color, and rotoscoping, a specialized studio structure, and pre-production planning (using storyboards) to efficiently construct a durable product. Disney, Warner Brothers, MGM, Paramount, and others produced theatrical cartoons during the 1930s, 1940s, and 1950s that would be run and rerun on television up to the present day—once the studios had overcome their fear of television in the late 1950s.

These theatrical films share a general aesthetic of naturalism, which was most aggressively propounded by the Disney studio. UPA contested that aesthetic with its abstract animation style: flattened perspective, abstract backgrounds, primary colors, well-defined character outlines, and limited animation.

The economic advantages of UPA-style animation necessitated its use in made-for-TV animation, which was inaugurated in syndication by *Crusader Rabbit* in 1948 and on prime-time network television by *The Flintstones* in 1960.

Cartoons quickly adapted to television's special demands. Made-for-TV cartoons rely heavily on limited animation, taming UPA's abstracted style into "radio with pictures." Because the visuals are so simple, dialogue comes to dominate the presentation of narrative, often duplicating what is presented in the image. Television cartoon segments are shorter than are theatrical cartoons, to allow for TV's interrupted and segmented form. Some shows use the serial form, posing enigmas to the viewer just before the commercial breaks began. Others are more like live-action series: broken into incomplete segments, but ending with a tentative conclusion. Shows that are compilations of new and old cartoons often use a host to bridge all the elements together.

The template for television animation was formalized by the early 1960s, but underwent significant changes in the 1980s and 1990s. Developments in computer-generated imagery (CGI) altered fundamental assumptions about how cartoons were made—changing the look of animation as well as its mode of production. CGI may eventually do away with the need for cels themselves. New economic pressures have also driven much animation work overseas and heightened the impact of merchandising. Social pressures have led animators to censor themselves—modifying old cartoons and inserting prosocial discourses into new ones. However, a new market for adult-oriented cartoons has arisen. In *The Simpsons* and *South Park* conservative values are challenged on a regular basis.

FURTHER READINGS

Little has been written specifically on the television cartoon. However, Charles Solomon, *Enchanted Drawings: The History of Animation* (New York: Knopf,

1989), does offer a well-illustrated chapter on the topic. Similarly, Leonard Maltin, *Of Mice and Magic: A History of American Animated Cartoons* (New York: New American Library, 1980), chronicles the advent of the TV cartoon after detailing the history of the theatrical cartoon. Solomon's and Maltin's approaches are historical and offer rudimentary critical analysis of the cartoons.

George W. Woolery, *Children's Television, the First Thirty-Five Years: 1946–1981* (Metuchen, NJ: Scarecrow, 1985), is a broad-based history of all children's programming, paying particular attention to cartoons.

Margaret Morse, *Virtualities: Television, Media Art, and Cyberculture* (Bloomington: Indiana University Press, 1998) examines many of the theoretical implications of CGI and its impact on television. However, the best resources for computer-based animation are on the Web—including sample images and animations. The addresses for these resources change quickly, however, and so we have placed them on *Television*'s companion Web site where they may be easily updated. Please see www.TVCrit.com for further information.

Most of the numerous books on theatrical cartoons are lightweight reading. Two books that do attempt a more rigorous critical and/or cultural interpretation of animation are Donald Crafton, *Before Mickey: The Animated Film, 1989–1928* (Cambridge, MA: MIT Press, 1982), and Eric Smoodin, *Animating Culture: Hollywood Cartoons from the Sound Era* (New Brunswick, NJ: Rutgers University Press, 1993).

ENDNOTES

[1] The speed of silent film was originally around 16 frames per second (f.p.s.), though by the 1920s it was above 20 f.p.s. The cameras were cranked by hand at that time, and the speed varied considerably. Once sound arrived the speed was standardized at 24 f.p.s.

[2] In both devices, one looks through slits to see drawings while the device turns. One views these individual drawings in quick succession, which leads the human percepetual system to translate the still images into motion pictures. The exact process is not fully understood, but it's thought that the phenomena of critical flicker fusion and apparent motion are what cause the illusion of movement. For more information, see David Bordwell and Kristin Thompson, *Film Art*, 6th ed. (New York: McGraw-Hill, 2000), pp. 2–3.

[3] Disneyland was opened in 1955. Disney's television program has been known variously as *Disneyland, Walt Disney Presents, Walt Disney's Wonderful World of Color, The Wonderful World of Disney, Disney's Wonderful World*, and *Walt Disney*. It was broadcast for 29 years on ABC, CBS and NBC; and is second only to *The Tonight Show* in longevity. The Disney cable channel was launched in 1983.

[4] Linda J. Obalil, "*Steamboat Willie*," *The International Dictionary of Films and Filmmakers: Films*, ed. Christopher Lyon (New York: Perigee, 1984), 451.

[5] The multiplane camera was still another of Disney's technological devices that was meant to increase naturalism. However, it had little impact on most cartooning of the 1930s.

[6] The U.S. Supreme Court ruled on the "Paramount Case" in 1948 and ordered the divorcement of the studios' exhibition operation from their production and distribution divisions. Studios were no longer permitted to own theaters and had to compete with independent producers to get their films shown.

7 To be accurate, some of the early Terrytoons were released to television before CBS's acquisition of Paul Terry's Studio in 1955. They had been seen on the network weekday afternoon program *Barker Bill's Cartoon Show* (1953–56).

8 George W. Woolery, *Children's Television, the First Thirty-Five Years: 1946–1981* (Metuchen, NJ: Scarecrow, 1985), 74–75.

9 As cited in Mark J. Wolf, "*Crusader Rabbit* and the Adaptation of Animation to Television," unpublished essay, 1991.

10 Rogier van Bakel, "Before *Toy Story* There Was . . . *ReBoot*," *Wired* 5.3 March 1997, 7 Nov. 2000 http://www.wired.com/wired/archive/5.03/reboot.html.

CHAPTER 12

The Television Commercial

Most television commercials are not bashful about their economic function. They exist to sell products and services. And they do so quite effectively. Huge corporations would not be spending one fourth of their advertising dollars— roughly $50 billion per year—on U.S. television if their market research did not show that viewers are positively affected by this avalanche of ads.[1] Corporations have come to depend heavily on television networks, and U.S. television networks have come to rely solely on advertising for their economic sustenance—unlike many other countries where television is government- or subscription-supported. Just as with radio before it, U.S. television's economic structure is undergirded by commercials.

To viewers, commercials are annoying, interruptive reminders of our economic bargain with corporate culture. U.S. television has always been "free," if we were willing to "pay" for it with our viewing time and our buying behavior when we visit the store. And so we invite advertisers into our homes to repetitively hammer away at us about the tastiness of Pepsi over Coke or the efficacy of the latest exercise machine or the sublime pleasure of Taco Bell's newest recombination of beef, cheese, and flour tortilla. But not all advertising is alike.

Not all television advertising seeks to persuade us through repetition and sledgehammer exhortations to buy, buy, buy! Not every ad uses the mind-numbing blunt approach of a Psychic Friends Network spot. Many advertisers understand what Paul Messaris calls the "value of indirectness."[2] They use humor and evocative imagery to persuade without attacking or numbing the viewer's sensibilities. And yet, they *all* still seek to persuade us in some fashion.

This chapter explores the form that that persuasion takes. It views commercials as televisual texts that have developed particular techniques of persuasion in order to serve the economic needs of the industry. We know that ads must sell us products in order to survive, but what the television analyst needs to understand is *how* that selling is accomplished. What ideologically loaded imagery do commercials use and how do they deploy it? How are commodities associated with particular lifestyles, values, and presumptions about the world? How are we encouraged to consume conspicuously? What visual and sound techniques are used to sell? In short, how do economics, ideology, aesthetics, and technology come together in the rhetorical form of the television commercial?

U.S. TV's Economic Structure

More than any other televisual texts, commercials are shaped by their economic context. Commercials are produced in a certain way due both to the current state of corporate, multinational economics and to specific aspects of the television economy. Thus, a basic understanding of television's economic structure is one key to understanding the commercial. Unfortunately, U.S. television's economic system in the 2000s is in a state of flux that is unparalleled since the rise to dominance of the major broadcast networks in the 1950s. Huge chunks of the audience that the socalled "Big Three" (ABC, CBS, and NBC) commanded have been lost to videocassette viewing, Web use, video games, cable networks, and newer broadcast networks (Fox, WB, UPN, etc.). The older broadcast networks have yet to start losing money, and so-called "dot-com" industries (i.e., Internet-based services) have yet to steal much advertising income from them, but it seems clear that the economic models of the past 50 years are fast changing under the impact of the convergence of broadcast television, theatrical film, cable, satellite, and computer-based technologies. No one truly knows where it will all lead, although venture capitalists are betting on the outcome with enormous sums of money. The next few years are going to be very interesting ones for the television industry.

Before we begin discussing commercials, we must make one additional caveat. Due to space limitations, we will focus on television advertising in the United States. Many countries have commercial-free television, while others blend commercially supported programs with non-commercial fare—resulting in distinctly different persuasive strategies. However, as socialist and communist systems find themselves increasingly challenged by a capitalist, market economy, we may find more nations adopting the U.S. model—for better or worse. Thus, the generalizations we make here about U.S. commercials may soon find application in many other countries.

In the complicated and quickly changing economic model of advertising-supported television, there are five principal players:

1. Production companies—who actually create TV programs.
2. Wholesalers—networks and syndicators.
3. Retailers—local over-the-air stations, cable systems, and DBS (direct broadcast satellite) systems.
4. Advertisers—national, regional, and local.
5. Consumers—that is, viewers.

We'll begin our consideration of commercials by outlining the basic structure of U.S. broadcasting and then explain how advertising fits into this structure.

Diverging Channels and Converging Corporations: Narrowcasting and Media Mergers

In the earliest years of U.S. television broadcasting, corporations produced and sponsored programs such as the enormously popular *Texaco Star Theatre* (1948–55). However, direct sponsorship of individual programs did not last long. An advertising model began to dominate in the 1950s in which production companies, advertisers, and wholesale/retail broadcasters were quite distinct and separate. Production companies were either independent producers or subsidiaries of large motion picture companies and were not owned by advertisers or broadcast networks. In the 1950s and 1960s, independent studio Desilu Productions, for instance, produced *I Love Lucy* and *Star Trek* (1966–69), among others (see chapter 9 for more information on independent producers). It rented these program's broadcast rights—for a specified length of time—to wholesalers such as CBS and NBC (in the cases of *I Love Lucy* and *Star Trek*, respectively) who provided them to their affiliated stations. The affiliates, most of whom were not actually owned by the networks, were the retail outlets that "sold" their wares to the consumers/viewers. (Certain key stations in large cities were owned and operated by the networks and known as O&Os.) After the initial broadcast run, the studios—not the networks—syndicated them directly to local stations or rented broadcast rights to wholesale syndicators, which handled distribution. From the 1950s to the 1980s, U.S. governmental regulation and economic tradition separated production companies, wholesalers, and retailers.

Synergy Within Multinational Corporations In the 1980s, the loosening of governmental regulation coincided with significant technological changes and colossal corporate mergers. At a time when the federal government was permitting large, merged corporations to stake a claim on more and more of the media terrain, there were also new technologies for delivering programming to television sets—principally, cable, DBS, and videocassette. The number of television channels received in the average U.S. home increased from less than 10 to dozens. In 1999, for instance, the average household could receive 62 diverse channels (ironically, the average viewer watched no more than 13 of those).[3] And, to complicate matters further, we've also seen the explosion of competing types of video screens—computer and video game monitors that are not even delivering conventional TV programming content. This divergence of programming and technology, however, has been matched by a convergence of media corporations. Fewer and fewer corporations are responsible for more and more programming. The largest corporations have their fingers in numerous media pies.

From the industry perspective, a diversity of holdings encourages a certain synergy among them. For example, Viacom has a media presence in over 100 countries and brought in revenues of nearly $13 billion in 1999.[4] Its subsidiaries—such as CBS, Paramount, and Blockbuster—can nurture one another. CBS-affiliated stations might run features to help support the release of the latest Paramount movie, which will then be featured on Blockbuster's shelves when it goes into videocassette/DVD release and may even wind up as the basis for a ride in a theme park. Synergy can be quite complicated and contradictory, however.

Mike Budd, Steve Craig, and Clay Steinman discuss an example of failed synergy within the Disney corporation:

> In 1997, Wind Dancer Production Group, a partner in *Home Improvement*, sued Disney, claiming that the company allowed ABC (its newly acquired network) to renew the show's contract for a smaller licensing fee than the program was worth, effectively cutting into Wind Dancer's profits. As the *Wall Street Journal* put it, 'Call it the dark side of synergy: the not-unanticipated consequence of having both the suppliers and the distributors of TV programs and movies under one single roof. In today's Hollywood, deal-makers are increasingly wrestling with a tricky question: How hard a bargain can you drive when, in essence, you're negotiating with yourself?'[5]

Moreover, synergy is undercut by longstanding contracts that predate mergers. Consider the example of *Frasier*. Even though Viacom owns both CBS and Paramount, which produces *Frasier*, the program is not broadcast on the CBS network. Rather, it appears on NBC where it began its run well before Viacom acquired CBS. And, of course, the syndicated version of *Frasier* appears on many stations that are not affiliated with CBS or Viacom.

TV Ratings: Coin of the Realm   Production companies, networks, syndicators, local stations—all of these entities rely on sponsors to make money. Some do so directly and others indirectly, but the ultimate source of most money in the U.S. television economic system is sponsors. Broadcasters ostensibly sell broadcast time to the sponsors, but, of course, what they are really selling is TV viewers and *their* time. Consequently, the value of broadcast time is determined by its **ratings**—by estimates of the number of viewers and, equally important, the types of viewers who are watching. On a regular basis, the one TV program that typically commands the highest price for its ads is the *NFL Super Bowl*, which is also the program that usually carries the highest ratings for the year. The *Super Bowl* has come to attract television's most innovative and prestigious commercials—beginning with a strikingly Orwellian commercial that heralded Apple's introduction of the Macintosh computer in 1984 (see description below). The commercials have come to be as much a part of the *Super Bowl* spectacle as the game itself, especially considering the frequently lopsided scores. It's not surprising, therefore, that broadcast, print, and online news media give substantial coverage to the commercials themselves. In 2000, *USA Today* even invited viewers vote for their favorites on the "*Super* Bowl" Ad Meter" on its Web site.

In contemporary television, the size of the audience is not the only determining economic factor. Lower ratings do not automatically mean less revenue. Many advertisers are looking for very specific audiences, for a particular **demographic** group. The explosion in the number of channels has resulted in a phenomenon known within the industry as narrowcasting. Instead of *broad*casting to a large but mixed audience, these channels narrowly define their viewing audience and hope to find a limited, but homogenous, demographic population for advertisers. MTV made its fortune on this premise—delivering a much smaller audience than did broadcast networks, but filling its audience with a young crowd with disposable income. It's easy to see how advertisers for music, cosmetics, hygiene products, and the like, would be attracted to MTV. A similar strategy prevails in other specialized channels: Food Network, Court TV, SciFi, Cartoon, Golf, and so on. Moreover, the Web is the ultimate in narrowcasting with entire sites devoted to topics as particular as *The Gallery of Ill-Fitting Pants, Modern Moist Towelette Collecting,* and *The Sheep Brain Dissection Guide.*[6]

As one might imagine, these narrowly defined channels necessitate advertising techniques that are distinctly designed for that limited slice of the audience pie. What persuades viewers of MTV is not the same as what persuades viewers of the Golf channel or of general interest networks such as ABC, CBS, and NBC. Since ratings and demographics define these narrowcasters, it is essential to understanding how ratings function during this era of increasing specialization.

Nielsen Media Research dominates TV audience measurement in the U.S. Arthur C. Nielsen began developing methods for measuring radio listeners in 1923. These methods were modified for use on television in 1950 and have been the ratings standard ever since. Nielsen ratings are a powerful force in the U.S. television economy. Networks use them to determine whether programs will live or die and what their advertising rates will be.

Anyone with a casual interest in the TV industry is familiar with the term, "Nielsen ratings," but it's worth noting that these "ratings" are not ratings in the sense that they evaluate or rate programs, as a TV critic might. They do not analyze the program's characteristics, as they are solely concerned with the behavior of the audience. Additionally, Nielsen ratings do not indicate how much or how little viewers enjoy a program or even whether viewers might dislike a program that they watch regularly. They also do not explain what meanings viewers construct from TV. The Nielsen data are exclusively quantitative measurements, indicating how many viewers watch and who they are by aggregating them into demographic groups.

Nielsen, like all audience research companies, compiles its ratings by tracking television use in a limited sample of U.S. homes. Obviously, it doesn't ask each of the nearly 276 million U.S. residents what they watch on TV. Instead, Nielsen records viewing behavior through People Meters it installs in 5,000 households—or roughly .05% of the 100 million households in the U.S.[7] People Meters are brick-sized devices that sit near the television set and automatically record that it is on and that it is tuned to a specific channel. The people in the vicinity of the TV are equipped with a remote control device with a button assigned to each of them. They push their assigned buttons to indicate when they start/stop watching TV.

People Meters are not the only method Nielsen uses to measure the audience. Four times a year, during periods known as **sweeps**, Nielsen selects viewers in **designated market areas (DMAs)**—cohesive metropolitan zones—to fill in diaries accounting for a week's worth of TV watching. The origin of the term, "sweeps," is rather obscure, but Nielsen provides the following explanation:

> These measurement periods are called "sweeps" because Nielsen Media Research . . . collects and processes the diaries in a specific order. The diaries from the Northeast regions are processed first and then swept up around the country, from the South, to the Midwest and finally ending with the West.[8]

In addition to diaries and People Meters, Nielsen also uses an additional type of television set meter in the 48 largest DMAs. These meters gather information only about the set's off/on status and its tuning, not who is in the room watching.

Through these processes, Nielsen is able, in theory, to measure who is viewing what. There are significant problems with these systems. As previously noted, they do not gauge viewers' feelings about programs and commercials. The Nielsen numbers tell us nothing about how viewers interpret the programs they watch. They only tell us where viewers are bobbing along in the television flow. And there is some controversy about how effectively Nielsen measures that. In order for People Meters and diaries to be accurate, viewers' must be both honest and diligent in recording their viewing habits. But there's little in the TV viewing experience that encourages diligence. How do we know that a viewer hasn't left the TV on while she takes a nap or he changes the baby's diaper? Or perhaps a viewer might listen to a soap opera playing in the living room while he is in the kitchen, washing dishes, and can't be bothered to push his button on the People Meter's remote control.

One may think of circumstances that might degrade the accuracy of the Nielsen ratings, but this has absolutely no impact on the television industry's acceptance of their validity when it comes time to determine advertising rates. As Nielsen explains: "... ratings are used like currency in the marketplace of advertiser-supported TV."[9] Despite the Nielsen ratings' inadequacies and problems, they are still the coin of the realm. Networks sell viewers to advertisers based on the Nielsen numbers. The Nielsen ratings thus establish the exchange rate under which advertisers purchase broadcast time. Using these numbers, broadcasters promise to deliver a certain number of viewers at a specific cost to the advertiser. Viewers are usually measured in thousands, but, oddly, this rate is not known in the business as "CPT," as in "cost per thousand." Instead, it takes the acronym **CPM** or **cost per mil**—which stems from *mille*, the Latin word for thousand.

As you can see in Table 12.1, which shows the top ten programs for the week of October 9 to 15, 2000, the Nielsen numbers actually consist of two

TABLE 12.1

Nielsen Media Research Top 10 Programs Week of October 9–15, 2000

RANK	PROGRAM	RATING	SHARE
1.	ER	19.2	30.0
2.	FRIENDS-SL(S)	18.0	28.0
3.	FRIENDS	16.6	27.0
4.	WILL & GRACE	15.8	23.0
5.	NFL MON NIGHT FOOTBALL	14.9	25.0
6.	MILLIONAIRE-TUE	14.5	23.0
7.	MILLIONAIRE-WED	13.9	22.0
8.	EVERYBODY LOVES RAYMOND	13.7	20.0
9.	MILLIONAIRE-SUN	13.5	20.0
10.	JUST SHOOT ME	13.3	20.0

Copyright 2000 Nielsen Media Research, reprinted with permission.

components: the **rating** and the **share**. Both are calculated as percentages of viewers.

The rating indicates the percentage of households with TV sets (or HUT—"households using television") that tuned into a specific program. Since TV households number approximately 100,800,000 in the U.S., the rating percentage shows how many households out of that 100,800,000 were actually tuned in. *ER* scored a 19.2 rating in our sample week, which made it the top-rated show. This rating indicates that 19.2% of TV households watched the program. We can thus calculate that 19,353,600 households (19.2% of 100,800,000) watched the program that night. And, based on additional data from its People Meters, Nielsen estimated that 29,330,000 viewers in those households were actually watching.

The share indicates the percentage of households with TV sets *turned on at that particular time* that tuned into a specific program. In our *ER* example, the program earned a 30 share—meaning that 30% of the households watching TV at that time were tuned in to the events at County General Hospital. Thus, while the *rating* number marks the percentage of a relatively stable number (total households with TV), the *share* number is the percentage of a constantly fluctuating number since the number of turned-on TV sets varies throughout the day and the year—with summertime being the season with the least viewing.

In light of the calculation of rating and share, it is interesting to consider just how precipitously viewing of the major broadcast networks has declined. In the 1952–53 season (the first one for which Nielsen ratings are available), ABC, CBS, and NBC had a combined average rating of 74.8. In other words, three quarters of the TV households in the U.S. watched these three networks all the time. In the 1998–99 season, that number fell to 26 or one quarter of the TV households. Additionally, the top program in that first ratings season was CBS's *I Love Lucy,* with a hefty 67.3 rating. Two thirds of the TV nation regularly watched it each week. In contrast, the top show from 1998–99 was NBC's *ER,* with a comparatively meager 17.8 average rating—approximately one fourth of *I Love Lucy's.* This means that only 17.8% of the TV nation watched *ER* during an average week. Broadcast networks and their programs clearly no longer command the enormous audiences they once did. The dispersion of the audience is obvious. Advertisers have had to adapt their commercials to this new world of increasingly narrow, but more homogenous, audiences.

Paying for "Free" TV

Every time you visit the store and buy Altoid mints that you saw advertised on television, you are paying for "free" TV. A portion of those mints' purchase price was added to the product to ameliorate parent company Philip Morris's advertising budget—which allocated over $787 million to television in 1998.[10] How do Philip Morris and other multinational corporations pay for television? For the most part, there is no direct contact between TV's sponsors and the companies that actually create TV programs—although there are significant exceptions to this such as sponsor Procter & Gamble's production of soap operas and the occasional instances of **product placement**, as when Budweiser paid to have Bud Light served to a castaway on *Survivor* (2000–). Instead of sponsoring/producing programs directly, most advertisers must deal with TV's wholesalers and retailers.

The TV and advertising industries classify advertising expenditures in five categories: network, syndication, national spot, cable, and local. Most of these categories are self-explanatory. "Network" refers to time bought on the four major broadcast networks while "cable" designates commercials on more specialized cable networks such as ESPN, MTV, and CNN. "Local" advertising is time bought on individual broadcast stations and cable services by local merchants. Network and cable purchases are not the only way advertisers reach a national audience. Advertisers may also buy time on syndicated programs that are aired nationwide on local stations and cable networks. Or they may place their ads directly on numerous local stations and cable services through "national spot" advertising. With spot commercials the advertiser may promote its products in specific regions without going to the expense of a full national or network campaign. Katz Television Group, for example, represents 350 television stations and 1,700 cable systems in DMAs across the U.S. Using Katz or another national representative, a manufacturer of air conditioners based in Phoenix could buy air time throughout the Southwest and South while minimizing its expenditures in New England.

Despite declining ratings, the general-interest broadcast networks still command a large portion of advertisers' dollars. In 1998, for instance, advertisers bought $13.7 billion worth of time on ABC, CBS, Fox and NBC, or approximately 29% of all advertising expenditures.[11] However, one recent trend in TV advertising has been to seek smaller, but more cohesive, audiences. This is reflected in the amount of money spent on cable networks. Although *all* categories of expenditures have continued to rise in the 1990s and 2000s, the percentage increases for cable networks have outpaced those of the traditional broadcast networks. In 1998, cable networks received less than half of the expenditures that broadcast networks got and only 12.6% of all U.S. TV ad expenditures, but their share of advertising revenue has continued to rise.

Which companies buy this time, buy these audiences? As you might well imagine, TV ad purchases are dominated by huge, diversified corporations. In particular, the top five advertisers on network television in 1998 were General Motors, Procter & Gamble, Johnson & Johnson, Philip Morris, and Ford Motors.[12] More interesting, perhaps, is the types of goods that are sold on television—as is shown in Table 12.2, *Advertising Age*'s classification of the top categories of network-TV advertising. In the U.S. at least, these are the products and services one sees most on network television. In the following section, we'll explore the meanings commonly associated with these commodities.

THE POLYSEMY OF COMMODITIES

Television advertising presents a discourse on modern life in a culture based on buying and selling. It tells us what it means to be a consumer and suggests activities we should pursue as consumers. Principally, it is telling us to buy

TABLE 12.2

Top Categories of Network-TV Advertising

1. Automotive
2. Food
3. Drugs and personal care
4. Fast food restaurants
5. Telephone
6. Retail
7. Financial services, insurance and securities
8. Beer
9. Computers
10. Entertainment[11]

"Top 10 categories by first-half 1998 ad spending,"
AdAge.com, 1999, http://www.adage.com/dataplace/
archives/dp289.html.

commodities, but often it does so in quite an indirect manner. Many ads conceal their function as advertising and simply appear to be short stories or evocative vignettes about the human condition. All ads—regardless of their bluntness or subtlety—are inscribed with packets of meanings for viewers to decode. All ads contain the fundamental meaning, "Buy this product," but they also suggest various other meanings that range from "Buy this product *and* you will become beautiful" to "Buy this product *and* you will be well liked" to "Buy this product *and* your dog's fur will really shine."

In this section we consider what comes after "buy this product." We look at the socially defined meanings, values, and illusions—the polysemy—that are commonly employed in the service of selling products. TV commercials present an ongoing discourse about objects and attempt to connect them to a range of meanings. We may identify eight broad categories of such meanings:

1. Luxury, leisure, and conspicuous consumption.

2. Individualism.

3. The natural.

4. Folk culture and tradition.

5. Novelty and progress.

6. Sexuality and romance.

7. Alleviation of pain, fear/anxiety, and guilt.

8. Utopia and escape from dystopia.

Although this list does not exhaust all of the meanings that commercials invoke, it does contain the principal values that advertisers use to entice consumers.

Luxury, Leisure, and Conspicuous Consumption

The end graphic in an ad for the Lincoln LS sedan reads simply, "Lincoln. American luxury." Car companies such as Lincoln, Cadillac, and Mercedes have long traded on their value as luxury goods. The same could be said of Rolex watches, De Beers diamonds, *haute couture* fashion and high-end electronics. When ads draw on the notion of luxury, they imply that the goods advertised go beyond filling basic human needs for food, clothing, and shelter. Luxury items, by definition, are ones that are not necessities, that one could do without and still subsist. In addition to providing material comfort and utility, luxurious cars, jewelry, clothing, and electronics serve a significant social function. Such goods offer a way for the consumer to emulate members of an elevated social class.

The emulation of higher classes was initially conceptualized by Thorstein Veblen as the 19th century came to a close. Veblen also coined the term "conspicuous consumption" to refer to the showy, excessive purchase of nonessential, luxury goods. In his book, *The Theory of the Leisure Class* (1899), he argues that members of the leisure class (persons who need not work for a living) must buy expensive commodities in a conspicuous manner in order to maintain their social status.[13] Conspicuous consumption becomes an emblem, a sign, of their wealth and power. Individuals who are not quite that wealthy, but aspire to be so, *emulate* the leisure class by consuming conspicuously.

Emulation need not just be about wealth. When consumers buy name-brand clothing in order to adopt a certain style of dress, for instance, they seek to belong to a specific social group. Tommy Hilfiger jeans are no better at keeping one's legs warm than are generic pants, but they serve an important function nonetheless. They allow the wearer to emulate members of a social group. Emulation is also the central strategy at work in all celebrity endorsements of products. Why would Nike have paid Michael Jordan huge sums of money and created a shoe line bearing his name (the Air Jordan) if it didn't think that viewers, especially young viewers, would want to emulate him and wear the same style shoes as he did? As the Gatorade campaign of the late 1990s suggested, many advertisers banked on teenage boys' desire to "be like Mike."

It's easy to dismiss such emulation and conspicuous consumption of luxury goods as crass social climbing and superficial status seeking, but, as Ellen Seiter writes (paraphrasing anthropologist Mary Douglas), "any distinction between necessary and unnecessary goods fails to account for the crucial importance of consumption for ceremonial purposes, for social cohesion, and for the maintenance of networks of support. ... To condemn people to a level of mere subsistence consumption is to exclude them from the basis for success and security within a social network."[14] In modern societies, what we own shapes where we fit into societies' networks of work and play. Moreover, as Seiter discusses, children acquire crucial social skills through "consumption events": "birthday parties, holiday celebrations, visits at friends' houses, and so on."[15] TV commercials thrive on and exploit the central function that consumption has come to have in social networking.

Individualism

One longstanding conflict in U.S. ideology is the rights of the individual versus those of the community. We enter into a social contract with the government and other citizens that holds that we will limit certain freedoms in exchange for a civil, well-ordered society. For instance, we have the capability of driving through the center of town at 80 m.p.h., but we don't. We observe traffic rules because we know that they serve the overall good of the community. Advertising, however, need not follow these rules as strictly. Many ads tacitly override the social contract in favor of individualist values—both good and bad. These individualist values are often based in the self: self-fulfillment, self-reliance, self-expression, self-absorption, even simple selfishness.

The U.S. Army entreats young men and women to "Be all you can be," to fulfill themselves and learn self-reliance through the military service—thereby repressing the discipline and obedience that attends that experience. Nike's "Just do it" campaign intimates that determination and self-expression will come to all who wear its clothing or shoes. And McDonald's has sold billions of Big Macs by telling viewers that it's okay to be a little self-absorbed and selfish: "You deserve a break today. So get up and get away to McDonald's." Leave behind your responsibilities to others, it implies, and escape to the comfort of a fast food restaurant.

Pitching individualism in a mass medium such as television is a tricky business. Consider the tag line of a Burger King campaign begun in 1973. "Have it your way" implies that the individual is unique and uniquely deserving of certain privileges—a hamburger prepared a certain way. (Burger King's jingle taunted McDonald's for its assembly-line approach, saying, "Special orders don't upset *us*.") But there is a fundamental problem when uniqueness is marketed by mass media. Burger King cannot provide hamburgers uniquely prepared a hundred million different ways. Rather, "your way" must be restricted to a fairly limited number of options within a very controlled environment. You can get your hamburger with or without tomatoes, but you cannot get it marinated overnight in an assortment of seasonings and broiled over dampened mesquite chips. Thus, the individualism that Burger King is selling is not unique. As it turns out, "your way" is the same way as millions of others. Similarly, Budweiser commercials may declare, "This Bud's for you," but TV viewers know that this is not literally true, that Anheuser-Busch didn't brew that bottle of beer to their own specifications.

"Advertising shepherds herds of individuals," notes Leslie Savan.[16] By this she means that television addresses viewers as individuals not as a group. It invites them to experience life as individuals, to break away from conformity and establish one's own identity. This leads to what she identifies as mass media advertising's "most basic paradox": "Join us and become unique."[17] Clothing and other fashion products often appeal to individualist values and suggest to viewers that they will stand out from the crowd if they purchase these products, but because commercials are simultaneously encouraging millions of other viewers to purchase those same products, they are perpetually creating or reinforcing fashion-based crowds of individuals. Thus, at the same time that commercials encourage viewers to be self-reliant individuals, they also entreat them to emulate others and join certain groups, enter certain networks.

A series of Gap commercials illustrates this paradoxical "herd of individuals" appeal. A group of models in their 20s sits or stands in front of a white background, faces the camera directly, and lip syncs to music such as Depeche Mode's "Just Can't Get Enough" (Fig. 12.1). Each ad concludes with the Gap's logo and an end line such as "Everybody in leather," "Everybody in cords," or "Everybody

FIGURE 12.1

in Vests." By suggesting (commanding?) "Everybody in ..." the Gap uses the appeal of networking and emulation—hoping the viewer will think, "I want to *be like* these models." But, significantly, these models do not interact with one another—in contrast to a contemporary series of Gap khaki ads in which dancers gleefully perform swing dances with each other. The "Everybody in ..." ads present a crowd of isolated individuals. They're all wearing leather/cords/vests, but in different ways. Their dress and body language (they all strike different poses) set them up as individuals even as the framing and song pull them to-gether as a group. Hence, they are paradoxically alone together—much like the millions of viewers simultaneously watching TV from their separate homes.

The Natural

Commodities may be associated with nature and aspects of the natural—wholesomeness, healthfulness, purity. Medical, food, and beverage products often emphasize their natural ingredients and thereby suggest that the products are wholesome, healthy, and pure.

Pertussin cough syrup was promoted in the 1960s as a "safe *natural* way to relieve night cough." Its ads resemble those of homeopathic medicine, claim-ing it is "made from nature's healing medicinals." The ads don't specify which medicinals, but they do stress that Pertussin does not contain "codeine, an-tihistamines, and nerve-dulling drugs." Post Grape-Nuts cereal was similarly advertised as the "Back-to-nature cereal" in TV commercials from the early 1970s featuring naturalist Euell Gibbons. He claims, "Its *natural*, sweet taste reminds me of *wild* hickory nuts" (emphasis added). Gibbons' comment is a bit disingenuous because Grape-Nuts contains no nuts—hickory or otherwise—but rather is manufactured from wheat and barley (which, granted, are natural ingredients).

In similar fashion, commercials for Coors Light beer make obvious con-nections between the natural qualities of the Rocky Mountains and Coors beer by suggesting that you "Tap the Rockies." Coors emphasizes its beer contains "Rocky Mountain water" and no additives or preservatives—alluding to nature's purity and repressing the company's exploitation of natural resources in order to make beverages. There have, however, been attacks on its use of the majestic images of the Rockies. In 1997, "Tap the Rockies" billboards in upstate New York were vandalized with the accusation, "Rape the Rockies, racist scum, toxic polluters."[18]

Another sense of naturalness is that which is opposed to the technological or artificial. Makeup products commonly present this illusion of the natural. An ad for Cover Girl Clean Sheer Stick, for example, promises, "It doesn't look like makeup—just great skin." As with many "beauty" products, the appeal of Clean Sheer Stick is its ability to conceal its artifice and appear natural. Makeup such as this promises to transform a person's natural face (just as certain bras and other undergarments promise to transform the body) while hiding the artificiality of that transformation.

It should be noted that the natural is not always viewed in a positive light. Advertising often qualifies its use of the natural world. Post's Grape-Nuts commercial extolled its "back-to-nature" virtues at a time when this phrase signified a new environmental consciousness, but in the early part of the 20th century Post seemed just as proud of the scientific processing of the natural world as it was of its naturalness. Text on Grape-Nuts boxes from then avers that Grape-Nuts is "a food containing the natural nutritive elements of these field grains *thoroughly and scientifically baked*" (emphasis added).[19] Nature is all well and good, apparently, but only if science is baked into it. Even natural beauty, as alluded to in the Cover Girl commercial, has not always been universally admired. In some circles, it is associated with coarseness and vulgarity, or seen as a trait of the presumably inferior working class. The royal court during Louis XVI and Marie Antoinette's reign (1774–92), for instance, preferred ostentatious powdered wigs and a blatantly artificial style of makeup and clothing. A more recent example is Goth fashion—including dyed hair, extremely pale complexions (often achieved through makeup), black lipstick and nail polish colors that are "not-seen-in-nature."[20] The Goths and the Louis XVI court have little interest in looking "natural." Instead of valuing the natural, cultures such as these emphasize otherworldliness, a certain sense of sophistication, refinement, and connoisseurship.

Folk Culture and Tradition

Closely allied to the imagery of naturalness is folk culture. Advertising calls on folk culture to represent traditional principles such as trustworthiness, simplicity, authenticity, and raw patriotism. "We make money the old-fashioned way," intones John Houseman in the Smith-Barney ad, "We earn it." Chevrolet's television commercials have long rested on folk associations—especially in its truck ads. In the 1980s, the "Heartbeat of America" campaign presented numerous images of folk life in the rural United States and thereby evoked the virtues of small-town life. Earlier, during the contentious 1970s, its ads sang the virtues of "baseball, hot dogs, apple pie, and Chevrolet". In this instance, small-town, folk values are blended with patriotism and nostalgia for a bygone era. Baseball ("America's pastime") and hot dogs connote the positive values of team sport (athletic prowess, cooperation, loyalty, courage in the face of adversity) while apple pie carries implications of motherly nurturing and down-home nutrition. The Chevrolet truck ad goes like this:

> In the years that I been livin' lots of things have surely changed. Lots of things have come and gone, some even came back again. But through all the many changes, some things are for sure. And you know that's a mighty fine feelin', kinda makes you feel secure. 'Cause I love baseball, hot dogs, apple pie, and Chevrolet.[21]

Irony is not normally associated with folk discourse, but Gallo Winery's Bartles & Jaymes wine cooler ads playfully parody folk narratives. They present the ostensible owners of the company as a couple of genial old codgers—Frank Bartles and Ed Jaymes. Actually, it is pure fiction, invented by Gallo's advertising agency, Ogilvy & Mather, in order to sell a new alcoholic beverage to young professionals. Over the course of 7 years (1985–92) and some 230 commercials, Bartles (played by David Rufkaur) chronicled their marketing endeavors (Fig. 12.2).

The First Bartles & James Wine cooler ad's text is as follows:

> Hello there. My name is Fred Bartles and this is Ed Jaymes. You know, it occurred to Ed the other day that between his fruit orchard and my premium grade wine vineyard, we could make a truly superior premium-grade wine cooler. It sounded good to me. So Ed took out a second on his house, and wrote to Harvard for an MBA, and now we're preparing to enter the wine cooler business. We will try to keep you posted on how it's going. And thank you very much for your support.

The folk values incarnated in the Bartles character included guilelessness, simplicity, and honest directness. Much like the Chevrolet spots that revel in the past as a gentler, "simpler" time, Bartles appears to be from another era where

FIGURE 12.2

selling products is a direct, honorable process. Sitting on his front porch with a wooden screen door behind him, he seems out of touch with the principles of slick contemporary marketing campaigns. There is considerable irony here, of course, since all of Bartles' guilelessness is a sham and the ad's honest directness was fabricated by a high-powered advertising agency.

Unlike many commercials that rely on folk culture, however, the Bartles & Jaymes' series presume that viewers are themselves wary of appeals based on baseball, hot dogs, and apple pie. The wine cooler was designed for sophisticated young professionals who might be skeptical of small-town values and bald-faced sentiment. The ads subtly play to that urban audience by softly parodying small-town perspectives—as when the first ad suggests Jaymes would write to Harvard for a Master's in business. The humor of many of the spots relies on the viewer's awareness of marketing jargon and strategies. "Thank you for your support" is a hollow phrase commonly used in marketing, advertising, and PR. When we hear it coming sincerely from the mouth of a country bumpkin, we laugh at the incongruity.

In a sense, the Bartles & Jaymes ads have it both ways: They appeal to viewers' desires for a simpler era and at the same time they chide the simplicity of that era—inviting the viewers in on the joke by alluding to the complicated machinations of modern marketing.

Novelty and Progress

The flip side of advertising's appeal to folk culture and tradition is its incessant hawking of the new and the merits of progress. Longstanding marketing research shows that consumers are drawn to packaging with the words "new" and "improved" prominent on it. To capitalize on this tendency, advertisers subject consumers to product improvements that are dubious at best. One commercial for "new mild, new formula" Zest soap promises "new lather," but it's hard to imagine what could be strikingly new about bubbles of soap. And the 2001 model of the Dodge Caravan closely resembled other minivans, but nonetheless a spot for it starts with a shot of tulips blooming, the title "Different," and the claim, "We began anew." It then lists several minor changes. "New, new, new! Dodge Grand Caravan, the best minivan ever." It concludes with the self-mocking question and a graphic: "And did we mention it's new? [pause] The All-new Dodge Caravan. Different." There is nothing that is literally "all-new" or completely different in the world of merchandise. If you changed everything in the design of a minivan, it would no longer be a "minivan." It'd be something completely new and different. Manufacturers and advertising agencies are not prepared to risk all-out newness.

Part of the appeal of newness and novelty stems from a positive attitude toward progress. Americans are accustomed to regular reports of scientific advances in medicine, physics, and other technological fields where the work of researchers builds on previous efforts and moves toward particular goals: a cure for AIDS, sending a human to the moon, a car that will get 1,000 miles per gallon. Applying the notion of scientific progress to soap, automobiles, or fashion is usually just hyperbole. Zest's new lather might well be different from its old lather (although even that is debatable), but that doesn't necessarily mean that it is an advance over the older lather. The new lather is different from—rather than an advance over—the old.

Coca-Cola's executives learned this lesson the hard way. New Coke received an enormous publicity campaign in 1985, but it turned into one of the biggest marketing fiascos of the century. Most Coke drinkers found the new, sweeter taste (designed to be closer to Pepsi's formula) was not to their liking. This led Coca-Cola executives to hurriedly reissue Coke's old formula under the name "Coke Classic"—a name that evokes images of a traditional soda fountain and all its folk associations. It's interesting to note that Coca-Cola's marketers changed the position of the word, "Coke," in the name when they released Coke Classic. That is, with "*New* Coke" they emphasized the newness of the product, but with "*Coke* Classic"—and not "Classic Coke"—they stressed its Coke-ness. There are no casual decisions in the naming of products. Deciding to put the word "Coke" first probably arose from hours of brainstorming and focus groups. Later, in 1992, "New Coke" became "Coke II." After 7 years on the market it was presumably no longer new, although it was still being presented as a successor ("II") to standard Coca-Cola.

Sexuality and Romance

It's no secret that sexuality and romance have been associated with thousands of products over the decades of TV's short history. "Sex sells," it has often been said in the advertising industry. One need not look far to find overt references to sex and sexual allure in television commercials—although, of course, U.S. network standards still prohibit nudity (which is quite common in European commercials) or graphic representation of sexual intercourse. Indeed, most of the networks still refuse to carry condom commercials. Still, ads for perfume or cologne, lingerie, bathing suits, shampoos, and cosmetics—which often feature women and men in revealing, tight-fitting clothing—are clearly banking on associating sex with their products.

The two most obvious ways that sexual imagery sells are (1) implying that the product will make the viewer more sexually appealing and (2) associating the product itself with sexuality and thereby stimulating a hormonal rush in order to draw the viewer's attention to it. The first type of appeal is evident in products such as perfumes and shampoos. The second comes into play in ads for beer and cars, designed for heterosexual men, that have attractive women posing by the products.

Victoria's Secret manages to incorporate *both* of these appeals in its commercials. During the 1999 *Super Bowl* between the Denver Broncos and the Atlanta Falcons, it advertised a Web-based fashion show by addressing itself principally to male viewers: "The Broncos won't be there. The Falcons won't be there. You won't care." The bulk of the ad consists of images of its minimally dressed models (Fig. 12.3). The "you" in this instance is the male viewer who might be sexually attracted to the women of Victoria's Secret. *Entertainment Weekly* attacked the ad as the "Worst Blatant Exploitation of T&A ["tits-and-ass"]" of the *Super Bowl* ads: "The plot: Jiggle, jiggle, jiggle, Web address. This embarrassingly

FIGURE 12.3

FIGURE 12.4

unsubtle spot announces an upcoming Internet fashion show for the lingerie catalog—because God knows we need more soft-core cyberporn."[22]

Evidently, the *Super Bowl* spot hopes to entice men to purchase lingerie for the women in their lives, but in an ad for its Natural Miracle Bra, Victoria's Secret mainly speaks to female viewers. The audio consists of various testimonials by women about the bra's effectiveness: "Makes you feel more natural. Makes you feel more confident as a woman. Very comfortable. Feels just like natural skin. When I wear the Natural I just feel feminine and more sexy. It gave me more cleavage . . . instant cleavage. I felt confident and sexy. You felt good about your body." (See the discussion above regarding the significance of the "natural.") The target viewers and the "you" of this ad's text are certainly women, not men. This water/glycerin-filled bra is thus marketed to women themselves. The heterosexual male viewer is not excluded from the appeal of this ad, however, as it features a large-breasted woman in the Natural Miracle Bra, modeling its cleavage-enlarging effects and presumably inciting his libido (Fig. 12.4). In true polysemic fashion, this commercial has room for several sexual interpretations.

Paul Messaris contends that such blatant appeals to sexual themes are matched by covert presentations of the subject in "at least three types of situations": "[F]irst, when sex is being used metaphorically and what the ad is really promising is something else; second, when the link between the product and sex is frowned upon; and, third, when the type of sex is socially unacceptable."[23]

One famous instance of metaphoric sex is a 1960s commercial for Noxzema shaving cream. In tight close-up, Gunilla Knutson, a former Miss Sweden, suggestively runs her lips across a string of pearls (Fig. 12.5). With her distinctly Swedish accent, she breathlessly intones, "Men, nothing takes it off like Noxzema Medicated Shave." A brass band then begins to blare "The Stripper," which accompanies close-ups of a man shaving his face (Fig. 12.6). "Take it off," Knutson commands, "Take it *all* off."

What is the source of the enduring appeal of this ad? Much like the Miracle Bra ad, this product ostensibly improves the sexual desirability of its user, but the strategy used in its pitch is a metaphoric one. The act of a man removing

FIGURE 12.5

FIGURE 12.6

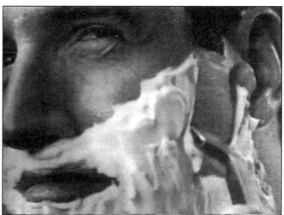

shaving cream is metaphorically linked to the act of a woman removing clothing: shaving = stripping. The phrase "Take it off" contains the literal meaning of shaving cream removal and the metaphoric meaning of clothing removal. In the 1960s, this was seen to be quite risque. Messaris argues that metaphoric sex and double entendres continue to be widely used in contemporary advertising as well—especially in commercials associating sex and food.

Messaris's second category of covert sexuality in commercials contains ads in which "the link between the product and sex is disparaged or condemned by public opinion. Cars, liquor, and cigarettes are among the most prominent examples of products in this category."[24] If advertisers were to state seriously that their cars, liquor, or tobacco products (which have been banned from U.S. TV ads since 1971) will enable men to attract women for the purpose of sexual activity, viewers would scoff or laugh at the ads. And yet that is exactly the implicit message of many commercials—especially local car commercials—in which conventionally attractive women pose beside various products. Messaris' point is that sexual associations with cars, beer, and other products have not disappeared from U.S. television. Rather, they have just been displaced from unabashed verbal statements to the more subtle language of the visuals.

Messaris's third category of implicit sexuality contains forbidden sexual themes. What qualifies as a sexual taboo on broadcast television advertising is, of course, quite tame and circumscribed when compared to premium channels (e.g., HBO or Showtime) or theatrical films. For instance, bondage and homosexuality are never unabashedly represented in U.S. commercials. They find their way into televisions commercials only through covert allusion—often cloaked in comedy or self-parody. In a Finish Line commercial for Reebok shoes, two young men are hiking through the jungle when one of them is bitten on the leg by a snake. The other begins to suck the venom from the wound, giving the appearance of oral sex (Fig. 12.7). A woman jogs by in Reebok shoes and the men disengage and look embarrassed. Allusions to gay sex and male homophobia are communicated through the visuals, but it's hard to imagine a sports shoe commercial that would verbally or directly present homosexual activity—especially considering sports culture's longstanding and virulent homophobia.

FIGURE 12.7

Child and teenage sexuality is similarly avoided in the manifest content of TV commercials. Messaris discusses what happened when an advertiser violated this particular taboo in the 1995 Calvin Klein jeans campaign.[25] The print and TV ads from that campaign feature very young, barely pubescent, models in revealing poses. Many critics of the ads argued that they appealed to the prurient interest of adult male viewers and thus qualified as child pornography. After considerable public protest, Calvin Klein withdrew the ads. Evidently, the commercials were not implicit enough for the U.S. media audience.

Alleviation of Pain, Fear/Anxiety, and Guilt

Numerous commercials use a simple narrative formula: Someone is in pain or feeling anxious and the ad's product alleviates that pain or anxiety. Case closed. All medicinal ads are based on this premise, as are many hygiene (e.g., deodorants, mouth washes, feminine douches) and food products. The Alka-Seltzer jingle, "Plop, plop, fizz, fizz. Oh, what a relief it is!" unmistakably exemplifies this approach.

Soap operas, several of which are produced by hygiene and food giant Procter & Gamble, are awash in this sort of commercial. It's interesting to consider how the soap opera narrative structure is the exact opposite of the narrative in its commercials (see chapter 2 for more on narrative). Soap opera stories never reach a definitive ending. Each small conclusion is the basis for a new enigma and further questions. But in the soap opera commercial, crises are quickly solved in 30 seconds. A child's cough is soothed. A woman's dandruff is controlled. A "tension headache" is eased. Hunger is satisfied. Commercials are small bits of closure inserted into soap opera's vast sea of open-ended narrative.

Guilt is often attached to issues of pain and suffering. Mike Budd, et al., explain how advertisers mount a "guilt campaign": "This involves airing commercials that imply that the viewer is not really a loving mother and home-maker unless she uses Downey to make her towels soft, Pampers to keep her baby dry, and Duncan Hines to bake cakes for her husband and children."[26]

Often the guilt is heaped on the woman by someone observing her not using the sponsor's product. A classic in this vein is the Wisk detergent commercials produced by the BBDO agency and begun in 1968. In this series, a wife and mother is repeatedly shamed for being unable to deal with the "ring around the collar" problem—until, that is, she learns to apply Wisk directly to the offending stains. Such ads encourage the viewer to seek alleviation of guilt through the purchase of commodities.

Utopia and Escape from Dystopia

In her consideration of children's advertising and consumer culture, Seiter argues, "Like most popular entertainments, commercials are utopian in many respects—portraying a childhood world more exciting, intense, and exhilarating than everyday life."[27] In Seiter's study she found that child-centered commercials often counterpose this utopian childhood world to the adult world of restraint and boring responsibilities. Of course, utopianism is not limited to children's commercials. Numerous commercials invite the adult viewer into a utopia of intensity of experience, exhilaration of emotion, and, frequently, unbridled hedonism (a total lack of responsibility).

Seiter draws on Richard Dyer's more general discussion of utopianism in film, television, and other mass entertainments. Dyer characterizes utopia as "the image of 'something better' to escape into, or something we want deeply that our day-to-day lives don't provide."[28] In contrast to the tensions and inadequacies of contemporary life, utopia offers:

- Abundance (elimination of poverty for self and others; equal distribution of wealth)
- Energy (work and play synonymous)
- Intensity (excitement, drama, affectivity of living)
- Transparency (open, spontaneous, honest communications and relationships)
- Community (all together in one place, communal interests, collective activity)[29]

Each of these traits can be found in television commercials.

An ad for the MCI Network explicitly alludes to utopia. It begins by explaining, "People here communicate mind to mind." Then it continues:

> Not black to white. There are no genders. Not man to woman. There is no age. Not young to old. There are no infirmities. Not short to tall. Or handsome to homely. Just thought to thought. Idea to idea. Uninfluenced by the rest of it. There are only minds. Only minds. What is this place? This place? Utopia? No. No. The Internet. The Internet. The Internet . . .[30]

MCI represents utopia as a community fostering the unfettered interchange of ideas; a place where nothing will constrict its citizens. Its ad insinuates that the Internet might be mistaken for utopia and that its networking can thus convey the customer to a utopian realm.

A commercial for a Mercedes-Benz roadster is less high-minded in its presentation of a utopian experience. In the ad, Peter Pan and Tinkerbell float into the bedroom of Michael, a middle-aged man. Michael is sleeping in respectable-looking pajamas next to a woman who is presumably his respectable spouse. Peter entices him, "Do you remember when we were 8 and we went flying?" When he protests that he can't fly any more, Peter corrects him, "It's never too late to fly!" We then cut to Michael, still in his pajamas, driving a roadster and shouting, "Woooo-hooo!" Notably, Peter and Tinkerbell are beside him, but his spouse is not. The spot fades to black as Michael shifts into high gear. Then the only text in the ad fades in: "Exhilaration" (followed by the Mercedes-Benz logo). With its allusions to Never-Never Land and the boy who won't grow up, this commercial associates its product with a utopian view of childhood pleasures and passions.

A dystopia is the exact opposite of a utopia. It's a land where freedoms are restricted and life is oppressive and colorless. Advertisers' products frequently promise to liberate consumers from such oppression. McDonald's modest suggestion that "You deserve a break today" could be viewed as an inducement to flee the dystopian home—soiled laundry, dirty bathrooms, and unfed children—and enter a world of culinary surplus and happy circus characters (Ronald McDonald).

The most unequivocal TV-commercial attack on dystopia is the Apple Computer spot that announced the release of the Macintosh computer in 1984. Apple drew heavily on George Orwell's *Nineteen Eighty-Four* (originally published in 1949), which contains the best known dystopia in 20th-century fiction. In it, Big Brother rules a harshly repressive totalitarian state where the Ministry of Truth rewrites history and the Thought Police arrest anyone who dares resist. The Apple "1984" commercial shrewdly transforms its arch rival, IBM, into Orwell's Big Brother—without ever mentioning IBM by name. IBM tyrannized the computer world at that time, and its corporate culture was a very conservative, contained one. Chiat/Day, Apple's advertising agency, chose to present the Mac as a liberating force, hoping to challenge IBM's monopolistic control of the computer industry. They hired feature film director Ridley Scott, who'd recently shot the dystopian *Blade Runner* (1982), to direct it. And they paid $500,000 for a one-time broadcast during the 1984 *Super Bowl*. (No other national broadcast time was purchased although the ad was screened repeatedly on news programs.)

In the ad, an audience of ashen-faced, shaved-head drones watches a large screen where their ruler harangues them about the "Information Purification Directives" and "Unification of Thought" (see Figs. 12.8–12.9).

> For today, we celebrate the first glorious anniversary of the Information Purification Directives. We have created, for the first time in all history, a garden of pure ideology. Where each worker may bloom secure from the pests of contradictory and confusing truths. Our Unification of Thought is more powerful a weapon than any fleet or army on earth. We are one people. With one will. One resolve. One cause. Our enemies shall talk themselves to death. And we will bury them with their own confusion. We shall prevail!

A young woman wearing a runner's outfit and wielding a sledgehammer sprints into the room, pursued by armed soldiers (Fig. 12.10). Her red shorts and

FIGURE 12.8   **FIGURE 12.9**

vigorous skin tone contrast sharply with the colorless minions. She flings the sledgehammer at the screen, which causes it to explode. Text scrolls over the image as the voiceover begins: "On January 24th, Apple Computer will introduce Macintosh. And you'll see why 1984 won't be like '1984.'"

When this ad ran, viewers had never seen Macintosh computers. The Mac is not shown in the commercial and no features of it are described. Viewers could have had no tangible sense of how Macs might differ from other manufacturers' computers. Instead, Apple relied entirely on the theme of liberation from dystopia to sell its new machine.

THE PERSUASIVE STYLE OF COMMERCIALS

As we have seen, commercials rely on a fairly predictable polysemy to persuade consumers to buy products. One clear persuasive strategy, then, is to build an

FIGURE 12.10

argument that a particular product is associated with positive meanings and images, or eliminates negative ones. But so far we have not concentrated on *how* that argument is built. What sound/image techniques and rhetorical strategies do commercials use to make products seem desirable? What, one might say, is the persuasive style of the TV commercial?

Some commercials persuade with a jackhammer-blunt style, while others so carefully hide their persuasion that viewers are left wondering just what was being advertised. As we examine the techniques used to persuade us, we'll find that they can be grouped into the following general categories. The list is not an exhaustive one and new persuasive styles will doubtlessly evolve in the future, but the majority of TV commercials rely on one or more of these persuasive devices:

1. Metaphor.
2. Utopian style.
3. Product differentiation and superiority.
4. Repetition and redundancy.
5. Extraordinary and excessive style: "televisuality" and counter television.
6. Graphics and animation.
7. Violating reality (special effects).
8. Reflexivity and intertextuality.

Let's examine how these tactics are employed in specific commercials.

Metaphor

Perhaps the most common way that advertisers assert the desirability of their products is to associate them with activities, objects, or people that are themselves desirable. Essentially, such association constructs a metaphor between the product and that desirable activity, object, or person. This may be accomplished in two ways. Either the product will enable the viewer to become similar to something else or the product itself is shown to be similar to something else. Our discussion of emulation shows how the former can be quite directly expressed through the commercial's script. Gatorade's suggestion to "be like Mike" by drinking its beverages is a clear-cut example of a simile where viewers are told they can become similar to someone else (Michael Jordan) by consuming a product. Thus, the product is offering to transform viewers from their mundane identities into something special and unique, or, at the very least, it is proposing to make them into a *simulation* of that unique person, Michael Jordan.

In commercials, a metaphor often links a product with an unexpected thing or activity. For example, Noxzema implies that shaving is metaphorically equivalent to stripping in the ad previously discussed, in which "The Stripper" plays and a seductive woman urges men to "take it all off." The metaphor in this case is created through the commercial's sound mix (the woman's dialogue and the music). By bringing normally incongruous sound and image together, Noxzema creates the metaphoric meaning. That is, the commercial's meaning is not a literal one ("The man is stripping"), but rather a metaphorical one ("Shaving is

FIGURE 12.11

FIGURE 12.12

like stripping in that something is removed in both cases"). It sounds bland and boring when summarized so bluntly, but to suggest that removing shaving cream is similar to removing clothing fastens a sexually provocative connotation to a normally routine activity.

Another method for generating metaphors is through a sequence of images—much as Russian filmmaker Sergei Eisenstein theorized 80 years ago. By bringing two or more images together in sequence, a filmmaker can imply that one image should be compared with the other and that there are similarities between them. A staunch socialist and revolutionary, Eisenstein advocated the use of visual metaphor or, as he called it, intellectual montage, for political causes. In the instance of his film, *Strike*, he intercut heroic striking workers being beaten by police with shots of a bull being slaughtered (Figs. 12.11–12.12) The metaphoric meaning is clear: strikers are cattle. And, further, it graphically argues that a gross injustice is being done.

Advertisers have usurped Eisenstein's principle to sell commodities. For instance, a commercial for a line of Hyundai cars begins with 10 images of exhilarating activities: a mountain climber topping a peak, a surfer negotiating a wave, children leaping into a swimming hole, a girl twirling in a water sprinkler, etc. (Fig. 12.13). These are followed by an equal number of shots of Hyundai cars on the road (Fig. 12.14). The final image is a group of mountain climbers on a summit (Fig. 12.15). The order of the images—cars sandwiched between swimming children and mountaineers—suggests that driving a Hyundai is the same as the other actions. Commercials are seldom satisfied only to hint at such meanings visually, however, and the significance of the images is often anchored by the sound. The Hyundai ad incorporates Cream's song, "I Feel Free," and thus makes clear what meaning ought to be generalized from this sequence of images.[31]

> There are those moments in life when absolutely nothing weighs you down. When you feel totally, completely free. This fall, Hyundai is introducing a exciting new line of vehicles that are a joy to drive and virtually effortless to own, thanks to America's best warranty plan. Because we believe freedom should be more than a feeling. It should be something you can actually touch.

FIGURE 12.13

FIGURE 12.14

It should be noted, however, that the narration does *not* explicitly state, "Driving Hyundai cars is like flying a kite or jumping in a creek." The sequentiality of the images, aided by the music, carries this meaning *indirectly*. As Messaris argues, indirectness is commonly used in advertising. He maintains that it has two advantages over direct approaches. First, an indirect, visual argument such as the Hyundai ad elicits a "greater degree of mental participation" from viewers.[32] It requires viewers to make the semantic connection between the product and the other objects (e.g., between Hyundai cars and children swimming). Messaris contends that viewers are more likely to retain the commercial's message because they themselves have helped to generate it. Second, Messaris contends, " . . . the [explicit] verbal claims made in advertisements tend to be held to much stricter standards of accountability than whatever claims are implicit in the ads' pictures."[33] His illustration of this is ads for cigarettes, which show happy, healthy-looking people smoking—thus making the indirect, implicit claim that smoking is a healthy activity when, of course, we know it is not.

FIGURE 12.15

Commercials can metaphorically suggest many things in the visuals that they would be prohibited from stating explicitly in the dialogue.

Utopian Style

We discussed earlier how commercials promise admission to utopia through the purchase of commodities—as when Michael escapes with Peter Pan to the utopia of a Mercedes-Benz roadster. Dyer contends that utopianism in mass entertainment is not just evident in the worlds it portrays. He takes the principle of utopianism a step further and finds it in the *style* of presentation, in aspects of mise-en-scene, cinematography, and, crucially, music.[34] That is, he argues that qualities of utopia (abundance, energy, intensity, transparency, and community) may be found in a medium's style. For Dyer, this is most evident in the film musical. Since music is fundamental to most, if not all, commercials, it seems reasonable that we might look for this utopian style in the television commercial.

Soda commercials offer particularly clear examples of utopianism's embodiment in style. To choose one instance among many, consider a Coca-Cola spot from 2000 that presents a rave party in the woods. A mass of people gyrate euphorically near a fire (Fig. 12.16) to the music of Basement Jaxx's "Red Alert". The handheld camera bumps and jumps within the crowd, occasionally craning above them. One stocky guy in a T-shirt and shorts is featured dancing quirkily by himself as three friends sit nearby (Fig. 12.17). There's no dialogue and the lyrics of the music are virtually indistinguishable. The only words in the ad appear on the bottoms of Coke cans. In total, they are: "Bliss . . . comes from . . . within. Enjoy" (Fig. 12.18). With so few words to anchor the meaning of this commercial, it must rely on elements of style (bass-heavy techno-styled music, dancing technique, camera movements) to signify its meaning. The utopian "bliss" that we are to associate with Coca-Cola imbues the image/sound style and encourages viewers to join the dance, figuratively speaking. Energy and intensity—in Dyer's sense of these terms—are embodied in the commercial's style.

FIGURE 12.16

FIGURE 12.17

FIGURE 12.18

Product Differentiation and Superiority

To survive in the marketplace, every product must distinguish itself from others in the same category. Coke must be perceived as different from Pepsi, Tide from Cheer, Ford from Toyota, Levi from Wrangler, and on and on. At the core of all advertising is the establishment and maintenance of a product's identity, its brand. The key to brand identity is a product's **unique selling proposition (USP)**, as advertising standard-bearer Rosser Reeves termed that certain something that separates a product from the rest of the field.[35] Even when there is very little actual difference between commodities, the USP principle holds that the advertiser must find or even fabricate one. Reeves is often quoted as explaining the USP this way: "Our problem is—a client comes into my office and throws down two newly minted half-dollars onto my desk and says, 'Mine is the one on the left. You prove it's better.'"[36] This lack of difference between products is called **brand parity**.

Reeves faced the challenge of brand parity in 1952 while developing an advertising campaign for Anacin, a pain reliever whose active ingredients consisted solely of aspirin (acetylsalicylic acid [ASA]) and caffeine. How was he to differentiate Anacin from regular aspirin? His solution was a series of cleverly worded commercials that feature a fanciful animated representation of an ailment he dubbed the "tension headache" (Fig. 12.19). A compressed spring and a jagged electrical spark metaphorically represent the overwrought human nervous system (several ads in the series include a small hammer pounding away, too). The ads' catchphrase of "fast, fast, fast relief" became part of the 1950s popular culture lexicon. But it wasn't enough for Reeves to explain how Anacin relieved pain. He also needed to "prove" that it lessened discomfort in a *different* manner from aspirin—even though aspirin was its main pain relieving agent. He needed to find Anacin's USP.

In one commercial from this long-running campaign, the announcer explains, "Aspirin has just one pain reliever. Add buffering, you still get just one. Only Anacin of the four leading headache remedies has special ingredients to relieve pain *fast*, help overcome depression *fast*, relax tension *fast*." Anacin's

FIGURE 12.19

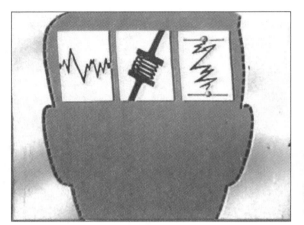

FIGURE 12.20

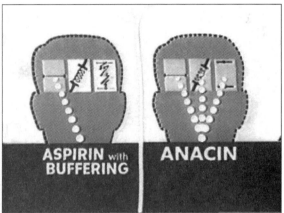

combination of ingredients composes its unique selling proposition, according to Reeves, because only Anacin has that particular recipe. To emphasize this point, side-by-side animation shows Anacin relieving headache pain that aspirin cannot alleviate (Fig. 12.20). Nowhere in this ad does the announcer reveal that the principal "special ingredient" in Anacin is aspirin itself. Instead, we're allowed to imagine that its ingredients are wholly different from aspirin. If we examine the text of the ad carefully, we find that the announcer does not deny that Anacin contains aspirin. He is just, let us say, less than forthcoming about the nature of its ingredients. In fact, one premise of the commercial is that "Three out of four doctors recommend the ingredients in Anacin." He doesn't specify what those ingredients are, but we may well suppose that the primary one is aspirin. Note also that the copy does not say that the doctors specifically recommend Anacin, but rather just that they recommend the ingredients Anacin contains.

If we were to rewrite this commercial without the need to create a unique selling proposition and in a more forthcoming, purely informational manner, it might go something like this: "Three out of four doctors recommend aspirin for headache pain. Anacin contains 325 mg. of aspirin and is also laced with 32 mg. of caffeine, which may speed the alleviation of your pain or may just give you the jitters." To be fair to Reeves, we should note that in his book, *Reality in Advertising*, he contests the suggestion that Anacin's USP is a made-up one. He argues that the difference between Anacin and aspirin is not "minuscule." He claims that distinguishing Anacin from aspirin is not based on a "deceptive differential," but rather is "the stuff and substance of good advertising."[37]

Advertisers currently express disdain for Reeves's hard-sell approach. It's said to be too simplistic for today's "sophisticated" consumers and yet television commercials continue to wage battles against brand parity. From the Apple Power Mac G4 commercials entreating computer users to "Think different" to the taste tests of the "Pepsi Challenge" to the Dodge ads beginning and ending with the word "Different," we see the persistent influence of Reeves's unique selling proposition and the need for advertisers to differentiate their products from those of their competitors.

Repetition and Redundancy

In addition to the USP, Reeves was also known as an advocate of blunt force repetition in television commercials. The Anacin spot above exemplifies this in its use of the word "fast." It appears eight times in the 30 second spot and three times in the tagline alone: "Anacin—for fast, fast, incredibly fast relief." Not only did Anacin's slogan contain repetition, but it was itself reiterated thousands of times in repeated airings of this commercial and in numerous different Anacin ads, which were also frequently aired. All successful advertising campaigns use repetition within ads, in repeated airings of ads, and across numerous other ads in the same campaign.

Repetition in advertising serves one major, obvious function: reinforcement. The first time you hear a word or see an image, you may not remember it. Each repetition of it makes recall more likely. But what, in general terms, are TV commercials reinforcing? They're doubtlessly reinforcing particular qualities of particular commodities, but in a more general sense they're reinforcing brand identity. If advertisers can get you to remember the names of their products when you visit a store, they feel they've achieved 75% of their goal. If they can get you to remember the superiority of their brands and subsequently purchase their products, they've achieved the remaining 25%.

Another technique that is closely related to repetition is redundancy. Most of the information that we hear and see repeated in TV commercials is redundant information. It exceeds what is necessary to make the point. Sound and image often redundantly convey identical information in commercials. For instance, in Apple's groundbreaking "1984" commercial (previously discussed) the narrator speaks the same words that we see crawl up the screen at the end. This is quite typical of the ends of commercials, where ads make their final bids to remain

---

Sidebar 12.1

Top Ten Slogans of the 20th Century. How many can you match with their products? (Answers below.)

1. Diamonds are forever.
2. Just do it.
3. The pause that refreshes.
4. Tastes great, less filling.
5. We try harder.
6. Good to the last drop.
7. Breakfast of champions.
8. Does she ... or doesn't she?
9. When it rains it pours.
10. Where's the beef?

1. De Beers 2. Nike 3. Coca-Cola 4. Miller Lite 5. Avis 6. Maxwell House 7. Wheaties 8. Clairol 9. Morton Salt 10. Wendy's. "The Advertising Century," *AdAge.com*, 2000, http://www.adage.com/century/slogans.html.

in the viewer's consciousness. Redundancy is common in much of television—as when soap opera characters redundantly rehash plot developments—but it exists at a much higher level and is absolutely crucial to the commercial.

Extraordinary and Excessive Style: "Televisuality" and Counter Television

Viewers do not seek commercials. They do not tune into television for the commercials (with the significant exception of home shopping channels). Indeed, they commonly use remote controls, videotaping, and channel browsing to avoid watching commercial breaks. And so, advertisers are continuously challenged to develop mechanisms for snaring viewers' attention, for hailing them, one might say, as one hails a cab. In other words, commercials must use techniques that say, "Hey, *you*! Watch me! Watch me *now*!" One way that hailing is achieved is through what John Caldwell terms "televisuality"—"defined by excessive stylization and visual exhibitionism."[38] He believes that much 1980s television and not just commercials is marked by televisuality, but we will limit our application of it to TV ads. This is a slightly different sense of the word than what we used before, as when the generic "televisual" is used as the adjectival form of the noun, "television."

In order to understand excessive or exhibitionistic television, we must recall its stylistic norm. By the 1970s, television found its own "classical" style, much like the cinema developed its classical style in the 1930s. Part Two describes this conventional television style in terms of mise-en-scene, videography, editing, and sound as they may be observed in sitcoms, soap operas, prime-time dramas, and other narrative and non-narrative programs. Central to this approach is that style should not draw attention to itself, that it should in a sense be invisible. What's meant by this is that style should support the narrative so effectively that the viewer may submerge into the story without being distracted by the style.

One of the quintessential principles of television commercials is that television classicism may be exceeded—and even violated—in order to attract the viewer's attention. Stylistic excesses and violations are used by commercials to snap viewers out of their dreamlike connection with television narrative, to shock them out of their television lethargy and make them sit up and take notice of the advertised products. Following Bertolt Brecht's "epic theater" and Peter Wollen's claims for a Brechtian "counter cinema" in radical films of the 1960s and 1970s, we might think of this disruptive stylistic approach as "counter television."[39] Although epic theater and counter cinema were both Marxist attempts to combat capitalism and consumerism and although the notion of Brechtian commercials may make Brecht spin like a top in his grave, it is impossible to deny that techniques once associated with experimental theater and film are now routinely used in television commercials.

Since we divided our consideration of television's classical style into chapters on mise-en-scene, videography, editing, and sound, we will illustrate the commercial's use of counter television with examples from each of these areas.

FIGURE 12.21

Daryl Myatt
Real Estate Agent

Mise-en-Scene. There are several unusual aspects of performance, of figure expression and movement, in television commercials. The most significant aspect in terms of the commercial's hailing function is the manner in which the camera is directly addressed. As discussed in chapter 4, news anchors and game show hosts typically address viewers directly by looking straight into the camera lens, but actors in fictional, narrative programs do not. Instead, actors in narrative programs look only at one another and *indirectly* address the viewer. Interestingly, commercials incorporate direct address in *both* non-narrative and narrative instances. In a non-narrative commercial for the Hair Club a client looks straight at the camera and details the benefits of its product (Fig. 12.21). It's evident that he's addressing viewers directly—specifically hailing men who feel anxious about hair loss. We find a more unconventional use of direct address in the narrative commercials for Bartles & Jaymes wine coolers. In this case we have fictional characters looking into the camera and speaking their lines (Fig. 12.2). These actors thus violate the taboo against direct-camera gazes, and they do so in a fashion that implores the viewer's return gaze.

Commercials' performance style is commonly pitched a notch or two higher than is the acting in narrative programs and the behavior of individuals in non-narrative programs. The goal of performers in many commercials is not so much plausibility or realism as it is noticeability. An excessive performance style can get commercials noticed during their 30-second bid for our attention. In the 1980s, Federal Express featured fast-talker John Moschitta, Jr. in a series of successful ads. Moschitta's ability to speak at the rate of 530 words per minute served a dual purpose for FedEx: to capture viewers' attention and to make a metaphoric connection between their delivery service's rapidity and Moschitta's speech. Excessive speed is also used in the selling of automobiles—where vehicles frequently careen recklessly around race tracks, desert trails, and mountain passes. A notice on such ads tells us that these are "professional drivers on a closed course" and that we shouldn't attempt such stunts ourselves, but if risky driving draws viewers' attention, then its persuasive function has been served.

FIGURE 12.22

FIGURE 12.23

Non-human figures also perform in unconventional ways in commercials. Animals frequently talk, sing, and dance. And objects that usually cannot move on their own commonly violate the laws of physics in commercial performances. We've seen singing raisins and talkative M&M candies, and we've been introduced to the Pillsbury Doughboy and Speedy Alka-Seltzer (Figs. 12.22, 12.23). By giving animals the human property of speech and by animating normally inanimate objects, commercials violate the behavioral rules of the real world.

Direct gazes at the camera, the excessive performance of actors, and the unconventional behavior of non-human "actors" all hail viewers—entreating them to pay attention and to be persuaded by commercials.

Videography and Cinematography. Despite the televisual exhibitionism Caldwell has found in several 1980s and 1990s programs, most television since the 1970s has adhered to television's classical conventions in terms of videography or cinematography. Music television, however, is a significant exception. When it arrived in the early 1980s, its stylistic flourishes and visualization of music had a major impact on the videography/cinematography of programs such as *Miami Vice* (1984–89) and the short-lived *Cop Rock* (1990). More important, it inspired a small revolution in the videography of commercials, which use music-video style to distinguish themselves from the program material they are interrupting. For commercial directors, counter-television videography is yet another way to draw the viewer's attention.

Table 12.4 counterposes the principal videographic elements of TV classicism with counter-television techniques that commercials use to catch our eye. Letterboxing, out-of-focus shooting, and imbalanced composition are all illustrated in a single commercial for MicroStrategy, a dot-com company specializing in business consulting (Fig. 12.24). Letterboxing was initially developed for transferring wide-screen movies to television and is also commonly used for videotape shot in the high–definition format. For example, compare the letterboxed version of *He Said, She Said* discussed in chapter 6 (Figs. 6.26–6.27) with the letterboxing of the MicroStrategy commercial. In both instances, the black bars at the top and bottom effectively reshape the aspect ratio of the

TABLE 12.4

Classicism Versus Counter-Television

CLASSICAL VIDEOGRAPHY	COUNTER-TELEVISION VIDEOGRAPHY
Image fills the frame	Letterboxing
Balanced composition	Imbalanced composition
(Objects centered)	(Objects at the frame's edges)
In-focus main figure	Out-of-focus main figure
Regular speed action	Slow motion and fast motion
Color	Black-and-white
Limited camera movement	Extremely active camera movement
Eye-level camera angle	Extreme low and high angles
"Normal" focal length	Extreme wide angle and telephoto

frame—making it wider than normal television. This width is emphasized in a later shot where the same woman is placed on the extreme left of the frame while a frazzled man appears in the background (Fig. 12.25). This image would be more conventional if she were moving toward the man and *into* the center of the frame, but she is not. Instead, she's walking to the left and out of frame. The result is a strikingly imbalanced composition. Also notable is the fact that two thirds of this shot is markedly out-of-focus and remains that way for the duration of the shot. That is, we do not pull focus to the man in the background (cf. Figs. 6.9–6.10).

Although variable speed action in commercials was partially inspired by music videos, television sports was more significant to its popularization. Ever since the 1960s—when advances in videotape technology enabled TV to replay action at variable speeds—slow motion has been an integral part of televised sports. As we have seen with mise-en-scene and videography, variable speed action is an attention grabber. Because narrative programs don't normally use variable speeds, slow motion and fast action make us attentive. They may also be used, as they are in sports programs, to emphasize strength and majesty and to show viewers actions that normally occur too quickly for the human eye to comprehend.

FIGURE 12.24

FIGURE 12.25

Consider the Mountain Dew commercial in which a cyclist chases a cheetah and pulls a can of soda from its throat—initially aired during the 2000 *Super Bowl*. Both fast and slow motion are used in this spot. The cyclist's pedaling as he gains on the cheetah is shown in speeded up action—making it seem faster than is humanly possible. Slow motion is used in several shots: the cheetah running, the bicyclist leaping on it, and the bicyclist's friends pouring Mountain Dew down their throats. By using slow motion, we are able to see details in the cheetah's running and the bicyclist's leap that we wouldn't discern at regular speed. And the slow-motion pouring enhances the appearance of the Mountain Dew—in theory making it more appealing.

As is explained in chapter 9, color came to television through a complicated and circuitous route. Once it was established in the 1960s, however, narrative programs discontinued use of black- and-white—with only very rare exceptions. Color was the last major technological component of TV classicism to evolve. Its arrival signaled the beginning of black-and-white as a counter-television component. Before color became the norm, it was capable of hailing viewers. Imagine how striking a color commercial must have seemed to viewers who were accustomed to black-and-white imagery.

Most frequently, commercials have used black-and-white or sepia-toned images to allude to the past. But, as in many music videos, the significance of black-and-white imagery is not always so clear. Take for example a spot about estrogen loss during menopause, sponsored by the pharmaceutical company American Home Products and broadcast, among other places, during the sit-com *Everybody Loves Raymond* (1996–), which, not surprisingly, is in color. Actress Lauren Hutton is shown cooking vegetables, running along the beach, and talking about menopause. Half of the shots are in color and half are in black-and-white. The black-and-white images are not supposed to be from the past and, indeed, there is no obvious meaning one can glean from the black-and-white cinematography—aside from the counter-television function of differentiating this commercial from the color programs during which it appears.

Extreme camera movement, angle, and focal length—the final three video-graphic elements in Table 12.4—are not as distinct as the other videographic techniques. Instead of being unambiguous violations of classical TV style, they are more exaggerations of techniques ordinarily used in conventional narrative programs. Where classical programs often include some camera movement (to follow action), slightly low/high angles, and various focal lengths (wide angle to telephoto), commercials incorporate camera gyrations, odd low/high angles, and focal lengths that are so extreme that optical distortion is evident. Unusually active camera movements are apparent in the Coca-Cola rave commercial previously discussed. And strange angles and focal lengths may be observed in the off-balance, low-angle shot of a scooter-rider in a WorldCom commercial (Fig. 12.26) and the wide-angle shot of an Infiniti car (Fig. 12.27). When distortion is this exaggerated, it draws attention to itself and violates the classical tenet of invisible, unobtrusive style. This, then, is the definition of Caldwell's televisual exhibitionism.

Editing. The first thing one notices about the editing of many commercials is the speed. The editing in commercials is typically paced faster than that in soap operas, sitcoms, and prime-time dramas. An average, 30-second

FIGURE 12.26

commercial contains 30 or more separate shots while a typical 30-second conversation scene in, for example, *As the World Turns* has approximately 10. Or, put another way, the average length of a commercial shot is 1 second or less, while the average shot length in narrative programs clocks in around 2 to 3 seconds. Rapid editing serves as a hailing device because each shot quickly presents new information for viewers to absorb. Additionally, viewers are constantly adjusting to different framing, composition, and camera angles. Each cut is a potential disruption as we instantaneously move from one camera position to another and new visuals are thrown before our eyes. This visual disorientation is used by commercials to jolt us into gazing at the advertised product.

Commercials, even narrative-based ones, are also not bound by the rules of classical, continuity editing and its pursuit of an invisibly seamless style. Jump cuts and breaches of the 180 degree rule abound in TV ads. A commercial for Aetna U.S. Healthcare illustrates the commercial's flexible use of continuity editing (and also alternates color with black-and-white). It tells the story of a fabric

FIGURE 12.27

TABLE 12.5

Aetna Commercial Editing

1. Long shot: the evident owner of the company works with a sewing machine on the floor (Fig. 12.28).
2. Medium long shot: she talks on the phone in her office (Fig. 12.29).
3. Long shot: she sorts balls of yarn (Fig. 12.30).
4. Medium shot: she smiles beside a worker (in black-and-white; Fig. 12.31).
5. Medium long shot: she examines a piece of fabric (Fig. 12.32).
6. Long shot: a loom (very quick shot; Fig. 12.33).
7. Long shot: another loom (very quick shot; Fig. 12.34).
8. Long shot: a room full of looms with the owner in the background staring out the window (Fig. 12.35).

company providing choices to its customers—which it offers as a metaphor for the new choices this HMO will offer its clients. In 30 seconds, the commercial presents 30 shots, some even less than 1 second long.

Its final eight shots are shown in Table 12.5. As you can see, the camera hops from the owner at one time/location to another—from sewing to talking to sorting to smiling to examining. If this editing were used in a conventional segment from a narrative program, it would seem weird or disturbing, but it works well in this commercial because it effectively conveys the spirit of this business and the value of free choice, and its editing style differentiates it from the narrative program it interrupted.

Jerky, discontinuous editing is not unheard of in narrative programs, but series of shots such as those in Table 12.5 would commonly be relegated to montage sequences where time and information are compressed (see chapter 7). Such montages are relatively rare in narrative programs and so their frequent use in commercials helps distinguish them from the program they're interrupting.

Sound. We have discussed sound in television in terms of speech and music (see chapter 8). The style of speech in commercials has been addressed previously at numerous points—including its importance to hailing and direct

FIGURE 12.28

FIGURE 12.29

FIGURE 12.30

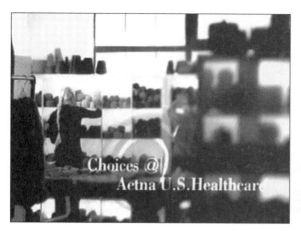

FIGURE 12.31

FIGURE 12.32

FIGURE 12.33

FIGURE 12.34

FIGURE 12.35

Sidebar 12.1

Top Ten Jingles of the 20th Century. How many can you match with their products? (Answers below.)

1. You deserve a break today.
2. Be all that you can be.
3. _____ hits the spot.
4. M'm, m'm good.
5. See the USA in your _____.
6. I wish I was an _____ wiener.
7. Double your pleasure, double your fun.
8. _____ tastes good like a cigarette should.
9. It's the real thing.
10. A little dab'll do ya.

1. McDonalds 2. U.S. Army 3. Pepsi Cola 4. Campbell's 5. Chevrolet (GM) 6. Oscar Meyer 7. Wrigley's Doublemint gum 8. Winston 9. Coca-Cola 10.Brylcreem hair cream. *AdAge.com*

2000, http://www.adage.com/century/jingles.html.

---

address. Unlike dialogue in narrative programs, commercial speech must be persuasive in some fashion, and it must be succinct because it doesn't have much time to persuade us. Also, the presence of an announcer's voice distinguishes commercial speech from narrative programs and aligns it with news and sports programs. As in news and sports, a voice that is not part of the commercial's diegetic world talks over it. It's a voice of authority—speaking directly to viewers and urging them to be convinced by the commercial's rhetoric.

The music of commercials is yet another rhetorical device that has less in common with narrative programs than it does with another television genre—specifically, the music video (see chapter 10). This is not surprising since music videos are essentially commercials for music and musicians. The principal similarity between commercial music and music videos and the crucial difference between it and nondiegetic music in narrative programs is a seemingly simple one: Both commercials and music videos use songs with lyrics while nondiegetic music normally does not (excepting nondiegetic music where it is clearly commenting on the action—as when a popular love song plays while lovers walk beside a river).

Why is this apparently modest distinction so important? Because the use of lyrics—jingles in the case of commercials—draws one's attention to the music itself, and classical, nondiegetic music isn't devised for that. Nondiegetic music strives for invisibility, hoping to shape the emotions of viewers without being noticed. Jingles, in contrast, are designed to be noticed and, of course, to be remembered. Many viewers recall commercial jingles decades later, but how many of them can say they remember the nondiegetic music of old programs?

Graphics and Animation

Almost every commercial on television contains some graphics (letters, numbers, cartoon characters, and corporate logos) on the screen. As we have seen exemplified in Apple's "1984" spot, the most common use of text is a redundant reinforcement of speech. Announcers speak their scripts and the same or similar words crawl up the screen—frequently at the conclusion of the spot and usually accompanied by the product's visual emblem, its brand identity further reinforced by its logo. In the case of "1984," the distinctive Apple logo (a rainbow-colored apple with a bite taken out) follows the concluding text.

Text is not limited to this redundant function, however. It may also supplement, clarify, and disclaim the explicit meanings of the dialogue and the implicit meanings of the images. The supplementing role of text is best exemplified in the nearly illegible legal qualifications included at the end of commercials for contests, car dealerships, and the like. Tiny on-screen text provides disclaimers and clarifications that the advertisers wish to downplay. Since the 1960s, the U.S. Federal Trade Commission has cracked down on misleading claims in medicinal and food advertising—leading to more and more disclaimers. Consequently, many ads now contain seemingly unnecessary warnings such as, "Use only as directed," in order to avoid legal liability. A Crest toothpaste commercial's spoken dialogue entreats us to "Get ready for a whole new level of clean. Introducing advanced cleaning from Crest Multi-Care." The dialogue implies that Multi-Care is measurably superior to other brands. However, in small text the ad clarifies that Multi-Care is only advanced "VS. CREST CAVITY PROTECTION"—that is, in comparison to other Crest products. It might well lag behind other brands in terms of toothpaste technology. The ad only certifies that it's advanced beyond *Crest's* previous level of cavity protection, just in case the FTC or the lawyers for Colgate may be watching.

One final example of textual disclaimers is found in the case of dramatizations. For instance, a Saran Wrap ad visually presents what appears to be a documentary—an unmanipulated record—of a test of its plastic wrap and that of its competitor, Reynolds Aluminum. A blind-folded woman sniffs an onion in both wraps and is repelled when the smelly odor escapes from Reynolds Wrap. But it's all a fiction, a dramatization. We must read the "fine print" to realize this. Only there does text disclaim what the images proclaim—that, despite appearances, this is an actor pretending to be repulsed (Fig. 12.36).

FIGURE 12.36

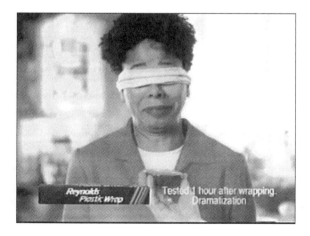

FIGURE 12.37

FIGURE 12.38

Redundant, reinforcing text and small-print disclaimers are important functions of TV graphics, but equally significant is the ability of graphics to catch viewers' eyes, to hail or entreat them to look at the screen. The most important device for graphical hailing is the ability of text and cartoon elements to be animated, for moving graphics are enormously more attention-grabbing than are static ones. Animation in commercials arrived with television's growth in the 1940s and early 1950s, but it was initially limited to techniques borrowed from the cinema. For example, a 1950s commercial for Philco refrigerators has a cartoon pixie flitting about the crisper and ends with text fading in over a seal of quality: "Philco famous for quality the world over" (Figs. 12.37–12.38). The animated pixie and the simple fading in of the characters were created on film, using an optical printer. (See chapter 11 for more on animation's evolution.) On most commercials, the graphical elements are sliding or floating or otherwise moving. Further, commercial graphics use an illusion of three-dimensionality to make letters and numbers appear to rise toward the viewer. Even in this 40-year-old spot, the 3D shading on the "Philco quality" letters gives them a more dynamic aspect.

As Margaret Morse explains in her overview of the history of TV graphics, the movement and three-dimensionality of graphic elements accelerated phenomenally with the development of computer technology in the late 1970s and 1980s. Today, hyperactive letters and logos often seem to be flying past us or us toward them. In the opening credits for *As the World Turns*—a program not known for its visual flourishes—the title comes from a virtual space *behind* us (Fig. 12.39), rotating and swooping toward a globe constructed out of images from the program (Fig. 12.40). The title then comes back toward us, and we ostensibly pass *through* the "o" of "World"(Fig. 12.41). "The viewer . . . seems to be freed from gravity in a virtual experience of giddy speed through a symbolic universe of abc's,"[40] notes Morse regarding similar sequences. In such a universe, the letters are far from flat or two-dimensional. The movement of the *As the World Turns* letters and their design makes them look like thick pieces of glass, with a sense of density and smooth texture.

FIGURE 12.39

Graphics flying toward the viewer are the visual equivalent of verbal direct address. Remember that in narrative programs the visuals are designed much like the theater—as if a fourth wall has been removed and you are peering into a room. This is particularly true in sitcoms and soap operas because their sets are constructed with a missing fourth wall, but it also holds true for prime-time dramas shot on location. Consequently, there is limited actor movement in depth—toward or away from the camera. The action mostly occurs on a plane perpendicular to the camera's and thus more left-and-right and less back-and-forth. Actors do not enter sitcom/soap opera sets from behind the camera the way the letters in the *As the World Turns* title sequence do. And actors do not exist by walking toward and past the camera the way the *As the World Turns* title does. When graphic elements behave this way, they, in a sense, say to viewers, "Pay attention! Here we come—right toward you. Duck!" As you can see, in commercials animated graphics serve a similar purpose to announcers speaking directly to the viewers. Both hail viewers—one through visually moving words and the other through verbally spoken ones. As Morse argues, these graphics

FIGURE 12.40

FIGURE 12.41

are predecessors of increasingly interactive computer environments, from first-person games (e.g., *Quake*) to virtual reality worlds.

A final and obvious form of animation in TV commercials is the use of cartoon characters. The Pillsbury Doughboy and Speedy Alka-Seltzer, previously discussed, are just two of the non-human entities called on to pitch products on television. The function of these characters (differentiating products) has not changed much over the past 50-odd years of television commercials. However, it should be mentioned that computer animation has had a major impact on the technology used to create these characters. Up until the 1990s, animated characters were either drawn or were created through stop-action animation (the frame-by-frame movement of dolls), as in the case with Speedy Alka-Seltzer (Fig. 12.23). Now, however, animated characters are just as likely to have been entirely computer generated—as in the current incarnation of the Pillsbury Doughboy (12.22).

Violating Reality (Special Effects)

"In a medium whose very essence is the ability to reproduce the look of everyday reality, one of the surest ways of attracting the viewer's attention is to violate that reality,"[41] contends Paul Messaris. What intrigues him is advertising's use of distorted imagery to make a viewer notice a product. Studies in cognitive psychology show that this distortion is most effective when it varies only slightly from a familiar object. As Messaris explains, ". . .if the discrepancy between the unfamiliar shape and some preexisting one is only partial, the mental task of fitting in the new shape becomes more complicated. As a result, such partially strange shapes can cause us to pay closer attention."[42] If an object is wholly different from what you are familiar with, you may ignore it completely or place it in a new visual category; but if it is partially similar then your cognitive processes work overtime trying to figure out whether or not it is a familiar object.

Messaris cites computer morphing as a prime example of this principle. A morph takes two dissimilar objects and creates a seamless transition from one to the other. In so doing, it creates a strange, reality-violating hybrid of two familiar objects. Morphing first came to viewers' attention in the films *Willow* (1988) and *Terminator 2: Judgment Day* (1991) where humans morph into various shapes, but it found its widest exposure in Michael Jackson's *Black or White* music video and television commercials in the 1990s. Notably, a Schick Tracer razor commercial morphs between a variety of faces—effectively communicating the idea that the Tracer will fit any shaped face and simultaneously getting viewers to concentrate on the ad by violating the reality of human physiognomy—as when a Caucasian man transforms into an African-American one (Figs. 12.42–12.43).

Morphing is just one example of violating reality through special effects. The advances in digital graphics of the 1990s facilitated the widespread incorporation of special effects in commercials. What makes digital special effects particularly successful is their uncanny resemblance to historical reality. To choose one example from many, consider a Cinnamon Toast Crunch cereal ad where a man is slaving away in his office cubicle. Suddenly, a giant, special effects hand reaches

FIGURE 12.42

FIGURE 12.43

down and starts pushing him around, giving him tasty cereal to eat and a video game to play with (Fig. 12.44). Initially, it looks like the familiar office scene, but then an incongruous and fantastic element intrudes into that reality. As Messaris might say, "It gives us a jolt, and it gets us to look."[43]

Reflexivity and Intertextuality

In chapter 4 we introduced the notion of reflexivity in non-narrative television. Commercials thrive on the televisual cannibalism that is reflexivity. TV commercials frequently parody films, television programs, other commercials, and even themselves in their efforts to market a product. Energizer batteries were featured in a series of advertisements where a plausible but sham commercial (usually a sly spoof of a familiar one) is interrupted by a battery-powered toy rabbit intruding into the frame. In one, a commercial for the nonexistent Nasatine

FIGURE 12.44

FIGURE 12.45

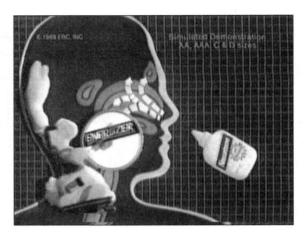

sinus medicine is suspended when the drum-beating bunny comes through (Fig. 12.45). In essence, the Energizer rabbit spots are commercials consuming other commercials. The Energizer spots were particularly remarkable for the accuracy of their parodies. The Nasatine spot includes Anacin-style animation and a copyright notice for a fake pharmaceutical company, Clow Laboratories (Fig. 12.46)! Reflexive commercials refer first of all to other television material, rather than referring directly to historical reality where their products actually reside. In essence, an extra layer of television has been added.

A close relation to parody is pastiche, the use of fragments of previous texts. Popular songs, for example, are regularly put to new uses by advertisers. The Knack's "My Sharona" was turned into "My Chalupa" by Taco Bell and Cream's "I Feel Free" (discussed earlier) sells Hyundai cars. Even the Beatles' "Revolution" has been used in a Nike shoe commercial (though it did result in a lawsuit against Nike). Pastiche in television commercials has reached

FIGURE 12.46

FIGURE 12.47

FIGURE 12.48

FIGURE 12.49

new heights of technological sophistication since the advent of digital special effects. One Diet Coke ad, for instance, has Paula Abdul dancing with and talking to film actors/characters Gene Kelly, Groucho Marx, and Cary Grant (Figs. 12.47–12.49).

Parody and pastiche are two examples of TV's high degree of intertextuality, drawing it away from historical reality and reflecting it back on itself (see the discussion of intertextuality in the context of TV stars in chapter 3). One television text (a commercial) refers to another (a program or previous commercial), which may well refer to another and another. Commercials are an integral part of this network of meanings and allusions. Familiar songs and images provide a shorthand for developing the persuasive argument for a product. Why write a new jingle when an old tune is already inscribed on the our minds? Why refer to historical reality when we are more comfortable with television reality? Commercials are nourished by intertextuality and reflexivity.

Summary: "Capitalism In Action"

At the start of a commercial break on ABC one evening in Fall 2000, a self-mocking title came up: "And now capitalism in action." On U.S. television, commercials are the most visible effect of the medium's underlying economic system. Multinational corporations strike deals with wholesalers (networks, syndicators, and national spot representatives) when they wish to buy TV time for national exposure. And local merchants buy TV time from individual stations and cable systems when they are shopping for exposure in a specific DMA. These purchases of time are essentially purchases of viewers' attention as it has been calculated by Nielsen Media Research. TV's wholesalers and retailers use the money they have exchanged for their viewers' time to rent programming materials from production companies, with the goal of attracting more viewers and/or viewers of a more desirable demographic. And that is U.S. TV capitalism in action.

Although it is evident that commercials signify the positive side of consuming, it would be wrong to say that that is their only meaning. Despite their often naked intent to sell, commercials also play host to a diverse polysemy. We have outlined eight components of commercial discourse and examined how they are used to persuade us to purchase products. These include luxury, individualism, the natural, folk culture, novelty, sexuality and romance, the alleviation of various forms of distress, and utopianism. Commercials endeavor to figuratively and literally associate their products with these values, and/or they make claims that their products will transform consumers if they buy them.

Commercials' styles may be rude and obvious or entertaining and obscure, but in some fashion they must always attempt to convince the viewer. We have identified eight persuasive strategies employed by commercials: metaphor, stylistic utopianism, product differentiation, repetition and redundancy, graphics and animation, special effects, and reflexivity and intertextuality. In many instances, we have seen that the style of commercials is excessive and exhibitionistic, and that it falls within John Caldwell's notion of televisuality. Commercial style, unlike classical narrative television and film, doesn't need to be invisible. Indeed, its forthright visibility may well help draw viewers' interest to the product.

FURTHER READINGS

There are many books analyzing advertising and its discourse, but only a few target television commercials specifically. The most comprehensive of such TV-commercial books is Mike Budd, Steve Craig, and Clay Steinman, *Consuming Environments: Television and Commercial Culture* (New Brunswick, NJ: Rutgers University Press, 1999), which details the structure of the TV industry and investigates the style and structure of commercials. Ellen Seiter, *Sold Separately: Children and Parents in Consumer Culture* (New Brunswick, NJ: Rutgers University Press, 1993) is more narrowly defined, but in its analysis of the discourses of commercials for children she provides many insights that may be applied to all commercials. The ideological analysis of commercials is undertaken in Sut

Jhally, *The Codes of Advertising: Fetishism and the Political Economy of Meaning in the Consumer Society* (New York: Routledge, 1987), which views television through the lens of political economy.

Of the general books on advertising, the most useful to television students is Paul Messaris, *Visual Persuasion: The Role of Images in Advertising* (Thousand Oaks, CA: Sage, 1997). Messaris considers the impact of images in both print and television advertising, and has useful insights into the function of visual style in the advertising process. The specific significance of words in advertising is assayed by Michael L. Geis, *The Language of Television Advertising* (New York: Academic Press, 1982) and Greg Myers, *Words in Ads* (London: Edward Arnold, 1994). The semiotic perspective of Robert Goldman and Stephen Papson, *Sign Wars: The Cluttered Landscape of Advertising* (New York: Guilford Press, 1996) applies to both images and words as signs. Their analysis includes discussions of intertextuality, reflexivity, and the process of hailing.

Another general book on advertising is Jean Kilbourne, *Deadly Persuasion: Why Women and Girls Must Fight the Addictive Power of Advertising* (New York: The Free Press, 1999). As is evident from the title, Kilbourne's book is a strong polemic on the influence of advertising and its discursive world. The analyses of Leslie Savan, the advertising columnist for *The Village Voice* are often perceptive and entertaining, although seldom fortified by academic research. They have been collected in *The Sponsored Life: Ads, TV, and American Culture* (Philadelphia: Temple University Press, 1994).

E N D N O T E S

[1] "1999 U.S. Advertising Volume," *Advertising Age*, 22 May 2000, http://www.adage.com/dataplace/archives/dp446.html.

[2] Paul Messaris, *Visual Persuasion: The Role of Images in Advertising* (Thousand Oaks, CA: Sage, 1997), 164.

[3] Nielsen Media Research, *2000 Report on Television* (New York: Nielsen Media Research, 2000) 17.

[4] "Facts and Figures," *Viacom*, July 2000, Viacom, Inc., http://www.viacom.com/factsandFig.tin.

[5] Mike Budd, Steve Craig, and Clay Steinman, *Consuming Environments: Television and Consumer Culture* (New Brunswick, NJ: Rutgers, 1999), 30.

[6] Laurie Ann Franks, *The Gallery of Ill-Fitting Pants*, 1999, Geocities. http://www.geocities.com/SoHo/Gallery/4905/pants.html; Michael Lewis, *Modern Moist Towelette Collecting*, America Online, 7 November 2000 http://www.members. aol.com/MoistTwl; and *The Sheep Brain Dissection Guide*, 6 September 1998, University of Scranton, http://www.academic.scranton.edu/department/psych/sheep.

[7] All figures are from the year 2000 and the 1999–2000 U.S. television season. Nielsen Media Research, *2000 Report on Television* (New York: Nielsen Media Research, 2000).

[8] "'The Sweeps'—Local Market Measurement," 2000, *Nielsen Media Research*, http://www.nielsenmedia.com/sweeps.html.

[9] "What TV Ratings Really Mean . . . And Other Frequently-Asked Questions," 2000, *Nielsen Media Research*, http://www.nielsenmedia.com/whatratingsmean.

[10] "100 Leading National Advertisers 1998: Profile of Philip Morris cos," *AdAge.com*, http://www.adage.com/cgi-bin/adage.cgi?profile, Philip%20Morris%20Cos.

[11] Robert J. Coen, MaCann-Erickson Worldwide, "1999 U.S. advertising volume," *AdAge.com*, http://www.adage.com/dataplace/archives/dp446.html.

[12] "100 Leading National Advertisers 1998: Sorted by Network TV in 1998," *AdAge.com*, 2000, http://www.adage.com/cgi-bin/adage.cgi?sort,27:43:59.

[13] Thorstein Veblen, *The Theory of the Leisure Class*, intro. John Kenneth Galbraith (Boston, Houghton Mifflin, 1973). Originally published in 1899.

[14] Ellen Seiter, *Sold Separately: Children and Parents in Consumer Culture* (New Brunswick, NJ: Rutgers University Press, 1993) 43–44.

[15] Seiter, 44.

[16] Leslie Savan, *The Sponsored Life: Ads, TV, and American Culture* (Philadelphia: Temple University Press, 1994) 8.

[17] Savan, 9.

[18] "World Wide Diary of Actions: United States 1997," *Animal Liberation Frontline*, 1997, http://www.animalliberation.net/doa/us/97.html.

[19] "Post Grape-Nuts and Grape-Nuts Flakes," *Kraft Foods*, 2000, http://www.kraftfoods.com/postcereals/gngnf.html.

[20] Elisabeth Van Every, "Goth Style," *Academia Gothica*, 2000, http://www.blarg.net/~icprncs/gothstyle.html.

[21] Quoted in Bernice Kanner, *The 100 Best TV Commercials—And Why They Worked* (New York: Random House, 1999), 17.

[22] A. J. Jacobs, "Remote Patrol," *Entertainment Weekly*, 7 Feb. 1999, 66.

[23] Messaris, 246.

[24] Messaris, 249.

[25] Messaris, 255–257.

[26] Budd, 79–80.

[27] Seiter, 115. Furthermore, she discusses the racism inherent in advertising's utopia: ". . . access to this child-centered utopia is restricted; full citizenship is denied to girls of all races and to boys of color" (Seiter, 115–6).

[28] Richard Dyer, "Entertainment and Utopia," in Bill Nichols, ed., *Movies and Methods*, vol. 2 (Berkeley: University of California Press, 1985) 222.

[29] Dyer in Nichols, 228.

[30] As quoted in Bob Garfield, "Is Internet Utopia? Good Heavens, No," *AdAge.com*, 20 Jan. 1997, http://www.adage.com/news_and_features/ad_review/archives/ar19970120.html

[31] See Messaris, 196–203, for further discussion of generalization in ads.

[32] Messaris, xviii.

[33] Messaris, xix.

[34] Dyer in Nichols, 222–226.

[35] Rosser Reeves, *Reality in Advertising* (New York: Alfred A. Knopf, 1961) 46–49. Moreover, he defined advertising as "the art of getting a unique selling proposition into the heads of the most people at the lowest possible cost" (121).

[36] Sut Jhally, *The Codes of Advertising: Fetishism and the Political Economy of Meaning in the Consumer Society* (New York: Routledge, 1987) 127; quoting Pope, D., *The Making of Modern Advertising* (NY: Basic Books, 1982), 287.

[37] Reeves, 62.

[38] John Thornton Caldwell, *Televisuality: Style, Crisis, and Authority in American Television* (New Brunswick, NJ: Rutgers University Press, 1995) 352.

[39] Bertolt Brecht, "The Modern Theatre is the Epic Theatre," in John Willett, ed., *Brecht on Theatre* (New York: Hill and Wang, 1964) 33–42; Peter Wollen, "Godard

and Counter Cinema: *Vent D'est,*" in *Readings and Writings: Semiotic Counter-Strategies* (London: Verso, 1982) 79–91

40 Margaret Morse, *Virtualities: Television, Media Art, and Cyberculture* (Bloomington, IN: Indiana University Press, 1998) 72.

41 Messaris, 5.

42 Messaris, 7.

43 Messaris, 7.

PART FOUR

CRITICAL ANALYSIS: METHODOLOGY

CHAPTER 13

Alternatives to Empirical Study

Empiricism has long dominated the study of television—as well as the study of other mass communication media such as radio and print journalism. Most of the research theories and methods taught in mass communication college courses are empirical ones. The basic tenet of the empirical approach is that we may understand a phenomenon through observation and experimentation—be it the pollination of tulips, the popularity of a political leader, or the effect of *Beavis and Butt-head* cartoons on children.

Several presumptions underpin this approach:

1. Knowledge about a phenomenon exists within that phenomenon itself; the researcher "uncovers" it through experimentation and informed observation.

2. Experiments should be repeatable, as in the natural sciences; that is, you should be able to get the same results if you follow the same procedure.

3. A phenomenon will be understood if enough facts about it can be gathered or its fundamental essence discerned.

4. Research results should be quantifiable; that is, they should be measured and expressed in numbers and formulas (this is true of much, but not all, empirical research).

5. Theory is used to generate hypotheses or ruminate about facts generated through empirical research.

When we apply empirical research to television, it can provide us with useful answers to some questions: How many people (and what kind of people) watched *Who Wants to Be a Millionaire* at 9:00 P.M., February 21, 2001, on channel 5? Or, do children act more violently after they watch violent cartoons?

Empirical research has been less successful in answering other questions: How does the narrative structure of soap opera differ from action drama? Or, how has the police show genre changed from *Dragnet* to *NYPD Blue*? Or, what are the sexual politics—the power relationships between men and women—in the situation comedy?

Empirical research falters when it must explain television's meanings, and it is also unable to explain how narrative and stylistic devices generate those meanings. To best cope with these questions, different analytical methods must be employed. Rather than using empirical methods derived from the natural and social sciences, we may tap the critical approaches used in film studies and literary criticism to cope with television's meaning systems. These research methods are used in **television criticism**, although obviously we're not talking about criticism on the level of *TV Guide* here.

For the sake of comparison and contrast, this chapter briefly comments on some aspects of empirical research but does not attempt a full-fledged critique of empiricism. Instead, it outlines approaches to the medium taken by television criticism—approaches that attempt to chart television's meanings and organize them within specific contexts. The critical approaches we discuss include auteurism, genre study, semiotics, ideological analysis, and feminism. This does not exhaust the nonempirical approaches writers have taken to television, but it does survey the principal trends. Even within this limited scope, we cannot hope to do justice to each method, but we will articulate each method's principal assumptions and suggest how that method might be used to mount an analysis of televisual texts. Readings are suggested at the chapter's end, but the most informative summary of contemporary critical methods is *Channels of Discourse, Reassembled*, edited by Robert C. Allen.[1]

EMPIRICAL RESEARCH AND TELEVISION

The Industry Perspective

The vast majority of empirical research performed on television is commissioned by the TV industry itself. Its principal questions are:

- What did viewers watch, and what type of viewers watched which shows?
- What will viewers watch in the future, and what type of viewers will be watching?

The first question is answered by corporations such as Arbitron and Nielsen Media Research, whose **ratings** are purchased by TV stations and networks so that they may use them to set advertising rates (See the weekly ratings in Table 12.1). Ratings not only calculate what was watched, but they also indicate the **demographics** of the audience: gender, age, income bracket, race, and so on. Demographics are meaningful to stations and networks because they are important to advertisers who want to target viewers to maximize the impact of their commercials—as is further discussed in chapter 12.

The second question posed by the industry is answered through market research techniques such as focus groups and cable testing, which ask a small number of viewers for their opinions of upcoming programs or commercials to predict the preferences of the viewing public at large.[2]

These research methods are of limited usefulness to the critical study of television. Ratings systems view programs as consumable products, without exploring their meanings. Viewers are not even asked *why* they watched a show, only *if* they did. And although market research will sometimes delve into what a program means to its test viewers, it is less concerned with meaning than it is with viewer preference. That is, the market researcher might show a test program to a group of viewers and ask them what they liked about it and why, but the main question remains *whether* they liked it enough to watch it regularly (and buy its advertiser's products). In one typical market research technique, known as auditorium testing, test viewers assembled in a room receive a device with a dial, numbered 1–5 (1=like; 5=hate; or some such scale). Then the test audience is shown a program. While the program is running, the viewers turn their dials to indicate their current enjoyment or annoyance level. This information is fed into a computer that can chart the responses and even overlay them on a videotape of the program. To approach information gathering in this fashion indicates just what is crucial to market researchers—the likability of a televisual product, not what it means to its viewers.

The Academic Perspective

Empirical studies of television conducted within academia are closely related to those within the industry. Many professors at colleges and universities hold positions as consultants to the industry. Academic empirical research is not powered by the same market demands as industrial empirical research, however. Academic researchers are relatively free to pursue "pure" knowledge about television, concerned only about review by their peers. In this endeavor they have cultivated theories for explaining television, and methods for articulating those theories. We will take time to sketch a few of them here.

Empirical Research Theories   The initial academic theories of television were particularly attentive to the impact of TV on the viewer. The **hypodermic needle** concept, which television research inherited from post-World War I studies of propaganda in newspapers and magazines, is one of the earliest of so-called **effects theories**. In this model, we are directly affected by what we see on TV as if we were injected with a hypodermic needle. Or, to borrow a metaphor from Pavlovian psychology, the bell rings and we salivate.

Subsequent theories of the mass media's influence have dismissed the hypodermic needle doctrine as simplistic behaviorism. Television programs are more complex stimuli than is Pavlov's bell, and our responses are not as predictable or crude as those of a hungry dog. Various attempts to refine the understanding of media impact have evolved: social learning theory, reinforcement theory, toleration/desensitization theory, vicarious catharsis theory, and so on. All of these may be gathered under the umbrella term **limited effects theories.** These theories hold that the media do indeed influence viewers and readers, but there are limitations to these effects due to the many variables involved. The hypodermic needle theory says that television will cause us to feel or behave in a certain way; limited effects theories suggest that certain television programs will cause certain viewers, under certain circumstances, to feel or behave in certain ways. The media are still seen to be affecting us, as in all effects studies, but those effects are no longer presumed to be as simple as a hypodermic needle injecting emotions or ideas into a spectator.

Not all empirical researchers view the spectator as passive. The **uses-and-gratifications** approach, for instance, attempts to chart the uses that we make of television and to quantify how it gratifies our needs. This style of research emphasizes the way that we employ television, seeking the emotional or intellectual purposes to which we put it. Both effects theories and uses-and-gratifications theory focus on viewers, but effects theories see them as entities that the medium influences, while uses-and-gratifications theory posits more active viewers who engage with texts and use them for their own needs.

Empirical Research Methods The above theories have been implemented through particular research methods. In this regard, academic research into television owes much to research in psychology and the social sciences. The methodology of those disciplines is rooted in the **scientific method:**

1. Derive a hypothesis, based on a particular theoretical perspective informed by an established body of knowledge.

2. Test the hypothesis with repeatable experimentation and observation.

3. Interpret the results:

- Do they confirm/contradict the hypothesis?
- Does this suggest a change in the body of knowledge related to this hypothesis? Has the understanding of this phenomenon progressed?

This is the ideal, at least, to which empirical researchers aspire in their analysis of television. Often, however, they fail.

Content analysis is one common empirical method that is modeled on the scientific method. Its procedure is straightforward. A textual component is selected based on the researcher's theoretical interests: for example, sexual behavior in prime-time programs, or sickness and death on soap operas.[3] The researcher observes the television text and counts the number of occurrences of this component in a program's **manifest content**—the characters and their actions. (Content analysis seldom addresses television's stylistic aspects.) These data are then "coded" (converted through categorization) into statistical form. From studies such as these we can learn that incidents of hugging in prime-time TV occurred at a rate of .80 per hour during the week of February 2–8, 1989, or that 5.3% of soap opera characters die in car accidents.

Content analysis often falls short in its attempt to interpret the significance of its statistical data. What does a .80 hugging rate signify? How do viewers interpret all that hugging or lack of hugging? Empiricism provides procedures for gathering information (through observation and experimentation), but its method of interpretation, of suggesting what these facts and figures mean, is not well defined. The researchers in content analysis studies often attempt to interpret their data by comparing them with real-life statistics and viewers' presumed attitudes. The problem with this technique, Robert Allen explains, is that it ignores the "transmutation" that a real-life experience undergoes when it is placed in the context of a fictional world.[4] Sexuality, sickness, and death mean something to us when we encounter them in the real world, but we cannot assume that they serve the same function when viewed in a TV program. Television and other art forms transmogrify life. The aesthetic text recontextualizes elements from real life in ways that give them new meanings. Directly comparing incidents from TV programs with similar incidents in reality, as do some content analyses, is misleading.

In sum, empirical research incorporates valuable descriptive tools for approaching television. Individual studies isolate small aspects of the television experience for observation and experimental testing. But this does not tell us how television generates meaning for its viewers. Television is a rather untidy system for producing meaning—a system that does not lend itself to quantification or breaking down into constituent elements. As Allen comments, "The harnessing of elements of an open system [such as television] so that they might be examined in isolation (from confounding variables) is, in the extreme case, tantamount to studying the operating of the automobile engine by taking out each component, one by one, and staring at it for a while."[5]

What we need is an understanding of how the televisual text functions as a meaning-producing text and how we understand that text. This is what television criticism aspires toward, although it has not been entirely successful.

THE AUTEUR THEORY

The **auteur theory** stems from the French term for author, *auteur*. Its basic precept is that a single individual is, and should be, the "author" of a work in order for it to be a good work. A book, poem, film, or television show should express this individual's personality, his "vision" (the masculine pronoun is significant; auteurist studies almost all focus on men). This notion stems from the Romantic image of the author as a Byronic figure who sits alone in a garret, scratching out angst-ridden poems with a quill pen. The tormented, misunderstood artist is a cherished character type, as can be seen in numerous portrayals of demented painters and writers in television programs.

The auteur theory originated in French film criticism of the 1950s and 1960s, where it was initially theorized that auteurs could be drawn from the ranks of producers, directors, scriptwriters, actors, and other filmmaking personnel.[6] However, the vast bulk of auteurist film criticism has been about directors: Alfred Hitchcock, John Ford, and Howard Hawks, among many others. In television, however, the director has much less influence than in film. Indeed, most series will employ several directors over the course of a season. Recognizing the diminished power of the director, television auteurism has taken a different tack and focused instead on producers and their "vision." Auteurist critiques have been published, for example, on producers Bill Cosby, David Lynch (*Twin Peaks*, which he also directed occasionally), Paul Henning (creator of sitcoms such as *The Beverly Hillbillies*), and Stephen J. Cannell (who created *The A-Team* and similar action programs).[7]

Whether they are discussing directors or producers, auteurist critics work along two interconnected lines. First, they discuss how an auteur's thematics, narrative structure, and stylistic techniques—the use of sound and image—are expressed in individual programs. Second, they articulate the entire career of the auteur, explaining how this particular program fits into the overall trajectory of the auteur's work. For the extreme auteurist critic, a bad program by an auteur is more significant than is a good program by an undistinguished director or producer, because the auteur's bad program may still tell you something about the auteur's thematics, narrative structure, and stylistic techniques.

For the auteurist critic, the auteur's vision or presumed personality furnishes the context within which the meaning of a particular element in a particular program will be understood. In David Marc's analysis of Henning, Jed Clampett (*The Beverly Hillbillies*) becomes a go-between, a "moral interlocutor." He divides and judges the contrasting worlds of city and country, the banker Drysdale and Jed's Granny, "modern culture" and "folk culture." Auteur Henning develops this thematic clash between modern culture and folk culture *over the course of several programs*.[8] The meaning of this character is thus determined by Henning's other work.

There are many problems with the application of auteurism to TV. The key issue is that its Romantic notion of the artist does not suit the corporate and collaborative realities of contemporary television. Bankers, market researchers, scriptwriters, actors, set designers, and others contribute to the production of any TV show. To single out the producer ignores the work of many. Plus, all television programs employ the conventions of the medium; there is nothing totally new on TV or anything totally unique to a televisual auteur. If there were, it would be incomprehensible to viewers as they would have no context in which to place it. Thus, the auteur does not work in an aesthetic vacuum. The conventions of the medium tend to overwhelm any television artist's individual creativity.

It is important to remember, however, that television's corporate/collaborative nature and its lack of uniqueness do not necessarily make it mediocre. The fact that medieval cathedrals were constructed by hundreds of artisans, over decades and even centuries, does not make them less significant. Equating personal genius with aesthetic quality is an outmoded concept that tells us little about television.

GENRE STUDY

Genres are probably the most common way that viewers label television programs. Without giving it a second thought, we call *Seinfeld* a situation comedy, *Gunsmoke* (1955–75) a Western, and *Columbo* a detective show. *TV Guide* and other television listing publications recognize this when they identify programs in the same fashion. To be useful as a method for interpreting television, however, genre study needs to be more precise in its understanding of the genre. Otherwise, generic boundaries blur. Critics devise awkward terms such as "dramedy," which was used to describe 1980s comedies such as *Frank's Place* (1987–88) and *Moonlighting* that took on a more serious tone.

The assumption underlying genre study is that television programs resemble one another and that grouping them together provides a context for understanding the meanings of a particular program. This would not seem controversial, but at a rudimentary level it becomes difficult to define what a genre is. Here is the dilemma: To conceptualize what a particular genre is, researchers must watch TV programs and induce the genre's characteristic thematics, narrative structure, and/or stylistic techniques; but researchers do not know *which* programs to view until they have some idea of what the genre's characteristics are. It's a classic chicken-and-egg problem: One needs to know the genre's characteristics to pick which programs to consider, but before one can do that one needs to have looked at programs within the genre to define its characteristics, but before one can pick programs one needs to know the genre's characteristics . . .[9] and around and around it goes.

To escape this debilitating dilemma, genre critics have adopted two strategies:

1. Define the genre's characteristics with a priori criteria drawn from a predetermined critical method; judge your criteria's usefulness after the study has been done.

2. Rely on a cultural consensus of what the genre's criteria are; a genre is thereby defined as "what most viewers think a genre is."

In practice, most genre critics combine these two strategies and create a genre's definition a priori from what they presume to be a consensual definition of the genre. From this they may devise a working definition of the genre. They may then measure programs by this standard to judge the applicability of the working definition.

Determining such a cultural consensus would appear to be a natural way that empirical methods (say, a survey research project) could be incorporated into the critical method. However, this is seldom, if ever, done in genre criticism. Instead, critics often depend on the slippery conception of the genre that derives from their own commonsensical understanding of it.

Historically, definitions of genre fall into three categories:

1. Definition by presumed audience response.

2. Definition by style—techniques of sound and/or image.

3. Definition by subject matter—both narrative structure and thematics.

These categories do not exist in isolation. They frequently overlap one another.

Audience Response. Several genres acquire their definitions from how the critic presumes the viewer will respond—usually without any empirical evidence as to how actual viewers responded. Comedy and horror are two such genres. Programs as different as *The Fresh Prince of Bel-Air* (1990–1996) and *Saturday Night Live* have been labeled "comedies." What groups these programs together? The presumption that the viewer will laugh at them.

Television comedies are even more clearly marked as such than are theatrical film comedies because television often includes audience response in the text itself. The television laugh track signals to the viewer what the response to the program "should" be. TV comedies are virtually unique in this regard. Theatrical film comedies never provide a laugh track and television's noncomedy programs are not normally accompanied by audience-response sound effects. Even television's horror programs, the flip side of comedies in terms of audience response, do not possess a "scream track" to cue the spectator when to respond in fear. The only other television programs that do include audience response within the text are non-narrative programs: game shows, talk shows, and similar presentations. But as far as fictional programs go, the sitcom is the only genre that responds to itself.

Style. The stylistic definition of a genre is probably the least common. There are a few genres, however, that link programs based on *how* the material is presented. The techniques of sound and image that are used to construct the program become critical to distinguishing it from other genres. Musicals tell stories through singing and dancing. For example, *Fame* (1982–87) told high school stories through song and dance, while the short-lived *Cop Rock* (September–December 1990) used the same technique to construct stories of police officers in action. The only thing linking these two programs generically is their musical style.

Subject Matter. Most programs are joined into genres on the basis of their content—the stories they tell and the thematic structure that underpins those stories.

In approaching the stories of a particular genre, the critic hypothesizes a narrative structure that is shared by the programs within the genre, and conventional characters that inhabit that narrative structure. The police show, for example, is populated by familiar figures: the police detectives, the uniformed officers, the victims, the criminals, and so on. These general types could be broken down even further. Television criminals, according to Stuart Kaminsky and Jeffrey Mahan, tend to be individual lunatics or organized crime figures.[10]

These character types are placed into action against one another in the police show narratives. Kaminsky and Mahan note that many police show narratives fit a common pattern or structure:

1. A crime is committed.

2. The police detective is assigned to the case by chance.

3. The destruction widens. The crime invades the detective's private world, and he (usually a "he") becomes irrational.

4. The detective encounters the criminal, but does not initially apprehend him or her.

5. The detective pursues the criminal, leading to a second confrontation.

6. "... the police destroy or capture the villain. The overwhelming tendency in television is not to destroy, but to capture, to contain and control the symbol of evil."[11]

Kaminsky and Mahan's narrative outline is general enough to provide for the variation within the genre, yet it provides specific information to distinguish the genre from others.

Genre analysis of narrative often relies on the concept of the narrative **function**, which was originally developed by Russian Formalists in the 1920s.[12] A function, in this sense, is a specific action or attribute of a character. A story, then, consists of a set of functions, as in the above list of police show actions. The critic strives to establish the nature of these functions and their order, analyzing how they affect one another.

Narrative structure is the first level of content in any fictional program. The second level would be the interpretation or **decoding**, in Stuart Hall's terms, of that narrative.[13] Critics have latitude in their interpretations of the genre narrative. The only constraint is the logic of that interpretation. In other words, does the interpretation follow from the narrative "evidence" at hand? There is, of course, no such thing as an "objective" interpretation/decoding of a generic narrative. There will never be one true and final interpretation of a genre. All interpretations are shaped by the ideology of the interpreter. Geoffrey Hurd, for example, sees the following binary oppositions in the British police series:

- Police vs. crime
- Law vs. rule
- Professional vs. organization
- Authority vs. bureaucracy
- Intuition vs. technology
- Masses vs. intellectuals
- Comradeship vs. rank[14]

Hurd's interpretation of narrative structure logically supports these oppositions, but it would be misleading to suggest that it is not without ideology, that his analysis is purely objective. Hurd's analysis bears the marks of structuralism, an interpretive method that strongly influenced British cultural studies (including television) in the 1960s and after (as well as auteurism). This method particularly stressed the importance of binary oppositions, much like Hurd's analysis. Thus, one could say that his analysis exists within the ideology of contemporary British cultural studies. This is not to say that it is wrong or useless, but rather to indicate some of the factors that shape analysis, even on an academic level.

Two of the most typical interpretive strategies to be applied to genres are **mythic analysis** and **ideological analysis.** Mythic analysis sees genres as 20th century myths, as stories shared by large segments of a culture, which offer the researcher evidence of that society's thought processes. The structural anthropology of Claude Lévi-Strauss—the basis of structuralism—is one form of mythic analysis. Ideological analysis also sees genres as representative of society, but differs from mythic analysis in that it defines societies in terms of social forces.

As previously suggested, genres' definitional categories do not exist in isolation. Their blending often leads to hybrid genres or cycles within genres. The situation comedy, for example, is defined as a comedy based on the presumption of audience response (encoded directly in the laugh track), but the "situation" part of sitcoms is a matter of the genre's content. The narrative dilemmas or situations in which the characters find themselves are the principal sources of humor in the genre—as opposed to comedies that generate their humor from physical pratfalls or verbal wit. Hence, its humor is predominantly situational. Of course, the sitcom is a rather "impure" genre; it doesn't generate humor *solely* through situational gambits. Physical humor, for example, is often a part of *I Love Lucy*—as when Lucy works on a fast-moving pastry conveyor belt. And the humor of *Friends* often arises from the characters' cutting remarks to one another. The point is, the sitcom is a genre that is not only defined by presumed audience response but also by its content.

In addition to articulating genres' presumed audience response, narrative and thematic structures, and audial/visual style, the genre critic is also interested in tracing a genre's evolution. Indeed, genres must evolve to maintain their audiences' attention. A new program within a genre, if it is to succeed, must balance familiar genre elements with innovations that pique viewer interest. When *Miami Vice* premiered, for example, it was immediately evident that it fell within the parameters of the police show. It had various familiar character types—police detectives and criminals and the like—and familiar themes such as order versus chaos. But it also changed the genre by incorporating rock music and music-video style. It succeeded largely because it blended the familiar and the unusual.

Many genres fall into an evolutionary pattern. Initially the genre's tenets are established, often after a trial-and-error period where unpopular options are discarded. The genre thereupon enters into what might be called a **classical period**, during which thematics, narrative structure, and aural/visual style solidify into relatively firm conventions, a **code** of the genre. At this point the genre becomes recognizable as a cohesive unit. After the classical period comes a time of **self-reflexivity** that is often accompanied by genre decay or even death, though not necessarily. In the self-reflexive period, the genre turns inward and uses its own conventions for subject matter. It becomes self-conscious, in a sense, and the result is often genre parodies.

These periods can be observed in the genre of the television soap opera. Initially, the soap opera made a rocky start on television. Although it had been immensely popular on radio, when it began its transition to television in the late 1940s it did not meet with immediate success. It wasn't until the 1950s that soap opera found a format that satisfied a large daytime audience (as well as the economic exigencies of television producers): unending stories of familial relationships, romance, birth and death; live broadcasts; half-hour long programs (originally they were 15 minutes long); and so on. Thus, the mid-1950s to mid-1960s would be the TV soap opera's classical era. Then, in the 1970s, the genre turned inward through parody: *Soap* (1977–81) and *Mary Hartman, Mary Hartman* (1975–78). As in any self-reflexive parody, the humor in these programs depended on a prior knowledge of the genre. *Soap* and *Mary Hartman* could not have existed if there had not been a classical period of the soap opera. A genre's self-reflexivity often accompanies a period of decline and, indeed, the soap opera was suffering from a glut of programs and reduced viewership in the early 1970s. Rather than become moribund, however, the genre rebounded by incorporating new themes (birth control, abortion, interracial romance, etc.) and younger character types, and enlivening its visual style and pacing (as exemplified by the innovative *The Young and the Restless* [1973–]). The consequence has been a revivified genre that continues to attract a large audience. So, genre evolution is not necessarily limited to the pattern we have delineated, but one can often observe the pattern's cycles in television genres.

In sum, genre criticism is not without its weakness. Crucial to the study of any genre is its definition, and it is there that critics must be most wary. And yet, it seems clear that in viewing TV programs, we—critics and viewers—do construct resemblances among programs, and in that resemblance is found meaning. When watching an episode of, say, *Friends* we bring to our viewing circumstance associations with dozens of other sitcoms we have watched. These associations influence the meaning that we decode from individual programs. Genre study provides one method of decoding.

SEMIOTICS

Semiotics is most briefly defined as the *science of signs*, but this does not tell us much about what semioticians actually do and what assumptions underpin their work. The basic premise of semiotics is that all forms of communication (television, movies, books, paintings, traffic lights, and so on) can be broken down into individual units of meaning. More important, they can be understood in terms of how they interact with other units of meaning. The smallest unit of meaning is the **sign**, which is combined with other signs into systems, which compose **texts**. (Our use of the term *text* for television programs already reveals the influence of semiotics on television studies.) The semiotician, then, tries to understand the sign systems in a text and postulates how those systems generate meaning.

"Pure" semiotics tends to be text-oriented. That is, it does not deal with the intentions of the producer of that text or with its reception by the reader/viewer, but rather focuses on the text "itself." More recent work has attempted to blend semiotics with Freudian psychology (i.e., psychoanalysis), theorizing the *relationship* between the reader/viewer and the text. The resulting analyses have been controversial. Psychoanalysis, as it has been rewritten by Jacques Lacan, has greatly affected literary criticism and film studies, but has yet to wield much influence over television studies.

Because the sign is the fundamental unit of meaning on which all semiotic study is based, there has been a great deal of discussion (and argument) about its characteristics. Our short overview cannot hope to canvas all of the definitions of the sign in all their complexity, so we will consider just one to provide the reader with a sample of the semiotic method. However, it is important to recognize that not all semioticians subscribe to the following definition of the sign.

C. S. Peirce (pronounced "purse") was among the founders of semiotics around the turn of the century. He theorized that the sign consisted of two components: the **signifier** and the **signified**. The signifier is the physical aspect of the sign: ink on a page (written language), the modulation of air waves in sound (spoken language), light and shadow on a screen (television and film), a blinking light (traffic lights), and so on. The signified, then, is that which is represented by the signifier. The signified may be a concept or an object or a visual field. A video image of the Grand Canyon on a TV screen is thus a signifier; its immediate signified is the physical space of the Grand Canyon. The key to such a process of signification is that the signified is *absent* and must be represented by the signifier to the reader/viewer.

Peirce categorizes signs into three main types, depending on the relationship of the signifier to the signified:

1. The indexical sign, or index.

2. The iconic sign, or icon.

3. The symbolic sign, or symbol.

In an **indexical sign** the signifier is physically caused by the signified. A footprint in the sand, for example, communicates the meaning, "presence of a human." The footprint is the signifier and it is physically caused by its signified, the human foot.

In an **iconic sign** the signifier resembles the signified.[15] Most images on television are icons, in this sense of the term, because the light and shadow emanating from the television set (signifier) resembles the visual field (signified; objects in a certain space) that was recorded by a camera. A filmed image of Jerry Seinfeld sitting on a sofa resembles the visual field of the real Seinfeld on the real sofa. That image is thus an iconic signifier of Seinfeld's appearance.

Finally, in a **symbolic sign** the signifier and the signified are linked solely through cultural convention. A religious signifier such as a cross or a Star of David is linked to the signified of Christianity or Judaism, respectively, by centuries of cultural convention. A crucifix, however, in which Christ is represented on a cross, would be both an *iconic* signifier of the crucifixion, since it actually resembles what it represents, and a *symbolic* signifier of the principles of and faith in Christianity, since the actual body of Christ represents those signifieds within many cultures (though certain African and Asian cultures do not share these). Most important, all written and spoken languages are comprised of symbolic signs. Cultural convention is all that ties a word such as *college* (the signifier) to the concept of college. There is no resemblance between *college* and its signified (as in the iconic sign); and its signified doesn't physically cause the signifier, *college* (as in an indexical sign). The noun, *college*, and all nouns are symbolic signs.

Thus, television consists of a variety of signs. The video image of someone or something is both an iconic sign and an indexical sign. The image resembles what it represents, but it also is caused by what it represents. Most video images are created by light bouncing off an object and striking a video pickup chip; in this respect, then, the signified causes the signifier, as in an index. The words and graphic characters displayed on the screen are symbolic signs. Moreover, on a secondary level, the video image may iconically signify a symbolic signifier. Sound confusing? All this means is that a videotape image (iconic signifier) could record something symbolic—say, the Emmy statuette—and represent it to the viewer. Objects within the iconic video image often have symbolic significance for the viewer.

Semioticians stress that meaning, signification, is achieved largely through the combination and contrast of signs. A word doesn't mean much, if anything, until it is placed in the context of a sentence. A single image of an actor on a piece of furniture has little significance until it is combined with other shots (signs) into a sequence of images. This is especially true on a symbolic level. Recall Hurd's thematic oppositions within the police genre. Without criminals and evil, police and good would have no meaning. It is from opposition that meaning arises.

In semiotics there are two principal ways that signs are combined: the syntagmatic and the paradigmatic. (Beware of confusing the semiotician's "paradigmatic" with the more conventional sense of the term, "paradigm," which is a model or pattern.)

The **syntagmatic structure** is the way that signs are organized linearly or temporally (over time). Words in a sentence written on a piece of paper follow

FIGURE 13.1

FIGURE 13.2

one another linearly, and their order shapes their meaning. Take the primitive sentence:

Dog bites boy.

If the linear order of the words is rearranged, the meaning is changed:

Boy bites dog.

Or even:

Boy dog bites.

Each of the three versions of this sentence expresses a different meaning even though the same words are used each time. The same holds true for the temporal order of shots on television, as can be illustrated by manipulating the order of shots in "China After Tiananmen," a *Frontline* documentary. Our first sequence of shots might contain (Figs. 13.1–13.3):

1. Medium close-up of a Communist official, who contends that most Chinese did not approve of the students' revolt in Tiananmen Square.

FIGURE 13.3

FIGURE 13.4

FIGURE 13.5

> **2.** Long shot of Tiananmen Square protesters.
>
> **3.** Long shot of persons waving from a window and applauding.

This sequence of shots suggests that the official is lying and that the applause is for the protesters. These shots could be rearranged (Figs. 13.4–13.6) so that the order is:

> **1.** Long shot of protestors.
>
> **2.** Medium shot of Communist official.
>
> **3.** Long shot of persons applauding.

In this order, a new meaning is signified: the people are applauding the official, and implicitly agreeing with what he is saying. In television, the order of images, their sequence, can have powerful effects.

In semiotics the smallest chunk of story, the smallest narrative unit, is called a **syntagm**. (Usually this corresponds to a *scene* in television and film.) Just as the arrangement of individual shots can change a scene's meaning, so can

FIGURE 13.6

the arrangement of individual syntagms/scenes change the meaning of the entire program. Each of Kaminsky and Mahan's components in their outline of the narrative structure of the police show would be a syntagm. Imagine how scrambling their order could result in different meanings for the genre.

The second way that signs are organized, according to semiotics, is via association, or paradigmatically. If the syntagmatic is linear or horizontal and temporal, then the **paradigmatic structure** is vertical and atemporal. The paradigmatic consists of the associations we make with a particular signifier that give meaning to that signifier. Let's return to our sentence from above and alter it slightly:

Doberman pinscher bites boy.

The signifier "Doberman pinscher" holds certain meanings (aggression, violence, even militarism) for readers because of the contrasting associations they make with potential substitutions for that breed of dog:

Chihuahua . . .
Terrier . . .
Collie . . .
Doberman pinscher bites boy.

Doberman pinscher carries its meaning partially because of the paradigm of "dog breeds" from which *Doberman pinscher* is chosen. Obviously, it has much different connotations from, say, *Chihuahua*.

There are many paradigms such as this operating in television. All the elements of mise-en-scene, for instance, derive meaning paradigmatically. Consider the use of sets and props. When a man pulls out an Uzi and begins raking pedestrians with it, the viewer understands that this is an evil character even before he begins to shoot because of the paradigm of weapons. Because the character uses an Uzi, rather than a Magnum .45 or a Winchester rifle or even a bow and arrow, the meaning "evil criminal" is signified. Where does this meaning come from? It comes from the gun's paradigmatic association with other weapons that could have been chosen.

It might appear that meanings generated from the syntagmatic and paradigmatic combinations of signs are limitless, open to infinite variation. This is where the semiotic concept of **codes** becomes significant. Codes consists of "rules," culturally based conventions, that govern sign systems. These codes may be very precise, such as the grammatical rules that govern language. But more often the codes are ambiguous and changeable, delimited by history and cultural context. Fashion, for instance, has its own mercurial code. A black tuxedo signifies solemnity and is associated with major life events and upper-class characteristics. A lime-green, 100% polyester tuxedo with large lapels signifies 1970s garishness and perhaps a bit of sleaze.

In television we can find both codes that are part of the general culture that television inhabits and those that are specific to the medium. The code of fashion exists in reality and also regulates the meaning signified by the clothing worn by actors on television. But the code of television and film editing, discussed in chapter 7, is specific to these two media alone.

In sum, semiotics offers ways of talking about meaning production in television, and aspires to a "science" of signs. It is not, however, a true science. Semiotic research seldom, if ever, employs the scientific method outlined above. The crucial component that semiotics lacks is the ability to repeat research projects and gather the same results each time. Without repeatability, conventional sciences will always view semiotics as an "impure," subjective science. What most prevents semiotics from confirming its interpretation through repeatable studies is an undeveloped theory of how viewers/readers understand the signs before them. Psychoanalysis and ethnography have offered some answers to this problem, but they are far from globally accepted.

IDEOLOGICAL CRITICISM

Ideology is a slippery term. In everyday use it has negative connotations. When politicians speak of "liberal ideology" or "conservative ideology" they usually imply brainwashing, suggesting that their opponents' political ideology clouds their views of the truth. Ideology, in this context, signifies a fraudulent and misguided image of reality. This sense of ideology stems from the original theorist of ideological criticism, Karl Marx. It is with Marxism, therefore, that we need to begin our consideration of ideological criticism.

For Marx, writing in the mid-1800s, ideology is **false consciousness**. It is a counterfeit image of the world that is determined by social class: **aristocracy** (the class of kings and queens), **bourgeoisie** (middle class), or **proletariat** (working class). These social classes are grounded in a person's relation to work, to labor. Aristocrats do not work; their power (what's left of it) is based in traditional laws of inheritance and ritual. The bourgeois own the factories, which Marx calls the **means of production**, where goods are created and where men and women work. The bourgeois therefore hold tremendous economic power. Proletarians must work to survive and thus must sell their labor to the bourgeois. Marx sees history as a struggle among these classes to control the means of production. During any one particular era, one of these three classes will be in control. One class, thus, will be the **ruling class**. Since the Renaissance, according to Marx, the bourgeoisie has increased its power and the aristocracy has declined. Hence, over the centuries the bourgeoisie has become the ruling class.

Marx's explanation of class is significant to his theory of ideology, because he sees ideology as being fundamentally delimited by class. A woman who owns a factory will interpret the world through bourgeois ideology. A worker in that factory will, presumably, interpret the world through working-class ideology. However, Marx contends, the class that controls a society's means of production and commands its economy also rules ideologically: "The ideas of the ruling class are in every epoch the ruling ideas, i.e., the class which is the ruling *material* force of society [that is, which controls the factories], is at the same time its ruling *intellectual* force."[16] This gives rise to the notion of a **dominant ideology**, a system of beliefs about the world that benefits and supports a society's ruling class. In most Western societies, the ruling class is the bourgeoisie; and its ideology, according to Marxists, is the dominant ideology.

For example, one tenet of bourgeois ideology is that everyone may become financially successful if they work hard enough. This obviously benefits the capitalist system, because it encourages proletarians to labor tirelessly—although economic success is more commonly based on the financial stature of the family into which one is born than it is on an individual's effort. As multimillionaire Malcom Forbes put it when asked by David Letterman how he earned his incredible fortune, "My father died."

So, Marx concludes, most workers will subscribe to the dominant (bourgeois) ideology because they have been intellectually bludgeoned into those beliefs by the agents of the ruling class: schools, the legal system, churches, the military, and so forth. The ideological **superstructure** of a society is supported and determined by its economic **base** or **infrastructure**. Ideology follows economics.

This view posits that television is an agent of the ruling class. Because huge, often multinational corporations own all television networks, the programs broadcast must toe the ideological line. In other words, television shows—both fiction and news—must necessarily support dominant ideology. Moreover, all viewers, whatever their class, are so inculcated with ruling class ideology that they are tricked into accepting this version of reality as truth. If the ruling class ideology becomes so pervasive that even people outside of the ruling class absorb its values as truth, then, contends Marxist theorist Antonio Gramsci, a state of **hegemony** has been achieved.[17] In an hegemony, people take ruling class values for granted—even when they don't serve their own interests.

One need not be a Marxist or a socialist to hold this view of television's ideological function. Indeed, political and moral conservatives also see TV as an ideological demon, but from a different perspective. To them the values represented on television are decadent and immoral, ideologically offensive because they are too liberal. And yet, they share the classical Marxist assumptions that:

1. Ideological apparatuses (such as television) contain a homogeneity of ideas; there are no contradictions within ideology.

2. The person exposed to the dominant ideology will necessarily accept it as truth.

The classical Marxist conception of ideology has been the topic of much debate over the past 30 years. During that time, a more limber theory of ideology has evolved. As far as television studies is concerned, there are two central components of the current notion of ideology.

First, a society's ideology consists of many conflicting sets of meanings— **discourses**—competing with one another. As John Fiske elaborates, a discourse is "a language or system of representation that has developed socially in order to make and circulate a coherent set of meanings about an important topic area."[18] The dominant discourse is the one that is taken for granted, is seen as the commonsense explanation of the world within a particular society or within a social group inside a society.

Second, the position of an individual within ideology has been reexamined. This, for some theorists, has involved the introduction of psychoanalytic theory into the discussion of ideology. In psychoanalytical Marxism, the individual in society is viewed as a **subject**, a psychological construct who enters the meaning-filled world of ideology through certain Freudian mechanisms (specifically, the Oedipal complex). Other theorists eliminate Freud (and his major revisionist, Jacques Lacan) from their theory of the ideological subject, but are still concerned with individuals' entries into the ideological world and their relationship to ideology. Regardless, contemporary ideological criticism contests the classical Marxist assumption of individuals who are molded solely by the circumstances of their class and the influence of ruling-class ideology.

What impact does this recent work have on the study of television?

Under the banner of **cultural studies** or **ethnography**, a group of theorists has been attempting to analyze television in the context of contemporary ideological criticism. Stuart Hall, of the University of Birmingham (England) Centre for Contemporary Cultural Studies (CCCS), initially led this effort, and his work has been elaborated on by David Morley, Charlotte Brundson, Ellen Seiter and other scholars in the United States, Australia, and elsewhere.

Hall argues that television texts are **encoded** with many meanings—many discourses—by the **television apparatus.**[19]

Television as "apparatus"—an idea that is not unique to cultural studies—deserves further elaboration. The television apparatus consists of bankers, media corporations, producers, directors, scriptwriters, et al. They create TV according to unspoken "rules" of genre, narrative, and technique, etc., as well as economic limitations imposed by television's mode of production. The apparatus includes all those factors—from flesh-and-blood bankers to ephemeral rules of editing—that construct the medium as a pleasurable viewing experience, as something viewers enjoy doing. "Apparatus" is thus a wide-ranging term to refer to the televisual experience and everything that goes into constructing it.

Hall rejects the wholesale condemnation of the television apparatus by classical Marxists who criticize TV as an ideological and hegemonic monolith, kowtowing to ruling-class ideology. Hall contends instead that television texts are encoded with many meanings, a **polysemy.** Television's meanings may even contradict one another, as is the case when a program about a promiscuous playboy is interrupted by a public service announcement urging sexual restraint.

Television's polysemy, however, is not completely free-ranging, according to Hall. He writes, "Any society/culture tends, with varying degrees of closure, to impose its classifications of the social and cultural and political world. These constitute a *dominant cultural order*, though it is neither univocal nor uncontested."[20] Television does not show us *everything*. It cannot signify *everything*. For years the life experiences of minorities were virtually invisible as far as television was concerned. With the notable exception of Ellen Degeneres and *Will and Grace* (1998–), gay characters and culture are still largely marginalized; their threat to the nuclear family remains too great. Many subcultures are simply unspoken, unable to be classified, repressed from the television world by the dominant cultural order.

In any event, a large part of television's pleasure can be attributed to its polysemic nature. With so many meanings being transmitted, viewers can largely pick and choose those that adhere to their own ideology. This brings up another tenet of Hall's theory: **decoding.** Viewers decode television texts from three different ideological positions:[21]

1. The dominant-hegemonic position. Viewers who fully subscribe to ruling-class discourse interpret television according to the **preferred reading**

that is encoded on the text by the television apparatus. Such viewers presumably include members of the class wielding economic control, but comprise also working-class viewers who, in hegemonic fashion, value the dominant system.

2. The oppositional position. Viewers whose discourse is totally foreign to ruling-class discourse fully reject the preferred reading of the text, lending it their own interpretation. Individuals who are aggressively disenfranchised from the benefits of the ruling economic system decode television texts in unique ways. This includes ghetto residents, recent immigrants who do not speak English, and so on.

3. The negotiated position. By far this is the most common decoding position. Most viewers are neither wholehearted supporters of dominant discourse nor wholly detached from it. The negotiated interpretation permits the dominant discourse to set the ideological ground rules, but it modifies those rules according to personal experience. Viewers select the meanings that apply to their personal situations.

Hall and other ethnographic researchers approach television from two tacks. They seek to understand the ideological discourses in the text and the preferred readings that the television apparatus elects, but they are also concerned with the ideological discourses of the viewer. The process of ideological criticism for ethnographic researchers is to comprehend the following:

- How are these discourses produced?
- Which discourses are privileged over others?
- Which social and economic interests are served by these discourses?
- How do the discourses of the text relate to the discourses of the viewer?

This last question has led ethnographic researchers to incorporate television viewers into their studies, unlike most of the critical theorists summarized in this chapter. Frequently, ethnographers conduct interviews with TV watchers as a significant part of their research. Such methods draw ethnographers closer to traditional empirical research, especially uses-and-gratifications theory, but still ethnography remains distinct from empiricism. Where empiricism assumes that the answers to research questions lie in the acquisition of quantifiable numerical data, ethnographers see research as a more mercurial and less quantifiable *interaction* between the discourses of the text, the discourses of the viewer, and even the discourses of researchers themselves. Knowledge about society is not pictured as being "out there," waiting to be dug up, and reduced to a few "thin" equations, but in flux, in a process of signification—a system of counterbalancing or competing discourses that is best represented through "thick" descriptions of viewers' experiences and their contexts.

IDEOLOGICAL CRITICISM AND FEMINISM

Although **feminism** has been a central component of critical studies—particularly literary criticism and film studies—since the 1970s, it has been slow to affect traditional mass communication research, including traditional work on television. Close on the heels of film feminism have been TV analyses from a feminist perspective—particularly in regard to the soap opera, one of the few genres designed specifically for women viewers. Feminist criticism, like ideological criticism, is concerned with social discourses. In particular, feminist criticism concentrates on the volatile province of gender discourse—on the way that women alone and women in relation to men are portrayed in language, literature, film, magazines, television, and other media.

Historically, the women's movement has centered on specific social and political concerns: women's right to vote, equal job opportunity, combating violence against women, abortion rights, affordable day care for children. In other words, feminism has long battled in the arena of **sexual politics**—as Kate Millett refers to the power relationship between men and women.[22] But feminists have not been concerned solely with this political agenda, with marching in the streets to protest for abortion rights or suffrage, or against domestic violence. Intertwined with feminist political concerns is an interest in the *representation* of women in the mass media and the *interpretation* of those images by viewers, both women and men. How are women's images used in the media? What is the significance of those images in television? What ideas, concepts, discourses are associated with or encoded on woman as defined by television? How do viewers interpret or decode those images?

"Image-of-women" Feminist Criticism. The simplest form of feminist television criticism presumes that television is a direct reflection of society. This approach searches for **stereotypes** on television, which are argued to be the result of ideologically defined social types of women that were prevalent at the time of the program's production. Donna Reed, for instance, is said to represent the stereotype of the 1950s American "housewife." More recently, the women of *Designing Women* or *ER* are said to represent the "liberated" social types of contemporary women.

This approach to women in television has been criticized for three reasons:

First, it overly simplifies the television-to-society relationship. A mass medium such as TV has a very complex relationship with the society that produces it. Television stories, for instance, do not automatically or naturally "reflect" the ideology of the society that produces them. Rather, they emphasize some factors while repressing or even inverting other elements. A society's ideology is mediated by several factors—scriptwriters' and directors' aesthetic concerns and network executives' economic preoccupations—as it makes its way into a television program.

Second, the image-of-women approach overly simplifies the television-to-viewer relationship, assuming that viewers accept and believe everything they see on TV, as in the discarded hypodermic needle approach. As Hall argues, the discourses of the viewer interact dynamically with those of the text, rather than the text's discourses simply being forced on the unwilling and unwitting viewer.

The third problem with this approach is that it does not account for the style with which women are represented in television. It focuses on what type of women are on television and neglects the way that that type is presented.

Other Forms of Feminist Criticism. Recently, feminist scholars have abandoned the image-of-women approach in favor of more subtle methods that attempt to explain how beliefs about gender circulate in a society and on television. These scholars start from the premise that a society run by men will probably encourage systems of beliefs that keep men in power, *but*—and this is crucial to contemporary feminist criticism—these systems of belief are not uncontested or monolithic. There are oppositional discourses that contradict patriarchal ideas, and patriarchal discourses are themselves riddled with contradictions. Moreover, contemporary feminist criticism has been strongly influenced by recent studies of the viewer, and has subsequently struggled to develop a theory of the female viewer's perception of television.

Soap opera, with its largely female audience, has proven to be the test case for the feminist analysis of television. In an early, groundbreaking essay, Tania Modleski writes about the soap opera in terms of the narrative pleasure it affords the female viewer.[23] She is also interested in the ways that women are positioned within the narrative. The constant interruptions, the lack of a conclusion, and other soap opera characteristics, she suggests, may qualify the genre as possessing a feminist narrative structure.[24] Her argument is typical of contemporary feminist criticism in that it articulates the ways that women are represented on television (specifically, through the narrative structure) and the position of the female spectator vis-a-vis the images that she sees on the screen. In so doing, Modleski is helping to define television viewing from a feminist perspective.

In sum, then, feminist criticism of television deals with a gendered discourse, with belief systems based on what have come to be known as women's issues. A feminist critique of any television show must remain alert to the program's sexual politics at the same time that it dissects the positioning of women *within* the text and the experience of female (and male) viewers before the TV set.

SUMMARY

As illustrated by the ethnographic approach to television, "critical" methods and "empirical" methods are no longer as separate as they once were. It is difficult to predict how far critical methods will venture in this direction, however. There has already been some retrenching on the part of ethnographic researchers as they confront the problems of survey or interview research: That interviewees don't consistently say what they mean, that their responses are always influenced by the style of the questions, and that people sometimes lie when filling out questionnaires or talking to interviewers. Still, it seems likely that researchers such as David Morley and others belonging to or influenced by the CCCS will continue to investigate audience research methods distinct from traditional empiricism.

Most of the critical methods surveyed in this chapter remain far removed from empiricism. Auteur theory, genre study, semiotics, ideological criticism, and feminism have historically focused their attention on the television text— its meanings and the construction of those meanings through specific narrative devices and audiovisual techniques. With the exception of semiotics, which aspires to be a science of signs, each of these methods provides a lens through which to view television's polysemy:

auteur theory	$\longrightarrow$	the producer/director's career
genre study	$\longrightarrow$	films linked by similar audience response, style, or content

ideological criticism $\longrightarrow$ class representation

feminism $\longrightarrow$ gender representation

More recently, the impact of psychoanalysis and its theory of the subject has forced proponents of these critical methods to rethink their concept of viewers and of their significance to the construction of meaning. And yet, auteurism, genre study, ideological criticism, and feminism are still distinguished by their emphasis on the text and the meanings it might communicate.

The brevity of this chapter has led to simplification (perhaps even oversimplification) of these critical methods. And we had to be selective in our choice of methods to present. Some contemporary critical methods that have been applied to television but are not considered here include rhetorical criticism, dialogic criticism, reader-oriented criticism, and post-structuralism. The diversity of television critical study prohibits sampling all of the critical methods currently being applied to television.

FURTHER READINGS

Several anthologies offer more extensive introductions to critical methods than could be presented in this short chapter. Of these, the most ambitious is Robert C. Allen, ed., *Channels of Discourse, Reassembled*, 2nd ed. (Chapel Hill: University of North Carolina Press, 1992). Separate chapters, with annotated bibliographies, cover semiotics, narrative theory, audience-oriented criticism, genre study, ideological analysis, psychoanalysis, feminism, and cultural studies. One chapter also outlines the debate over postmodernism and television.

Similarly, Leah R. Vande Berg, Lawrence A. Wenner, and Bruce E. Gronbeck, eds., *Critical Approaches to Television* (Boston: Houghton Mifflin, 1998) introduces the reader to numerous separate critical methods, some of which have been influenced by a speech communication perspective. Although it does touch on several of the same topics as *Channels of Discourse*, it also provides space for hermeneutic, mythic, rhetorical, and sociological critical methods. *Critical Approaches to Television* furnishes applications of each method.

Other general anthologies are less explanatory in their presentation, but do offer the reader a sampling of critical methods: Tony Bennett, Susan Boyd-Bowman, Colin Mercer, and Janet Woollacott, eds., *Popular Television and Film* (London: Open University Press, 1981); Todd Gitlin, ed., *Watching Television: A Pantheon Guide to Popular Culture* (New York: Pantheon, 1986); Andrew Goodwin and Garry Whannel, eds., *Understanding Television* (New York: Routledge, 1990); E. Ann Kaplan, ed., *Regarding Television: Critical Approaches* (Frederick, MD: University Publications of America, 1983); Colin MacCabe, ed., *High Theory/Low Culture: Analysing Popular Television and Film* (New York: St. Martin's Press, 1986); Patricia Mellencamp, ed., *Logics of Television: Essays in Cultural Criticism* (Bloomington: Indiana University Press, 1990); Horace Newcomb, ed., *Television: The Critical View*, 6th ed. (Austin: University of Texas Press, 2000).

There are a several books organized around specific critical methods within television studies. Two anthologies devoted specifically to a cultural studies' perspective are Stuart Hall, Dorothy Hobson, Andrew Lowe, and Paul Willis, eds., *Culture, Media, Language* (London: Hutchinson, 1980); and Ellen Seiter, Hans Borchers, Gabriele Kreutzner, and Eva-Maria Warth, eds., *Remote Control:*

Television, Audiences, and Cultural Power (New York: Routledge, 1989). Significant feminist TV essays are collected in Charlotte Brunsdon, Julie D'Acci, and Lynn Spigel, eds., *Feminist Television Criticism: A Reader* (Oxford: Clarendon Press, 1997). In addition, two books providing overviews of feminist work on TV are: Bonnie J. Dow, *Prime-Time Feminism: Television, Media Culture, and the Women's Movement Since 1970* (Philadelphia: University of Pennsylvania Press, 1996) and Charlotte Brundson, *The Feminist, the Housewife, and the Soap Opera* (Oxford: Clarendon Press, 2000).

John Ellis, *Visible Fictions: Cinema: Television: Video* (Boston: Routledge, 1992) is particularly valuable for its correlation of television with the cinema. Other books offering helpful overviews of television criticism include John Corner, *Critical Ideas in Television Studies* (Oxford: Clarendon Press, 1999); John Fiske, *Television Culture* (New York: Methuen, 1987); Christine Geraghty and David Lusted, eds., *The Television Studies Book* (London: Arnold, 1998); and Paul Monaco, *Understanding Society, Culture and Television* (Westport, CT: Praeger, 2000).

Finally, Ellen Seiter, "Making Distinctions in TV Audience Research: Case Study of a Troubling Interview," in Newcomb, 495–518, offers insights into the difficulties of performing ethnographic research.

E N D N O T E S

[1] Robert C. Allen, ed., *Channels of Discourse, Reassembled*, 2nd ed. (Chapel Hill, NC: University of North Carolina Press, 1992).

[2] In "focus groups" a few individuals are gathered in a room, shown a program/ commercial and then asked for their opinion of it. The technique of "cable testing" has selected viewers watch an unreleased program/commercial in their own homes, over their cable TV systems. (Only particular viewers may view the program/commercial; it is not shown to everyone on the cable system.) Then those selected viewers are interviewed over the phone.

[3] Barry S. Sapolsky and Joseph O. Tabarlet, "Sex in Primetime Television: 1979 Versus 1989," *Journal of Broadcasting and Electronic Media 35*, no. 4 (Fall 1991): 505–516; Mary Cassata, Thomas Skill, and Samuel O. Boadu, "Life and Death in the Daytime Television Serial: A Content Analysis," in *Life on Daytime Television: Tuning-In American Serial Drama*, eds. Mary Cassata and Thomas Skill (Norwood, NJ: Ablex, 1983), 23–36. The latter is critiqued in Robert C. Allen, *Speaking of Soap Operas* (Chapel Hill, NC: University of North Carolina Press, 1985), 36–38.

[4] Allen, *Soap Opera*, 37–38.

[5] Allen, *Soap Operas*, 42.

[6] The term is based in the phrase "*la politique des auteurs*" ("the policy or polemic of the author") that appeared in a 1954 *Cahiers du Cinéma* essay by François Truffaut. It was translated into "auteur theory" by American film critic Andrew Sarris in the early 1960s.

[7] David Marc, "The Situation Comedy of Paul Henning: Modernity and the American Folk Myth in *The Beverly Hillbillies*," in *Demographic Vistas: Television in American Culture* (Philadelphia: University of Pennsylvania Press, 1984), 39–64; Bishetta D. Merritt, "Bill Cosby: TV Auteur?" *Journal of Popular Culture 24*, no. 4 (Spring 1991): 89–102; Robert Thompson, "Stephen J. Cannell: An Auteur Analysis of the Adventure/Action Genre," in *Television Criticism: Approaches and Applications*, eds. Leah R. Vande Berg and Lawrence A. Wenner (New York: Longman, 1991), 112–126.

[8] Marc, 46, 62.

[9] Andrew Tudor terms this the "empiricist dilemma," because it is an observational question, a question of which programs to observe. In order to make the distinction between empirical studies and critical studies clearer, I have avoided using his term. But it should be noted that critical studies do have empirical aspects, just as empirical studies do have critical aspects. See Andrew Tudor, *Theories of Film* (New York: Viking, 1973), 135–138.

[10] Stuart M. Kaminsky, Jeffrey H. Mahan, *American Television Genres* (Chicago: Nelson-Hall, 1985), 56.

[11] Kaminsky and Mahan, 61–62.

[12] V. I. Propp, *Morphology of the Folktale*, translated by Laurence Scott, with an introduction by Svatava Pirkova-Jakobson (Austin, TX: University of Texas Press, 1968).

[13] Stuart Hall, "Encoding/Decoding," in *Culture, Media, Language* (London: Hutchinson, 1980), 128–138.

[14] Geoffrey Hurd, "The Television Presentation of the Police," in *Popular Television and Film*, eds. Tony Bennett, Susan Boyd-Bowman, Colin Mercer, and Janet Woollacott (London: British Film Institute, 1981), 66.

[15] Iconic signs are the most confusing and the most controversial within the study of semiotics. Some of the confusion stems from the use of the term "icon" or "ikon" in art history and religion to refer to an object with symbolic significance. The semiotic controversy revolves around the very question of iconicity. Many semioticians reject the notion of resemblance between signifier and real-world objects, contending that all signification is *constructed* by human interpretation and that "resemblance" implies an impossible, "natural" or necessary correspondence between signifier and signified. Ferdinand de Saussure, another one of semiotics' founders, is among those who reject the entire principle of iconicity.

[16] Karl Marx, Frederick Engels, *The German Ideology*, Part One, edited and with an Introduction by C. J. Arthur (New York: International Publishers, 1947), 64. Originally written 1845–46.

[17] Antonio Gramsci, *Prison Notebooks* (New York: Columbia University Press, 1991).

[18] John Fiske, *Television Culture* (New York: Methuen, 1987), 14.

[19] See Hall, "Encoding/Decoding", 128–138.

[20] Hall, 134.

[21] Hall, 136–137.

[22] Kate Millett, *Sexual Politics* (Garden City, NY: Doubleday, 1970).

[23] Tania Modleski, "The Search for Tomorrow in Today's Soap Operas," in *Loving with a Vengeance* (Hamden, CT: Archon, 1982), 85–109. Originally published in 1979. See also Tania Modleski, "The Rhythms of Reception: Daytime Television and Women's Work," in *Regarding Television: Critical Approaches*, ed. E. Ann Kaplan (Frederick, MD: University Publications, 1983), 67–75; and Charlotte Brunsdon, "Crossroads: Notes on Soap Opera," in Kaplan, ed., 76–83.

[24] Modleski, *Loving*, 105.

Sample Analyses

Over the course of *Television*, we have suggested a variety of techniques for look-ing at television critically. In so doing, we have drawn examples from assorted television programs to illustrate analytical theories that remain rather abstract. The best way to make these theories concrete is to apply them to individual television programs. The acid test of any TV-analytical method is whether or not it helps you understand television.

This appendix presents the outlines of two assignments in TV criticism—one for narrative and the other for non-narrative programs. We encourage you to apply the questions here to a program of your own choice and see what results your analysis yields. These analytical questions can also help guide in-class discussions—providing a structure for your dissection of television programs.

One great advantage to TV analysis in the digital age is the ability to grab frames from video for illustrations. All of the frames in *Television* were captured using relatively modest Windows and Mac computers. Basically, frame grabs are done by (1) hooking a VCR to your computer using a special video card (e.g., ATI All-in-Wonder) or an external device (e.g., Snappy), (2) digitizing images from videotape, and (3) using image-editing software (e.g., Adobe Photoshop or Jasc Paint Shop Pro) to touch up the images and store them in appropriate formats (JPEG for the Web; TIFF for printing). Then insert the images into your word processing document to illuminate your discussion of lighting, set design, objective correlatives, performance, and so on.

You'll find several samples of critical analyses and detailed instructions on doing video frame grabs on *Television's* Web site: www.TVCrit.com.

SAMPLE NARRATIVE ANALYSIS

I. Analysis of polysemy

This is the core portion, the most important part, of your analysis. In this segment you should analyze the ideas that underpin programs.

A. What meanings, what discourses, are encoded on the text, presented for the viewer to decode? Outline the issues involved and then flesh out that skeleton with details from the program.

B. Are some meanings emphasized over others? Are some presented positively and others negatively? How? In other words, what attitude or perspective toward those meanings does the show take? Does the program seem to have a "message"? For example, if it's a program telling a story about a woman getting an abortion, does it support or condemn her decision?

C. What characterizes the preferred viewer of this program? That is, what sort of viewer does this program seem to be designed for? What potential does the program offer for alternative interpretations, for what might be called "against-the-grain readings"?

II. Analysis of Program Structure: Flow, Segmentation, and Interruption

To effectively analyze a text's polysemy you must break down its overall structure and visual/sound style. This is where you explain how a program takes a perspective toward a certain meaning or issue.

A. What recurring dilemma underpins the narrative of every episode? That is, what general dilemma is repeated every week? What is the program's continuing narrative problematic?

B. Using one or two episodes to illustrate your argument, explain how a specific enigma is played out in one narrative on a particular week/day. How does this one individual episode illustrate the general dilemma of the program? How does the narrative come to an (inconclusive) conclusion?

C. How is the program segmented? Where are the commercials inserted? How is the narrative segmented in order to fit between the commercials? (It would probably be useful for you to list the timing of all of the scenes and commercials in this episode as you prepare your analysis.)

D. What do the commercials suggest about the target audience, the preferred viewer, of the program? Does the polysemy of the commercials support or contradict the meanings of the program?

III. Analysis of Visual/Sound Style

Begin by choosing a single scene from one episode of your program. List all of the shots for that scene. Draw a bird's-eye-view diagram of the positions of the actors, furniture and cameras.

A. How does the mise-en-scene contribute to this episode's narrative? In other words, how do the elements of mise-en-scene communicate aspects of the story to the viewer?

B. Which mode of production was used—single-camera or multiple-camera? What advantages/disadvantages does this mode offer the program? How does it affect what the program can and cannot do?

C. How does the organization of space through editing support the narrative? How does the variation of framing (long shot, close-up, etc.) influence our understanding of the scene? What sort of rhythm (fast? slow?) is used in the scene and why? Does the editing pull us closer to the characters or distance us?

D. How do elements of music, dialogue, sound perspective, or sync help to construct the story in this episode? What do they emphasize or de-emphasize?

E. What do the credits tell the viewer about the program? Specifically, what do they indicate about the show's narrative or polysemy? What do the credits re-establish each week?

SAMPLE NON-NARRATIVE ANALYSIS

I. Analysis of polysemy

(This portion is essentially the same as for narrative programs as both analyses seek to deconstruct television's meanings.)

A. What meanings, what discourses, are encoded on the text, presented for the viewer to decode? Outline the issues involved and then flesh out that skeleton with details from the program.

B. Are some meanings emphasized over others? Are some presented positively and others negatively? How? In other words, what attitude or perspective toward those meanings does the show take? Does the program seem to have a "message"?

C. What characterizes the preferred viewer of this program? That is, what sort of viewer does this program seem to be designed for? What potential does the program offer for alternative interpretations, for what might be called "against-the-grain readings"?

II. Analysis of Non-narrative Structure

A. Discuss which modes of representation your text utilizes. Be sure to cite specific examples illustrating the mode.

B. Explain the implied relationship between the television world and the historical world in your text. How do the two interact?

C. Explain the implied relationship between the text and the viewer. How does the text address the viewer?

D. What principles dictate how the text presents its information about the historical world? In other words, how is the text organized?

III. Analysis of Visual/Sound Style

A. Begin by choosing a 2-minute segment (shorter, if you choose a commercial) from your text. List all of the shots for that segment. If it helps to understand the segment, draw a bird's-eye-view diagram of the positions of the social actors, historical world, and camera.

B. How does the historical world mise-en-scene of this segment contribute to the text's meaning? In other words, how do the elements of mise-en-scene communicate aspects of the text's meaning to the viewer?

C. Which mode of production was used—single-camera or multiple-camera? What advantages/disadvantages does this mode offer the text?

D. How does the editing support the text's meaning? In other words, why were the shots presented in the order that they were? How does that order affect meaning?

E. How, in this segment, does the manipulation of sound help to construct the text's meaning?

Compiled by Rosemary McMahill

abstract animation

An aesthetic tenet of animation that sees animation as consisting of lines, shapes, and colors, abstract forms to be manipulated by the animator at will. The opposite of *naturalistic animation*.

act (segment)

A portion or segment of the narrative presented between commercial breaks. Consists of one or more *scenes*.

actor movement

Typically referred to by the theatrical term *blocking*.

actualities

Events from the *historical world* used in news and sports programs.

additive color

In video, the combination of red, green, and blue *phosphors* to generate all other colors.

ADR

See *automatic dialogue replacement*.

Advanced Television Systems Committee (ATSC)

Formed in the early 1990s to set standards for U.S. digital television, including HDTV.

aesthetic

A philosophy of the beautiful; criteria that define art (or television) as good or bad. Also used to refer to determining factors of television that are neither technological or economic.

ambient sound

Background sounds of a particular room or location.

analog sound

An electronic replica of a sound wave on audio or video tape; the sound wave is converted into an electronic copy or analog. This type of sound recording is being replaced by *digital sound*. Vinyl albums and audio cassettes create sound through an analog process; compact discs, DVDs, and digital audio tape (DAT) store sound digitally.

anamorphic

A widescreen film process (under such trademark names as CinemaScope and Panavision) used to create an image wider than conventional television's. The *aspect ratio* of most films made with anamorphic lenses today is 1:2.35, while the conventional television image's aspect ratio is 1:1.33.

antagonist

Character and/or situation that hinders the protagonist from achieving his or her goal(s).

anti-naturalist performance

Performance style in which the viewer is kept aware that the actor is pretending to be a character.

aperture

In terms of a narrative: an ambiguous ending. The opposite of *closure*. In terms of video and film cameras: the opening through which light passes.

arcing

A term used in television studio production to refer to the semi-circular sideways movement of the camera.

aristocracy

In Marxism, the most elite social class—consisting of individuals who do not work and hold power through inheritance: kings, queens, princes, princesses, and so on. According to Marx's analysis of history, the aristocracy controlled European countries until the *bourgeoisie's* rise to power in the decades after the Renaissance.

aspect ratio

The ratio of height to width of a screen. The conventional ratio for television has been 1:1.33 (or 3:4), but that may change to 1:1.78 (or 9:16) with the advent of *high-definition* television.

ATSC

See *Advanced Television Systems Committee.*

automatic dialogue replacement (ADR)

The replacement of lines of dialogue during post-production. Also known as looping.

auteur theory

Posits that directors are the authors of films/television programs in the same manner that writers are the authors of novels. Directors are seen as injecting their personal artistic visions into films/television programs, and, over time, certain stylistic and thematic tendencies are discernable in directors' work.

axis of action

In the *continuity (or 180°) system*, the line of action around which the space of the scene is oriented.

back light

In the *three-point lighting* system, the source of illumination placed behind and above the actor. Its main function is to cast light on the actor's head and shoulders, creating an outline of light around the actor to distinguish him or her from the background.

balance

In video and film, the blending of three colors (red, green, and blue in video; yellow, magenta, and cyan in film) to produce a spectrum of colors. Different video processes and film stocks favor some colors over others, resulting in various types of color balance.

base

In film production terms, the celluloid backing of a piece of film to which the *emulsion* adheres. In Marxist terms, a society's economic system, on which is built its *superstructure*.

blocking

The actor's movement around a set; the director's incorporation of the actor into the *mise-en-scene*.

blue screens

On a television studio set, areas of the background that are blue (or green), onto which live images or maps are substituted through the *chroma key* process.

boom operator

The sound technician who physically operates the *overhead boom microphone*.

bourgeoisie

In Marxist terms, the middle class; owners of the *means of production* and employers of the *proletariat*.

brand parity

In the context of advertising, when all products are essentially the same. Contrast with a product's *unique selling proposition*.

Brechtian performance

Anti-naturalist, confrontational performance style based in the theories of German playwright Bertolt Brecht. He demanded that the viewer constantly be made aware of the fact that he or she is watching a play and that he or she should be distanced from the characters (see *distanciation*).

brightness (luminance)

In the context of television's image quality, how bright or dark a color is.

broadcast standards and practices (BSP)

The units within TV networks that make sure offensive material is not broadcast— TV's internal censors.

bug

A small network or station logo superimposed in a corner of the frame.

camera obscura

A darkened chamber with a hole in one wall through which light enters, creating an image of the outdoors on the opposite wall. It was the earliest form of a "camera," and is where the name derives.

camera operator

The person who actually handles the camera.

cardioid microphone

A *unidirectional* microphone with most of its sensitivity aimed toward the front, and a *pickup pattern* that resembles an inverted heart.

cathode ray tube (CRT)

A television picture tube. The cathode ray excites the *pixels* to create the video image.

cause-effect chain

In narrative structure, the way one event leads to (causes) another and is the result (effect) of a previous event.

cel (celluloid)

A transparent sheet of plastic, on which images are drawn and painted in the production of animation.

chiaroscuro

A *low-key lighting* style, usually in reference to theatrical productions or the dark paintings of Rembrandt.

chroma

See *chrominance*.

chroma key

An electronic special effects process, specific to video, used to insert one image into another, often using blue screen making a single color (usually blue or green) transparent so that one image may be inserted into another—as in weather maps with a forecaster superimposed over them.

chrominance

The level of *saturation* of a color; the color's purity, how much or little grayness is mixed with it.

CinemaScope

A *widescreen, anamorphic* film process with an aspect ratio of 2.35 to 1.

cinematographer

The person overseeing all aspects of the film image—including lighting and the operation of the camera.

cinematography

The process of making a film image, and the characteristics of the film image.

classical Hollywood cinema (Hollywood classicism)

A conventional style of filmmaking with a particular model of narrative structure, editing technique, mise-en-scene, dialogue, music, etc. Narrative is presented in a clear cause-and-effect chain, with definite *closure*.

classical period

In the history of theatrical cinema, the 1920s–1950s when the Hollywood studio system of film production held total power and evolved the classical style of filmmaking. In a genre's evolutionary pattern, the stage during which thematics, narrative structure, and audial/visual style are solidified into firm conventions, a recognizable cohesive unit.

close miking

The positioning of a microphone very close to the performer's mouth—often used by radio and TV announcers.

close-up (CU)

A framing that presents a close view of an object or person—filling the frame and separating the object or person from the surroundings. Conventionally, a TV close-up of a person is from the shoulders or neck up.

closure

In terms of narrative: a fully resolved conclusion, in which all of the narrative's questions are answered. The opposite of *aperture*.

code

A set of rules; an historically and/or culturally based set of conventions.

color announcer

A type of television sports announcer; often he or she is a former athlete and/or coach, with first-hand expertise.

compositing

The *post-production* combination of two or more video/film/digital sources in a single image.

computer-generated imagery (CGI)

Images that are created digitally, usually through computer modeling with *wire-frame* objects.

content analysis

An *empirical* method of analysis that selects a specific textual component, counts and codes the number of occurrences of this component into a statistical form, resulting in quantifiable data that usually cannot be interpreted beyond the data itself.

continuity editing (invisible editing)

A style of editing that creates a continuity of space and time out of the fragments of scenes contained in individual shots; the shots are arranged to support the progression of the story, thus editing technique does not call attention to itself. Based on the 180° rule.

continuity person

The person in a production responsible for maintaining consistency in all details from one shot to the next, including action, lighting, props, and costumes.

copyright

The exclusive legal rights to perform or sell a song, book, script, photograph, etc. To use copyrighted material (e.g., a piece of music) in a TV program, a fee or *royalty* must be paid to the copyright holder. If there is no copyright, the material may be used for free and is said to be in the *public domain*

cost per mil (CPM)

The advertising rate charged to TV sponsors, which is quantified per thousand viewers. "Mil" equals "thousand," from the Latin word *mile*. Thus, the CPM is the cost per thousand viewers.

CPM

See *cost per mil.*

craning

A movement deriving its name from the mechanical crane on which a camera may be placed. A crane shot is one in which the entire camera, mounted on a crane, is swept upward or downward.

cross-fade

Akin to a *dissolve*, one sound fades out while the other fades in, resulting in a brief overlap.

CRT

See *cathode ray tube.*

cultural studies (ethnography)

A critical approach that argues that viewers decode television texts based on their specific ideological position in society; it looks at the interaction between the ideological *discourses* of the texts and those of the viewers.

decoding

In cultural studies, the reader/viewer's interpretation of a text that has been *encoded* with meaning by its creators.

deep focus

When all planes (foreground, middle-ground, and background) of an image are in *focus*.

deep space blocking

A type of blocking associated with single-camera productions, particularly those shot on *location*. The depth of the "set" is emphasized by the ability of one actor to be positioned near the camera and another far away; the actors may move toward one another, or participate in independent actions.

definition

In terms of the image quality of television, film and definition refers to the capability to separate and depict detail. This is sometimes termed *resolution*.

demographics

The characteristics of an audience, usually broken down in terms of age, gender, income, race, etc.; used with *ratings* to set advertising rates.

depth of field

The range in front of and behind the *focus distance* that is also in focus.

Designated Market Area

Cohesive metropolitan areas that *ratings* companies use to define television markets.

dialogue

Speech among characters, which does not usually address the viewer. Also, a type of interview in which the voices of the interviewer and the interviewee are both heard, and both persons may be visible on camera.

diegesis

The world in which the narrative is set. In other words, the world fictional characters inhabit.

diegetic sound

Dialogue, music, and sound effects that occur in the *diegetic space* of the television program; that is, sound that is part of the characters' world.

diegetic space

The physical world in which the narrative action of the television program takes place.

digital audio workstation (DAW)

A computer-based system for digitally editing sound.

digital sound

A technology (e.g., CDs) that converts sound into numbers; this allows computers to process and/or change the recorded sound. It has been replacing analog sound processes (e.g., vinyl albums and audio cassettes).

digital television (DTV)

Television broadcast in a digital format—in contrast to analog format such as *NTSC* and PAL. Permits *HDTV, multicasting*, and *enhanced TV*.

digital video (DV)

Any video format that relies on digital technology for recording and/or editing. For example, video recorded with a digital camera or edited on a *nonlinear editing* system.

digital video effects (DVE)
Special effects created with digital, computer-based technology. Compare with *electronic effects*.

director
A person who is in charge of a television show, on the set or in a control booth, during the actual production process.

discourse
Socially-based belief structures. The viewer brings discourses to the *reading* of the television *text*, which itself contains discourses that match or clash with the viewer's.

dissolve
A special effect wherein simultaneously one shot fades out as the next fades in, so that the two images briefly overlap.

distanciation
A technique of *Brechtian performance* style wherein actors retain the sense of themselves as actors; thus viewers and actors alike are distanced from characters rather than identifying with them.

DMA
See *designated market area*.

dolly
A wheeled camera support that permits a rolling camera movement. In conventional television usage, dollying refers to forward or backward movement and *trucking* (which is accomplished with a dolly) refers to sideways movement.

dominant ideology
In Marxism, the system of beliefs about the world propagated and supported by the society's *ruling class*.

DTV
See *digital television*.

dubbing
The replacement of one voice for another.

DV
See *digital video*.

DVE
See *digital video effects*.

DVD
A disc the size of an audio CD that can store a feature-length film and include interactive features. There's no consensus on what "DVD" stands for, but when it was introduced to the consumer market in 1997 it was known variously as the "digital video disc" and the "digital versatile disc."

dynamic range
A range of sounds from soft to loud. A measurement of the limits of microphones, recording and playback machines, and other audio equipment.

Editech
The first electronic editing system for videotape—invented and marketed by Ampex.

effects theory
A type of communication theory (e.g., *hypodermic needle concept*) that proposes that, because viewers are passive, television directly affects them.

electron gun

A mechanical device, located in the rear of a television's picture tube, which fires an electron beam at the *pixels*, scanning line-by-line across the lines of the television image, causing the pixels to glow and create the television image.

electronic effects

Special effects (including *fades, dissolves, and keying*) created on video using an analog special effects generator. Compare with *digital video effects (DVE)*.

electronic news gathering (ENG)

The video recording of news events or *actualities*.

emotional memory

Technique of *method* acting wherein the actor draws on memories of previous emotions that match the emotions of the character.

empiricism

A theoretical approach that advocates the understanding of a problem through systematic and controlled observation/experimentation, with research results measured and expressed in numbers and formulas.

emulsion

The mixture of photosensitive chemicals with a gelatin medium attached to the *base* of a piece of film.

encoding

In cultural studies, the creation of meaning within a text by a cultural institution such as the television industry. Readers/viewers may *decode* these preferred meanings when exposed to texts, or they may take a position opposing them.

ENG

See *electronic news gathering*.

enhanced TV

In *digital TV*, the addition of interactive functions to standard TV programs.

epic theater

Brechtian theory of theatrical presentation in which the viewer is alienated from the character.

establishing shot

A long shot that positions characters within their environments, and helps to establish the setting.

expository mode

Mode of television that presents an argument about the *historical world*; the "facts" of that world are assertively or even aggressively selected and organized and presented to the viewer in a direct address.

exterior scenes

Scenes set outdoors, often in particular *location settings*.

extreme close up (XCU)

A framing that presents a view closer than a conventional close-up—For example, a shot of an eye that fills the entire screen.

extreme long shot (XLS)

A framing that presents a distant view of an object or person—For example, an aerial shot of a car on a street

eyeline match

An editing principle of the *continuity system* that begins with a shot of a character looking in a specific direction, then cuts to a second shot that shows the area toward which the character was looking.

fade out/fade in

A special effect often used for scene-to-scene transition. In a fade out the image darkens until the screen is black. In a fade in, the image starts out black and then gradually becomes visible.

false consciousness

In Marxist terms, a counterfeit image of the world determined by one's social class.

feminism

A critical approach that concentrates on gender *discourse*, the manner in which the male–female relationship is portrayed.

fill light

In the *three-point lighting* system, a source of illumination used to fill the shadows created by the *key light*. It is directed obliquely toward the actor from the opposite side of the key light, at approximately the same height (or a little lower), and is generally half as bright as the key light.

film stock

The specific type of film used to record images.

filter

In lighting, a colored *gel* placed in front of a light source. In cinematography or videography, an optical device (colored, polarized, etc.) attached to the lens.

fine grain

A type of film stock in which the *grain* is smaller, resulting in a higher image *definition*.

flashback

A disruption of the chronological presentation of events, in which an event from the past is presented in a program's present. See *flashforward*.

flashforward

A disruption of the chronological presentation of events, in which an event from the future is presented in a program's present. See *flashback*.

flow

Television's sequence of programs, commercials, news breaks, and so on. The overall flow of television is segmented into small parcels, which often bear little logical connection to one another.

focal length

The distance from the lens' optical center to its *focal point*, usually measured in millimeters. There are three conventional types of focal length: *wide angle, normal, and telephoto.*

focal plane

The plane within a camera where the light strikes the film or electronic pick-up.

focal point

In a camera lens, that spot where the light rays, bent by the lens, converge before expanding again and striking the film or electronic pickup at the focal plane.

focus

The adjustment of the camera lens so that the image is sharp and clear.

focus distance

The distance from the camera to the object being *focused* on.

Foley

A *post-production* process wherein sound effects are fabricated for a previously recorded scene while the Foley artist watches a shot projected on a screen.

format

In film, refers to the film width itself and is measured in millimeters (e.g., super-8, 16mm, and 35mm). In videotape, the combination of the width of the tape, measured in inches, (e.g., 1/2″, 3/4″, and 1″) and the process used to store the images on tape (e.g., VHS, Beta).

framing

Determines what the viewer can and cannot see due to the manipulation of the camera frame (the edge of the image).

frequency response

A range of sound frequencies from low to high. A measurement of the limits of microphones, recording and playback machines, and other audio equipment.

function

In narrative study, a single action or character attribute. Based in Russian Formalism and the work of Vladimir Propp.

gel

A piece of plastic or gelatin placed in front of a light source to change its color.

genre

Groupings of television programs defined by their narrative structure, thematic content, and style of sound and image.

grain

The silver halide crystals suspended in the _emulsion_ of a piece of film. When struck by light and chemically processed, these crystals change color, resulting in the film image. The smaller the grain, the higher the _definition_ of the image (i.e., the sharper the image).

hand-held

A technique in which the camera is held by the camera operator, rather than fixed to a camera mount such as a tripod or _dolly_.

hard light

Direct, _undiffused_ light; the result is the casting of harsh, distinct shadows.

hard news

Refers to news stories that examine events that affect society as a whole (e.g., national politics and international relations).

high angle

A shot in which the camera is placed higher than the filmed actor or object, so that the camera looks down on the actor or object.

high-definition television (HDTV)

A broadcast technology in which the number of _scan lines_ of the video image is increased and the size of the _pixels_ decreased (as well as reshaped)—resulting in a clearer, better _defined_ image.

high-key lighting

A lighting style in which the ratio in intensity of _key light_ to _fill light_ is small. The result is an evenly lit set, with a low contrast between bright and dark areas.

historical world (historical reality)

The reality that is processed, selected, ordered, and interpreted by nonfiction television programs.

hypodermic needle theory

An _effects theory_ that purports that viewers are passive, and directly and immediately affected by what they see on television.

hue

A specific color from within the visible spectrum of white light: e.g., red, green, blue.

hypercardioid microphone

A highly *unidirectional* microphone, for which the *pickup pattern* is narrower than that of a *cardioid microphone.* So-called "shotgun" microphones have a hypercardioid pattern.

icon

Generally speaking, an object that represents a theme or an aspect of the character or the like. In the specific context of *semiotics,* a type of *sign,* wherein the *signifier* physically resembles the *signified.* For example, a photograph (*signifier*) is a mechanical reproduction of what is photographed (*signified*).

iconography

The objects that signify character and themes of the narrative.

ideological criticism

An area of *television criticism,* concerned with class and gender representation, that studies society's competing *discourses* and the position of the individual within society.

illusion of depth

The ability of the two-dimensional television image to create an illusion whereby space seems to recede into the image. A *telephoto lens* creates a small illusion of depth and a *wide-angle lens* creates a large one.

improvisation

Technique of *method* acting style used mostly in rehearsal; actors put themselves into the minds of the characters, place the characters into imagined situations, and invent-dialogue and action.

indexical sign (index)

In *semiotics,* a type of *sign* in which the *signifier* is physically caused by the *signified.* For example, where there is smoke, there is fire. Thus the *signifier* (smoke) is physically caused by the *signified* (fire).

infrastructure

See the Marxist definition of *base*

interactive mode

Type of television text in which the historical world is mixed with that of the video/film maker—according to Bill Nichols's approach to nonfiction television and film. This occurs in one of two ways: the *social actor* is brought into a television studio; and/or a representative of television enters the historical world to provoke a response from social actors. In another context, interactive is coming to refer to the capacity of the viewer to respond to or affect what is seen on television, for example, through home shopping services and video games.

interior scenes

Scenes set inside, in particular on *studio sets,* though also including location interiors.

intertextuality

The intertextual, self-reflexive quality—as when one television *text* (e.g., a commercial) refers to another (e.g., a program or commercial) or to other types of *media texts.*

jump cut

An editing technique wherein one shot does not match the preceding shot, resulting in a disruptive gap in space and/or time.

key light

In the *three-point lighting* system, the main source of illumination and the most intense light on the set. It is normally positioned above the actors' heads and several feet in front of them.

keyframe

In animation, the essential frames used to construct a character's movement. If the animation is computer aided, the animator designs the keyframes and the computer automatically generates the frames in between (see *tweening*).

keying

A special effects process, specific to video, in which an image or text is inserted into another image. See *chroma key*.

kinescope

A film copy of a television program; made by aiming the film camera at a television screen. Used during the early years of television (before videotape) to record programs that were broadcast live.

laugh track

A soundtrack of prerecorded laughter, usually added in the *post-production* process to a comedy program with no studio audience.

lavaliere microphone

A small microphone often clipped to a performer's tie or shirt.

lead

In news stories, the reporter's opening comments—designed to capture viewer attention.

letterbox

A process by which a *widescreen* film is presented on video. The top and bottom of the video frame is blackened, and the *widescreen* film frame is reduced to fit into this frame-within-the-video-frame. Also used to present *high-definition video* on conventional TV sets.

lighting color

The color of a light source, which may be manipulated with *gels*.

lighting diffusion

The hardness or softness of a light source. *Hard light* casts a sharp, definite shadow.

lighting direction

The positioning of lights relative to the object being shot. The norm for lighting direction is *three-point lighting*.

lighting intensity

The power of a light source. Regarding the relative intensity of lighting sources, see *three-point lighting*.

linear perspective

A method of drawing or painting that converts the three dimensions of reality into two dimensions. Originally developed during the European Renaissance, it formed the foundation for how lenses represent a visual field.

limited effects theory

A type of communication theory (e.g., social learning theory, vicarious catharsis theory) that regards media as having conditional influences on the viewer; due to intervening variables, the effects of media on the viewer are limited.

lip sync

Synchronizing a performance to recorded speech or music; most frequently found in music videos, wherein the performers mouth the words to the prerecorded song while they are filmed or videotaped.

live-on-tape

A video production that is recorded live, with most of the editing done while the scenes transpire (rather than in *post-production*).

location settings

Pre-existing settings that are chosen as backgrounds for television programs.

long shot (LS)

A framing that presents entire objects or persons—situating them in a setting.

loudness (volume)

How loud or soft a sound is. See *dynamic range*.

low angle

A shot in which the camera is lower than the recorded actor or object; thus the camera looks up at the actor or object.

low-key lighting

A lighting style wherein the *key light* is so much more intense than the *fill light* that there is a high contrast between bright and dark areas. The bright areas are especially bright and the dark areas are very dark.

luminance

The brightness or darkness of a color. See *chrominance* and *saturation*.

magnetic tape

A ribbon of plastic with a coating on it that is sensitive to magnetic impulses created by electricity. In *analog* technology, these magnetic impulses are modulated on the tape in a fashion parallel to the sound wave's modulation. In *digital* technology, magnetic tape is used to record sounds encoded as a string of numbers that will later be converted into sound.

manifest content

In a *content analysis* of a television text, the characters and their actions.

masking

A *non-anamorphic widescreen* film process. In masked films, blackened horizontal bands are placed across the top and bottom of a 1:1.33 frame, resulting in a wider *aspect ratio* of 1:1.85.

match cut

A principle of *continuity editing* that maintains continuity by fitting ("matching") the space and time of one shot to that of the preceding shot.

match-on-action

A *continuity-editing* technique wherein a cut is placed in the midst of an action, so that the action from one shot continues to the next.

means of production

Marx's term for the locations (factories and the like) at which goods are produced and men and women labor.

media text

Any item in the mass media (e.g., a TV commercial or program, film, magazine, interview, public appearance, etc.).

medium close up (MCU)

A framing in between *medium shot* and *close-up.*

medium long shot (MLS)

A framing in between *long shot* and *medium shot.*

medium shot (MS)

A framing that presents a moderately close view of an object or person. Conventionally, a TV medium shot of a person is from the thighs or kness up. Two common types of medium shots are the *two shot* and the *three shot.*

method

Naturalist performance style that encourages the actor to become the character, at which point the gestures/dialects necessary for the performance will emerge organically; approaches used to achieve this union between actor and character are *emotional memory, sense memory,* and *improvisation.*

mise-en-scene

The staging of the action for the camera. All of the physical objects in front of the camera and the arrangement of those objects by the director. The organization of setting, costuming, lighting, and actor movement.

mixer

A machine that blends various sound sources.

mode of production

An aesthetic style of shooting that relies on a particular technology and is governed by a certain economic system. Television's two principal modes of production are single-camera and multiple-camera.

mode of representation

Manner in which a non-narrative television program depicts *historical reality* and addresses itself to the viewer about that version of reality; modes include *expository, interactive, observational,* and *reflexive.*

motion-caption device

A system by which the movement of three-dimensional objects or humans is traced by a computer.

motivation

In narrative structure, a catalyst that starts the story's progression—a reason for the story to begin (usually a character's lack or desire).

MOW (movie of the week)

Industry shorthand for any film produced specifically for television and not shown initially in theaters.

multicasting

In *digital TV,* individual broadcast stations may simultaneously transmit four or more programs.

multiple-camera production

A *mode of production* common in television wherein two or more cameras are used to record the scene, enabling simultaneous and/or *post-production* editing. The mode used in most sitcoms and all soap operas, game shows, sports programs, and newscasts.

multi-track recording

In the sound editing process, recordings are digitally or electronically divided into four (or many more) separate *tracks.* On each is a sound category (dialogue, music, effects) separated from the others, allowing the sound editor to manipulate individual soundtracks before producing a finished soundtrack.

music television

Generally refers to a system, such as a cable or satellite service (e.g., MTV, CMT), through which recorded music is delivered.

music video

A visual representation of or accompaniment to a song or other musical selection that usually exists independently as a recording.

musical director

Person who selects and arranges the music for a program.

mythic analysis

An interpretive strategy of *genre* analysis that approaches genres in terms of archetypes, stories shared by large segments of a culture that offer the researcher evidence of that society's thought process.

narration (voice-over)

When a character's or omniscient narrator's voice is heard over an image.

narrative enigma

A question that underpins a story and will (in classical films) or will not (in soap opera) be answered at the conclusion.

narrative function

A specific action or an attribute of a character in a narrative—according to the narrative theory of V. I. Propp.

narrative image

A particular representation of a program created by advertising and promotion in order to entice viewers.

National Television System Committee (NTSC)

A committee established by various manufacturers of television equipment in order to develop a set of standards that would render color transmission and reception compatible to black-and-white television sets. The initials NTSC are also commonly used to refer to the 525-line broadcast standard used in the U.S.

naturalistic animation

An aesthetic tenet of animation that advocates that animation replicate live-action film/video as much as possible; cartoon characters should resemble objects in reality and our view of these characters/objects should resemble the view of a camera. The opposite of *abstract animation*.

naturalistic performance

Performance style in which the actor attempts to create a character that the audience will accept as a plausible and believable human being, rather than as an actor trying to portray someone.

negotiated reading

In cultural studies, the interpretation of the text that partially accepts and partially rejects the meanings that the text emphasizes.

NLE

See *nonlinear editing*.

nondiegetic sound

Sound that does not occur in the *diegetic space* (the characters' world), such as music that is added in *post-production*.

nonlinear editing (NLE)

Editing performed on a computer, in which shots do not have to be placed one after the other (i.e., in a linear fashion).

non-narrative television

Televisual texts (e.g., news and sports programs, game shows, some commercials) that present reality to us without using conventional narrative structures. Instead, non-narrative television relies on *expository, interactive, observational,* and/or *reflexive modes of representation.*

normal lens

A type of *focal length* that seems to most closely approximate the human eye's range of vision (in actuality the range of vision is narrower in a normal focal length lens, with less *illusion of depth*).

NTSC

See *National Television System Committee.*

objective correlative

An object that comes to represent an aspect of a character—for example, Bart Simpson's skateboard representing his carefree and spontaneous lifestyle.

observational mode

Type of television text wherein a television producer's presence is not obvious to the viewer, and his or her manipulation of the historical world is minimal.

omnidirectional microphone

A microphone that picks up sound equally from all directions.

180° rule

A *continuity-editing* principle that dictates that cameras remain on one side of the *axis of action* in order to preserve the scene's spatial continuity and *screen direction.*

oppositional reading

In cultural studies, the interpretation of the text that is wholly contrary to the text's dominant meanings.

overhead boom microphone

Held on a long arm by a *boom operator,* positioned above the actors' heads and out of view of the camera, it is equipped with a *hypercardioid* microphone so that sound from the direction in which it is pointed will be recorded and ambient sound will be minimized.

package

In television journalism, an 80–105 second news story shot in the field and filed by a reporter.

pan-and-scan (scanning)

A process by which a *widescreen, anamorphic* film (1:2.35) is reduced to television's smaller 1:1.33 aspect ratio. The most significant part of the original frame is selected, and the pan-and-scan frame can slide, or "scan," left or right across the original frame.

panning

The action of physically rotating the camera left and right, on an imaginary vertical axis. Only the tripod head is moved, not the entire support. Pan also refers to the resulting horizontal movement of the image

paradigmatic structure

In *semiotics,* a manner in which *signs* are organized and meaning created. Paradigmatic structures create meaning through association, in contrast to *syntagmatic* structures that create meaning through sequence or chronological order. For example, in baseball, the players that might replace one another in the syntagmatic batting line-up are in paradigmatic relationship to one another.

pedestalling

The raising or lowering of the camera on the vertical post of the camera support. Pedestal is also the term given to the moveable camera support (the shaft in the center of a dolly) used in studio television production.

perfect fit

In the study of television stars, a matching of a particular role's characteristics to a star's *polysemy*.

phosphors

See *pixels*.

pickup pattern

In microphones, the shape of the space in which the microphone is sensitive to sound. Common patterns include *omnidirectional and cardioid*.

pilot

A program, sometimes an *MOW* that introduces a new *series*.

pitch

How high or low a sound is. See *frequency response*.

pixels (phosphors)

Phosphorescent dots, arranged in horizontal lines on the television screen, which produce the video image when struck by a beam from the *electron gun*.

play-by-play announcer

A television sports announcer, usually a professional broadcaster, who functions as narrator of the game's events, keeps track of game time, prompts the comments of the *color announcers*, reiterates the score, modulates the passage of time, and may lead into commercial breaks.

point-of-view shot

A shot in which the camera is physically situated very close to a character's position; thus the resulting shot approximates the character's point-of-view.

polysemy

Literally, many meanings. Refers to television's ability to communicate contradictory or ambivalent meanings simultaneously. See *structured polysemy*.

post-production

Everything (e.g., editing, sound effects) that transpires after the program itself has been shot.

preferred reading

In cultural studies, the interpretation of the text that is stressed by the text itself. Marxists presume this reading aligns with the *dominant ideology*.

pre-production

The written planning stages of the program (script preparation, budgeting, etc.).

problematic fit

In the study of television stars, a complete mismatch of a particular role's characteristics with a star's *polysemy*.

product placement

The appearance of a trademarked product (e.g., Budweiser beer or Apple computers) in a program—when the sponsor pays for such placement.

production

The shooting of the program itself.

proletariat

In Marxist terms, the working class; this least powerful group works to survive, selling its labor to the *bourgeoisie.*

promotion

A *media text* (e.g., an appearance on a talk show) generated by stars and their representatives in a deliberate attempt to shape the star's image.

pseudomonologue

An interview in which the interviewer and his or her questions are not evident in the text; only the interviewee's answers are included.

public domain

Material (e.g., a piece of music) that is not *copyrighted,* which may be used in TV programs without paying a fee or *royalty.*

publicity

A *media text* (e.g., an unauthorized biography) that presents information outside the control of stars and their representatives.

pulling focus

See *racking focus.*

racking focus (pulling focus)

Shifting the *focus* from foreground to background, or vice versa.

rating

In the context of TV *ratings,* the percentage of all homes with television sets that are tuned to a specific program. Usually used in conjunction with ratings *share.*

ratings

Based on a random sample of television viewers, the calculated amount and percentage of viewers watching a particular program on a particular station or network. Usually expressed in terms of *rating* and *share.*

reading

The viewer's active interpretation of a *text*—whether written (e.g., a book) or visual (e.g., a television program or film).

re-establishing shot

A long shot that once again positions the character(s) within the environment of the scene, helping to re-establish character and/or setting; also used as a transitional device.

reflexive mode

A non-narrative television text that draws the viewer's attention to the processes, techniques, and conventions of television production.

remote control device(RCD)

A device that allows one to operate a television without directly touching it.

repertory

Naturalist performance style in which the actor constructs a performance by selecting particular gestures and spoken dialects.

rhythm

The timing of speech, music, sound effects, or editing.

rotoscope

A device used in animation wherein a single frame from a live-action film is rear-projected onto a light table with a semi-opaque glass in the center; the animator traces the images cast by the film onto a cel; the tracings are rephotographed, resulting in an animated film that duplicates live-action images.

royalty

A fee paid for the use of *copyrighted* material.

ruling class

Marx's term for the social class in control of a society's *means of production*; the class that controls the *means of production* controls the society overall.

saturation (chroma or chrominance)

In terms of television's image quality, the level of a color's purity (or how much or little grayness is mixed with the color).

scan line

Lines of glowing *pixels* that make up the television image. In the *NTSC* system used in the United States, there are 525 lines in the TV image. PAL, developed in Germany, and SECAM, from France, are 625-line systems. *HDTV* has a variety of formats; all of which contain hundreds of additional scan lines.

scanning

See *pan-and-scan*.

scene

The smallest piece of the narrative action; a single narrative event that occurs in continuous space over continuous time.

scientific method

An *empirical* approach that advocates developing research questions and hypotheses based on an established body of theoretical knowledge, investigating them with replicable methodology, and explaining the results in terms of their contribution to the established body of knowledge.

Scopitones

Produced in the 1960s, short films of performances by popular musicians presented on coin-operated machines akin to jukeboxes.

screen direction

From the camera's perspective, the direction a character is looking and/or an object is moving in a shot.

screenplay

Generally speaking, a written description of a program, wherein the action and dialogue are described scene-by-scene. (Terms used to describe different types of scripts vary considerably within the television and film industries.)

screen time

The duration of a program—which is normally shorter than the time represented in the program's narrative (that is, its *story time*). For example, the story time of one soap opera episode is typicallly a day or two, but its screen time is less than 60 minutes.

segue

A transition from one sound to another. (Pronounced "WAY")

selective use

In the study of television stars, a use of selected parts of star's *polysemy* in a particular role.

self-reflexivity

A program that refers back to itself or similar programs. In a genre's evolutionary pattern, the stage during which the genre turns inward and uses its own conventions for subject matter, often in the form of a parody.

semiotics

An area of _television criticism_ that breaks down all forms of communication into individual units of meaning or signs that are studied in terms of their singular characteristics as well as their interaction with other units of meaning.

sense memory

Technique of _method_ acting style in which the actor draws on memories of physical sensations of an emotional event in order to generate _emotional memory._

serial

A narrative form of television that presents daily/weekly episodes, with a multiple set of recurring characters and simultaneous story-lines. Because each episode specifically links to the next, narrative _closure_ is rare.

series

A narrative form that presents weekly episodes, usually self-contained, with a defined set of recurring characters.

set designer (scenic designer)

Person who builds or selects elements in constructing the setting of a television program.

sexual politics

In _feminist_ studies, the power relationship between men and women.

shallow focus

A small _depth of field,_ with just one plane (foreground, middle-ground, or back-ground) in _focus._

shallow space blocking

A type of _blocking_ associated with _multiple-camera, studio set_ productions, where, due to the shallow sets, the actors mostly move side-to-side, rather than up-and-back.

share

In the context of TV _ratings,_ the percentage of homes with turned-on television sets that are tuned to a specific program. Usually used in conjunction with _ratings._

shooting script

Generally speaking, a written description of a program, where each scene is described shot-by-shot. (Terms used to describe different types of scripts vary considerably within the television and film industries.)

shot-counter shot (shot-reverse shot)

A _continuity-editing_ principle that alternates shots, particularly in conversation scenes between two characters. It is a mainstay of the _180° rule._

sign

In _semiotics,_ the smallest unit of meaning—comprised of a _signifier_ and its _signified._

signified

The meaning communicated by the _signifier;_ can be an object, a concept, a visual field, and so on.

signifier

The physical aspect of a _sign,_ such as ink on a page, chalk on a chalkboard, stop sign, light emanating from a TV screen, etc.

signs of character

The various signifiers—viewer foreknowledge, character name, appearance, _objective correlatives,_ dialogue, lighting, _videography_ or _cinematography,_ and action—that communicate the character to the viewer.

signs of performance
> The actor's facial, gestural, corporeal, and vocal signifiers that contribute to the development of character.

simulcasts
> Programs that are simultaneously broadcast on both radio and television.

single-camera production
> A *mode of production* wherein one camera operates at a time and the shots are done in the most economically efficient order. On television, the main mode used in creating prime-time dramas, *MOWs*, music videos, and commercials.

social actor
> "Real" people as used in nonfiction television programs; people "performing" according to social codes of behavior in order to represent themselves to others.

soft focus
> An entire image that is slightly *out-of-focus*.

soft news
> News stories that examine the personal, such as gossip, scandal, murder, mayhem, and "human interest stories."

soft light
> A *diffused* light source, resulting in indistinct, blurred outlines and minimal shadows.

sound bite
> In a news *package*, a short piece of audio that was recorded on location.

sound editor
> Technician who, in *post-production* manipulates a program's soundtrack.

Soundies
> Produced in the 1940s, short films of performances by popular musicians presented on coin-operated machines akin to jukeboxes.

sound stage
> A large room designed for the recording of programs. Sets are arranged on the stage in a variety of ways, depending mostly on the presence/absence of a studio audience.

stand-up
> A feature of a television news *package*, in which the reporter stands before a site significant to the story while narrating it.

star image
> A representation of an actor that is fabricated through the *media texts* of *promotion*, *publicity*, television programs, and criticism.

Steadicam
> Registered trademark for a gyroscopically balanced camera mount that attaches to a *camera operator's* body, which produces smooth camera movement without the use of a *dolly*.

stereotype
> A conventionalized character type that is demeaning to a particular social group.

story time
> The amount of time that transpires within a program's narrative. See *screen time*.

storyboard
> A written description of a program consisting of small drawings of individual shots.

stripped syndication

A programming strategy in which *syndicated* shows are scheduled Monday through Friday in the same time slot.

structured polysemy

The organization and emphasis/repression of meanings within television's *polysemy*.

studio set

Three-walled, ceilingless set erected on a *sound stage*; this type of set is usually shallow, normally wider than it is deep, and rectangular rather than square.

subject

In contemporary psychoanalysis, the human psyche—formed chiefly through the Oedipal Complex. In contemporary Marxism, an individual viewed as a psychological construct who enters the ideological world and must be considered in relationship to this ideology.

subjective shot

A shot wherein the camera is positioned as if it were inside a character's head, looking out of his or her eyes.

subtitling

The process in which the original dialogue of a film or television program is both heard and printed at the bottom of the screen. Subtitling is often used for foreign-language films. In television it is also used, as closed-captions for viewers with impaired hearing, on conventional programs.

subtractive color

The process wherein, as white light passes through a piece of film, yellow, magenta, and cyan colors are filtered out, leaving the many colors of the spectrum.

sweeps

Time period during which Nielsen Media Research conducts seasonal *ratings* of network television programs.

superstructure

In Marxist terms, a society's ideological constructs, which grow out of its economic *base*.

sweetening

A *post-production* sound effects process wherein the sound technicians add more applause and laughter to those of the actual studio audience.

switcher

A technical device that allows a director to change between various video cameras while recording a scene.

symbolic sign (symbol)

In *semiotics*, a type of *sign* in which the *signifier* and the *signified* are connected solely through cultural convention. For example, Christianity (*a signified*) represented by a cross (*signifier*) or Judaism(*signified*) by a Star of David (*signifier*).

sync (or synch)

The synchronization of sound and image. See *lip sync*.

syndication

The distribution or leasing of television programs to stations and networks by their production companies. It refers both to the second run of a program after a network's initial license period (e.g., *I Love Lucy* [1951–57]) and a program that was created specifically for syndication (e.g., *Baywatch*[1989–99]). See *stripped syndication.*

syntagm

In *semiotics*, a first level ordering of signs—for example, in narrative television, an individual *scene.* The sequence of scenes is their *syntagmatic structure.*

syntagmatic structure

In *semiotics*, the manner in which *signs* are linearly and/or temporally organized. For example, the batting line-up in baseball is in syntagmatic order. See *paradigmatic structure.*

take

A single shot, lasting from the starting to the stopping of the camera.

teasers

On television news, brief announcements of upcoming stories used to maintain viewer attention.

Technicolor

A type of color film process, used mostly from the late 1930s to the 1950s.

telephoto lens

A long *focal length* that creates a narrow, but magnified view of an object or person.

Telescriptions

Produced by Louis Snader in the 1950s, short films of musical performances that were marketed to television stations for use in variety shows or as filler material.

television apparatus

The combined work of all of the various factions (bankers, media corporations, directors, scriptwriters) that create television programs and the viewing experience itself—including the psychological mechanisms at work during TV viewing.

television criticism

Non-empirical, analytical methods (e.g., *auteurism, genre study, semiotics, and feminism*) employed to understand systems of meaning on television. The term is also used in the popular press to refer to evaluative reviewing of television.

televisual

Characteristic of television. Also used by John Caldwell to refer to excessive or exhibitionistic style in television.

text

A segment of the *televisual flow*, such as an individual program, a commercial, a newscast, even an entire evening's viewing. In *semiotics*, any coherent system of *signs.*

theatrical film

Films originally designed to be shown in theaters, as opposed to made-for-TV films. See *MOW.*

three-point lighting

An *aesthetic* convention in which an actor or object is lit from three sources or points of light of varying intensity. There is one main source of illumination (*key light*), one source filling shadows (*fill light*), and one source backlighting the actors (*back light*).

three shot

The framing of three characters in a medium shot.

ticker

Information moving across the bottom of the secreen—such as sports scores and weather updates.

timbre (tone)

A characteristic of sound referring to the tonal quality of a note and/or voice.

tilting

The action of rotating the camera up and down, on a horizontal axis in a stationary body. *Tilt* also refers to the resulting vertical movements in the image.

track

An area along the length of recording tape (like the lanes on a highway) in a *multi-track recording*, in which speech, music, or sound effects are individually recorded. Similarly, computerbased, *nonlinear editing* (*NLE*) also relies on the metaphor of tracks of sound and image.

tracking

Any sideways or forward/backward movement of the camera *dolly*—sometimes on actual tracks.

treatment

A written description of a program, containing only a basic outline of the action; the first stage of the scriptwriting process.

trucking (crabbing)

In television studio production, any sideways movement of the camera.

two shot

The framing of two characters in a medium shot.

tweening

A process in animation by which frames are created that constitute a character's movement. These frames come in between the *keyframes* the amimator has designed and can be automatically generated by a computer.

typecasting

When the *star image* perfectly fits the character he or she portrays.

unidirectional microphone

A microphone that picks up sound from a specific direction.

unique selling proposition (USP)

Rosser Reeve's term for that certain something that distinguishes one product from all the others.

uses-and-gratifications

A research method that sees the viewer as an active user and attempts to chart the way that viewers employ television; this method quantifies how television fulfills viewers' emotional or intellectual needs.

USP

See *unique selling proposition.*

vaudeville

Anti-naturalistic performance style in which the actor reminds the viewer that the character is not a real person, often by directly addressing the viewer.

verisimilitude

The impression of truth or reality.

videographer

The person overseeing all aspects of the video image—including lighting and the operation of the camera.

videography

The characteristics of the video camera.

volume

How loud a sound is. One of three main characteristics of television sound. See *pitch* and *timbre*.

wide angle lens

A *focal length* that generally provides a wide view of a scene and increases the *illusion of depth*, so that some objects seem to be far apart from one another.

widescreen

An *aspect ratio* wider than television's original standard of 1.33:1 (that is, 4:3). Television widescreen (a part of the *high-definition* format) is 16:9 or 1.78:1. Common variations of widescreen in theatrical films are *masked* (1.85:1) and *anamorphic* (2.35:1).

wipe

A special effect used as a transition device between scenes, in which a line moves across the screen, apparently erasing one shot as the next replaces it.

wireframe

A stage in *computer-generated imagery* wherein the surface of objects is represented with polygonal lines (wires). The wireframe will be covered with surfaces when the animation is rendered.

zoom in or zoom out

A function of the *zoom lens* wherein the *focal length* is varied from *wide angle* to *telephoto* (zoom in), thereby magnifying the object as the angle of view is narrowed—or vice versa (zoom out).

zoom lens (variable focal length)

A lens with a variable *focal length*, allowing the operator to shift immediately and continuously from *wide angle* to *telephoto* (or vice versa) without switching lenses.

INDEX